SHAKESPEARE
IN HIS AGE

BEAUCHAMP CHAPEL,
ST. MARY'S CHURCH, WARWICK

The Earl of Leicester's Tomb against the wall

SHAKESPEARE
IN HIS AGE

by

F. E. HALLIDAY

No man is an *Iland*, intire of it selfe;
every man is a peece of the *Continent*;
a part of the *maine*.

JOHN DONNE

THOMAS YOSELOFF, PUBLISHER
NEW YORK

© 1956 by F. E. Halliday
First American Edition 1964

6068
Printed in the United States of America

TO
TOM GAUNT
TO WHOM
I OWE SO MUCH

CONTENTS

Chapel Children again—The second Blackfriars
theatre—*Twelfth Night* at Whitehall—Rebellion
and execution of Essex.

Part Three—1603–1616

LIST OF ILLUSTRATIONS

PREFACE

I T is no easy matter to find three or four words that serve as summary and abstract of a hundred thousand, yet *Shakespeare in his Age* does, I think, epitomise what I have set out to do—to relate Shakespeare to the epoch in which he lived. No man is an island, not even, or rather least of all, Shakespeare, and adequately to understand him we must know something of the continent, the main, of which he was a part. But a general and comprehensive survey of that territory is inevitably static, often irrelevant and apt to be confusing and remote; a shadowy tapestry, a drop-scene by no means always adding significance to the action of the player.

Such a picture was not my purpose. I wanted to discover and describe what was happening in England, and even further afield, while Shakespeare was doing this and writing that. We all know that he was finishing *Henry V* at the time of Essex's Irish campaign; but what was happening, what were other men doing—statesmen, courtiers, churchmen, sailors, poets and composers—when he married at the age of eighteen, when he arrived in London, when he was writing *Love's Labour's Lost*, *Macbeth* and *Pericles*, and when he was collaborating with Fletcher? The only thing that matters, of course, is the writing, but it follows that anything that illuminates it is of some value, and such a synthesis seems to me to be particularly illuminating. *King John* gains by being seen in the light of the death of Drake, the Cadiz Raid, the Islands Voyage and the poetry of Donne, and *Lear* in that of the Hampton Court Conference, Gunpowder Plot and *Volpone*. Then, against this shifting scene Shakespeare himself becomes a more comprehensible figure, and, after all, the scene itself is not the least interesting in our history.

My method therefore has been, first, to account for and describe the England into which Shakespeare was born, his political and cultural inheritance, without some appreciation of which the rest would lose so much of its significance; then, to follow year by year the course of events in that wonderful half century of his life, noting the forces that helped to determine, the pressures that must have modified, his development and his work. I have tried to place myself in the position of Shakespeare, and describe the things that he saw, the plays and music that he heard, the books that he read, the men whom he met and the ideas that he encountered, so weaving, contrapuntally as it were, into a single narrative the main political events of the period, the progress of the arts—architecture, painting and music, as well as poetry and the drama—the development of the theatre and the fortunes of the dramatic companies. Shakespeare, then, is only a subordinate figure in this history, yet he is always at the centre, the hub about which all other things revolve and to which all else is related.

There is another reason for his being but a minor figure. One of the most striking things to emerge from this study is the small part that he played in London life—an intensely competitive life—outside the theatre. Unlike most of his contemporaries, he seemed to make no effort to advance himself by writing pageants and entertainments for the City or adulatory poems and masques for the Court. The reason is, I think, quite simple. He was by nature tolerant and easy-going, and then so successful from the start of his career in London that there was no need to bother with trifles that interfered with the art to which he had dedicated himself and the success of the fellowship to which he was devoted. The thin strand of his career, therefore, is apt to be obscured by the coarser web of obtrusive events and more necessitous and assertive men, and I can only hope that I have succeeded in tracing that delicate and precious thread as it was being woven into the broad fabric of history, and relating it to that grand pattern.

Perhaps I should finish with a word of warning. My description of the Elizabethan stage is by no means the orthodox one. We really know very little about the subject, for unfortunately the Elizabethans themselves told us next to nothing about it, and all accounts derive mainly from hint and allusion, often obscure and sometimes contradictory. But by approaching the problem from a new direction I have been able to adduce some fresh evidence, and it is on this that my reconstruction is based.

F. E. H.

St. Ives, Cornwall
30th September, 1955

ENGLAND IN 1564

IF ever poet was fortunate in his age it was Shakespeare. Although for the greater part of Elizabeth's reign England was engaged in undeclared or open war with Spain, never since the Roman occupation had it enjoyed such a period of domestic peace, never before had its people been so united, so true to themselves, so loyal to their leaders and their sovereign, so conscious of their powers and their common destiny. The fifty years of Shakespeare's life are a period of comparative calm between two storms: when he was born, the disorders and excesses of the Reformation were over, and when he died, although a wise man might bethink him of his cloak, the clouds of an even more violent tempest had scarcely begun to gather. The England of Elizabeth has the quality of an April day, fresh, boisterous and invigorating, its sudden glooms and brilliant bursts of sun, and we see her people, after the shocks and frustrations of an economic, social and religious revolution, quivering with energy, like greyhounds straining upon the start.

This was the inheritance into which Shakespeare entered. Had he been born fifty years earlier, it is quite possible that we should never have heard of him at all; for what chance would there have been for a poor provincial boy to make his name in the world of literature? There was then no theatre, no drama for which he could write; there was not even any poetry of the new age to serve him as a model. Despite his genius, we should have had at best only another curiosity of literature. Had he been born fifty years later, the Elizabethan impetus would have spent itself, his inheritance would have been the enervated drama of Fletcher and the Jacobeans, and the theatres would have been closed in his face as soon as he began to write for them, and remained closed for the remainder of his active career. He would have been a brilliant lyric and epic poet, inspired perhaps by the King's cause, though not by any religious conviction, and broken perhaps by the Commonwealth. Though he might have been the rival of Milton, in more senses than one, the age was not for him, and a

Shakespeare of the mid-seventeenth century would be but the shadow of the Shakespeare we know.

It is always dangerous to discount the continuity of history. The lives of the great mass of people are swept due on in time's compulsive current, but there are periods when the surface suffers such violent change that the depths are disturbed and the course of life is noticeably affected. Such a period was the early sixteenth century in England. The old feudal nobility had destroyed itself in the Wars of the Roses; the medieval structure of society, based on guild and manor, had broken down; the Medieval Church had been pillaged and shaken to its foundations. A new social, economic and religious order had to be erected, at the same time as a new world beyond the Atlantic beckoned for exploration, and vistas of a new world of the spirit were revealed by the rediscovery of the civilisations of Greece and Rome, the invention of printing, the dissemination of the new learning and the new art of Renaissance Italy. The revolutionary period was over by the middle of the century, and the Elizabethans were left to tidy up and piece together their shattered medieval inheritance, and make a synthesis of old and new. Consolidation and organisation were followed by physical and economic expansion, and by an expansion of the spirit so rapid, so violent, that it could find adequate release only in the arts, a liberation that precipitated a secondary revolution in poetry and the drama, the art which, above all else, reflected the strenuous and heroic action of the age.

It was a brave new world that had been revealed for exploration beyond the seas and in the mind of man, yet even England remained to be discovered, and the same impulse that compelled Hawkins and Drake to follow the course of the westering sun urged less adventurous, though more disinterested, minds to explore the wonders of their own country. The work had been begun in the late years of Henry VIII by John Leland, who explored every county in England and Wales, and bequeathed a mass of material to his successors, William Harrison, John Stow and William Camden, greatest of English antiquaries. William Lambarde and Richard Carew contributed detailed surveys of their native counties, Kent and Cornwall, while Christopher Saxton, John Norden and John Speed added the maps, by no means the least beautiful part of the Elizabethan legacy to the visual arts. We know, therefore, a great deal about Shakespeare's England, far more than we know about any previous period.

When Elizabeth succeeded Mary as Queen in 1558, the population of England and Wales was something over four million, more than four-fifths of whom were thinly spread over the countryside. Much of the land was still unreclaimed waste, marsh or forest, and the greater part of the remainder cultivated in open fields, so that we must imagine a typical landscape as a patchwork of unhedged strips surrounding a village, separated from its neighbours by swamp, common or wood, and linked by roads so bad and narrow as to be almost impassable for wheeled traffic. But some of the land had already been enclosed, particularly in the south and along the Welsh border, a movement that had been intensified by the dissolution of the monasteries, when their vast estates had been engrossed by the enterprising class of merchants, the new gentry and the new nobility. Enclosure for the sake of better and more economical methods of cultivation, though it might lead to some dislocation and distress, was a beneficial process, but enclosure of the open fields for sheep was another matter. This led to unemployment and vagrancy, two of the main problems of Tudor times, and was frowned upon by the government. Thomas Bastard describes how,

> Sheep have eat up our meadows and our downs,
> Our corn, our wood, whole villages and towns,

but his contemporary, Thomas Tusser, in the homely rhymes of his *Hundreth Good Pointes of Husbandrie*, a book that Shakespeare, like every other countryman, must have read, stoutly defends enclosure and the new farming, though there seems to have been little advance on medieval implements and technique. Warwickshire was scarcely affected by the enclosure movement, and in his boyhood Shakespeare might wander at will through the Forest of Arden, which covered much of the north-western half of the county, or cross the Avon by the many-arched bridge into the open fields of the plain that lay between the river and the honey-coloured limestone of the north Cotswold escarpment.

Stratford was a typical market-town of some two thousand inhabitants, who lived in rows of half-timbered houses, backed by gardens and orchards. For nearly four hundred years they had enjoyed some rights of self-government, and the religious Guild of the Holy Cross had become an additional organ of government, caring for the poor, maintaining an almshouse and exercising control over the school attached to the Guild Chapel and buildings in the centre of the town. These had been rebuilt towards the close of the fifteenth century by Sir Hugh Clopton, who also built the fine house opposite, New Place, and the bridge across the Avon. To the south, mirrored in the river, rose the great grey church of the Holy Trinity, and close by was the College that housed the chantry priests. Shakespeare was fortunate in his birthplace as in his age, as well he knew. Its recent history was typical, and illustrates admirably the impact of the Reformation on similar towns. In 1547 Guild and College were dissolved, and two years later the Bishops of Worcester were deprived of the manor of Stratford, which remained with the Crown until 1562, when Elizabeth granted it to one of her favourites, Ambrose Dudley, Earl of Warwick. The inhabitants were compensated by the grant of a charter of incorporation; there was to be a bailiff and fourteen aldermen and fourteen capital burgesses, the bailiff and one alderman acting as justices of the peace, and the bailiff presiding over the Court of Record with jurisdiction in civil cases up to £30. Part of the Guild property was transferred to the corporation, and out of it they had to maintain the almshouse, and pay the schoolmaster and vicar, appointed by the lord of the manor, who also had the right of objecting to the bailiff elected by the council; for the bailiff, unlike a mayor, was in theory the servant of the lord of the manor. It was a satisfactory settlement—at the expense of the Church. The townsmen had gained control of their own affairs, and the centralising Tudor government had strengthened its grip. The poor were to be cared for and the children educated, and there is no reason to doubt that all burgesses with Protestant sympathies were satisfied.

But the future of England did not lie in its agriculture, and while Stratford dreamed away the years, other towns began to outstrip it. The neighbouring manor of Birmingham was just beginning to stir, as were Manchester and Leeds and other villages in the West Riding. Though it is scarcely true to say that the Industrial Revolution began in Elizabeth's reign, industrial evolution was rapid, and there were significant advances in weaving, in the mining and smelting of metals and in coal-mining. Newcastle grew apace, and the seamen learned their craft carrying 'sea coal' from the north to London, as well as in the fishing fleets of the West Country, now venturing as far afield as Newfoundland, and in those of Yarmouth, off whose shores vast shoals of herring had recently and lucratively appeared, soon to be celebrated by Thomas Nashe in his spirited *Lenten Stuff*. Plymouth, strategically placed at the Channel approaches, was growing; but as yet by far the biggest towns apart from London were Norwich, the main centre of the worsted industry, enriched by an influx of skilled Flemish weavers, York, the ancient capital of the north, and Bristol, which exported prodigious quantities of cloth. These had populations of nearly twenty thousand.

Oxford and Cambridge were scarcely more populous than Stratford, but their numbers were swollen by some fifteen hundred members of the university. Both universities had suffered under the Reformation, when the numerous monks and friars had been expelled, and they emerged, as we should expect, poorer and more secular and more orderly institutions. This new discipline was the result largely of the college system. The medieval college was for graduates, under-graduates being lodged about the town, but now the old buildings were extended and new colleges founded—Jesus at Oxford, Sidney Sussex and Emmanuel at Cambridge—until all members of the university were housed in them. At the same time a tutorial system was de-veloped, every undergraduate being placed in charge of one of the fellows, who acted both as tutor and guardian, for boys still came up at the age of thirteen or fourteen. This stricter control encouraged the governing class to send their sons to the university where, in the course of seven years, they had the chance to learn much logic and Latin, and some mathematics and Greek. Sidney and Raleigh were at Oxford; the Cecils and Bacons, Essex and Southampton, Walsingham and Gresham at Cambridge. The government kept a watchful eye on the universities, as on everything else; William Cecil was himself Chan-cellor of Cambridge, and his rival, Leicester, Chancellor of Oxford.

Nor were the schools neglected. Like the universities and so many other institutions, they suffered a set-back at the time of the Disso-lution. Monastic foundations disappeared, not all guild schools were as fortunate as Stratford, and there was for a time an understandable reluctance to make new foundations. But Elizabeth was a scholar, a humanist and an educationist—had she not learned her Latin and Greek from the great Roger Ascham himself?—and by the end of her reign there were nearly four hundred grammar schools in the country, as well as a considerable number of new elementary schools. That astonishing woman seemed to conjure up genius in every walk of life, and her age produced a galaxy of headmasters. Thomas Ashton founded the fortunes of Shrewsbury, which was entered in the year of Shakespeare's birth by Fulke Greville and his friend Philip Sidney from Ludlow Castle. For twenty years, before succeeding to the headmastership, William Camden was second master at Westminster, where one of his pupils was Ben Jonson, who was to dedicate *Every Man in his Humour* to his 'most learned and honoured friend', and gratefully and gracefully to acknowledge his debt to his old master:

> Camden, most reverend head, to whom I owe
> All that I am in arts, all that I know
> (How nothing's that?), to whom my country owes
> The great renown, and name wherewith she goes.

A schoolmaster could scarcely hope for greater recognition than that. Under the enlightened Richard Mulcaster, Merchant Taylors' became one of the leading schools; a staunch supporter of education for women and of the English tongue, he numbered among his pupils Lancelot Andrewes, Thomas Lodge, Thomas Kyd and Edmund Spenser, before he left to become High Master of St. Paul's at the end of the century.

Education has led us to London, as indeed almost any other theme eventually would have done, for here was by far the greatest industrial and commercial centre in the kingdom, the centre of so many other activities besides, and just outside its walls lay the seat of government itself. For we must distinguish between London proper, the bourgeois City, and aristocratic Westminster, between which lay more than a mile of almost open country. When Elizabeth came to the throne, London was a city of a hundred thousand inhabitants, five or six times the size of Norwich; when she died the population had doubled. The growth was a healthy one and not at the expense of the rest of the country, and it is in some sort a measure of the achievement of the age. The City was the home of the merchants and master craftsmen, their apprentices and journeymen, and was governed by a Lord Mayor and Corporation elected by the twelve great Livery Companies, jealous of any interference with their privileges by the Privy Council and Court at Westminster, though they were themselves continually striving to extend the area of their own authority. This was confined virtually to the area within the walls, but even here there were small 'liberties' such as that of Blackfriars, which were for the most part beyond their jurisdiction.

In the early days of the reign, most of the citizens lived within the walls, which ran approximately as a semicircle from the Tower, a royal stronghold, to the Fleet Ditch, a mile to the west, a mile of river frontage crowded with wharves and shipping. The streets were narrow; so, too, were the medieval gabled houses, built of timber and clay with plaster, a shop in front, a kitchen or parlour behind and a court or garden beyond; unimpressive to the foreigner, but 'neat and commodious within'. The Reformation had left its mark: gaps where old monastic foundations had been destroyed, but on the hill just within Ludgate, one of the many gates that pierced the walls, rose the Gothic bulk of St. Paul's Cathedral, spireless since it was struck by lightning in 1560. Through the maze of lanes two main thorough-fares cut across the city, dividing it into four parts: from east to west, from Aldgate to Newgate, ran Leadenhall Street, Cornhill, Cheapside; from Bishopsgate in the north ran Gracious Street down to the only bridge that spanned the river, fabulous London Bridge with its twenty arches, through which the waters silently flooded, and roared again at the ebb, and bearing almost another city on their backs. Gracious Street and Bishopsgate were the streets of the great inns— the Bull, Cross Keys, the Bell and the Boar's Head—and there Sir Thomas Gresham built his great house.

Across the river was the borough of Southwark with its church of St. Mary Overie, where old John Gower lay, and the Bankside and Paris Garden. For a spectator standing here, opposite the recently plundered priories of Blackfriars and Whitefriars, the view of the great city across the river must have been one of the fairest in Europe, and away to the west was the noble sweep of the Thames, where the great houses and their gardens bordered the water. But first, on this shore of silver-streaming Thames, like Spenser he would see

> those bricky towers,
> The which on Thames' broad aged back do ride,
> Where now the studious lawyers have their bowers,
> Where whilom wont the Templar Knights to bide.

These were the Middle and Inner Temple which, with Lincoln's Inn and Gray's Inn behind them to the north, made London into a third university town. They were colleges frequented largely by the sons of the nobility and gentry, for whom a knowledge of law was an essential part of their education. But they were something more than schools

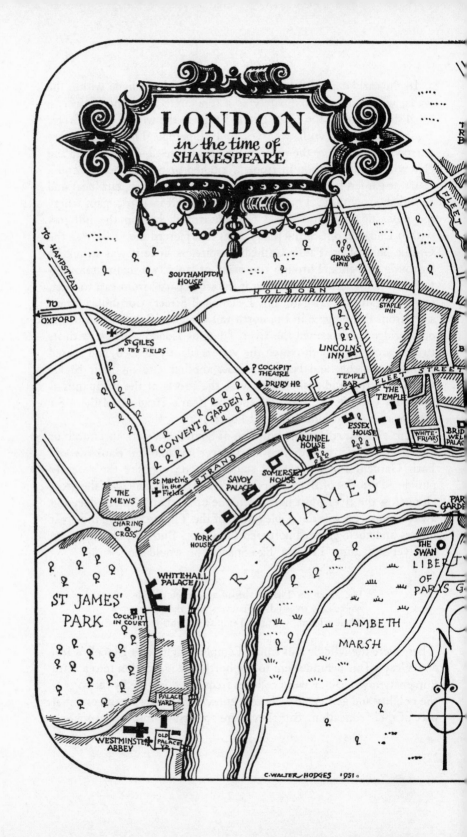

St Leonard's Chu.

SHOREDITCH

THE THEATRE

THE CURTAIN

THE FORTUNE

ARTIL- LERY GARDEN

BISHOPSGATE STREET

BARTHOLOMEWS PRIORY

St GILES

CRIPPLEGATE

MOOR- FIELDS

MOORGATE

BETH- LEHEM HOSPITAL

LONDON WALL

BISHOPSGATE

ALDERSGATE

MOUNTJOYS HOUSE

GUILDHALL

LOTHBURY

BULL INN

GATE

PAUL'S

CHEAPSIDE

MERMAID TAVERN

WATLING STR.

CHURCHYARD

THREADNEEDLE STR.

CORNHILL

CROSS KEYS

LEADENHALL STR.

ALDGATE

LOMBARD STR

GRACIOUS ST.

FENCHURCH STR.

BELL INN

EASTCHEAP

BOAR'S HEAD

TOWER STR.

EAST SMITHFIELD

QUEEN HYTHE

LONDON BRIDGE

ST MARYS STR.

BILLINGS GATE

THE TOWER

KSIDE

BEARGARDEN (LATER THE HOPE)

THE ROSE

St SAVIOUR'S

NE

THE GLOBE

LIBERTY OF THE CLINK

SOUTHWARK

TABARD INN

0   1   2   3   4   5   6   7   8

FURLONGS

of law; there was music and dancing and acting, too, 'so that these hostels, being nurseries or seminaries of the Court, are therefore called Inns of Court'. Like the Oxford and Cambridge colleges, the inns had territorial and family connections; thus many West Countrymen entered the Middle Temple: Raleigh was there, and his cousins the Carews, and it seems to have been the favourite inn of many of those coming up from Stratford and its neighbourhood; Fulke Greville, the Combes, Henry Rainsford of Clifford Chambers and Thomas Hales of Snitterfield, where the Ardens and the Shakespeares came from.

West of the Temple was Leicester House, and beyond that again lay Arundel House, Somerset House, the Savoy, old Durham House, and the long frontage of Wolsey's York Place, reconstructed by Henry VIII and renamed Whitehall, now the principal London residence of the sovereign, for

> You must no more call it York Place, that's past;
> For since the Cardinal fell, that title's lost;
> 'Tis now the King's, and called White Hall.

Old Westminster Palace had been partially destroyed by fire, but the great Hall of Rufus and Richard II remained, backed by the bulk of the Abbey, with its recent addition, the delicately traceried Chapel of Henry VII.

The royal occupant of Whitehall was now Elizabeth, when Shakespeare was born, a young woman of thirty; tall, fair, well-favoured, high-nosed, neat of limb and feature and learned beyond common belief. But, beset by bewildering difficulties, she was by her courage and inscrutability, by her almost masculine intelligence and altogether feminine intuition, already in process of becoming a legendary figure—Gloriana, the Faery Queen. She trusted her own judgment implicitly, fortunately for England, and never questioned the divine origin of her rights as Queen, though she knew when to yield gracefully—over trifles—the better to gain her end in matters of moment. She was a despot, but a popular, almost idolised despot, because, like Shakespeare, she could divine what lay about men's hearts, and it was this understanding of, this deep sympathy for her people, her essential *Englishness*, that roused their devotion and made them think of her as the symbol of their country.

She had made no mistake about her first minister. William Cecil had been of service to the Protector Somerset in the reign of her

brother, Edward VI, and when she succeeded she chose this unob-
trusive young man—he was only thirty-eight—to be her Secretary.
She well knew what she was doing, for Cecil was a man of absolute
integrity and immense industry, with a prodigious grasp of detail; above
all, one who understood her, as well as anybody could understand that
enigmatic woman, and the partnership that lasted almost till the end
of the century was perhaps the most fortunate and fruitful in the whole
history of England.

The executive power lay with the Privy Council, a body of men
responsible, not to Parliament but to the Queen, under whom it
became virtually confined to the chief officers of state, the Lord
Chancellor, Lord Treasurer, Lord Privy Seal and Lord Admiral,
with those of the Household, the Lord Chamberlain, Lord Steward,
and Master of the Horse—and the Secretary. The official status of the
Secretary was inferior to that of the others, but under Cecil and his
son inevitably the office became the key position, the link between the
Crown and the Council, and the real power behind the throne.

In the less settled parts of the kingdom the government was
represented and strengthened by subsidiary bodies, the Council of the
North and the Council of Wales, the one based on York, the other on
Ludlow, where Philip Sidney's father, the gentle and much-loved
Sir Henry Sidney, was Lord President. No longer was the government of the country dependent on the goodwill of a feudal nobility
with almost royal powers in various parts of the kingdom; all was now
firmly controlled from the centre, by the Queen, Cecil and the Privy
Council. But to enforce their orders a host of officials was necessary,
the more economical the better, and such a body of men was found in
the new class of landed gentry, many of them snappers-up of the con-
fiscated monastic estates, with everything to gain, therefore, by
strengthening the Tudor dynasty. These were the men who freely
gave their time to the work of local government, carrying the decrees
of the Council into the uttermost skirts of the kingdom, enforcing the
provisions of the Poor Law, fixing wages, examining recusants and
administering justice, for many of them were Justices of the Peace.
Many of them were members of Parliament as well.

For Elizabeth the function of Parliament was to vote supplies and
she called it only for that reason, or to add the weight of its authority
to some important course of action on which she had already determined. Although Parliament had no direct control over the Privy

Council and policy making, yet it held the purse-strings when sub-
sidies were needed to amplify the royal revenue. In normal times the
sovereign was expected to run the country on his personal income, and
it is easy to see how, in a time of rapidly increasing responsibilities and
soaring prices, this body of four hundred and fifty men who composed
the Commons, members of the most influential class in the country,
for so they soon became, might grow into a source of danger to the
Crown.

Elizabeth managed them with tact, but towards the end of her
reign they were becoming critical and restive, an ominous mood for
any successor who claimed her prerogatives but lacked her authority
and charm. But such troubles lay within the dark abysm of the future.

When, on that gloomy November morning of 1558, the unhappy
Mary Tudor died, the new Queen must have faced the future with
more misgivings than her London subjects, who lit bonfires in the
streets, fetched out tables, ate and drank and made merry, and set all
the church bells in the City ringing, for it was an amiable foible
of these Elizabethans, having got a glass in their heads, to go up
into some belfry and ring the bells for hours together, for the sake
of exercise.

Most urgent of solution was the religious problem. There were
still as many Catholics as Protestants in the country, and if religious
strife was to be brought to an end and national unity preserved, a
settlement that both sides could accept was imperative. Elizabeth had
no strong religious convictions, and was guided primarily by political
expediency. On the one hand, she saw that the democratic organisation
of the Church preached by Protestant extremists was a threat to the
throne (No bishop, no queen!), and she had, in any event, a fastidious
distaste for their bleak services; on the other hand, there could be no
question of submission to Rome, no interference by a foreigner in
English affairs could ever again be tolerated, and here she knew she
had the overwhelming support of her people. Parliament was called
and the Act of Supremacy passed, though in a form less provocative
than her father's original measure; whereas Henry VIII had insisted
on being called 'Supreme Head of the Church', Elizabeth was to be
merely 'Supreme Governor of the Realm in all causes as well ecclesiastical as civil'. It came to the same thing, but it allowed a greater
elasticity of conscience to the Laodicean. Then, it was no longer trea-

son to refuse the oath; the recusant was merely precluded from office. The Act of Uniformity, which followed, reintroduced the second and milder Prayer Book of Edward VI, with further modifications in wording and ritual which made it more acceptable to the Catholics though offensive to Protestant zealots. At the same time, attendance at church on Sundays and Holy Days was enacted on pain of a fine of a shilling for each offence. The success of the settlement may be measured by the fact that only two hundred clergy resigned, though all but one of the Marian bishops refused the oath and were replaced by new men of a middle way. Unerringly Elizabeth selected the modest and scholarly Matthew Parker as her Archbishop of Canterbury, a man who disliked the reforming zeal of Knox and Calvin as much as she did, and whose firm moderation smoothly carried through the religious settlement, though not without some trouble from the Queen herself, in whose chapel the forbidden crucifix and lighted tapers were wont to appear and disappear according as her foreign policy inclined to the Catholic or the Protestant side.

The second problem was economic. Her father's extravagance, her brother's debasement of the currency and her sister's disastrous war with France had reduced the treasury to the verge of bankruptcy, while the collapse of the medieval social structure, under which the worker had been cared for by his manor or his guild, had led to the startling modern problem of widespread unemployment. The first thing was to restore the currency. Once again Elizabeth found and backed the man for the job. Sir Thomas Gresham had been financial agent to the Crown in Antwerp, the greatest commercial centre in the world; dismissed on religious grounds by Mary but reappointed as indispensable, this financial genius was at Elizabeth's command. In 1560 the debased coins were called in and replaced by new ones; confidence was restored and the value of English money on the foreign exchange was almost doubled. Gresham was to live—in princely style —for another twenty years, and it was in no small measure due to him that England was financially prepared for war with Spain.

Three years later the challenge of unemployment was met by the Statute of Apprentices. All contracts for employment were to be for at least a year, all craftsmen were to serve a seven years' apprenticeship under a master who was responsible for their welfare as well as their tuition, and the enforcement of the Act was entrusted to the Justices of the Peace, who were empowered to fix wages in their own districts. The state had taken over the regulation of agriculture, industry and labour; the drift from the towns was stayed, for the worker could now practise his craft wherever he wished, unfettered by guild restrictions; the skilled foreign immigrant was welcomed instead of discouraged, and a new field of industry and commerce was opened to the enterprising Elizabethans, comparable to, and indeed the complement of, the new world that was yet to be explored and developed.

There remained one problem that Elizabeth could not solve. For every devout Catholic she was illegitimate, the child of a second woman, born while her father's wife was still alive, and she had even been declared illegitimate by her father and the courts when her mother, Anne Boleyn, had been executed as an adulteress. It is true that she had been reinstated in the line of succession by her father's will, confirmed by Parliament, and that her own Parliament had hastened to declare her the lawful sovereign, an authorisation sufficient for all good Englishmen, yet for anybody who cared to deny its validity, the legitimate heir to the throne was Mary Stuart, granddaughter of Henry VIII's sister and James IV of Scotland. Mary had become Queen of Scotland a week after she was born, but from childhood had been brought up in the corrupt and brilliant French Court, and six months before the accession of Elizabeth had married the heir to the French throne. The beautiful girl of sixteen was, therefore, not only Queen of Scotland, but also presumptive Queen of France, with a claim to be Queen of England strong enough to warrant her assumption of its arms.

Scotland was in danger of becoming a French dependency. For the last six years Mary's mother, Mary of Guise, had been regent, and a French army of occupation garrisoned its strongholds in defence of the Catholic faith. It was Mary of Guise and Mary Tudor whom John Knox denounced in his *Blast against the Monstrous Regiment of Women*, and the Scots, nobles and peasants alike, rallied to the Protestant cause, which had also become the cause of liberty and patriotism. By the end of 1559 the main French force was beseiged in Leith, where it awaited reinforcements; if it were relieved the Protestant and nationalist cause might well be lost, and urgent appeals for aid were sent to England. Cecil implored Elizabeth to send help; but she hesitated, she did not wish to offend her Catholic subjects or to risk a war with France. At the last moment she agreed; an English fleet blockaded the Forth, an English army helped to reduce Leith and the French were expelled from Scotland for ever. It was an historic occasion, the first on which England and Scotland had worked together; and Protestantism had been saved, though Elizabeth looked askance at the democratic Presbyterianism imposed by Knox on the country to whose rescue she had come.

Meanwhile, for a few delirious months Mary had been Queen of France; but her husband was killed in 1560, and in the following year the nineteen-year-old widow returned to her native country. She had lost one throne, but there remained the chance of another south of the Border if she played her cards intelligently. Much might depend on whom she married as her second husband, and on whom her cousin of England married as well.

For the question of Elizabeth's marriage was one of supreme consequence. She was now almost thirty, almost, according to Elizabethan standards, middle-aged. In 1562 she very nearly died of small-pox, being saved only at the last moment by the unwilling attentions of a German quack, a mining engineer turned physician. Her single state set a premium upon her life, and if she should be killed the heir to the throne was the ardent and romantic Mary, and there was no saying what her matrimonial adventures might be. Elizabeth must marry and have children; but Elizabeth thought otherwise. Philip II of Spain offered his hand, gallantly but not entirely disinterestedly, only to be decisively rejected, though for a time she played off his cousin, the Archduke Charles, against the Earl of Arran, Catholic against Protestant, and henceforth her coquetry with foreign princes was the most delicate device in her diplomacy. At home there was, of course, Lord Darnley, whose claim to the succession both of the English and the Scottish thrones led her to detain him in England; he was 'a proper and well-proportioned long man', but he was a fool and twelve years her junior, a vicious youth fit for Mary, whose chances he might ruin if she let him go north. Then there was a properer man than Darnley among her courtiers, a real man of her own age, the tall, handsome and dashing Robert Dudley. They had met in the Tower, where they had both been imprisoned by her sister, Mary, when he had been sentenced to death after the attempt of his father, the Duke of Northumberland, to put Lady Jane Grey on the throne. However, he had been pardoned, and now that his wife, poor Amy Robsart, had so unfortunately, though opportunely, fallen down stairs and broken her neck, he was an eligible widower. She was fascinated; she danced with him, made him a Knight of the Garter, granted him the castle of Kenilworth and lands in Warwickshire and Wales, and in 1564 created him Earl of Leicester. Cecil was on tenterhooks, for he distrusted the man; ugly stories were being whispered concerning the death of his wife, and his marriage with the Queen might split the country. Suddenly Elizabeth declared that she had no intention of marrying her favourite, and even recommended him as a husband for her cousin Mary. However, it was Darnley, not Dudley, whom she sent to Scotland.

This, then, was the domestic scene in 1564. Thanks to Cecil's able diplomacy, Elizabeth was firmly established on the throne with virtually all her people behind her; thanks to Gresham the country was entering a period of unprecedented prosperity, and, under the tolerant Parker, Catholics were becoming reconciled to the Anglican doctrine and ritual. England was at peace, but abroad the scene was very different. In France, civil war had broken out between the Catholic Guise faction and the Protestant Huguenots; after furious fighting and a series of assassinations, a truce was patched up, but both sides were waiting for a renewal of the conflict. In 1562–3 Elizabeth had tried to repeat her successful Scottish policy, and intervened on behalf of the Huguenots; but her insistence on the return of Calais, lost by Mary, as the price of her help only alienated her allies. In any event, the Catholics had the better of the fighting, and Elizabeth had to acquiesce in the permanent loss of Calais. The episode taught her a lesson, and there were no more European adventures for more than twenty years. In the Netherlands, approximately the modern Holland and Belgium, another religious war was imminent. Originally independent states, they had become, by inheritance, the most valuable part of the Spanish possessions, and now that the Pope and the Council of Trent had demanded the merciless repression of heresy, the fanatical and pedantic Philip II was determined to carry out his orders. In 1564 the storm was breaking; Gresham, than whom nobody was better informed, was withdrawing from Antwerp, and a stream of Flemish craftsmen was flooding into England, which was soon to wrest the commercial supremacy from the Netherlands. England was being enriched both relatively and absolutely by her rivals' troubles. Meanwhile Elizabeth remained unmarried and, apparently, fancy-free, while Darnley prepared for his northward journey.

LONDON in 1600, from *CIVITAS LONDINI*, by JOHN NORDEN

QUEEN
ELIZABETH I
AND THE
GODDESSES
by
Hans Eworth, 1569

When Shakespeare was born, the fortunes of England were in the ascendant. But what was his cultural heritage? What was the condition of the arts? Broadly speaking, we may say that, just as the sixteenth century was politically and economically an age of transition, a period in the course of which England emerged from the medieval into the modern world, so it was with the arts. At the end of the fifteenth century the principal patron of the arts was still the Catholic Church; its finest architecture was ecclesiastical, its style the soaring Perpendicular Gothic of King's College Chapel at Cambridge, of Henry VII's Chapel at Westminster, and of innumerable additions to cathedrals and parish churches, including the chancel of Holy Trinity at Stratford, where Shakespeare was destined to lie at last; its sculpture was the canopied saints of niche and portal, of spandrelled angels, of marble bishops and alabaster princes recumbent upon their tombs, of the crucified Christ above the carved wooden screen that separated chancel from nave; the peculiar glory of its painting was the stained and storied glass that gilded the light falling from the great windows; its grandest music was its motets, unaccompanied sacred songs for many voices intricately linked; its drama was the miracle and morality play.

The Reformation put an end to this. The Church was impoverished, its sphere and power of patronage curtailed, and ecclesiastical building almost ceased until the Laudian revival a century later. But it was not only that artistic activity was checked; many of the existing works of art were destroyed; Henry VIII ordered the despoliation of the monasteries and chantries, the removal of shrines and monuments of miracles, and his minions added carvings, stained glass and other treasures to their agreeable labours of destruction. Thanks to the iconoclasts of the sixteenth century and their even more destructive descendants of the seventeenth, we have to go to Fairford in Gloucestershire, or St. Neot in Cornwall, to see a parish church whose medieval glass is virtually complete. And we have only to go to Salisbury, loveliest of cathedrals without, bleakest of buildings within, to realise how thirteenth-century architects thought in terms of coloured glass when designing their internal bays.

It was only just before the beginning of these destructive decades that the influence of the Renaissance on the visual arts began to be felt in England. The result was that the English Renaissance was almost entirely a secular movement; patronage passed from the Church to the Court, to the new nobility and wealthy gentry, who vied with one another in the enrichment of their environment. But the foreign art that influenced England most was not that of the great period in Italy. There the Renaissance, inspired directly by classical models, had spent itself in the course of the fourteenth and fifteenth centuries, and by the time of the Reformation was declining into mannerism, an imitative art of variation without progression, formally ingenious but spiritually impoverished. The English Renaissance, therefore, was inspired only indirectly, or at many removes, by classical antiquity; there were very few Englishmen who had seen a Greek or Roman building, fewer still who had seen a Greek statue, and the influence was mainly that of contemporary Italy, France and the Netherlands. We can see this best in Tudor and Elizabethan architecture, which almost symbolises the transition from the medieval to the modern age. There is little or no understanding of classical form beyond a growing awareness of symmetry, and structures essentially Gothic are progressively overlaid with classical or pseudo-classical ornament of questionable function. This does not mean that these great houses are ugly, they are among the most beautiful buildings in England; but it does mean that they are not classical, they are Tudor, Elizabethan or even Jacobean, brilliant hybrids and somehow essentially English.

In architecture we can trace the development of the taste for the 'antique' from the middle of Henry VIII's reign. The hall of Hampton Court is a purely medieval structure, buttressed and pinnacled, and looking from the outside like some late Perpendicular chapel built of brick; yet there is carving in the hammer-beam roof that is unmistakably Renaissance in origin and apparently English in execution. More remarkable was the southern of the two gatehouses built across what is now Whitehall to connect the old York Place with its extension to the west. Typically Tudor in design, a central opening flanked by corner turrets with arched passages for pedestrians, it was faced with classical detail: Doric and Ionic pilasters, pediments and cornice, the turrets crowned with cupolas instead of crenellations. But the Tudor building most significant for the future of English architecture was Somerset House, built about 1550 by John Thynne for the Protector Somerset. Its plan was of the traditional courtyard type, an inward-facing house, derived from the days when exterior walls were primarily defensive; but at one end of the court was something new in

English architecture, a Renaissance loggia. Even more interesting was the Strand front, with central gatehouse and projecting bays in which the windows were grouped in pairs beneath a pediment, in the French manner. The classical influence in this façade is something more than a veneer; but, then, it is exceptional and John Thynne was something of a genius. Somerset House was a portent and a challenge, a challenge that was taken up by the statesmen of the period, and the age of the building of great country-houses began. William Cecil started the restoration of Burghley, his family home in Northamptonshire, and the building of Theobalds, a new house in Hertfordshire; William Herbert, first Earl of Pembroke, built Wilton House; while Somerset's great rival, the Duke of Northumberland, sent one of his men to study architecture at its classical source, and in 1550 John Shute set off for Italy. The fruit of his labours appeared in 1563 as *The First and Chief Grounds of Architecture*, though his researches seem to have been more among books than buildings, and his chief authority the recently published *Architettura* of Sebastiano Serlio. Both these books, with their illustrations of the orders, were widely read, but the Elizabethans were not purists and preferred their own variations and adaptations to classical originals. Moreover, during the early years of Elizabeth's reign, Englishmen were at last free to travel in Europe, and inevitably brought back with them the foreign fashions that Shakespeare was later to laugh at. Inevitably, too, they brought back new fashions in the arts, but the fashion that swamped all others came from the Netherlands, for Antwerp did a brisk trade in art as well as in more prosaic merchandise, and now that the Spanish persecution was upon them, builders and masons joined the throng of craftsmen who fled to England. In the hands of the Flemings classical design had assumed strange irresponsible shapes, intricate, curly and spiky, and it was these, particularly the 'strap' ornament, so called because it looks like strips of leather, that Elizabethan artists and builders seized on for the embellishment of their buildings. We can understand why Sir Thomas Gresham, when he began his great Royal Exchange in London in 1566, took the Antwerp Bourse for his model, employed a Flemish overseer, and imported his material from Flanders; but even Sir John Thynne, or his inspired master mason Robert Smythson, was taken somewhat with the manner, for Longleat has Flemish detail lacking in Somerset House, from which it derives, though with a difference; Somerset House was medievally introspective, inward-looking,

Longleat has the right Renaissance outward look, its windows—and there is as much window as wall—face the world, so that, apart from being one of the most beautiful, it may be said to be the first of our great modern country-houses. Kirby, Wollaton, Worksop, Wimbledon, Montacute, glorious Hardwick Hall and many others followed in the course of the reign.

Elizabeth herself was no great builder; she had her palaces of Whitehall, Windsor, Hampton Court, Richmond and Greenwich, where she was born, but in the summer she liked a change of air, and then it was that, accompanied by her Household, she made her stately progresses, and the great houses went up to receive her. It was an honour, but it was an expense; Cecil reckoned that her twelve visits to Theobalds cost him 'two or three thousand pounds every time'. It was also an anxiety, and not all her subjects were as eager as the Secretary to entertain their sovereign, for whom he was always prepared to exceed his purse and to whom he consecrated his house. Thus, when she proposed visiting Petworth, the Duke of Northumberland wrote, 'her Majestie will never thank him that hath perswaded this progreyse, considering the wayes by which she must come to them, up the hill and down the hill, so as she shall not be able to use ether coche or litter with ease, and those ways also so full of louse stones'; and he was careful to add, 'nether can ther be in this cuntrey any wayes devysed to avoyd those ould wayes'. The noble duke was no psychologist, and the indomitable woman came.

The year 1563 was one of plague, and Elizabeth's summer holiday was little more than a visit to the Earl of Arundel at Nonsuch, the great Surrey palace built by her father, and which 'of all other places she liked best'. But 1564 was propitiously clear of infection, and the year of Shakespeare's birth witnessed the first of the royal progresses on the grand scale; the queen went as far afield as Cambridge and Leicestershire, visiting more than twenty of her subjects, the first of whom was Cecil at Theobalds, and the last Sir Thomas Gresham at Osterley.

It is strange to reflect that if Shakespeare never went abroad he never saw a purely classical building. The first in England was begun in the year of his death: the Queen's House at Greenwich. His architectural environment was essentially a medieval one. There was little expansion in Stratford and Warwick in the sixteenth century, and the buildings that would impress him most in his youth would be

Holy Trinity, the church and castle at Warwick, and, a little farther afield, Kenilworth, though he would see examples of the contemporary style at Charlecote, rebuilt by Sir Thomas Lucy in 1558, and at Kenilworth, where Leicester added new buildings in 1571. Although there was almost feverish building activity in London during the twenty years of his residence there, it was mainly to house the so rapidly growing population; everywhere the suburbs were encroaching on the country north of the walls, but there was little new building of architectural importance, and it is probable that he saw nothing more classical than Somerset House and the Doric arcade in the courtyard of the Royal Exchange. Of course he knew other parts of England besides Stratford and London, and was probably acquainted with many of the new country-houses, but nowhere would he find a strictly classical building; even monumental Audley End, completed at the time of his death, was characterised by an Italian as inclining 'to the Gothic, mixed with a little of the Doric and Ionic'.

Milton saw the partial transformation of London into a Renaissance city after the return of Inigo Jones from his epoch-making Italian tour in 1614; he saw the classical buildings going up, and his Pandemonium could scarcely be mistaken for anything Elizabethan:

> Built like a temple, where pilasters round
> Were set, and Doric pillars overlaid
> With golden architrave; nor did there want
> Cornice or frieze, with bossy sculptures graven.

Shakespeare saw none of this, though he may have known the works of Shute and Serlio, and the *Architectura* of the Fleming, Vredeman de Vries; but it was ever his way to describe what he had actually seen, what he knew at first hand, and his architectural description is of another age:

> This castle hath a pleasant seat . . .
>   no jutty, frieze,
> Buttress, nor coign of vantage, but this bird
> Hath made his pendent bed and procreant cradle.

His imagery, too, is in terms of medieval building,

> Hath nature given them eyes
> To see this vaulted arch and the rich crop
> Of sea and land?

And that he was at his ease with the architect's vocabulary is witnessed by Romeo's splendid pun on 'lantern':

> I'll bury thee in a triumphant grave
> A grave? O, no, a lantern, slaughtered youth;
> For here lies Juliet, and her beauty makes
> This vault a feasting presence full of light.

The elaborate comparison of the setting up of a kingdom to the building of a house in 2 *Henry IV* (I. iii) is a reflection of the everyday scene in London towards the end of the century, intensified perhaps by his own restoration of New Place. His first-hand knowledge of classical architecture was confined to its detail; this he prized, and his description of Imogen's bedchamber must be that of the Renaissance interior of one of the great houses that he knew:

> the chimney-piece,
> Chaste Dian bathing . . .
> The roof o' the chamber
> With golden cherubins is fretted: her andirons—
> I had forgot them—were two winking Cupids
> Of silver, each on one foot standing.

It was in the field of interior decoration, carving and sculpture that Renaissance art reached England. Henry VIII was a Renaissance prince, an accomplished musician with a talent for writing verses, developed no doubt by his tutor John Skelton, and a patron of the arts, if not always a very discriminating one. About the time of his accession in 1509 a group of Italian artists was in England, the chief of whom was Pietro Torrigiano, the Florentine sculptor who, after breaking Michelangelo's nose in a fit of temper, more constructively fashioned the magnificent bronze effigies of Henry VII and his Queen in Westminster Abbey. Wolsey too, employed Italian artists, but most of them seem to have left the country soon after his fall, and it is uncertain whether the screen of King's College Chapel, erected about 1534 and perhaps the finest piece of wood carving in Europe, is the work of Italian or French masters. After the Reformation the province of wood carving and the plastic arts was primarily secular, but there was little immediate demand from the new patrons for statuary to embellish the exterior of their houses, or even the interior, where plasterwork was all the fashion; and English sculpture never recovered the grand simplicity of its golden age, the thirteenth century, the century in which William Torel made the bronze effigy of Queen Eleanor in Westminster Abbey, one of the masterpieces of the world. Though very fine, John Orchard's bronze of Edward III, and the Richard II and Anne of Bohemia by Nicholas Broker and Godfrey Prest, are not equal to Torel's work, and in the fifteenth century the simple idealised form gave way to the elaborate irrelevancy of dramatic portraiture and realism, well exemplified in the, admittedly charming, series of statues in Henry VII's Chapel, whose prophets, evangelists and apostles read their books with the aid of pince-nez. However, if the nobility, gentry and moneyed merchants forgot the sculptors in their lives, they were determined not themselves to be forgotten in their deaths, and an ever-increasing number of monumental effigies enriched and encumbered the churches, some of them of much more than common merit, as are those at Framlingham in Suffolk. There is the tomb of the Duke of Richmond, Henry VIII's illegitimate son, and the effigies of the third Duke of Norfolk and his wife, of the two wives of the fourth Duke, executed by Elizabeth, and there, too, lie his mother and father, the poet Earl of Surrey, done to death by Henry VIII, their three children in red robes and ermine capes kneeling behind them. Then there is the later work of Robert Smythson, greatest of Elizabethan architects, of Epiphanius Evesham, Nicholas Stone and other English masters. In the sixties the traffic in foreign works of art began in earnest, and with the sculptures from the Netherlands came the sculptors, Maximilian Colt, Joseph Hollemans and the rest, who filled the niches over the arcade of the Royal Exchange with statues of the English kings. The builders of the great houses followed suit: the roundels at Longleat were filled with carvings; Wollaton was to have had its niches graced with statues from Italy, unhappily lost at sea; but Montacute was more fortunate, and the niches of its main front house the pleasing, though not altogether convincing, figures of the Nine Worthies. One of the Flemish master masons who fled the Spanish terror was Gheerhart Jannsen, naturalised as Gerard Johnson. He established himself on the Bankside in London, where he died in 1611, leaving his business to his four sons, one of whom, Bernard, designed Audley End, and another, Gerard the younger, in 1616 received a commission to make a monument for the parish church at Stratford, where his acquaintance, perhaps his friend, William Shakespeare had recently been buried.

The one artist mentioned by Shakespeare in his work is 'that rare Italian master, Julio Romano' on whom he fathered the reputed statue of Hermione. Romano was really a painter and architect, the favourite pupil of Raphael; but Vasari quotes an epitaph that credits him with skill as a sculptor as well, and it is quite possible that Shakespeare saw one of his carvings in England. He once had a prodigious reputation, but his work is now forgotten or best forgotten. Romano was an unfortunate choice, but Shakespeare had a genuine feeling for sculpture, which was the inspiration of some of his noblest lines, particularly in his early poetry, and when we read the splendid opening of *Love's Labour's Lost*,

> Let fame, that all hunt after in their lives,
> Live register'd upon our brazen tombs,

or the yet more splendid *Sonnet 55*,

> Not marble, nor the gilded monuments
> Of princes, shall outlive this powerful rhyme,

we are present with Shakespeare in Westminster Abbey, beside Torel's bronze effigy of Queen Eleanor, or Torrigiano's gilt bronze of Henry VII.

It was fortunate for the art of England that, just at the time that the Reformation put an end to religious painting, a great artist should appear to open up a new and lucrative field, that of portraiture, a form of art that had a peculiar appeal to the new patrons; for not only did portraits make pleasant patches of colour on the walls, they also offered a more cheerful kind of vicarious immortality than the monumental tombs that they would never see. Hans Holbein, a German well acquainted with the art of Italy and the great master of the northern Renaissance, was in England most of the time from 1526 until he died, 'choked by pest', in 1543. Erasmus introduced him to Sir Thomas More, indirectly therefore to Henry VIII, and the result was a series of paintings and drawings of More and his circle, of the King and his Court, which brings the age to life more fully perhaps than any other in our history.

There was nobody of comparable stature to succeed Holbein, but Henry managed to secure as Court painter a fashionable and competent Netherlander, Guillim Scrots, one of whose best works is a full-length portrait of Henry Howard, Earl of Surrey, the poet who was executed on a fantastic charge of treason a few days before the blood-besotted King himself expired. Scrots appears to have left England on the accession of Mary, and for the next twenty years Court painting—and there was little elsewhere of importance—was dominated by another Netherlander, Hans Eworth of Antwerp. His portraits include a Holbeinesque 'Mary Tudor', a strangely moving one of Lord Darnley and his little brother standing in the deserted gallery of some Tudor house, and an allegorical one of Queen Elizabeth, in which the goddesses recall the work of 'that rare Italian master, Julio Romano'. This, dated 1569, may be the first painting of Elizabeth as Queen, the first of a series that grew more and more fantastic and remote, gathering legendary accretions as the reign progressed, and culminating in the extraordinary portrait painted to commemorate her visit to Ditchley in the nineties.

Although it is to anticipate, some mention must here be made of the most important figure in English painting in the latter half of Elizabeth's reign, Nicholas Hilliard, a Devonshireman. The illumination of manuscripts had been almost killed by the invention of printing, but, by adapting the old technique to the new subject-matter, Holbein kept the art alive in the form of miniature portraits, called 'limnings', a corruption of 'illumination'. In the hands of Hilliard miniature painting became the visual counterpart of the poetry of the age; his limnings have the jewel-like and enamelled quality of Sidney's sonnets and Spenser's odes, the same delicately compounded artifice and freshness, like 'meadows painted with delight', and at the same time a Shakespearean power of characterisation that sometimes equals that of his master, Holbein. In 1572 he was appointed limner and goldsmith to the Queen; his work became immensely popular at Court, and lords and ladies of the capital carried his miniatures on chains about their necks. Donne knew his worth, and wrote,

> a hand, or eye
> By Hilliard drawn, is worthy an history
> By a worse painter made.

And when Shakespeare made Hamlet say of his uncle, 'those that would make mows at him while my father lived, give twenty, forty, fifty, a hundred ducats apiece for his picture in little', he was thinking of Hilliard—or of Hilliard's young rival, Isaac Oliver.

In his *Treatise concerning the Art of Limning*, Hilliard generously acknowledges his debt to Holbein and 'the most excellent Albert Dürer . . . doubtless the most exquisite man that ever left us lines to view for true delineation'; and he adds, 'Of truth all the rare sciences, especially the arts of carving, painting, goldsmiths, embroiderers, together with the most of all the liberal sciences, came first unto us from the strangers, and generally they are the best and most in number'. By 'strangers' he meant primarily Flemings, and it is important to appreciate the debt that Shakespeare's England owed in the visual arts as well as in industry to the Netherlands. There were many itinerant and refugee Flemish painters in the country in Elizabeth's reign, but the most important visiting artist was an Italian, Federigo Zuccaro, who was here for about a year in 1574–5, when he painted full-length portraits of Elizabeth and Leicester. On the strength of this, any unsigned Elizabethan portrait is liable to be fathered on Zuccaro, and many of these have hopefully been claimed as portraits of Shakespeare; but as at the time of Zuccaro's visit Shakespeare was a ten-year-old Stratford schoolboy, such claims seem scarcely justified.

The graphic art with which the youthful Shakespeare would be best acquainted was such stained glass as had escaped the zeal of the reformers, and the line illustrations in books, the title pages of which were often embellished with the Flemish strap ornament and cartouches that the masons so gaily carved into three-dimensional forms. Most of the wall painting in the churches had been erased or decently covered with a coat of whitewash; but there were wall paintings in some of the Stratford houses, and Shakespeare would certainly know those at the White Swan, painted shortly before his birth and illustrating the story of Tobias and the Angel. Such paintings, though not normally of religious subjects, were superseding tapestries as decorations for the walls: 'And for thy walls', says Falstaff, 'a pretty slight drollery or the story of the Prodigal, or the German hunting in waterwork, is worth a thousand of these bed-hangings and these fly-bitten tapestries'. Simple, non-representational designs and stencil work were cheaper than tapestries; but then tapestries, like wainscoting, had a utilitarian as well as an æsthetic value—they kept in the warmth, or rather they kept out some of the cold.

Like so many other forms of art, tapestries came principally from the Netherlands; 'arras' indeed being the Elizabethan name for them, though Arras had long been superseded by Brussels as the great centre of manufacture. But tapestries were manufactured nearer to Stratford than Brussels. Early in the sixteenth century, William Sheldon of Beoley, near Henley-in-Arden, sent one Richard Hicks to learn the art in the Low Countries, and then set up looms at Barcheston and in the dissolved abbey of Bordesley, with Hicks as master weaver, 'the only auter and beginner of tapestry and Arras within this realm'. Richard was succeeded by his son Francis, who was responsible for a series of tapestry maps of the counties, and the celebrated 'Hatfield Seasons', a set of four hangings dated 1611, now at Hatfield House. One can see the Flemish influence in the landscapes with figures, and it is not unlikely that the designer worked with one of the pictures of the elder Brueghel in his mind. If Shakespeare saw them, and he probably saw a great many of these Warwickshire tapestries, he would like them, for he had the same eye for humorous and realistic detail as Brueghel; and it is tempting to think that in London, or possibly at Titchfield or Wilton, he saw paintings by that great Flemish master, which had been shipped over from Antwerp. He would always pause to sketch a scene that would have delighted Brueghel, and we have only to compare this from *Lucrece*,

> Here one man's hand lean'd on another's head,
> His nose being shadow'd by his neighbour's ear;
> Here one, being throng'd, bears back, all boll'n and red;
> Another, smother'd, seems to pelt and swear;

with Brueghel's *Adoration of the Kings* in the National Gallery to see the affinity between the two. That Shakespeare was intensely interested in painting is certain, and his part in the designing of Lord Rutland's *impresa* suggests that he may even have been an amateur painter like his friend Burbage. But the whole question of Shakespeare and painting remains to be explored.

We can be more confident about Shakespeare's musical experience. The sixteenth century, the golden century of English music, was given a splendid send-off by its Tudor rulers—Henry VIII was a composer and player of many instruments, Edward VI a lutenist and Mary Tudor and Elizabeth both skilful players of the virginals. But the English had ever been singers, singers of folk-songs and ballads and carols, and the peculiar glory of the Tudor age was not its instrumental music but its song. The art of counterpoint, the harmonious weaving together of two or more melodies, had been almost mastered by the English and Netherlandish composers of the fifteenth century, and it was this contrapuntal sacred music for unaccompanied voices, the motet, that Thomas Tallis brought to such perfection in the early years of Elizabeth's reign. To hear the confluent melodies and rhythms of his motet *Spem in alium*, written for eight five-part choirs, is as celestial an exaltation as most of us will ever experience in this life. His pupil, William Byrd, joined him at the Chapel Royal, and together they published their *Cantiones*, a collection of Latin motets for five and six voices. Both these great men remained staunch Catholics, and most of their music was religious, though Byrd wrote important work for the virginals and is sometimes called the father of the English madrigal, but it is, above all, his three great Masses, published with some secrecy in the year of the Armada, that justify his claim to be called the greatest composer of the age.

The effect of the Reformation on English music had been profound. The Dissolution involved the expulsion of musicians from the monasteries—Tallis himself was expelled from Waltham Abbey—and led to the dissemination of music throughout the country, a process quickened by the printing press of Wynkyn de Worde. There was a liberation of the old liturgical forms, new rhythms had to be found to suit the agile English that replaced the formal and sonorous Latin cadences, and, as in the other arts, there was a parallel process of secularisation, stimulated by the demand of the Court for ceremony and delight, and of the great country-houses for entertainment. The result was a rapid development of instrumental music, for lute, viol, virginals and recorder, and the transformation of the motet into the madrigal, for the madrigal is essentially the motet secularised and writ small.[1] 'Next unto the motet this is the most artificial, and to men of understanding, the most delightful', wrote Thomas Morley. 'If, therefore, you will compose in this kind, you must possess yourself with an amorous humour, for in no composition shall you prove admirable except you put on and possess yourself wholly with that vein wherein you compose. So that you must in your music be wavering like the wind, sometime wanton, sometime drooping, sometime grave and staid, otherwhile effeminate, and the more variety you shall show the better you shall please'.[2]

[1] It is worth noting that the form was developed by the Netherlandish musicians in Rome, and is another of the debts that English art owes to the Low Countries.
[2] *A Plaine and Easie Introduction to Practicall Music*, 1597.

Shakespeare's life coincided with the zenith of this wonderful era. When he was born, Byrd was organist of Lincoln Cathedral, Tallis organist of the Chapel Royal, where the Master of the Children was Richard Edwards, whose poem *In Commendation of Musique* is quoted in *Romeo and Juliet*:

> Then music with her silver sound
> With speedy help doth lend redress.

Richard Farrant was Master of the Children of Windsor and organist to the Queen at St. George's Chapel, and Sebastian Westcott Master of the choir school of St. Paul's. Then, born within a few years of Shakespeare, was a whole galaxy of composers: Thomas Morley, the pupil of Byrd and friend of Shakespeare, for whom he composed the setting of 'It was a lover and his lass'; John Dowland, writer of airs and the greatest lutenist of his age,

> whose heavenly touch
> Upon the lute doth ravish human sense;

John Bull, first Professor of Music at Gresham College, famous for his compositions for the virginals, who ended his career as organist of Antwerp Cathedral; Thomas Campion, physician and poet, who died leaving all that he had, and 'wished that his estate had bin farr more', to Philip Rosseter, lutenist to the Royal Household and, like his friend, a rare composer of songs; Thomas Tomkins, last of the madrigalists, and John Wilbye, perhaps the greatest, who passed his life in the service of the family of Sir Thomas Kytson, the builder of Hengrave Hall in Suffolk; and Thomas Weelkes, organist of Winchester College and Chichester Cathedral, composer of music for viols and of madrigals. Rather later was Orlando Gibbons, one of the most versatile of this illustrious company, whose death in 1625, while going to welcome the bride of Charles I, brought to an untimely end the greatest age of English music, an age that has only recently been rediscovered.

In the Middle Ages the aristocratic toughs and noble hooligans, made so familiar to us in Shakespeare's early histories, had regarded music with contempt, as an accomplishment fit only for priests and women, but the civilising Renaissance had altered all that. Thus, in Castiglione's *Cortegiano*, a book written in the form of a discussion on the qualities that go to make the ideal gentleman, a soldier who refuses to join in dance and music receives from a lady the stinging rebuke: 'I should think that as you are not at war, nor in any likelihood of fighting, it would be a good thing if you were to have yourself thoroughly well oiled and put away in a cupboard with all your fighting gear until you were wanted, so as not to get more rusty than you are already.' And, according to Thomas Morley, anybody who was unable to take part in a madrigal at sight was considered unfit for polite society. We may be sure that his friend Shakespeare was not one of these, but that he could sing an air with the best of them, and probably accompany himself upon the lute as well. After poetry, music appears to have been his next love, and his plays are full of musical allusions and images, from the early comedies and histories to *The Tempest*, in which the discord beating in men's minds is resolved by the music of the magic island and sweet sounds that give delight. And who but a musician could have written the last act of *The Merchant of Venice*, most musical of plays?

> The man that hath no music in himself,
> Nor is not mov'd with concord of sweet sounds,
> Is fit for treasons, stratagems and spoils;
> The motions of his spirit are dull as night,
> And his affections dark as Erebus.

When Henry VIII died, there was nothing to suggest that the reign of Elizabeth was to be an age even richer in its poetry than its music. Though the century 1450–1550 is the most brilliant in the literature of Scotland, it is the most barren in that of England; and yet it is a period that made possible the full development of its future triumphs. 'I haue practysed and lerned at my grete charge and dispense to ordeyne this said book in prynte after the maner and forme as ye may here see, and it is not wreton with penne and ynke as other bokes ben, to thende that euery man may haue them attones: for all the bookes of this storye named the Recule of the Historyes of Troyes thus enpryntid as ye here see were begonne in oon day, and also fynysshid in oon day.' Thus casually did Caxton introduce the revolutionary invention of printing to his countrymen. Chaucer's clerk of Oxford had dreamed of a library of twenty books, twenty manuscript volumes involving far more than as many months in the making, but now ten times the number could be turned out in a single day, and for the first time the riches of medieval literature were placed within reach of all men who could read. The *Recuyell of Troye* was printed at Bruges in 1474, but within two years Caxton had set up his press in Westminster, and before he died in 1491 had printed many of the medieval classics, including Gower's *Confessio Amantis*, Chaucer's *Canterbury Tales*, *Troilus and Criseyde* and *House of Fame*, some of Lydgate's poems and Malory's *Morte d'Arthur*, which he himself edited. His work was carried on by his pupil Wynkyn de Worde, and by the royal printer Richard Pynson, the finest printer to practise in England before the appearance of John Day in the last year of Henry VIII's reign.

The dramatic poetry of Chaucer and romantic prose of Malory were by no means idle and unprofitable reading for a future dramatist, but we can imagine the boy Shakespeare somewhat impatient of medieval literature and eagerly seeking that of his own so different and so much more exciting age. He would soon close, if ever he opened them, the works of scholars such as John Colet, Thomas Linacre and other apostles of the new learning, and might well shudder at the mention of William Lyly, the author of the *Latin Grammar* that he used at school; but he would devour the work of one of Linacre's pupils, the *Utopia* of Sir Thomas More, a political treatise set within a story of exploration and adventure, the original Latin of which was ably translated by Ralph Robinson fifteen years after More's execution. Then there was Lord Berners' translation of the *Chronicles* of Jean Froissart, a picturesque account of European chivalry in the fourteenth century, and one of the numerous romantic histories and historical romances issued by the early printing presses, which were to have such an influence on the poets of the next generation.

But the most important prose work of the period was the English version of the Bible. The *Great Bible* of 1539, 'apoynted to the vse of the churches', was largely the work of Miles Coverdale, but its special glory was the New Testament of William Tyndale, whose simple and noble language set a new standard for English prose. During the Marian persecutions another version was prepared by refugee reformers in Geneva, and in 1560 the *Genevan Bible* [1] was published. Everything was done to make it easy and attractive to read; it was printed in a clear roman type instead of black letter;

---

[1] This is sometimes known as the *Breeches Bible*, from its rendering of *Genesis* iii. 7: 'They sewed fig tree leaves together and made themselves breeches.'

chapters were divided into verses; there were illustrations: pictures of the crossing of the Red Sea and the vision of Ezekiel, maps of the Holy Land and a nostalgic glimpse of Paradise; and the text was illuminated by a lively marginal commentary. It was a triumph for the left-wing Protestants, and its popularity was such that scores of editions were issued in Elizabeth's reign, in spite of its not being recognised for use in churches. The official *Great Bible* could not compete, and as a result Archbishop Parker ordered its revision by 'able bishops and other learned men', their work being published in the magnificent folio of 1568, known as the *Bishops' Bible*. Several editions followed, but it failed to dislodge the Genevan version from the affections of the people, and though the one was read aloud in church, the other was studied privately in the home. We can scarcely exaggerate the effect of the reformed church service in training the literary taste of the people, as Sunday after Sunday they unconsciously absorbed the grand language of the Bible, and grew accustomed to the grave cadences of Cranmer in the Book of Common Prayer, and joined together in singing the psalms, even though they were in the stumping metrical version of Sternhold and Hopkins, 'human hymns' as yet being considered improper. It was their children, brought up on this language and these rhythms, who were to form the theatre audiences that listened to the verse of Marlowe at the time of the Armada.

Most of the important prose works of the first half of the sixteenth century were translations, and even *Utopia* has to be judged as English literature in Robinson's translation. There were exceptions, of course; Sir Thomas Elyot's *Governour*, a guide to the education of the ruling class, written in a self-conscious and forward-looking style, and Thomas Wilson's *Art of Rhetorique*, a young man's defence of English and, what is more, of plain English: 'Among all other lessons this should first be learned, that we never affect any strange inkhorn terms, but to speak as is commonly received; neither seeking to be overfine, nor yet living overcareless, using our speech as most men do, and ordering our wits as the fewest have done.' Sound sense, though soon to go unheeded, but Roger Ascham, tutor to the Princess Elizabeth, agreed with Wilson, and his *Toxophilus*, a dialogue on the art of shooting with the long-bow, is as lucid as it is delightful, and in it English prose, discarding the artless romanticism of the Middle Ages, assumes a new classical discipline.

If there was a little original prose of the first order written, or at least published, in the first half of the sixteenth century, there was even less poetry. The splendid ballad of the *Nutbrown Maid* appeared in 1502, but it was really a late medieval poem, the product of the previous century when so many of our ballads appear to have been composed, and the only considerable poet of early Tudor times was John Skelton. A Cambridge graduate well spoken of by Caxton and Erasmus for his learning, he was appointed tutor to the future Henry VIII, and in 1504 rector of Diss in Norfolk. There, in an age of celibate clergy, he scandalised his parishioners by a secret marriage, and with his biting wit made for himself many influential enemies. His *Colin Clout* was an attack on the greed and incompetence of the clergy in general, but in *Speak Parrot* and *Why Come Ye Not to Court?* he turned his invective on the great Wolsey himself; then, to escape his vengeance, sought sanctuary in Westminster Abbey, where he died in 1529. Skelton was in revolt against the obsolescent civilisation of the Middle Ages, and his impatience is reflected in his verse, which bubbles and tumbles from his pen in a stream of short lines, foaming with alliteration and frothing with rhyme:

> For though my rhyme be ragged,
> Tattered and jagged,
> Rudely rayne beaten,
> Rusty and moughte eaten,
> If ye take well therwith,
> It hath in it some pyth.

Some pith indeed! and at his best he manages his flexible 'Skeltonics' with the greatest dexterity; they are an admirable medium for the scathing satire of *Colin Clout*, and equally effective in the coarse and vigorous *Tunning of Elinor Rumming*:

> Her face all bowsy,
> Droopy and drowsy,
> Scurvy and lousy.

And he manages them with a comparable delicacy in his best-known poem, *The Book of Philip Sparrow*, and in his address to:

> Merry Margaret, as midsummer flower,
> Gentle as falcon or hawk of the tower.

In the sixteenth and seventeenth centuries, Skelton was generally regarded as a figure of fun; in the eighteenth, by Pope and Warton, as an object of contempt, and his genius has only recently been re-discovered, though it was recognised by Ben Jonson, who introduced him as 'The worshipful poet laureate to King Harry' in his masque *The Fortunate Isles*. In spirit Skelton belonged to the new age, but his equipment was inadequate for its expression; he had no knowledge of the new forms, and could only rebel against the dreary stumbling verse of his contemporaries by quickening the old alliterative line and barbing it with rhyme. We would not have it otherwise, for Skelton is unique; but because he was an eccentric his influence was slight, and later poets had little to learn from him but liveliness and vigour. The prose of Nashe owes more to Skelton than does all the poetry of the Elizabethans.

For almost thirty years after Skelton's death virtually nothing occurred to ruffle the waters of English poetry, and then, in the last year of Mary's reign, in 1557, came an unpretentious book that was destined to be as influential as any in our literature: *Songes and Sonnettes, written by the ryght honorable Lorde Henry Haward, late Earle of Surrey and other*, edited by Nicholas Grimald, and printed by Richard Tottel, from whom it takes its familiar name of *Tottel's Miscellany*. Grimald had collected some three hundred poems by various authors, many of them as worthless as his own over-liberal contribution, but fortunately almost half the volume was made up with the work of Surrey and Sir Thomas Wyatt. Henry Howard was the Earl of Surrey who had been painted by Guillim Scrots shortly before his execution in 1547, when he was barely thirty; Wyatt was the older man, but he, too, died young, early enough for Surrey to write of him, 'Wyatt resteth here, who quick could never rest'. Apart from the very real merit of much of their work Wyatt and Surrey are of the first importance as innovators, the men who supplied the form that Skelton had lacked. What they did was described by George Puttenham in his *Art of English Poesy* thirty years later: 'Having travelled into Italy, and there tasted the sweet and stately measures and style of the Italian poesy, as novices newly crept out of the school of Dante, Ariosto and Petrarch, they greatly polished our rude and homely manner of vulgar poesy from that it had been before, and for that case may justly be said the first reformers of our English metre and style.' This, of course, is the dead hand of classical pedantry, and strikes a chill; it is too like Dryden's polishing of that rough diamond Chaucer; but though it may be urged that Wyatt and Surrey took some of the life out of English poetry by their strict scansion and artificial forms, it is quite certain that English poetry stood in sore need of discipline, and, however clumsily it may at first have been applied, it led eventually to the music of *The Faerie Queene* and the rhythms of *The Tempest*. Wyatt introduced the sonnet into English, though not in the strict Petrarchan form, but with the final rhyming couplet characteristic of the Elizabethans. Surrey, too, wrote sonnets, but his great contribution was his translation of part of the *Aeneid* into blank verse, the first as far as we know to be written in English, and soon to be taken over by the dramatists and developed into the grandest measure in our poetry. It was no small achievement of these young men to have presented the Elizabethans with their two favourite verse forms, but their own best work was in their lyrics, of which Wyatt was the more accomplished master. He had the gift of weaving a poem about a memorable line, repeated as a refrain, as in the rondeau, or varied at the end of each verse: 'Forget not yet'; 'And wilt thou leave me thus?'; 'My lute, be still, for I have done'; and few lyrics of the Elizabethan, or of any age, surpass that beginning, 'They flee from me, that sometime did me seek'.

Another important literary event took place in 1557. The medieval brotherhood of Stationers had been all very well in an age of manuscripts, and might safely be left to manage its own affairs; but the multiplication of printed books called for a stricter control of the trade, and Mary, with the Tudor passion for centralisation, incorporated the Stationers' Company by royal charter. Under an elected Master and two Wardens, ninety-four booksellers and printers were enrolled as 'freemen of the mystery or art of a stationer'. The Company was given the monopoly of printing for the whole of England, save for those allowed to print by royal warrant, and by entering their 'copy' in the Stationers' Register and paying a fee of 4*d.*, the freemen secured the sole right of printing or selling a book. Two years later the charter was confirmed by Elizabeth, with strict provision that no 'book or paper' was to be printed without being licensed by the Privy Council or their deputies. Like so many other institutions and activities in Tudor England, the book trade was made responsible to the sovereign for its own good government.

One of the licensers of printing was the Archbishop of Canterbury. The good Matthew Parker was a lover of books; he had rescued many that might have perished with the monasteries, therewith enriching the libraries of his beloved Cambridge, and now, with his new authority and wealth, he encouraged printers to cut new founts of type and to turn out books that would at least not be shamed by the masterpieces of Antwerp, Leyden, Paris, Geneva and Venice. Parker's favourite was John Day, the finest and most enterprising English printer of the period, who cut a fount of Saxon type for his patron's use. He had been sent to the Tower by Mary at the beginning of her reign 'for pryntyng of noythy bokes', but he was active again by 1557, when he was enrolled as a freeman of the Stationers' Company, and published Tusser's *Hundreth Good Pointes of Husbandrie*. This he followed with Sternhold and Hopkins' *Whole Book of Psalms*, which marks the beginning of music publishing on a commercial scale, and in 1563 issued one of the most influential books of the age, John Foxe's *Actes and Monuments . . . wherein are described the great Persecution and horrible Troubles that have been wrought and practised by the Romishe prelates*, commonly known as *Foxe's Book of Martyrs*. It was scarcely calculated to reconcile the rival religious factions; the Catholics at once attacked its exaggerations and inaccuracies, while the Protestant hatred of Spain and the Inquisition was further inflamed by its vivid and often very moving descriptions of martyrdom. A copy of a second corrected edition was ordered for every collegiate church, and in most Protestant homes the *Book of Martyrs* took its place beside the Genevan version of the Bible. Foxe had been for a time tutor in the Lucy household at Charlecote, and it is probable that his book was even more popular in the Stratford district than other parts of the country, though possibly not in the home of John Shakespeare.

The same year saw the publication of the first great poem of the new reign. *A Mirror for Magistrates*, a dismal collection of stories by various authors, on Lydgate's theme of the *Falls of Princes*, had appeared in 1559. It was almost worthless, but the second edition of 1563 included two new poems by Thomas Sackville, *The Complaint of Buckingham*, prefaced by an *Induction*. Sackville was a very young man when he wrote them, and the wonder is how he wrote them with such assurance, such accomplishment. There is no fumbling, no stiffness, as in the experimental verse of Wyatt and Surrey, and the *Induction* has something of the incisive dramatic quality of Chaucer's description of the Temple of Mars in *The Knight's Tale*. Yet more striking than the medieval echoes is the new overriding music, for the *Induction* is more than a preface to the falls of princes, it is the preface to the poetry of the Elizabethan age, the entry into the enchanted country of *The Faerie Queene*, and a fitting salute to the great poet who was to be born in the following year. Sackville was to live to see all but the final triumphs of Shakespeare; a statesman whose distinguished service was rewarded with the Earldom of Dorset, he was also part author of the first regular English tragedy, *Gorboduc*.

When Shakespeare was born there were no public theatres, for the very good reason that there were no plays, in the modern sense of the word, to perform in them. The medieval miracle plays, dramatised Biblical stories that were the counterpart of those in the stained-glass windows, were still desultorily performed by the guildsmen, either on movable 'pageants' in the streets of the bigger towns, or in open-air amphitheatres in smaller towns and villages. Thus, in 1566 at Coventry, one of the towns with a large cycle of miracles, the tanners' pageant stood at St. John's Church, the drapers' at the Cross, the smiths' at Little Park Street End, and the weavers' at Much Park Street. Coventry is only twenty miles from Stratford, and it may well have been here that John Shakespeare introduced his two-year-old son to the drama.

The fifteenth century invented a variation of the miracle play. Biblical characters gave place to personifications of qualities, such as Beauty, Penitence and Pride, and the old stories became moral allegories in which Vices struggled with Virtues for the soul of man. Because of this conflict, these morality plays may be more dramatic than the miracles, but they are also more didactic, more remote and generally infinitely tedious, though the best-known one, *Everyman*, is much the finest play before the birth of Shakespeare. Skelton tried his hand at them, but only one of his plays has survived, *Magnificence*, a wearisome affair published with apparently unconscious humour as 'a goodly interlude and a mery'. But then, an interlude was meant to be merry, merrier at least than a morality. By the time that Skelton wrote, about 1520, the term had come to be applied to any kind of dramatic performance, but originally it was a comic episode played between two serious scenes, or light fare offered in the intervals of some other form of entertainment, like Thomas Medwall's 'godely interlude' of *Fulgens and Lucrece*, performed in two parts between the rounds of feasting in the hall of Cardinal Morton, probably at Lambeth Palace.

The interlude was the answer to the demand of the late fifteenth century for matter more amusing than the morality, from which it was nevertheless derived, for it normally retained something of its didactic character, though it added farce from the folk-plays and comedy from the popular interpolations in the miracles, and above all, substituted real characters for remote personifications and abstractions. An interesting exception to this is the *King John* of Bishop Bale, written about 1550, for here real characters rub shoulders, if the phrase may be used, with abstractions: 'Privat Welth cums in lyk a Cardynall' (so much for the papal legate Pandulph and a by-blow at Wolsey), and John is poisoned by a monk called Dissimulation. *King John* is little more than a moral interlude, but the little more makes it into our first historical play. Of about the same date is *The Four P's* of John Heywood, in which a Palmer, a Pardoner, a Pothecary and a Pedler wager as to who shall tell the biggest lie, the Palmer winning the prize by asserting that he has never seen a woman out of patience. It is all very childish and elementary; it is also far removed from the propaganda of the miracles and the exhortation of the moralities. But as yet the native drama was unaffected by classical models.

While the vigorous and sprawling popular interlude was thus developing in Tudor times, a different kind of dramatic evolution was taking place in the schools and universities, where the new learning had led to the study of classical or, rather, Latin plays, for there was little or no first-hand knowledge of the Greek. The comedies of Plautus and Terence were read, and the strange closet versions of Greek tragedy, written by Seneca, who 'improved' Æschylus, Sophocles and Euripides, much as Dryden and lesser men than he were to write what they considered improved versions of Shakespeare. It was a short step from the reading to the acting. The first record of a performance of a classical play is of 'a goodly commedy of Plautus' at Greenwich Palace in 1519, and within a few years the boys of St. Paul's, Eton and Westminster were performing the plays of Plautus and Terence as part of their regular curriculum. The writing of Latin plays at the universities followed as a matter of course, and then in the middle of the century came the epoch-making experiment of writing English plays on classical models. The two parallel streams of dramatic development were to be brought together; the lawless native interlude was to be given shape and coherence by the academic drama with its classical principles of construction.

The first of these 'regular' English plays was *Ralph Roister Doister*, written in rhyming doggerel about 1550 by Nicholas Udall, head-master of Eton, where he cruelly tormented young Tom Tusser, and later of Westminster. It has the five acts of a classical play, and the complex and skilfully contrived plot derives from Plautus, as does the vainglorious Ralph himself, but most of the incidents and minor characters are mere English, and lifted out of the interlude. A similar play, written at about the same time and acted some years later at Christ's College, Cambridge, is *Gammer Gurton's Needle*. Though the plot owes nothing to Plautus and it is much broader in treatment and coarser in tone than *Ralph Roister Doister*, the uproarious story of the very English Gammer and her man Hodge is firmly controlled within a classical frameworth. If *Ralph Roister Doister* is the first regular English comedy, *Gammer Gurton's Needle* is the first regular English farce.

Unfortunately the first regular English tragedy is English merely in its language and its legend. Only the last two acts of *The Tragedy of Gorboduc* are by Sackville, the first three being by Thomas Norton, who was later to inveigh against the 'unnecessarie and scarslie honest resortes to plaies', and to perish shortly after his release from the Tower, where his fanatical puritanism had got him. *Gorboduc*, or *Ferrex and Porrex* as it was later called, was first performed in the Inner Temple at Christmas 1561, before being presented three weeks later 'in her highnes Court of Whitehall', the occasion on which the dashing Christopher Hatton, builder of the great house of Holdenby, danced himself into Elizabeth's heart. What the Queen and Hatton and Dudley and the rest of that gay company thought of the play when the dancing was done we do not know, but we do know on the authority of John Day, who published the second edition, that the authors never intended to publish at all. They were right, for *Gorboduc* is monumentally dull, dull in a new and classical way. All the paraphernalia of Senecan tragedy save ghosts are artfully deployed. The theme is one of blood and revenge of the cumulative kind, like the ballad of the horseshoe-nail for want of which a kingdom was lost; yet, with rare delicacy, not a drop of blood is shed on the stage. Indeed, nothing happens on the stage save words, in speeches of a hundred lines or more in length; the murder of Ferrex by Porrex, of Porrex by his mother, of mother and father by· the people, the slaughter of the people by the nobles and of the nobles by themselves, are all reported by messengers, and all but the last of the five acts are clinched by the moralising chorus of four 'ancient and sage men of Britain'. The wheel had come full circle; the interlude had escaped from the morality play only to be threatened by the drearier, because merely pedantic, morality of neo-classicism. The danger was a real one; the literary mannerists of Italy, Castelvetro and the rest, had petrified their own drama by their perverse misinterpretations of the *Poetics* of Aristotle, on whom they fathered their own pernicious 'rules' for the writing of tragedy. They had their followers in England, and Sackville and Norton were themselves inspired by Jasper Heywood, the Jesuit son of the interlude writer, whose translations of Seneca's *Troas*, *Thyestes* and *Hercules Furens* appeared shortly before the production of *Gorboduc*. Even as late as the 1580's Philip Sidney, most liberal of the neo-classical school, whose heart was moved more than with a trumpet by the reading of some old Border ballad, could write, '*Gorboduc* . . . is full of stately speeches and well sounding phrases, climbing to the height of Seneca his style, and as full of notable moral- ity, which it doth most delightfully teach, and so obtain the very end of poesy', and then go on to grieve that 'it might not remain as an exact model of all tragedies, for it is faulty both in Place and Time'. The doctrine that the action of a tragedy should occur in one place within twenty-four hours was the darling 'Unities' of Castelvetro, on whom Sidney had been wasting his own all-too-precious time. Had he lived another year he would have seen his theorising blown all to pieces by the production of *Tamburlaine* in the public theatre, while Kyd, lamentably lacking in the nice refinement that post-Renaissance pedants attributed to the Greeks, joyously swooped on the sensational elements in Senecan tragedy—revenge, blood and ghosts—and swept them from the wings on to the stage. In the end the native stock proved much too lusty a growth to be confined by neo-classic bonds, but it was twenty years or more before it was able to assert itself.

All the early plays, miracles, moralities, interludes and comedies had been written in verse, rhyming verse of indeterminate metrical form, often alliterative and ranging from the comic short lines of the *Second Shepherds' Play* in the Towneley cycle,

> He was takyn with an elfe;
> I saw it myself.
> When the clok stroke twelf
> Was he forshapyn;

to the beautiful three-, four- and five-beat lines of *Everyman*,

> Alas! wherto may I truste?
> Beaute gothe faste awaye fro me.
> She promysed with me to lyve and dye;

and the doggerel of *Ralph Roister Doister*,

> To mine own dear coney bird, sweetheart, and pigsny,
> Good Mistress Custance, present these by and by.

But *Gorboduc* was written in blank verse, humdrum and stumping it is true, yet nevertheless the basic measure of *Hamlet* and *Antony and Cleopatra*. It was fortunate, after all, that a piratical publisher got hold of the script and printed it.

It is clear that this development of the secular drama involved considerable changes in the places where it was played and in the status of the actors who performed it. The miracles were still performed in the traditional English manner on mobile pageants, or they were acted in open-air arenas surrounded by wooden stands, or in permanent stone or earthen amphitheatres, such as those at Perranzabuloe and St. Just in Cornwall. These are the only medieval theatres that have survived, and very impressive monuments they are. That at St. Just is 126 feet in diameter, surrounded by a bank of seven steps, each one foot high, the top one forming a platform seven feet wide. The whole was originally cased with granite slabs, and a ditch ran round the outside wall, pierced on one side by an entrance. Perran Round is even bigger, the arena itself being 130 feet across, though its banks do not appear to have been cased with masonry. From the ample stage directions and the five plans included in their manuscripts, we know pretty well how the Cornish miracle plays were produced; and they were still being performed, though in a degraded manner, as late as 1602. Ranged round, and sometimes within the arena, or 'plain', were small tents standing on shallow platforms, each representing some locality in the play, and in these tents the characters remained when they were not performing. Good characters, such as saints and Solomon and David, were on the south side, powerful worldly rulers, such as Roman emperors, were on the west, and 'because evil approacheth out of the north', evil characters occupied that side; thus, the position of the popular comic executioners was at the north-east, while Hell, not a tent but a huge lath-and-

PERRAN ROUND

canvas monster's mouth belching fire and smoke and devils, was due north. Heaven was at the east, a more elaborate structure than the canvas tents, probably of wood, for it had an entrance with doors that could be opened, and apparently 'rooms' on either side in which the angels played and sang. Its stage was much bigger than the others, perhaps thirty feet long and twenty broad, but only about one foot high, so that a character could easily step down into the arena. Towards the back were a few steps mounting to a small platform, the *pulpitum* or upper stage, on which was the throne of God in front of the mansion of Heaven. In Perran Round there is a trench that once ran under the shallow stage, connecting Heaven with a circular pit just in front of it, a contrivance for sudden appearances, such as the creation of Adam, and called the 'conveyor'.

The play was conducted almost like a choir by the prompter, or 'ordinary' [1] as he was called, for he seems to have followed the players about the plain, prompting them when necessary, and, at the conclusion of a scene, turning to the tent of the next character due to appear, and summoning him to come in, or rather, to come out. When a character appeared for the first time, he would emerge from his tent and parade on his little stage before announcing in a loud voice who he was, and 'going down'. This simple, basic form of action can easily be illustrated from the play of *St. Meriasek*, the only surviving saint's play in our literature. Thus, when Meriasek has cured a number of sick men, we get the stage direction, *Let them go off. Here Meriasek waits at Camborne.* The theatre is now empty of actors except for Meriasek, who is praying near his chapel, a tent in the centre of the plain. Suddenly the flap of a tent on the north-west opens, and *hic Teudarus pompabit*, 'here Teudar shall parade', and the infidel tyrant shouts:

> Teudar I am called,
> Reigning lord in Cornwall;
> That Mahound be honoured
> Is my charge without fail.

Messengers come in and tell him of Meriasek's miracles, and Teudar 'goes down' and argues with the saint. Of course, Meriasek gets the better of the argument, and Teudar goes up again to his scaffold, where

---

[1] In Cornwall the 'play-book', the authoritative text of the play, was called the *Ordinale*, from the liturgical *Ordo*, the written directions for a dramatic church service, and the man in charge of this manuscript was the *Ordinary*.

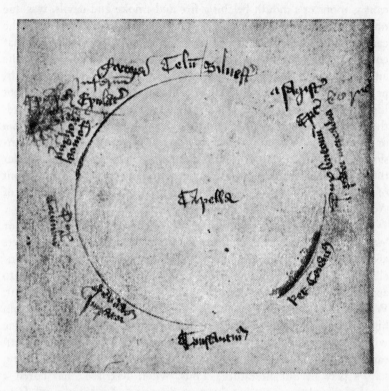

STAGE FOR THE FIRST PART OF *ST. MERIASEK*

Key

HEAVEN

Torturers	Silvester
Hell	Schoolmaster
Outlaws	Bishop of Cournouaille
Bishop Poly	Duke of Brittany
Count of Rohan	*i.e.* father of Meriasek

CHAPEL

Duke of Cornwall	King Conan
Emperor	
Teudar	

Constantine

he shouts, 'Executioners, come into the plain!' Their tent, it will be remembered, is at the extreme north-east, almost as far away as it can be, and Teudar shouts again, 'Hi, hi, hi! What, do you pay no heed? They must be fetched.' He goes down, the prompter adding, 'here yerdis [sticks] aredy for Teudar & hys men', and the executioners are hauled out and soundly beaten. Most of the action took place towards the middle of the plain, so that all had a fair chance of hearing what was said, and then a large space was essential for many of the spectacular episodes, as when the Duke of Cornwall's host of twenty men defeats the rather smaller army of Teudar, who escapes on horseback, or when the great dragon with a gun and fire in its mouth swallows some of the soldiers who are sent to destroy it. The main stage was normally reserved for very exalted action in which God took part when he descended the steps from his throne on the pulpit.

The Cornish cycle, known as the *Ordinalia*, was probably written early in the fifteenth century by a member of Glasney College at Penryn, and would be acted by its secular canons and vicars choral, assisted by local craftsmen and other laymen. After the Dissolution they, as well as innumerable saints' plays, now lost, were probably performed under the direction of parsons by their parishioners in villages and towns, many of which had their own rounds, for a performance meant an influx of strangers, and strangers meant money. No wonder the playing-places were surrounded by a ditch filled with water, to discourage those who would fain see a performance without paying their penny.[1]

Presumably the stationary production of miracles was similar in other parts of the country, in wooden amphitheatres long since perished; of moralities as well, at least the early ones. Certainly the earliest that we possess, *The Castle of Perseverance*, written about 1450, was performed in this way. Fortunately it is illustrated by a plan similar to the Cornish ones, the only plan descriptive of the English, as distinct from the Cornish, medieval drama. The 'place' is bounded by two concentric circles, representing the spectators' seats or standings, between which is written, 'This is the watyr a bowte the place, if any ditch may be mad ther [where] it schal be pleyed, or ellys that it be stronglye barryd al a bowte'. Within the circle is the castle, above

---

[1] In this description of the production of 'gwary miracles' I have helped myself liberally from the Introduction to my *Legend of the Rood* (Duckworth, 1955).

which is the legend, 'lete no men sytte ther for lettynge of syt [obstructing the view] for ther schal be the best of all', and below is written, 'Mankynde is bed schal be under the castel, & ther schal the sowle lye under the bed tyl he schal ryse and pleye'. Outside the circle are directions for the stages with their tents: God is at the east, Covetousness north-east, Belial north, the World west, and Flesh, the best of a bad lot, south. Some episodes took place on the stages, but most of the action was in the 'place', which was kept clear of spectators by stewards, but 'nowth over many'. A week before the production, criers went round the villages announcing its performance 'at N on the grene in ryall aray'.

The secularisation of the drama led to fresh developments. Latin plays and native interludes were performed indoors before select and educated audiences; schoolboys acted Plautus and Terence and *Ralph Roister Doister*; graduates and undergraduates acted classical and neoclassical plays, *Gammer Gurton's Needle* was produced at Cambridge, and *Thersites*, a delightful mock-heroic interlude, at Oxford; Inns of Court men presented *Gorboduc*; choirboys performed at Court, as did adult players, who also entertained the princely clerics and nobility in their great halls, as when *Fulgens and Lucrece* was played before Cardinal Morton. Then there were the masques, which were not without their influence on the drama. Originally they were entertainments in which friends, wearing masks, carrying torches and accompanied by musicians, unexpectedly visited a house and danced before the host and his guests, afterwards inviting them to take part. By Tudor times the spectacular and mimetic elements had become so emphatic and elaborate that the masque was little more than a combination of pageantry and interlude, in which the spectators took no part. These courtly entertainments were known as 'disguisings' to distinguish them from the masque proper, and from which indeed they were now divorced; but by the middle of the century the various elements were fused, and the masque of Elizabeth's reign combined the original dancing and 'commoning' of performers and spectators with the pageantry, generally allegorical, of the disguisings.

Some thirty interludes have survived from the first half of the sixteenth century, and were presented, as we should expect, something in the manner of the miracles and moralities in the medieval rounds. On informal occasions in the halls of the sovereign and the nobility, the feasters still sitting on the dais, the tables and benches below would be pushed to the wall, leaving a space for the players, who would thus be surrounded by spectators on all sides, as in the open-air amphitheatres. Very few of the early interludes had any change of scene or need of anything but the simplest properties; but if more than one scene had to be represented the medieval method of multiple setting was employed, and folding 'houses' of painted wood and canvas, similar to the 'tents' of the miracles, were set up on the floor. On more formal occasions at Court, tiers of seats were sometimes erected to accommodate the spectators, as at Greenwich in 1527, when 'the chambre was raised with stages v degrees on every side'.[1] Though this was for the pageantry of a foot-tourney and masque, the same arrangement was probably made for a play. As scenic effects became more elaborate and trap-doors and other quaint devices were called for, stages were built either in the middle of the hall or against one of the end walls; thus at Whitehall, for the Christmas Revels of 1601, 'a broad stage' was set up in the middle of the hall, but when Elizabeth visited Oxford twenty-five years earlier, the stage in Christ Church hall was at the dais end, and the Queen sat beneath a gilded state, or canopy, probably about the middle of the hall. These early stages seem to have been quite small—that at Richmond in Armada year was only fourteen feet square—and the players would use the floor beside the stage, probably for outdoor and distant scenes. There would be houses both on the stage and the floor and in them the players awaited their cue, as in the medieval tents, on hearing which they opened the door —for the houses at Court had practicable doors—stepped out, and the action took place outside, again as in the medieval open-air theatres, the whole playing-place being imaginatively transformed into the neighbourhood of that house, or if necessary, into its interior. Possibly too, the houses were arranged, where feasible, with good characters on one side and bad on the other.

There is no reason to suppose that the presentation of plays in the halls of schools, colleges and private houses differed fundamentally from that at Court, though few of the halls could emulate the hundred by forty-five feet of Whitehall, and that the players were often embarrassed by cramped and makeshift quarters is indicated by a stage direction in William Percy's *Aphrodysial*, 'Here went furth the whole Chorus in a shuffle as after a Play in a Lord's howse'.

[1] The word *stage* must be treated with caution. Here it means *scaffolding* (for a tier of five seats). The actors' stage was originally called the *scaffold*.

The actors in the medieval religious drama were amateurs, though the guildsmen were paid for their services; amateurs too, of course, were the undergraduates and Inns of Court men who presented the classical plays and politer interludes; but the secularisation of the popular drama naturally led to a big increase in the number of professional actors. In the Middle Ages troupes of professional entertainers, clowns, minstrels, acrobats and jugglers wandered about the country, performing in town halls, monastery halls, inn yards, open-air rounds and any place where a profit was to be made. Most profitable of all were wealthy private patrons, and some of the more respectable troupes were retained by the nobility as interlude players. The Earls of Essex had a company by 1468, and the first royal company, consisting of four men, was established by Henry VII, and increased to eight by Henry VIII. Their services were normally required only in mid-winter, and for the rest of the year they were free to go on tour, competing with the irregular troupes of permanent wanderers, varying their interludes, most of which must have been wretched knock-about farces, with tumbling and other 'feats of activity', which were their real speciality.

Many of these itinerant 'rogues and idle persons', as they were called, were naturally drawn to the rapidly growing and prosperous capital, where they made their temporary, and sometimes almost permanent, headquarters at the City inns, the earliest record of a performance being at the Boar's Head, Falstaff's tavern in Eastcheap, in 1557. The inn yard made an ideal playing-place, a ready-made round, or rather square, and we must imagine the spectators in the galleries, and those on the ground roped off behind the supporting pillars, as in the medieval rounds,[1] while the players performed their medley of acting and tumbling about the yard, set with tents in the traditional manner.

Queen Mary was too fanatically preoccupied with religion to be interested in interludes, and Elizabeth much too fastidious to relish the uncouth horseplay of the eight men whom she had inherited, and though she kept them on her establishment she allowed them literally to die off. They performed at Court at Christmas, 1559, but 'the plaers plad shuche matter that they wher commondyd to leyff off'. That was positively their last appearance at Court, though they can

---

[1] 'for a lynge when they were about the playne' (*Borough Accounts* of St. Ives, Cornwall, 1574).

be traced in the provinces until 1573—they were at Stratford in 1569
—and the last of the Queen's Interluders died a few years later.

To whom, then, did the young Queen turn for her winter entertainment? Robert Dudley was not slow to exploit an easy way into
her favour. He formed his own company, composed of the most skilful actors he could find, made them rehearse the wittiest of the interludes, and offered them to the Master of the Revels for presentation
before the Queen. And sure enough, 'Lorde Robte Dudleyes players'
performed at Court, though what they performed we do not know, at
Christmas, 1560, and the two following years. There were no plays in
the plague winter of 1563, but in 1564 'therle of Warwickes players' gave
two performances. Ambrose Dudley, now Earl of Warwick, had lost
little time in following his brother's example. These were the only
men's companies at Court between 1560 and the end of 1566, and no
doubt the Queen appreciated the flattering attention of her favourites,
but when she wanted something more intelligent it was to the boys'
companies that she turned, and while Dudley's and Warwick's men
gave five performances, the 'Children of Powles' gave nine. Like the
men, they were paid £6 13s. 4d. for each performance—though they
had to supply their own 'sugar candee, comfetts and butterd beere,
being horse'—and this remained the standard fee until 1575 when,
after a little characteristic wavering, it was raised to £10.

The Children of Paul's were the boys of the choir school attached
to St. Paul's Cathedral, and were trained by their enterprising Master,
Sebastian Westcott, not only in singing, but also, in their private
circular theatre 'at Paules', in the lucrative art of acting as well.
Westcott had enlisted the aid of the best interlude writer of the day,.
John Heywood, and Elizabeth had already seen the fruits of their
collaboration, once at Hatfield in her brother's reign, and again at
Nonsuch in 1559, when she was entertained by the Earl of Arundel
with 'a play of the chylderyn of Powlles and ther Master Sebastian,
and Master Haywood'. The rough and not over literate adult interlude players could scarcely hope to compete for Elizabeth's favour
with the boys, who could sing like angels, speak Plautus and Terence,
and were trained by an accomplished musician to perform the plays of
Heywood. In the first eighteen years of the reign, that is before the
building of the first public theatre in 1576, adult players gave thirty-
two Court performances to the boys' forty-six, and of these, twenty-
one were by the Children of Paul's.

The greatest rivals of the Paul's boys were the Children of the Chapel. The Chapel Royal was not a building, but part of the establishment of the Royal Household, consisting of a dean, a number of gentlemen musicians, two of whom were Tallis and Byrd, and another the Master of the Children, the choirboys, of whom there were twelve. Great pains were taken to secure the finest singers, and agents travelled about the country listening to cathedral choirs and pressing their best boys into service. Members of the Chapel accompanied the formal progresses of the sovereign, and they were, for example, with Henry VIII at the Field of the Cloth of Gold. William Cornish was then Master of the Children, and it was he who first formed them into a dramatic company, supplying them with his own plays, unfortunately lost, for performance at Court. After his death little is heard of their dramatic activities until the reign of Elizabeth, when, under their new Master, Richard Edwards, they performed at Court at the first Christmas celebrated by the infant Shakespeare.

PART ONE
1564–1588

I

1564–1572

ELIZABETH AND MARY

On February 15th, 1564, Galileo was born in Pisa, three days later Michelangelo died in Rome, and in May Calvin died in Geneva. On February 6th Christopher Marlowe was born in Canterbury, and in April, probably on the 23rd, William Shakespeare was born in Stratford, the first surviving child of John Shakespeare, a prospering tradesman, and of Mary, daughter of Robert Arden of Wilmcote. Francis Bacon and George Chapman were three years old, Philip Sidney, Fulke Greville and John Lyly boys of ten, Walter Raleigh and Edmund Spenser some two years older.

A stream of Protestant refugees from the Netherlands, augmented by a trickle of Huguenots from France, was pouring into England, bringing with them their art, their craftsmanship and their skill. One of these was the Queen's coachman, William Boonen, who in 1564 built the first coach in England. Another was Mistress Dinghen Vanderplasse, who in the same year introduced starch to the English housewives, and taught them, to her own great profit, the art of stiffening ruffs. And in 1564 John Hawkins sailed on his second voyage to the Spanish Main, bringing back with him the profits of his trade in slaves, and the American weed—tobacco. Elizabeth had a stake in the venture, and he was rewarded with a coat-of-arms, with a negro, chained, as his crest. If,

> Hops, Reformation, bays and beer,
> Came into England all in one year,

Shakespeare may be said, and with greater exactness, to have come in with coaches, starch, tobacco and the word 'Puritan', a nickname coined by Archbishop Parker to describe the whole body of extreme reformers, whether followers of Calvin or not.

It might with equal truth be said that Shakespeare and the Elizabethan Age came in together. In 1564 Cecil began the building of Theobalds, the precocious Nicholas Hilliard was painting his miniature of Mary Queen of Scots, Byrd was about to join Tallis at the Chapel Royal, Sackville's *Induction* to the *Mirror for Magistrates* had just been published, *Gorboduc* had recently been performed, and its script was in the hands of the printer. The art of the Middle Ages had been fertilised by that of Greece and Rome, no matter at how many removes, and a new and vigorous art comparable to that of the Italian Renaissance was about to blossom. What the Doge's Palace, Giotto and Petrarch were to fourteenth-century Italy, so were Hardwick Hall, Hilliard and Spenser to sixteenth-century England. It is true that in the field of painting and sculpture Elizabethan England produced nothing that approached the work of the Italian masters of the *trecento*, but then Italy produced no drama that approached that of the Elizabethans. This, however, is not the point; the important thing is that in both countries the grafting of the classical on to the medieval stock led to a fresh flowering of the arts in which the Gothic and the Greek were miraculously blended, in Italy most apparent in the visual arts, in England in poetry and the drama. But whereas in Italy the Renaissance had two centuries of vigour, in England its course was run in fifty years, the fifty years of Shakespeare's life; by 1616 its spontaneity and initial inspiration had been lost, the medieval element had been swamped by the classical, and soon the unique miracle was irrecoverably over. The delicate Gothic line of Hilliard gave place to the commonplace chiaroscuro of Isaac Oliver, the piercing sweetness of motet, madrigal, lute and viol was drowned by the coarser music of the organ, Inigo Jones, for all his genius, could only invent variations on classical themes, and Milton, disowning the medieval impishness of *L'Allegro* sombrely laboured at the lines that Shakespeare had written so lightly. The drama had an even shorter course to run, from the first of Marlowe's plays to the last of Shakespeare's; for it was twelve years after their birth before the first theatre was built, twenty-five years before the blank verse of *Gorboduc* was transformed into the poetry of *Tamburlaine*, and by the time of Shakespeare's death the best work of Jonson and Webster was over, and little remained but a shadow.

Elizabeth was staying at Richmond when Shakespeare was born, in the palace rebuilt by Henry VII to replace the medieval Sheen. She was still distressingly a virgin queen, though her thoughts at the time must have been much on marriage, both her own and that of her cousin Mary of Scotland. At the end of July she began her summer holiday. Preceded by three or four hundred carts bearing her baggage, accompanied by a host of members of her Household, and followed by more carts with the royal furnishings, she travelled in her new coach, at the rate of ten or twelve miles a day, to visit the loyal gentlemen of the eastern Midlands. Her first stop was at Theobalds, where she picnicked with Cecil, and by August 5th she was at Cambridge, where she was submitted to a gruelling ordeal by classical drama. The plays were in King's College chapel, across part of the western end of which a stage was built five feet high from wall to wall, so that the actors could use the doors of two chapels on the north side for their entrances. The Queen sat in her canopied throne, or 'state', at the other end of the stage, which was lit by the torches of her guard standing on either side. On Sunday there was a three hours' performance of the *Aulularia* of Plautus, on Monday a Latin tragedy of *Dido*, on Wednesday *Ezechias*, an English comedy by the late Nicholas Udall, on Thursday—but Elizabeth had had enough, and flatly refused to hear a Latin version of the *Ajax Flagellifer* of Sophocles. On taking her leave the next day she congratulated Thomas Preston, a Fellow of King's, on his theological disputation with the puritanical Thomas Cartwright, and on his performance in *Dido*. A Thomas Preston was the author of *Cambyses*, 'a lamentable tragedy mixed full of pleasant mirth', but it is a nice point whether a Cambridge don could have written this piece of knockabout nonsense, in which the comic villains, Huff, Ruff and Snuff, hobnob with the great King of Persia himself, in the native manner that was not to be put down by any number of classical models. By the middle of September Elizabeth was back in London, or rather at her country-house of St. James's, built by her father on the site of an old leper hospital. At the beginning of December, as was her usual custom, she moved to Whitehall for the Christmas Revels.

The traditional season for the Revels was from All Saints (November 1st) to the beginning of Lent, but under Elizabeth the greatest concentration of plays was during the twelve days of Christmas, the period of ancient licence that culminated in the feast of Epiphany on Twelfth Night. Excluding Christmas Day itself, there were nearly always performances on the feasts of St. Stephen, St. John and the Innocents (December 26th, 27th, 28th), on New Year's Day and on Twelfth Night (January 6th). Then might come a play at Candlemas (February 2nd) followed by one or two at Shrovetide, before the austerities of Lent put an end to revelling. The greatest number of plays performed before Elizabeth in one season was eleven, the average being about seven.

In 1564 the Revels began with two plays by Warwick's Men (one would like to know what they were), another by Sebastian West-cott's Children of Paul's, and then the Children of the Chapel presented a play by their Master, Richard Edwards, *Damon and Pythias*, the 'tragecall comodye' of two faithful friends, written in doggerel and enlivened with an interlude of Grim the Collier of Croydon. In January the boys of Westminster School performed the *Miles Gloriosus* of Plautus, and possibly the *Heautontimorumenos* of Terence as well. At Candlemas the Paul's boys gave another performance, and on February 18th Sir Percival Hart's sons made a masque, for which the Revels Office supplied 'diuers devisses and a rocke or hill ffor the ix musses to singe vppone'. (Darnley was on his way to Scotland.) Then at Shrovetide the gallants of Gray's Inn presented a comedy, in which the question of marriage was debated by Juno and Diana, the one advocating matrimony, the other chastity. When Jupiter was asked for his opinion he gave his verdict in favour of marriage, and Elizabeth, leaning towards the newly appointed Spanish ambassador, de Silva, whispered, 'This is all against me'. It was indeed, for rumours were already arriving of Mary's marriage to Darnley. They were true, though the ceremony had been a secret one, celebrated with Catholic rites. Elizabeth ordered Darnley to return, but, after nursing the stupid young athlete through an attack of measles, Mary re-married him publicly in July. The union of the Catholic Stuart cousins not only threatened Knox's Presbyterian Church settlement, it might also rally the English Catholics in support of their succession to Elizabeth's throne.

Although Elizabeth did not go on progress in 1565, the round of Court life went on much as usual. In November she attended the wedding of the Earl of Warwick and Lady Anne Russell, and in February 1566 that of the Earl of Southampton and Mary Browne, daughter of the first Viscount Montague. And it was probably in the February of this year, while she was staying at Greenwich Palace, that she saw the tragedy of *Tancred and Gismund*, written and presented by the gentlemen of the Inner Temple. She must have been gratified, for despite its Senecan paraphernalia it has situations and flourishes of poetry that anticipate the triumphs of the eighties. It is the first Elizabethan tragedy. The play was published in 1591, after much revision by the chief author, Robert Wilmot, and the transformation of the original rhyming quatrains into blank verse. The Inner Temple already had *Gorboduc* to their credit, and their lead was followed by Gray's Inn, where, some time in 1566, George Gascoigne presented his tragedy of *Jocasta*, and his comedy *Supposes*. Gascoigne was a Cambridge graduate, a dissolute hanger-on at Court, who had recently repaired his wasted fortune by marrying a wealthy widow, the mother of the poet Nicholas Breton. There is nothing very remarkable about the two plays; both are translations or adaptations from the Italian, but *Jocasta* is important as the second English blank verse tragedy, and *Supposes*, adapted from Ariosto's *I Suppositi*, as the first English prose play, and the probable source of the Bianca sub-plot in *The Taming of the Shrew*.

Meanwhile Scotland was in a state verging on civil war, and in October 1565 the leader of the Protestant party, the Earl of Murray, Mary's illegitimate half-brother, was driven to find refuge in England, when Elizabeth, having secretly helped him with money, publicly rated him as a rebel. Mary had wisely refused to grant Darnley the crown matrimonial, thus excluding him from all important affairs of state, and in this had been supported by her Italian secretary, David Rizzio. The jealous and vicious titular king was easily persuaded by his followers that the secretary's influence was dangerous, and on March 9th, 1566, they dragged Rizzio out of Mary's presence and murdered him. Darnley at once denounced his accomplices; Mary made a show of reconciliation, and on June 19th gave birth to a son, the future James I of England. (A few weeks later, Mary Shakespeare gave birth to a second son, Gilbert.)

The Stuart claim to the English succession was strengthened. But Elizabeth had never admitted it, and how could she allow it now, though there was no real alternative, short of a child of her own body? With thoughts of Mary, Darnley and the infant James uppermost in her mind, she began her summer progress, and it was a strangely ironical twist of fortune that brought her, at the end of July, to Fotheringay in Northamptonshire. She was impressed by the strength of the castle where Richard III had been born, but more interested in the dilapidated church, in which Richard's brother, Rutland, his father, third Duke of York, and his great-uncle, the Aumerle of Shakespeare's *Richard II*, were buried. She found their tombs in ruins, and ordered the erection of new monuments. By the middle of August she was at Coventry, where the guildsmen gave a special performance of their Corpus Christi cycle of miracle plays, and from Coventry went to Kenilworth to spend two delightful days with Robert Dudley, now Earl of Leicester. Thence she went to visit his newly married brother at Warwick, only five miles away, and so to Stratford, where she stayed at Charlecote with Thomas Lucy, whom she rewarded with a knighthood. On the last day of August she reached Oxford, and the members of the university strove their best to outdo the entertainment she had received at Cambridge two years before. Perhaps they succeeded, for twenty-six years later Elizabeth returned to Oxford, but never again to Cambridge. A series of plays was given in Christ Church hall, on a high stage at the upper end, approached by a flight of steps. The Queen sat in her state, and the rest of the audience on tiers of seats and galleries erected round the walls. She was not present at the first play, a comedy in Latin prose called *Marcus Geminus*, but she attended the Latin tragedy of *Progne*, and was there to see the two parts of the English play *Palamon and Arcite*, translated from the Latin by her old friend Richard Edwards, Master of her Chapel Children. The play has been lost, but it seems to have been a dramatised version of Chaucer's *Knight's Tale*, and may later have been used by Fletcher and Shakespeare when writing *The Two Noble Kinsmen*. The performance was marred by an unfortunate accident; the great press of undergraduates crowding the stairs broke down a wall, killing a cook and two other people. The Queen expressed her grief, but the performance went on and when all was over she congratulated Edwards on the excellence of the play and the actors, one of them being John Reynolds, then a boy of seventeen, who took the part of Hippolyta. Two months later Edwards was dead.

He was succeeded as Master of the Children by one of the Gentlemen of the Chapel, William Hunnis, a freeman of the Grocers' Company, and Keeper of the Orchard and Gardens at Greenwich, in which capacity he supplied the Court with flowers. He was also a writer of interludes, well lost if we may judge by his poems, some of which were published along with those of Edwards and others in *The Paradise of Dainty Devices* of 1576, some under separate titles, such as *A Hive Full of Honey* and *Seven Sobbes of a Sorrowful Soule for Sinne*, which sufficiently indicate their quality. Hunnis did not bring the Chapel Children to Court that Christmas (in November

Lettice Knollys, Countess of Essex, gave birth to a son, Robert Devereux), but there were plays by the Paul's and Westminster boys, and on February 11th of the new year, 1567, another company made its first appearance, the Children of Windsor, under their Master Richard Farrant. The next day came the staggering news from Scotland: the house where Darnley was sleeping in Edinburgh had been blown up, and his strangled body found in a neighbouring garden.

Whether Mary took any part in the plot will probably never be known, but that she was aware that some plot was afoot can scarcely be doubted. The murderer was the handsome, reckless ruffian, the Earl of Bothwell, to whose love and protection she so completely surrendered herself that, within three months of the crime, she married him. This seemed conclusive evidence that she had been Bothwell's accomplice in the murder, and even the cynical, unprincipled nobles were revolted by her conduct. At Carberry Hill the royalist forces deserted their Queen; Bothwell fled, and Mary surrendered to the rebels, who confined her in Lochleven Castle. In July she was made to abdicate in favour of her infant son, and Murray was appointed Regent. Elizabeth held advanced ideas about the sanctity of princes' persons, and demanded Mary's release, at the same time suggesting that she should have the custody of James; but Murray pursued his own anti-Catholic course, and James remained in his keeping, Mary in Lochleven Castle.

Meanwhile Hawkins had sailed on his third slaving expedition to the Spanish colonies in America, taking with him his young cousin Francis Drake, whose guardian he had been. At about the same time, the Duke of Alva arrived in the Netherlands with an army of 10,000 men, to put down the anti-idolatry rioting; he was as thorough as his master, Philip II, could have wished, and some 6,000 heretics were executed. Elizabeth and Cecil watched uneasily, for they could scarcely afford to see a powerful Spanish base established within a few miles of the Kentish coast, particularly now that Calais had been lost. There could be no question of open intervention, but it was no business of theirs if English volunteers chose to serve against Alva, and English privateers to sail under the Huguenot flag with a commission to wage war on Papist ships, whether those of France or any other nation.

There were seven plays at Court that winter, and at Shrovetide, 1568, William Hunnis made his first appearance with the Chapel

Children. Perhaps their play was the *Tragedy of the King of Scots*, for which the Revels Office supplied a 'Pallace and a gret Castell one thothere side'. The play was an appropriate one, for the curtain was rising on another act in the real tragedy of the Queen of Scots. In May, Mary escaped from Lochleven Castle, to be joined by a half-hearted body of troops, who were easily scattered by Murray at Langside, and on the 16th she escaped over the Solway and landed on English soil. She was an embarrassing guest. Elizabeth could not very well force the nation that had ejected her to take her back, yet if she detained her in England she would almost certainly become the centre of Catholic intrigue. Eventually she promised that if Mary could prove her innocence she would restore her—on conditions; which meant that Murray would remain the real ruler of Scotland. An inquiry was held, but its findings were inconclusive; Mary could not be proved guilty, yet neither could she herself prove her innocence, and she remained a prisoner in England, first at Bolton Castle, then at Tutbury Castle, near Stafford.

Earlier in the year, Drake, followed a few days later by Hawkins, had returned after a fearful homeward voyage across the Atlantic. They had kidnapped negroes on the Guinea coast, shipped them off to the Spanish Main, where they forced the Spaniards of Rio de la Hacha to buy them, contrary to the regulations of Philip II, then, driven west by storms, put in at the Mexican port of San Juan d'Ulloa to refit. While they were there a fleet of thirteen Spanish sail arrived, bringing the new viceroy, who, after professing friendship, treacherously attacked them. Only two of the English ships escaped, a hundred men being left to the mercy of the Spaniards, who accused them, not of being smugglers engaged in an iniquitous traffic, which they were, but of being heretics, which was nothing to the point. Those who were not killed were reserved for a worse fate at the hands of the Inquisition. The English were being treated like the Netherlanders under Alva. Small wonder that Drake vowed vengeance and refused to accept the Pope's ruling that the New World was the property of Spain.

In the summer the Netherland revolt broke out in earnest, and the Protestant leaders were sent to the block. Alva asked Philip for money, who borrowed a large sum from the Genoese bankers and sent it off by sea, but his treasure ships were attacked by the privateers, including English, based on Rochelle, and driven to seek refuge in Plymouth Sound. The Spanish ambassador asked for a safe-conduct, but Elizabeth, persuaded by Cecil, told him that she had decided to accept the Genoese loan herself. Alva at once seized all English goods in the Netherlands, to which Elizabeth replied by seizing all Spanish and Flemish goods in England. She had much the better of the bargain. Cecil had struck a shrewd, and profitable, blow on behalf of the Netherlands, but relations with Spain were becoming, to say the least, strained. They were not improved by William Allen's foundation of the English College at Douai for the training of Catholic missionaries to undermine Elizabeth's religious settlement.

In addition to the *Bishops' Bible*, a few books that were to prove of some importance to Shakespeare and his contemporaries were published during the years 1567–8, all of them translations. William Painter, clerk of the ordnance in the Tower of London, where he considerably enriched himself by peculation, is remembered as the author of *The Palace of Pleasure*, a hundred and one stories translated from classical and Italian writers, notably Boccaccio and Bandello. The book was a storehouse for the Elizabethan dramatists, and partly accounts for the Italian themes of so many of their plays. Shakespeare took from it Boccaccio's story of *Giglietta di Nerbone* for his *All's Well that Ends Well*, and probably used it for *Romeo and Juliet* and *Timon of Athens*. Another translator of Bandello, but indirectly by way of Belleforest's French version, was Geoffrey Fenton, whose *Certain Tragical Discourses*, written in a rhetorical and revoltingly moral vein—he was knighted by Elizabeth for his services as an informer against his colleagues in Ireland—supplied Shakespeare with matter for the main plot of *Much Ado about Nothing*. A more attractive character was Arthur Golding, who, torn between humanism and Calvinism, reconciled his translations of the anything but puritanical stories of Ovid's *Metamorphoses* by drawing a Christian moral from them. The story of *Venus and Adonis* comes from the *Metamorphoses*, which prompted Francis Meres to write, 'the sweete wittie soule of Ovid lives in mellifluous and hony-tongued Shakespeare', but it is impossible to say how much Shakespeare owed to Golding's translation, as he would almost certainly read much of the original Latin while at school. However, we may be sure that as a boy he did read the clumsily managed fourteeners of Golding, and even in the last and loveliest of his plays remembered the lines beginning, 'Ye airs and winds, ye elves of hills, ye brooks and woods alone'.

In 1568 John Shakespeare was elected bailiff of Stratford.

Elizabeth had been ten years on the throne, and with the aid of Cecil had imposed a new order on the country in place of the old disorder favoured by the feudal aristocracy. But the forces of this old disarray had not been destroyed, and now that Mary was in Elizabeth's hands feudal anarchy once more raised its head. The great Catholic lords of the Border, the Earls of Northumberland and Westmorland, having learned nothing from the fate of their ancestors in the reign of Henry IV, proposed to marry Mary to the Duke of Norfolk and place her on the throne. Norfolk, at heart a Catholic, but a weak and vacillating man who had readily conformed to the Established Church, was not averse from marrying Mary, but hesitated to take up arms. He was confined in the Tower, and the northern earls were forced to act before their plans were fully prepared. Advancing to release Mary from Tutbury Castle, they met with little support; their forces deserted them, and Northumberland fled to Scotland, Westmorland to Spain. The insurgents were severely dealt with, and the last feudal rebellion in England was over. Scotland, less fortunate than England, plunged still further into anarchy when, in January 1571, the Earl of Murray was assassinated. John Knox preached the funeral sermon, and within two years he, too, was dead.

In the spring of 1570 a vicious blow was struck at the harmony of the English people; the Pope, Pius V, issued a Bull declaring Elizabeth a heretic and illegitimate, excommunicate therefore, and deposed. Nothing could have been better calculated to rouse the resentment of English Protestants, to fan their patriotism into a passion and unite them in fanatical loyalty to Elizabeth. But for the Catholics it was a disaster; they were faced with the cruellest of dilemmas, for they could not be loyal both to the Queen and to the Pope, and henceforth every Catholic was suspect, a potential traitor, and the period of religious toleration was brought perforce to an end. Events moved rapidly to a crisis. An Italian banker, Ridolfi, tried by means less crude than rebellion to achieve the end so muddled by the northern earls. Philip of Spain agreed to back the marriage of Mary and Norfolk and ordered Alva to prepare plans for the invasion of England; but Ridolfi's agent was intercepted and the plot uncovered. Norfolk, who had been released, was rearrested, convicted of treason by his peers and sentenced to death. The Spanish ambassador was ordered to leave the country, and his last act was an attempt on the life of Cecil. Norfolk was executed after some months' delay, in June 1572, and

Parliament not unnaturally demanded the attainder of Mary. But Elizabeth knew that she had no real right even to detain Mary, much less bring her to trial, although she was a constant threat to her own life, and compromised by consigning her to Sheffield Castle and the charge of the Earl of Shrewsbury, who, almost broken-hearted, had had to pronounce the sentence of death on Norfolk.

Cecil, now Lord Burghley and Lord Treasurer, had been helped in the unravelling of the Ridolfi plot by his protégé, Sir Francis Walsingham, who symbolised both the triumph of the new order over the old and the new policy which the breach with Rome and Spain had brought about. A convinced Puritan, with great faith in the rack as an instrument for persuading men to tell the truth, his policy was one of open defiance of Spain at the risk of immediate war, a policy fortunately checked by the cautious Burghley and circumspect Queen; but his methods were secret and labyrinthine, and before long all the courts of Europe were enmeshed in a subtle web of espionage. In 1570 he was appointed ambassador at Paris with the task of trying to reconcile the religious factions in France, and bring about an Anglo-French alliance that would check the power of Spain, detach the Netherlands and the New World from her empire and establish Protestantism as the dominant power in Europe. The first stage in the plan seemed to be completed when in August 1572 the Huguenot prince, Henry of Navarre, married the sister of the French King, Charles IX.

Meanwhile, Elizabeth toyed with the idea, or rather appeared to toy with the idea, of a marriage with Charles's brother, the Duke of Anjou; then, the match having gone the way of all the others, with his still younger brother, Alençon, a singularly unattractive youth, whom she used to call her Frog when he came awooing her. In June 1572 she entertained the French ambassador with a bear-baiting, masque and tourney in the banqueting-house at Whitehall. Such banqueting-houses were temporary affairs, erected for some exceptional entertainment, when more space was required than was afforded by the hall of a palace. This one was covered with canvas, decked with birch and ivy, fretted with flowers, painted and gilded with heraldic devices, and strewn with rose leaves sweetened with sweet waters, William Hunnis supplying seventy-nine bushels of roses for the occasion, as well as pinks, honeysuckle and privet flowers.

A month later Elizabeth went on progress. She stayed three nights with Burghley, who presented her with a picture of Theobalds, then three nights with the corpulent Sir Nicholas Bacon, her Lord Keeper, at his newly built house of Gorhambury, Tudor brick with ornate classical porch. In some distress he had written to his great friend and brother-in-law Burghley, asking him 'what you thinke to be the best waye for me to deale in this matter: ffor, in very deede, no man is more rawe in suche a matter than my selfe'. His youngest son, Francis, a delicate boy of eleven, was probably at home at the time. After Sir Nicholas at Gorhambury, the Earl of Bedford at Woburn Abbey. The good earl, too, had written to Burghley: 'I trust your Lordship will have in remembraunce to provide and helpe that her Majesties tarieng be not above two nights and a daye; for, so long tyme do I prepare.' Elizabeth stayed three nights and two days. She seemed unable to tear herself away from Warwickshire. After staying at Warwick Castle, she spent two days at Kenilworth with Leicester, where there were 'such princely sports as could be devised', then back to Warwick for the fireworks and country dancing, and north again to Kenilworth, where she remained for the best part of a week. On Saturday, August 23rd, she arrived at Stratford, and was asleep at Charlecote when, in the early morning of Sunday, a bell tolled in Paris as a signal to begin the work that was to finish the prospect of an Anglo-French alliance.

Paris was full of Huguenots celebrating the marriage of Henry of Navarre, when the Queen Mother, fearful that she was losing her influence over her weak-willed son, made a last desperate attempt to regain her ascendancy, and persuaded Charles to agree to the treacherous attack of St. Bartholomew's Day. The fanatically Catholic mob was turned loose on the sleeping Huguenots, and before dawn the city was a shambles. The massacre spread to the provinces, and some twenty-five thousand Protestants perished in the fearful slaughter. The melancholy Philip of Spain was heard for once to laugh aloud, and the new Pope, Gregory XIII, celebrated the event with a *Te Deum*; but when Elizabeth at last consented to receive the French ambassador, she and all her Council were clothed in mourning, and Walsingham, who had seen the massacre and told the French what he thought in no uncertain terms, was recalled. Charles IX, henceforth a prey to constant nightmares and visions, was an old man at the age of twenty-two, and died two years later.

England prepared for war, for everybody, from the Queen down, thought the massacre was part of a great Catholic plan concerted with Philip and Alva, and the prelude to invasion. But there was no interruption of the Revels, and that Christmas there were a number of innovations. The Children of Eton gave a play, their only Court performance of the reign, and 'Richard Mulcaster with his Scholers', two of whom may have been the fourteen-year-old Thomas Kyd and Thomas Lodge, made the first of his six appearances during his enlightened headmastership of the newly founded Merchant Taylors' School. More interesting and more important were the three performances given by Leicester's Men; evidently there had been profitable discussion about the drama during the week that Elizabeth had stayed at Kenilworth. In January of that year a proclamation had been made enforcing the statutes against unlawful retainers, which prohibited the granting of livery by a lord to any but his domestic servants, a necessary precaution after the northern rebellion and the Norfolk affair. This had been followed by an Act of Parliament, part of the Poor Law legislation, directed against sturdy vagabonds, rogues and strumpets, charmingly catalogued by William Harrison as 'rufflers, uprightmen, hookers or anglers, rogues, wild rogues, priggers or prancers, palliards, fraters, abrams, freshwater mariners or whipjacks, dummerers, drunken tinkers, swadders or pedlars, jarkmen or patricoes; demanders for glimmer or fire, bawdy-baskets, morts, autem morts, walking morts, doxies, dells, kinching morts, and kinching coes'. The Act is less picturesque in its phraseology, and classes as rogues and vagabonds 'all Fencers Bearewardes Comon Players in Enterludes & Minstrels, not belonging to any Baron of this Realme or towardes any other honorable Personage of greater Degree, whiche shall wander abroade and have not Lycense of two Justices of the Peace at the leaste'. The penalties for vagabondage were ferocious; for the first offence, 'to bee grevouslye whipped, and burnte through the gristle of the right Eare with a hot Yron of the compass of an Ynche about'; for the second, to be deemed in all respects as a felon, for the third, death. The Act was to come into force on the Feast of St. Bartholomew. As all companies had to travel for part of the year, for they made their living not by wages but by their earnings, this meant that reputable players had to find a patron among the nobility, though, as most of them had already done so, the effect of the Act was to strengthen the position of the genuine player and his company. However, as a result of the Proclamation and the Act,

Leicester's Men wrote a letter to their patron, 'humblie desiringe your honor that you will now vouchsaffe to reteyne us at this present as your houshold Servaunts, not that we meane to crave any further stipend or benefite but our lyveries as we have had, and also your honors License to certifye that we are your houshold Servaunts when we shall have occasion to travayle amongst our frendes as we do usuallye once a yere, and as other noble-mens players do. Your Lordshippes Servaunts most bounden, James Burbage, John Perkinne, John Laneham, William Johnson, Robert Wilson, Thomas Clarke.' Here we have a first glimpse of the players who up till now have been no more than walking shadows; Robert Wilson, famous for his 'extemporal wit', was to become a minor playwright; and James Burbage was already the father of two boys of five or six, Cuthbert and Richard, whose fortunes were to be inextricably interwoven with those of Shakespeare. Leicester's, specially favoured by the Queen, were to be the leading company for the next ten years.

Two companies had visited Stratford in the summer of 1569, the Earl of Worcester's and the unfortunate Queen's Interluders, banished from Court since their deplorable exhibition of ten years before and now nearing the end of their run. This was during the bailiffship of John Shakespeare, to whom the players would have to report, from whom they would have to obtain a licence, and before whom they would give their first performance, known as the 'Mayor's play', for which they received a few shillings. After that they were free to play to the public at some appointed place, an inn yard perhaps, or in the wooden round where the miracles and moralities were still performed by amateurs. John Shakespeare was doing very well, and in 1569 a daughter, Joan, was born, destined to outlive the rest of her family by thirty years, and two years later, another daughter, Anne. William was then aged seven and a half, and no doubt already a pupil at the free grammar school, from which the master Walter Roche, had just resigned to practise as a lawyer in the town. He was succeeded by Simon Hunt, recently down from Oxford, a Catholic who stayed four years before going to Douai, later becoming a Jesuit and succeeding Robert Parsons as Penitentiary at the English College in Rome. Shakespeare would be under his tuition at a very impressionable period of his life.

Shakespeare and the Elizabethan Age were growing up together. In 1572 Tallis and Byrd, master and pupil, joint organists of the

Chapel Royal, and both inspired by the old faith, were composing the labyrinthine harmonies of their Latin motets. Middle Temple Hall, a Renaissance modification of a traditional form, was completed; Longleat and Kirby Hall were almost finished; Dr. John Caius, a physician much travelled in Italy, France and Germany, was erecting the strange medley of Tudor Gothic and Flemish classicism, the Gate of Honour, at his old Cambridge college, Gonville Hall, for which he also secured an annual licence for the dissection of the bodies of two malefactors; and in January 1571 Elizabeth had dined with Sir Thomas Gresham at his great house in Bishopsgate Street, and opened his London Bourse with a flourish of trumpets and the name Royal Exchange. She had recently had her first portrait painted as Queen: Hans Eworth's allegory, in which she plays the part of Paris and confounds the three rival goddesses by awarding the apple to herself, a form of flattery that was to be elaborated by the poets; and in 1572 Nicholas Hilliard painted her miniature, and was appointed limner and goldsmith to the Queen. In the same year John Donne and Ben Jonson were born and Drake set out on the first of his great expeditions to the New World. The classical pattern of the Elizabethan Age was beginning to take shape, but there was still no sign of a literary revival.

II

1573–1580

THE FIRST THEATRES

THERE was no war, after all, for the very good reason that none of those ultimately responsible for such things wanted one. Though the gloomy Philip had gloated over the St. Bartholomew Massacre, the news had come as a pleasant surprise, for there had been no collusion with the Queen Mother of France, who, now that she had enfeebled her country by widening the breach between Catholics and Huguenots, was above all eager for reconciliation with England. Alva and Philip, relieved that the projected Anglo-French alliance had come to grief, were equally eager to profit by France's discomfiture and to placate Elizabeth, provided she would not interfere in the Netherlands. Elizabeth, in her turn, by no means approving of rebellion and supporting the Netherlands only because they were a drain on the Spanish power, was quite prepared for more cordial relations with Spain, provided there was a resumption of the Flemish trade. She overruled Burghley and Walsingham, now Secretary of State and a member of the Privy Council, and in 1573 a treaty was arranged; Alva was recalled, a more conciliatory policy pursued in the Netherlands and trade with England restored, while in return Elizabeth ordered home the English volunteers in Flanders, restrained the privateering and piratical activities of her sailors and even emphasised the ground common to Anglicanism and Catholicism by persecuting the Anabaptists, two of whom died at the stake 'in great horror, roaring and crying'.

The return of Drake from the New World would have embarrassed Elizabeth if she had been capable of such an emotion. With a hundred men in three tiny ships he had sacked the Spanish town of Nombre de Dios, crossed the isthmus of Panama and caught his first glimpse of the Pacific, seized two mule-trains of gold and silver, and in the summer of 1573 sailed into Plymouth with his plunder. In any event, the Spanish honeymoon did not last long; Philip insisted on treating captured English sailors as heretics by handing them over to the Inquisition, and Elizabeth dallied as long as she dared with the offer of sovereignty that the Netherlands made her. However, a Spanish ambassador was again accredited to England—after Drake had been allowed to slip out of Plymouth and down the Channel in December 1577.

With the recession of the war scare, the Court resumed its normal routine. Elizabeth saw nine plays in the winter of 1573–4, five of them given by boys, and three by Leicester's, whom she honoured in May by issuing a patent under the Great Seal, authorising them to perform plays anywhere in England, including the City of London, provided they had been approved by the Master of the Revels, and were not performed at the time of common prayer or when there was serious plague in the City. This was a blow to the City Corporation, as it overrode, in the case of one company at least, the Royal Proclamation of 1559 confirming the traditional privilege of all civic authorities to license entertainments. It was the thin end of the wedge, and, as the Corporation complained, 'a precedent far extending to the heart of our liberties'. They bowed to the inevitable, but not without a protest and a code of regulations, the preamble to which summarises their case against plays:

Wheéaras hearetofore sondrye greate disorders and inconvenyences have benne found to ensewe to this Cittie by the inordynate hauntyinge of greate multitudes of people, speciallye youthe, to playes, enterludes, and shewes, namelye occasyon of ffrayes and quarrelles, eavell practizes of incontinencye in greate Innes, havinge chambers and secrete places adioyninge to their open stagies and gallyries, inveglynge and alleurynge of maides, speciallye orphanes and good Cityzens Children vnder Age, to previe and vnmete Contractes, the publishinge of vnchaste vncomelye and vnshamefaste speeches and doynges, withdrawinge of the Queenes Maiesties Subiectes from dyvyne service on Sonndaies and hollydayes, at which Tymes suche playes weare Chefelye vsed, vnthriftye waste of the moneye of the poore and fond persons, sondrye robberies by pyckinge and Cuttinge of purses, vtteringe of popular busye and sedycious matters, and manie other Corruptions of youthe and other enormyties, besydes that allso soundrye slaughters and mayhemings of the Quenes Subiectes have happened by ruines of Skaffoldes, fframes, and Stagies, and by engynes, weapons, and powder used in plaies; And whereas in tyme of goddes visitacion by the plaigue suche assemblies of the people in thronge and presse have benne verye daungerous for spreadinge of Infection. . . .

However, plays would be tolerated, provided they contained no unfit or uncomely matter, were not performed at times of plague and divine service, and were first 'perused and allowed' by the Lord Mayor and

Court of Aldermen, who reserved the right to approve the actors and license the places where they played. It was the first round in the struggle between the Privy Council and the City Corporation for the control of public entertainment in London. They were at one over the question of disturbances and the spreading of plague, but the Queen and her Council were emphatically opposed to the Puritans in and behind the Corporation, who wished to prohibit plays on religious and moral grounds, the main reason for their antagonism. Elizabeth had no sympathy with those who wished to cramp creative activity; besides, she wanted to be amused, and the public performance of plays in the City inns was the rehearsal for and prelude to performance at Court.

It was not often that foreign players were seen in England, but in 1574 Elizabeth was entertained by Italians who accompanied her progress and made pastime at Windsor and Reading, the Revels Office supplying them with a gallimaufry of devils' coats and heads, a scythe for Saturn, and horsetails for the wild man's garments. Their performances wrung a protest from Thomas Norton, Sackville's collaborator in *Gorboduc*, at the 'unchaste, shamelesse and unnatural tomblinge of the Italion Woemen'. Tumblers, or acrobats, were the most important members of the English companies, but they were not women, and the London aldermen made a note of Norton's offended susceptibilities. Elizabeth pursued her leisurely way over the enchanted uplands of the Cotswolds—Woodstock, Burford, Sherborne—and at the beginning of August dropped down into the western combe that enfolds Sudeley Castle. It was here that she had stayed as a girl of fourteen with her stepmother, Catherine Parr, and her second husband, Lord Seymour, who had made over-hearty and indelicate advances, and been executed for his ambitions by his brother, the Protector Somerset. Then, by way of Gloucester, Berkeley Castle and Bristol, she went to see the wonders of the all-but-finished Longleat, and the former Comptroller of her Household, Sir John Thynne, son-in-law of Gresham. Thence to stay with the Earl of Pembroke at Wilton, where she met the twenty-year-old Philip Sidney to whom she gave a lock of her hair.

Wherever the Queen stayed some form of entertainment was expected and duly provided by her hosts, but all previous entertainments paled before the princely pleasures with which she was diverted by Leicester at Kenilworth in 1575. She arrived on Saturday, July 9th, to be greeted by 'armonious blasterz' on silvery trumpets, and speeches by Hercules, a Sibyl, the Lady of the Lake and a Poet, possibly George Gascoigne, who, with William Hunnis, was mainly responsible for the dramatic episodes. On Sunday afternoon there was dancing with a 'lively agility and commendable grace', for dancing was loved above all things, and after that a firework display. On the 11th Elizabeth hunted and listened to a dialogue between a Savage Man and Echo. The 12th and 13th were devoted to music, dancing and hunting, and on the 14th these strange, civilised and barbaric, finely sensitive and callous Elizabethans forgot their music in the bestialities of bear-baiting, a sport that was followed by fireworks and feats of tumbling by an Italian. After two days of rest the festivities were renewed on the 17th with rustic sports: a bride-ale, morris dancing, tilting at the quintain and a performance of their Hocktide play by the men of Coventry, who had urgently petitioned for the privilege of performing before the Queen. In the evening there was an interlude and an 'Ambrosiall Banket', which was so prolonged that there was no time for a projected masque. The climax came on the 18th, when, after hunting, there was a water-pageant of the Delivery of the Lady of the Lake, in which Triton rode upon a mermaid and Arion on a dolphin's back. (Shakespeare must have played truant on that Monday afternoon.) In the evening the Queen held an investiture, and touched the poor for the 'king's evil'. The next day there was a repetition of the Coventry play, but on the 20th an expedition to see a device prepared by the Earl of Warwick had to be cancelled owing to bad weather. Elizabeth stayed another week, but there were no more major diversions, and it may have been now that Zuccaro made the drawings for the portraits that he is said to have painted of Elizabeth and Leicester. The drawings are in the British Museum, but the paintings, if they were ever made, have been lost. The princely pleasures were over, and on July 27th Elizabeth left Kenilworth to the presentation of a pretty device by Gascoigne and Hunnis, *The Farewell of Silvanus*. She and her Court and retainers had been there for nearly three weeks, and a hundred and sixty had sat at table with her host; it had cost Leicester £6,000 (£150,000 of our money), but rumour had it that he was not without his compensations.

It may have been while he was performing in the makeshift theatres at Kenilworth that James Burbage conceived the idea of building a permanent playhouse for Leicester's company and any others who might care to rent it. He was in the prime of life, an experienced actor and had been a joiner; just the man for the job if only he could raise the capital. In April 1576, shortly before Shakespeare's twelfth birthday, he took a lease of a plot of land, just to the north of Bishopsgate, in the rapidly growing suburb of Shoreditch. It was part of an estate, formerly a priory of Benedictine nuns, with a holy well, from which it took its name and status, the Liberty of Halliwell, outside the jurisdiction of the City, therefore, and its troublesome regulations. The lease was for twenty-one years at a rent of £14, renewable for a further twenty-one within the first ten years, the tenant being allowed to take away any theatrical buildings erected on the site, and the ground landlord and his family having free seats 'in some one of the vpper romes'. As Burbage was worth only £60 or so, the next thing was to find the money, and this he did by the sweet and continual persuasion of his sister's husband, John Brayne, a wealthy grocer. Burbage assured his brother-in-law that the playhouse would cost no more than £200, but by the time Brayne had advanced £500, and he and his wife had laboured at the building with their own hands, there was scope for misunderstanding, and once at least they went together by the ears with such a will that they could scarcely be parted. Burbage's reputation for being a stubborn fellow was not undeserved. However, The Theatre, as it was proudly called, was finished by 1577, and Leicester's Men were in occupation.

We know very little about the structure and appearance of the Theatre, and any imaginary reconstruction is based mainly on our knowledge of its successors, of which there are a number of exterior, though conventional, views, and one sketch of an interior. We know that it was built mostly of timber, had 'about' three galleries, either the middle or top one, or both, having 'rooms' or boxes for the spectators, that there was a tiring-house or dressing-room for the actors, and, according to de Witt, writing twenty years later, that it was an amphitheatre. And that is all. For a public open-air playhouse Burbage had two models to work from: the yard of one of the City inn-theatres with its surrounding galleries, and the medieval amphitheatre with its tiers of timber steps. The auditorium of the Theatre seems to have been a compound of the two: the covered galleries of the square inn yard, in the circular, or possibly polygonal, shape of the medieval 'wooden O's'. It has already been suggested that the staging of plays at the inns (as also, with modifications, in the halls of palaces, colleges and houses) was derived from that of the stationary miracle plays and moralities, such as the Cornish cycle and *The Castle of Perseverance*, the audience being confined to the galleries and the area round the walls immediately below them, so that the actors had the whole yard for their hotchpotch of histrionics, horse-play and acrobatics; for we must remember that many of these early plays, probably most of them, were something in the nature of a circus and, like a circus, demanded an arena. Our conception of the presentation of an Elizabethan play has been governed by that of a yard or pit thronged with spectators pressing right up to the edge of an apron stage on which all the action took place. But it is most improbable that it would ever occur to Burbage to put part of his audience in the yard, for that was the traditional and proper place for the performance of a play, as the traditional and proper place for spectators was on the surrounding benches that he had provided. That there were no spectators in the yard is suggested by the description of the accident at the Beargarden in 1583. Admittedly, we should scarcely look for an audience in the arena with the bears, but the Bearhouse was a similar building to the theatres, and a distinction is made between 'the yard, standings and galleries'. The 'gallery was double and compassed the yard round about'; this collapsed, and naturally 'they were most hurt and in danger which stood under the galleries on the ground'. The original groundlings then, or at least some of them, stood under the galleries, and there is no evidence that they stood anywhere else until twenty years after the building of the Theatre, by which time plays were very different from those for which Burbage had to cater.

We should then, I believe, conceive the Theatre as an elaborated version of the medieval round, something on the lines of the following imaginary reconstruction. A circular yard of about sixty feet in diameter was surrounded by three galleries, each about ten feet high and twelve feet deep. In the lowest were 'standings' for the ground-lings, and three or four rows of seats in the upper ones. On one side was the wall of the tiring-house (actors' quarters), in front of which projected a stage almost into the middle of the yard. This was prob-ably about four feet high, as the region beneath had to accommodate hell, which communicated with the upper world by trap-doors in the manner of the old conveyor. A door led on to the stage from either side of the tiring-house wall, and between these, from another entry on the level of the middle gallery, descended six or seven steps, the top

THE THEATRE

one forming a platform, the medieval *pulpitum*, extended perhaps into a gallery some five feet wide, on which was the central property, the throne, a secularised version of the throne of God in the miracles.[1] There is evidence for this in the *English Wagner Book* of 1594, in

[1] Compare *Julius Cæsar*, III. ii :
    Enter Brutus and goes into the Pulpit.
    Citizen. Let him go vp into the publike chaire,
    Wee'l heare him: Noble Antony, go vp.

which Faustus's servant, Wagner, conjures up a vision of his master's death, though, as it is a vision, the description is correspondingly inflated, and cannot be accepted as accurate in all its details:

They might distinctly perceive a goodly stage to be reared ... Therein was the high throne wherein the king should sit, and that proudly placed with two and twenty degrees to the top ... There might you see the ground-work at the one end of the stage, whereout the personated devils should enter in their fiery ornaments, made like the broad wide mouth of an huge dragon.

It might almost be a picture of a medieval round, though the conveyor pit and hell's mouth have been combined, the devils emerging from under the stage into the yard. On either side of the upper entry were small 'rooms' for musicians, again as in the miracles. Heaven, or 'the heavens', was probably moved to the level of the top gallery, for the production of effects and such appropriate sounds as thunder, though we do not know that it projected over the stage as it did later, for there is no indication that the stage of the Theatre was originally sheltered by a canopy. There were probably two doors into the yard, in which were tents or 'houses' representing various localities, according to the play, and within them the appropriate characters could wait when not performing. If a scene began at one of these houses, an audience brought up on medieval conventions of staging would understand that the whole arena might become that locality so that the action flowed freely 'below' and 'above', over yard and stage, steps and pulpit, 'conducted' perhaps by the book-holder with his prompt-copy, in the manner of the Cornish 'ordinary'.

There is valuable evidence of the use of the steps and gallery in the last scene of *Sir Thomas More*, a play of the nineties:

More. Is this the place?
I promise ye it is a goodly scaffold. . . .
Well, let's ascend a God's name.
In troth methinks your stair is somewhat weak. . . .
                              (*As he is going up the stairs*)
Truly here's a most sweet gallery . . .
                                        (*Walking*)
Point me the block; I ne'er was here before.
Hangman. To the east side, my lord.
More. Then to the east.   (*Exit with Hangman*)

Here also is one indication that the theatres, like the medieval rounds, were orientated, for as the only exit faced the top of the steps the

stage must have been at the east. The medieval tradition and nomen-
clature—scaffold, throne, heavens, hell—died very hard, as we
should expect. As late as 1598 Henslowe had 'j Hell mought' at the
Rose.

The charge for admission to the Theatre was 1*d.*, which gave
access to the bottom gallery where the groundlings stood, another 1*d.*
or 2*d.* paid at an inner door securing a seat in one of the upper galleries,
or in a 'room'. The admission pennies were the players' profits, the
gallery takings the owners' rent, both being collected by 'gatherers'
with boxes, Burbage himself being at the inner door dealing indirectly
in the pennies, and thrusting 'some of the money devident betwene
him and his ffellowes in his bosome or other where about his bodye'.
The trick was a new one then, unless the same method of collection
was employed in the medieval rounds, but it persisted until the closing
of the theatres in 1642, by which time prices had risen enormously,
and gatherers 'seem to scratch their heads where they itch not, and
drop shillings and half-crown pieces in at their collars'.

It was not long before Burbage and Brayne had a rival. By the end
of 1577 one Henry Laneman had built the Curtain—the name was
taken from the curtain wall enclosing Holywell Priory—a few
hundred yards south of the Theatre, strategically placed therefore to
entice wavering citizens walking from Bishopsgate to sample its
alternative delights. In a recently discovered view of Shoreditch, made
soon after the demolition of the Theatre in 1599, the Curtain is
shown as a circular or polygonal building with the 'heavens' at the
east; another indication, therefore, that Burbage and Laneman preserved the convention, derived ultimately from the time when plays
were performed in churches, of orientating their playhouses so that
stage and throne were at the eastern side. We cannot say what companies rented the Curtain in its early days; possibly the Earl of
Sussex's, who were then performing fairly regularly at Court; possibly Lord Howard's, soon to achieve immortality under their later
name of the Admirals'.

There was a third and different kind of theatrical venture in 1576.
In the south-west corner of the City were the remains of a Dominican
priory that gave the name of the Liberty of Blackfriars to the area
lying between Ludgate Hill and the river. After its suppression by
Henry VIII the priory estate had been split up into a number of
holdings, one of which, the long building on the west side of the

cloisters, belonged to Sir William More, who leased part of the upper
storey to Richard Farrant, Master of the Children of Windsor and
organist to the Queen at St. George's Chapel. He had just been
appointed Deputy Master of the Chapel Children under Hunnis, and,
being an enterprising sort of man, converted the long narrow room
into a private theatre where the Chapel boys could rehearse their
Court plays and give public performances, as did the Paul's boys under
Westcott. It was a wise move, for with the opening of the Theatre
and the Curtain the competition of the adult companies became much
more severe, and in the course of the next fifteen years the position at
Court was reversed, the men performing two plays for every one by
the boys.

Distinction must be made between the boys who played women's
parts in the men's companies and the boys who played all the parts at
Blackfriars. The former were apprenticed to, and trained by, the men;
chosen for their acting ability, though it was an advantage to sing
tolerably well, they generally became professional actors when their
voices broke. The others were choirboys whose acting might be indifferent, but as singers they were the pick of the country and trained
by accomplished musicians. But nearly all boys can act, at least before
they reach a self-conscious adolescence, though not all with the distinction of Solomon Pavy, 'a child of Queen Elizabeth's Chapel',
whose epitaph Ben Jonson wrote:

> Years he numbered scarce thirteen
>   When fates turned cruel,
> Yet three filled zodiacs had he been
>   The stage's jewel;
> And did act, what now we moan,
>   Old men so duly,
> As sooth, the Parcae thought him one,
>   He played so truly.

The adult companies consisted of eight or ten men, known as sharers,
because they owned all the stock and shared the profits according to
their holdings, a few hired men who were not full members and two
or three boys. They still performed in the old inn-theatres, but now
in the open public playhouses of Shoreditch as well. There, because
of the difficulty of artificial lighting, the plays were given in the
afternoon; the flag fluttered above the hut on the tiring-house, and
at two o'clock, after the third sounding of a trumpet, the Prologue

in a cloak of black velvet stepped on to the stage and the performance began. The large room at Blackfriars where the children played was roofed, and for that reason, and because its higher prices made it more exclusive, was called a private theatre. As artificial light was needed in any event, performances were not confined to daytime, though they were normally given in the afternoon, daylight being supplemented by candles and torches. Music, of course, was a much more important part of the entertainment than in the public theatres.

The theatres had come to London, but where were the plays? And where were the playwrights? There was George Gascoigne, who, in the year of the Kenilworth entertainment, published his *Glass of Government*, a 'tragicall comedie' adapted from Terence. But the reward of virtue and punishment of vice in speeches of epic proportions was no fare for the public theatres, no 'Bellsavage fayre', as he himself admitted, or rather insisted, for after his volunteering exploits in the Netherlands he had turned respectable, maintaining that 're-formed speech doth now become us best'. It did not, and the *Steel Glass* of 1576, by which he is chiefly remembered, is little more than medieval moralising in blank verse. His best is his pioneering work, and he was a pioneer in many ways; *Supposes* is the first English play in prose, as it is the first to acclimatise the Italian theme so dear to the later dramatists. In his *Notes* on the writing of verse, itself one of our earliest critical essays, he insists on the necessity of some fine invention in the making of a delectable poem, 'for it is not enough to roll in pleasant words, nor yet to thunder in *rym, ram, ruff* by letter'. And his own verse, some of his lyrics at least, have a grace and invention achieved by none of his contemporaries. He died in 1577, before he was fifty, at the house of his friend George Whetstone, who wrote a long, lugubrious elegy on his well-employed life and godly end.

Whetstone knew; for the two had been companions in fortune, squandered their youthful patrimonies together, served together in the Netherlands, and in middle age arrived together at a soberer view of life. The result was the publication in 1578 of the two parts of his play, *Promos and Cassandra*, an adaptation of a story in Cinthio's *Hecatommithi*, later to be Shakespeare's main source for *Measure for Measure*. Much more interesting than the play, ostentatiously didactic, is the *Epistle* to William Fleetwood, the puritanical Recorder of London, describing the contemporary drama. The English playwright, he maintains, 'first grounds his work on impossibilities, then in three hours runs he through the world, marries, gets children, makes children men, men to conquer kingdoms, murder monsters, and bringeth gods from heaven, and fetcheth devils from hell'. There are really two criticisms, or gibes, here: one against the medieval, knockabout farcical element in the popular plays, the other against the abuse of the imaginary classical decorum and neo-classical unities, a theme that was soon to be developed, in almost identical terms, by Philip Sidney. *Promos and Cassandra* was no more Belsavage fare, or Theatre or Curtain fare, than *The Glass of Government*, and neither Gascoigne, if he had lived, nor Whetstone, if he had not abandoned drama for seafaring and soldiering (he sailed with Humphrey Gilbert and fought at Zutphen), was the man that the theatres were waiting for. George Peele and Thomas Lodge were still at Oxford, Robert Greene at Cambridge, Thomas Kyd had just left Merchant Taylors', and Marlowe and Shakespeare were schoolboys of twelve.

Stratford was becoming a regular centre, not only for the provincial companies but also for the London companies when they went on tour; Leicester's were there in 1573, Warwick's and Worcester's in 1575 and Leicester's and Worcester's in 1576. Shakespeare's second brother, Richard, was born in 1574, and in the following year his schoolmaster, Simon Hunt, went off to Douai, to be succeeded by Thomas Jenkins, a Welshman whom Shakespeare remembered with affection if, as is most probable, he is the original of Sir Hugh Evans in *The Merry Wives of Windsor* and, with a difference, of Fluellen in *Henry V*. Shortly before this, in October 1573, Henry Wriothesley, the second son of the Earl of Southampton, was born at Cowdray House in Sussex.

The two worst enemies of the actors were plague and Puritans. Fortunately there was no severe outbreak of plague in the critical years that followed the opening of the two new public theatres, though in 1577 they were closed in August and September for fear of spreading infection, and the London companies had to go on tour in the provinces, a much less lucrative occupation than playing in the capital. In the same year the Puritan attack on the theatres opened in earnest. These early Puritans were not necessarily dissenters, many of them indeed were clergymen, but they disliked or detested with varying degrees of intensity the high Anglican ritual on which Elizabeth insisted and the whole apparatus of the episcopal hierarchy. The movement had received an impetus from the Marian persecutions and the contact of Protestant exiles with Calvinism in Geneva, and in the early seventies controversy had broken into print and pamphlet, John Whitgift and Thomas Cartwright, whom Elizabeth had heard dispute at Cambridge, being the chief protagonists. It was just at this time that the firm hand of Archbishop Parker was withdrawn. He died in 1575, and was replaced by Burghley's nominee and crony, Edmund Grindal, who sympathised with the Puritans' demand for free speech in their preachings and prophesyings. Elizabeth, for whom these things were an abomination bordering on sedition, ordered Grindal to suppress them. He gently remonstrated but firmly refused, and the Queen, who could not very well depose an archbishop without undermining her own authority, had to content herself with suspending him from his jurisdictional functions. Fortune was favouring the Puritans.

Their attack on the theatre began with a sermon preached at Paul's Cross by Thomas White, vicar of St. Dunstan-in-the-West, in November 1577. 'The sumptuous Theatre houses' (Burbage must have felt flattered) are 'scholes of vice, dennes of theeues, and Theatres of all leudnesse'. There was still some plague about in London, and, as the cause of plague is sin and the cause of sin is plays, he had little difficulty in demonstrating with inexorable logic that the cause of plague is plays. In the following month John Northbrooke, a Gloucester clergyman, published his *Treatise wherein Vaine playes or Enterluds, commonly used on the Sabboth day, are reproued*: 'Satan hath not a more speedie way, and fitter schoole to work and teach his desire, to bring men and women into his snare of concupiscence and filthie lustes of wicked whoredome, than those places, and playes, and theatres are; and therefore necessarie that those places and players shoulde be forbidden and put downe by authoritie'. Even the miracle plays, 'histories out of the scriptures', are condemned, 'for the long suffering and permitting of these vaine plays hath stricken such a blinde zeale into the heartes of the people, that they shame not to say that playes are as good as sermons'. Here we have it, underlined as well, the Puritan's lament that his passion for preaching is not appreciated, for 'many can tarie at a vayne playe two or three houres, when as they will not abide scarce one houre at a sermon'. However, he would allow schoolmasters very occasionally to practise their scholars in plays, provided they were in the chastest Latin, and not performed publicly for profit, a hit at Farrant and the Blackfriars theatre.

Stephen Gosson's *School of Abuse* followed in 1579. Gosson was a young Oxford man whose 'pleasant invective' against poets and players was probably prompted by disappointment at his own lack of success as actor and dramatist, rather than by any moral convictions, though he did later become a parson. His book has some pretensions to literary merit (he dedicated it, without permission, to Philip Sidney), is relatively moderate and not altogether indiscriminate in its condemnation. He casts a jaundiced eye on those actors who 'jet under gentlemens noses in sutes of silke', but admits that some of them are sober, discreet, honest householders and citizens. Nor are all plays to be condemned, and he singles out two for special commendation, good plays and sweet plays, worthy to be sung of the Muses. One of them was his own *Catiline's Conspiracies*. Thomas Lodge, just down from Oxford, and recently admitted into Lincoln's Inn, began his literary career with a modest *Defence of Poetry, Music and Stage Plays*, in reply to *The School of Abuse*. More sweeping in its denunciation and swashing in its blows was the *Blast of Retreat from Plays and Theatres*, almost certainly by the egregious opportunist Anthony Munday. Not only is the theatre the school of abuse, it is also the school of bawdry, nest of the devil, sink of all sin, 'the meere brothel house of Bauderie and consultorie house of Satan'. Actors are 'roisters, brallers, ildealers, bosters, louers, loiterers, ruffins', and when he saw 'by them yong boies, inclining of themselves unto wickednes, trained up in filthie speeches, unnatural and unseemlie gestures, to be brought up by these Schoole-masters in bawderie, and in idlenes', he could not 'chuse but with teares and grief of hart lament'. Having helped to hound Edmund Campion to his death, and written a profitable little eye-witness account of the proceedings, he returned 'againe to ruffle upon the stage', from which he was hissed, and went into the playwriting business at the lowest level, as hack to Philip Henslowe.

Elizabeth's attention was diverted from the Puritan campaign by a far more serious threat from the other flank. Though Philip, the champion of the Catholic Church, prudently refused to make another Netherlands of England, the Pope had other and less costly schemes for bringing about the destruction of the heretic Queen. A little deft diplomacy might restore the Catholic ascendancy in Scotland, and wrest the young King James from the hands of the Protestant Regent, the Earl of Morton; if Protestant volunteers served in the Netherlands, Catholic volunteers might serve in Ireland, ever in a state of incipient or open rebellion; and though armed invasion of England was beyond the papal means, there was nothing to prevent a secret penetration by Catholic priests and Jesuit missionaries from the English colleges of Douai and Rome.

In 1579 the Catholic Duke of Lennox arrived in Scotland. Walsingham, well aware of what was afoot, counselled extreme measures, but Elizabeth held him back, knowing that French intervention was improbable so long as she dangled the bait of marriage before the grotesque Alençon. Within a few months Morton was duly done to death, and a period of more than customary anarchy supervened, until Lennox was expelled and some sort of order restored by the Earl of Arran. Meanwhile papal volunteers, reinforced by some eight hundred Spanish and Italian adventurers, landed in south-west Ireland. Munster was ablaze with rebellion, and the new Deputy, Lord Grey de Wilton, firing the villages and slaughtering their inhabitants, advanced on Smerwick where the foreigners had entrenched themselves. They were forced to surrender at discretion, and all but the officers, who were held to ransom, perished in the ensuing massacre. One of the English officers responsible for the slaughter was Walter Raleigh, a tall dark, handsome man of twenty-eight, whose splendid bearing, romantic presence and ready wit found favour with Elizabeth at Court in the following year. Lord Grey's new secretary at Dublin was another young man of the same age, equally eager for the spoils of Ireland, Edmund Spenser.

By this time the Jesuits were at work in England, proselytising and persuading the faithful that professed loyalty to the Queen was justified on the grounds that they would the better be able to help in her deposition when the time came. The leading members of the mission had arrived in the summer of 1580, the brilliant backstairs intriguer, Robert Parsons, and the saintly Edmund Campion, whose official business it had been to welcome Elizabeth to Oxford fourteen years before. Walsingham, too, was at work, but for months his quarry eluded him, until at last Campion was caught in Berkshire. Taken to the Tower and racked, he died the atrocious death reserved for traitors, without any betrayal of his confederates, and protesting to the last his loyalty to the Queen. Parsons escaped to continue his work by directing the mission from Rome, where he died thirty years later as Rector of the English College and a disappointed man.

Campion and Parsons were still at large when, on September 26th,

1580, Drake put in to Plymouth, having 'extended the point of that liquid line, wherewith (as an emulator of the sun's glory) he encompassed the world'. He had sailed with a hundred and seventy men and five small ships, but by the time he had passed the Straits of Magellan had lost touch with the others, and the *Golden Hind* alone began the journey up the west coast of South America, in waters never before entered by an Englishman. After stuffing his ship with Spanish plunder, he sailed in search of a north-east passage, but having reached the haven of what is now San Francisco, turned west and crossed the Pacific to the Spice Islands, and so, by way of the Cape of Good Hope, back to Plymouth, which he had left almost three years before. It was a tremendous achievement, and Drake was the idol of England. His plunder was an invaluable addition to the national wealth so carefully acquired under the directions of Gresham, who just failed to live to welcome him; but Elizabeth herself was there when he put in at Deptford, and knighted him on board the *Golden Hind*. Philip protested, but Elizabeth had only to point to Ireland, where the Spanish forces had recently landed. There was little to choose between the irregularities of the two, but Philip was not a monarch to be offended with impunity; he was now King of Spain and of Portugal as well, of Portugal with the Indies, ruler of virtually all the newly discovered territories of the world.

Both within the country and without, the Catholic menace was mounting, and when Parliament, increasingly Puritan in complexion, met in January 1581, it passed a ferocious Act making it high treason to proselytise or join the Roman Church; anyone celebrating or attending Mass was liable to a heavy fine and a year's imprisonment; and a fine of £20 a month (a crippling sum) was the price of abstention from the Anglican service. It was under this Act that Campion was hanged, disembowelled and quartered. The persecution of Catholics, which had been prosecuted with a desultory mildness since the Papal Bull of 1570, now began in earnest; there were fifteen Catholic martyrs in 1584, thirty-five in Armada year and altogether some three hundred perished in the last thirty years of Elizabeth's reign.

What was the effect of the persecution on the affairs of the Shakespeare family we cannot say, but the Ardens were Catholics, and there is some reason to believe that John Shakespeare was a Catholic, too. In any event, his fortunes began to decline towards the end of the seventies; he no longer attended meetings of the town council, and, in his embarrassment, sold part of his wife's estate and mortgaged the remainder. His daughter, Anne, died in 1579, and a year later a fourth son was born, Edmund, almost certainly an unexpected and unwanted child. William was then sixteen, the age at which a grammar school education was completed, and, though all is conjecture, it is reasonable to suppose that he joined his father in his business. Marlowe left King's School, Canterbury, at the same time, to go up to Cambridge as a scholar of Corpus, and shortly before this, Shakespeare's acquaintance or friend, Richard Field, son of a tanner with whom his father did business, left Stratford for London where he was apprenticed to Thomas Vautrollier, one of the finest printers in the country. About this time, too, died a man whom Shakespeare may have met, Raphael Holinshed, steward of the manor of Packwood, near Stratford.

Holinshed's *Chronicles of England, Scotland, and Ireland* had been published in 1577, a work based on, frequently transcribed from, the histories of his predecessors, Berners' *Froissart* and the *Chronicles* of Hall and Grafton. More interesting reading and far more original writing is the informative, humorous and confidential chatter of William Harrison, who contributed the *Description of England* to Holinshed's history. He dislikes affectation as much as foreign fashions: 'The short French breeches make a comely vesture that, except it were a dog in a doublet, you shall not see any so disguised as are my countrymen of England. . . . Then we must put it on, then must the long seams of our hose be set by a plumbline, then we puff, then we blow, and finally sweat till we drop, that our clothes may stand well upon us.' But, on the whole, he is full of wonder and admiration for his England and his English: 'It is a world to see' the increase in our exports and imports (including the unspeakable venerous potato); 'it is a world to see' the improvement in our diet, education, inns and houses, and 'for strength, assurance, nimbleness, and swiftness of sailing, there are no vessels in the world to be compared with ours'. Hawkins was just about to be placed in charge of the naval dockyards. Christopher Saxton's maps of England and Wales and the counties were originally intended as illustrations to the *Chronicles*, but were published separately in 1579, the first national atlas to be produced by any country, and perhaps the most beautiful. In the same year as the *Chronicles* came Richard Eden's *History of Travel*, from which Shakespeare got the name of Setebos, a Patagonian god, and in 1580 the cheerfully indigent John Stow published his *Chronicles of England*, later re-issued as the *Annals*.

But the wonderful year, or the first wonderful year, for all were wonderful when Shakespeare started writing, was 1579, which ushered in the long-awaited literary revival with North's *Plutarch*, Lyly's *Euphues* and Spenser's *Shepherd's Calendar*. The *Lives of the Noble Grecians and Romanes*, printed by Vautrollier, was a translation of a translation: Sir Thomas North's version of Jaques Amyot's rendering of Plutarch's Greek. North's prose is noble and serene, so admirable indeed that when Shakespeare came to use his book for the Roman plays, he frequently accepted it with little alteration, though rarely without some touch that transfigures the whole; thus North's somewhat pedestrian, 'As the dolphin shows his back above the water, so Antony always rose superior to the pleasures in which he lived', is transformed by Shakespeare into:

> his delights
> Were dolphin-like, they showed his back above
> The element they lived in.

But the comparison is hardly fair; the rocking and rhyming sentence is not characteristic of North, but of Lyly.

John Lyly was a lively spark recently down from Oxford, very different from his grave grandfather, William Lyly, of Latin Grammar fame. His *Euphues; The Anatomy of Wit* is professedly a romance, the scene Naples, a sordid little love-story, swollen with unwholesome moralising and distended by a kind of verbal dropsy. His style added the word 'euphuism' to the language, though the manner was not new, and had been seeping into English prose for more than half a century; what was new was its concentration, its extravagance. The framework is the balanced sentence and antithetic clause; its decorative devices, alliteration, classical and mythological allusions, and similes drawn from natural and unnatural history. Thus Euphues makes love to his friend's betrothed: 'Though the stone Cylindrus at every thunder clap roll from the hill, yet the pure sleek stone mounteth at the noise; though the rust fret the hardest steel, yet doth it not eat into the emerald; though Polypus change his hue, yet the salamander keepeth his colour', and so on, through Proteus and Pygmalion, Æneas and Dido, Troilus and Cressida. Was ever woman in this humour won? Euphuism became the fashion and affected all forms of Eliza-

THE LIVES OF THE
NOBLE GRECIANS AND RO-
MANES, COMPARED TOGETHER BY THAT
graue learned Philosopher and Historiogra-
pher, Plutarche of Chœronea.

Theseus.

A   LIKE as historiographers describing the world(frende *Sossius Senecio*) *Sossius Sene-*
doe of purpose referre to the vttermost partes of their mappes the *cio a Senatur*
farre distant regions whereof they be ignoraunt,with this note:these *of Rome.*
contries are by meanes of sandes and drowthes vnnauigable, rude,
full of venimous beastes, SCYTHIAN ise, and frosen seas. Euen so
may I (which in comparing noble mens liues haue already gone so
farre into antiquitie, as the true and certaine historie could lead me)
of the rest, being thinges past all proofe or chalenge, very well say:
that beyonde this time all is full of suspicion and dout, being deliue-
red vs by Poets and Tragedy makers,sometimes without trueth and likelihoode, and alwayes
B without certainty. Howbeit, hauing heretofore set foorth the liues of *Lycurgus* (which established the lawes of the LACEDÆMONIANS)and of king *Numa Pompilius:*me thought I might
go a litle further to the life of *Romulus*, sence I was come so nere him. But considering my selfe
as the Poet *AEschilus* did:

    VVhat champion may vvith such a man compare?
    or vvho(thinke I)shalbe against him set?
    VVho is so bold? or vvho is he that dare
    defend his force,in such encounter met?

                                A

bethan literature, from the prose of the pamphleteers to the verse of
the dramatists. Its influence may be seen in the early work of Shakespeare, particularly in *Love's Labour's Lost*, but he was never taken
with the manner, and Falstaff sluiced euphuism out of the plays along
with King Cambyses' vein. Lyly exploited the success of his best-seller
with a sequel, *Euphues and his England*, but he was to do better than
this, for euphuism, purified and distilled and purged of its slabby
moralising, made a medium of sheer delight for the sophisticated
fantasy of his comedies.

At Pembroke, Cambridge, Spenser had formed a friendship with
a Fellow of the college, some ten years his senior, Gabriel Harvey,
an irritable, irritating, ambitious and dissatisfied pedant, with a passion
for imposing classical metres on English verse. Fortunately Spenser
was proof against such seductive Harveian hexameters as,

> What might I call this tree? A laurel? O bonny laurel,
> Needs to thy boughs will I bow this knee, and vail my bonneto;

though when Harvey introduced him to the Earl of Leicester he was
subjected to still greater pressure by the coterie of literary reformers
that he found at Leicester House—among others, Edward Dyer,
Fulke Greville and Philip Sidney. The craze for classical metres can
easily be understood; something had been wrong with English prosody
for the last hundred and fifty years, and perhaps the quantitative
system of the so-delightful Latin poets was the answer. Spenser might
well have been carried away by the exalted society in which he found
himself, but he kept his head, obstinately refused to look back any
further than Chaucer for his verification, and in 1579 published his
Shepherd's Calendar, a series of twelve eclogues, one for each month
of the year. It is not a great poem, but it has claims to be considered
the best longish poem (excluding the Scottish writers) since the time
of Chaucer, no very difficult feat. The diction is archaic and uncouth,
befitting, so Spenser thought, the bucolic characters, and there is
overmuch of the old *rim, ram, ruff* by letter: 'And sooth to sayn,
nought seemeth sike strife', but there is in places an entirely new
music, prefiguring the poetry of the *Faerie Queene*:

> Colin, to hear thy rhymes and roundelays,
> Which thou wert wont on wasteful hills to sing,
> I more delight than lark in summer days,
> Whose echo made the neighbour groves to ring.

Here at last was the Elizabethan poetry. Spenser dedicated his work to Philip Sidney, 'most worthy of all titles both of learning and chivalry', and set off for Ireland.

Sidney had been in Ireland with his father in 1576, when the Earl of Essex died there mysteriously, some said by poison, and on his death bed expressed the wish that he, Sidney, might marry his daughter, Penelope Devereux. The next year his sister Mary married Henry Herbert, Earl of Pembroke, and from then on Sidney was a constant visitor at Wilton House, engaged in writing *Arcadia*, which he delivered sheet by sheet to his 'most dear lady and sister'. In the following May, when the Queen visited his uncle, the Earl of Leicester (for his mother was Leicester's sister, Mary Dudley), he wrote *The Lady of May* for her entertainment in the garden of Wanstead House, a piece in which the schoolmaster, Rombus, 'one not a little versed in the disciplinating of the juvenall frie', delightfully resembles the Holofernes of *Love's Labour's Lost*. It was shortly after this that Leicester secretly married the widowed Countess of Essex, and ugly stories began to circulate; the feud that had existed between Leicester and Essex was notorious, and people, remembering Amy Robsart's misadventure, drew sombre conclusions. It was not until the spring of 1579 that Elizabeth was told—by de Simier, the envoy of Alençon, to whose marriage with the Queen Leicester was opposed. She was furious, and there was talk of sending the Earl to the Tower; but the cloud passed, and there were three visits to Wanstead that summer. Sidney incurred a more lasting disgrace. There was a quarrel in the tennis-court at Whitehall; the violent and techy Earl of Oxford, a favourite of the Queen's and a supporter of the Alençon match, called Sidney a puppy. Sidney challenged him, but the Queen forbade the duel because of the disparity of rank, and ordered him to apologise. He refused; then, to make matters worse, wrote her a long letter elaborately stating the case against a marriage with a young repulsive Catholic prince. Nothing could have been better calculated to infuriate her; she dismissed him from Court, and he retired to Wilton.

Sidney's loss was posterity's gain, for in his enforced retirement he began the revision of *Arcadia*, wrote *The Defence of Poesy*, and many of the sonnets to Stella. The main story of the *Arcadia* is the wooing of Pamela and Philoclea, daughters of King Basilius of Arcady and his guilty wife Gynaecia, by Musidorus and his friend Pyrocles, disguised as a woman. The leisurely progress and desultory manner of the telling allow of innumerable songs, including the well-known lyric, 'My true love hath my heart', and the splendid double sestina in the second Eclogue, beginning:

> Ye goat-herd gods, that love the grassy mountains,
> Ye nymphs, that haunt the springs in pleasant valleys,
> Ye satyrs, joy'd with free and quiet forests,
> Vouchsafe your silent ears to plaining music,
> Which to my woes gives still an early morning,
> And draws the dolour on till weary evening.

Then, in the manner of the Spanish and Italian romances that were Sidney's model, many minor themes are woven into the main plot. Such a one is the story of the blind and outcast king, cared for by the loving son whom he had done his best to destroy:

> This old man (whom I leade) was lately rightfull Prince of this Country of *Paphlagonia*, by the hard-hearted ungratefulnesse of a Sonne of his, deprived not only of his Kingdome (whereof no forraine forces were ever able to spoile him) but of his sight, the riches which Nature grants to the poorest creatures. Whereby, and by other his unnaturall dealings, hee hath beene driven to such griefe, as even now hee would have had mee to have ledde him to the top of this rocke, thence to cast himselfe headlong to death.

Out of this Shakespeare created the Gloucester sub-plot in *King Lear*. He also borrowed a number of names for his other plays, Leonatus for example, and Pyrocles himself is probably the original of Pericles, Prince of Tyre. The *Arcadia* is the first major work of our literature in which the medieval element, impregnated and fertilised by the spirit of the Renaissance, flowers into a great work of art that is unmistakably Elizabethan.

The Defence of Poesy was Sidney's reply to Gosson and the Puritans. He had first to try to convince his opponents that fiction is not the same thing as lying, and his main defence of feigning poetry is that it teaches, or should teach, virtue both by precept and example, the true poet, the maker, being more philosophical than the philosopher. He defends the drama on the same grounds, though, with more than a touch of Leicester House pedantry, he deplores the breaking of neo-classical 'rules', and the native romantic plays that mingle kings and clowns. Had he lived to see *Henry IV* and *Hamlet*, he would have changed his mind. He is on surer ground, indeed the surest ground, when, instead of writing from his head, he looks in his heart and

writes that poetry is all for our delight, for the poet 'commeth to you
with words set in delightfull proportion, either accompanied with, or
prepared for the well enchaunting skill of *Musicke*, and with a tale
forsooth hee commeth unto you, with a tale which holdeth children
from play, and old men from the Chimney corner'.

Now that Sidney was no longer Leicester's heir, he was not the
eligible young man that he had been (in 1580 he was still only twenty-
six, ten years older than Shakespeare), and Penelope Devereux was
married against her will to the wealthy and unlovable Lord Rich.
Sidney had already written sonnets to Stella, as he called her, though
not very passionate ones, and it was only when it was too late that he
found that he really loved her:

> I might, unhappy word, O me, I might,
> And then would not, or could not, see my bliss;
> Till now, wrapped in a most infernal night,
> I find how heavenly day, wretch, I did miss.
> Heart, rent thyself, thou dost thyself but right;
> No lovely Paris made thy Helen his,
> No force, no fraud, robbed thee of thy delight,
> Nor Fortune of thy fortune author is;
> But to myself myself did give the blow,
> While too much wit, forsooth, so troubled me
> That I respects for both our sakes must show,
> And yet could not by rising morn foresee
> How fair a day was near; O, punished eyes,
> That I had been more foolish, or more wise.

He turned savagely on the 'rich fool' who had married her, and then
poured out his heart in a century of sonnets, the best of which are
among the best in our language, and all the more dazzling if we think
away Shakespeare's and all the other sequences that followed *Astrophel
and Stella*, and try to see them as they were when they were written,
with no companions save the faint pilot stars of Wyatt's and Surrey's
songs. The golden age of Elizabethan poetry comes in with Sidney
rather than Spenser, yet, though all these works were written round
about 1580, none of them was published until after his death: *Arcadia*
in 1590 and 1593, *Astrophel and Stella* in 1591 and *The Defence of
Poesy* in 1595.

Soon after Sidney went to stay at Wilton, in 1580, his sister, the
Countess of Pembroke, gave birth to a son, William Herbert. A year
later Henry Wriothesley, whose elder brother was already dead, be-

came the third Earl of Southampton on the death of his father. He
was barely nine at the time. Robert Devereux, Penelope's brother and
Leicester's stepson, had been Earl of Essex since he was ten, when he
went up to Trinity, Cambridge. He was now fourteen, and just about
to take his degree of Master of Arts. The younger generation of the
nobility, who were to play such a brilliant, or disastrous, part in the
closing years of the reign, were beginning to take the stage.

At the same time, new companies of actors, encouraged by the
opening of the Theatre and Curtain, were beginning literally to
take the stage. Lord Howard of Effingham's, the Countess of Essex's,
the Earl of Derby's and Lord Strange's Men all made their first
appearance at Court between 1576 and 1580, and the last three
visited Stratford as well. Ferdinando Stanley, Lord Strange, was the
eldest son of the Earl of Derby, and his company seems to have been
primarily a troupe of acrobats, for they were paid for 'certen feates of
Tumblinge by them done before her Majestie'. The adult companies
were overtaking the boys' in popularity and the royal favour. Poor
Sebastian Westcott was in trouble; while he was rehearsing for the
Revels of 1575, one of his boys, 'being one of his principall plaiers,
was stolen and conveyed from him', and to add to his distress the Court
of Aldermen sent a protest to the Dean of St. Paul's 'that one Sebastian
that wyll not communicate with the Church of England kepes the
playes and resorte of the people to great gaine and peryll of the corupt-
inge of the Chyldren with papistrie'. The protest appears to have had
little effect, for two years later he was 'commitid to the Marshalsea'
for his Romish activities, and spent his Christmas there. There was no
performance by the Paul's boys in 1578. Tallis and Byrd of the
Chapel Royal were more fortunate, but then their office did not
render them so liable to corrupt the children with papistry. In 1575
Elizabeth granted them jointly a twenty-one-year monopoly of music
printing, and on their behalf Vautrollier issued their thirty-four
Cantiones Sacræ, Latin motets for five and six voices. This was the
last of Tallis's music to be published in his lifetime, but his work was
to be carried on by the next generation: in the following year Byrd's
nineteen-year-old pupil, Thomas Morley, composed the motet,
Domine non est.

In 1579, the year that saw the last performance of the York
miracle plays and the birth of John Fletcher, Edmund Tilney was
appointed Master of the Revels. He was a distant connection of Lord

Howard of Effingham, to whom he probably owed his preferment, and the author of *A Brief and Pleasant Discourse of Duties in Marriage*, dedicated to Elizabeth, which is precisely what he claims it to be, pleasant and brief. As Master of the Revels he was responsible to the Lord Chamberlain, the Earl of Sussex at the time of his preferment, then his kinsman Lord Howard until he became Lord Admiral in 1585. The Royal Household was, as it still is, divided into three departments, each in charge of a great officer; the Master of the Horse was concerned mainly with things out of doors; the Lord Steward with affairs below stairs, with food and drink, light and fuel; the Lord Chamberlain with all things above stairs, with the Queen's accommodation, wardrobe, travel, reception of guests and entertainment. Parsimonious as Elizabeth was in most things, the splendour and trappings and etiquette of her Court were the wonder of Europe, and its two essential elements, the Presence Chamber and Privy Chamber had somehow to be contrived wherever she stayed on her progresses, even if it meant the Lord Chamberlain's sleeping in the garret. Access to the royal presence was difficult. At Whitehall there was first the Great or Guard Chamber, in which plays were sometimes given; then the Presence Chamber with its Esquires of the Body, Gentlemen Ushers, and Grooms; and finally the Privy Chamber, to which were attached the six Maids of Honour, and various Ladies, Knights, Gentlemen, Ushers, Grooms, Squires, Pages and Messengers. For all these the Lord Chamberlain was responsible, as well as for the Chapel and the Revels Office.

The function of the Master of the Revels, with his staff of clerks, yeoman and groom, was originally to arrange and organise the Court Revels, but the powers of the Master were gradually extended, partly because of the Privy Council's policy of centralisation, partly because it was to the Master's advantage. Thus already the royal patent for Leicester's Men authorised them to play in the City of London, subject only to the allowance of the Master, and in course of time Tilney came to exercise very wide and almost independent powers over the public theatres. For Court performances of plays the erection of the stage and seating accommodation was the province of the Office of Works, but the Revels Office was responsible for the making of costumes, 'houses' and any other scenery or properties. Until 1608 its headquarters were at the dissolved priory of St. John of Jerusalem in Clerkenwell, and a memorandum drawn up by Tilney when he was firmly entrenched in his office gives a good idea of the work done there:

Which Office of the Revells Consistethe of a wardropp and other severall Roomes for Artifficers to worke in (viz. Taylors, Imbrotherers, Properti makers, Paynters, wyerdrawers and Carpenters), togeather with a Convenient place for the Rehearshalls and settinge forthe of Playes and other Shewes for those Services.

He did not forget to add the important note, 'In which Office the Master of the Office hath ever hadd a dwellinge Howsse for him self and his Famelie'. The official salary was only £10 a year, but 'fees and other perquisites'—perhaps a gratuity for licensing a play in Lent, or even a pair of gloves for his wife—brought in another £100, some £2,000 to-day.

Accounts showing expenses incurred were made out by the Revels Office and submitted to the Treasurer of the Chamber who, on a warrant from the Privy Council, paid the Queen's semi-personal reckonings, including the Keepers of Paris Garden, musicians, rat and mole takers and players. The Chamber Accounts give the name of the company paid, and sometimes that of their representative who actually received the cash; John Symons, for example, being the payee for Strange's tumblers. The Revels Accounts give the name of the company, and generally the title of the play; thus, in the first year of Tilney's Mastership, 'A history of Alucius' was given 'on St. Johns Day by the Children of her Maiesties Chapell'. Unfortunately the Revels Accounts are missing for the critical years 1589–1603, from the very year in which Shakespeare began his career as a dramatist till after that of the writing of *Hamlet*.

By 1580 English actors were as far afield as Denmark, performing at the Court of Frederick II. In the same year is the first mention of a theatre at the Surrey village of Newington, where the archery butts were, about a mile to the south of London Bridge. Again in the same year Warwick's Men, headed by the Dutton brothers, whose frequent and easy changes of allegiance earned them the name of chameleons instead of comedians, deserted their old patron for the new Court favourite, Oxford. They took possession of the Theatre while Leicester's were on tour, but got into trouble for assaulting the gentlemen of the Inns of Court, and Laurence Dutton found himself in the Marshalsea. Altogether it was an exciting season at the Theatre. In February Burbage and Brayne were charged before the

Middlesex magistrates with bringing together an unlawful assembly, which committed tumults, affrays and other misdemeanours and enormities. The great earthquake followed on April 6th, and the Puritans were not slow to draw a moral and let it be known that not only 'the great stage and theatre of the whole land' had been shaken, but also 'the scenical Theatre as well'. The triple event occasioned a characteristic letter from the Lord Mayor to the Privy Council, suggesting that players and tumblers and such like were a very superfluous sort of men, and that plays should be wholly stayed and forbidden in the City and in the liberties outside the Corporation's jurisdiction. Fortunately the Privy Council stood firm, but their hands would have been strengthened had there been a dramatist of whom they could say that it would be a crime against the spirit of man to prevent the public performance of his plays.

III

1581–1587

THE NEW DRAMATISTS

ALTHOUGH the theatre had as yet produced no playwright of genius or even of distinction, the young men who were to revolutionise the stage in the course of the most rousing decade in our history were gathering in London. The eldest, and somewhat apart from the rest, was witty John Lyly, aged twenty-five or twenty-six, who had gracefully neglected his Oxford studies to accept the wreath of bays offered him by Apollo. Lord Burghley himself had shown him favour, and he was now in the service of Burghley's son-in-law, the Earl of Oxford. The young 'raffineur de l'Anglois' was the most fashionable writer of the period, every beauty at Court was expected to be able to parley Euphuism and every author to write it; he had been half-promised, if Elizabeth's evasive hints could be called half-promises, the succession to the Mastership of the Revels; everything seemed possible and the future full of delight. Thomas Lodge was about four years younger. The son of a former Lord Mayor of London, gone bankrupt, he had been at Merchant Taylors' under Mulcaster, who had doubtless taught him a great deal about acting and the theatre as a means to 'good behaviour and audacity'. After taking his B.A. from Trinity, Oxford, he entered Lincoln's Inn and, according to the not unprejudiced Gosson, plunged into dissipation, becoming 'looser than liberty, lighter than vanity itself', and certainly he was hauled up before the Privy Council and admonished in the summer of 1581. A kindred spirit of the same age was George Peele, the son of a clerk of Christ's Hospital, where he was educated before going up to Oxford. Shortly after taking his degree, the school governors ordered their clerk 'to discharge his howse of his sonne George Peele', and by 1581 he was in London seeking his fortune, soon securing a small one by marrying a girl with some property, which he as speedily dissipated. Another restless young man prepared to riot it in the capital was Robert Greene. Born in Norwich a few months before Elizabeth's accession, he went to St. John's, Cambridge, where Gabriel Harvey added him to his extensive list of enemies, and, having consumed the flower of his youth among wags as lewd as himself, picked up further depravity abroad before settling in London to earn his living by his wits and to spend it in debauchery. The respectable and already successful Lyly stands apart from these three younger and anything but respectable adventurers, but at least they were all university men; whereas Thomas Kyd, after leaving Merchant Taylors', where he must have known Spenser and Lodge, seems to have followed his father in the profession of scrivener before taking seriously to literature. They were a strange crew, these reckless, dissolute and brilliant University Wits who were to rescue the drama from the stranglehold of University Academics, and prepare the way for the genius of Marlowe and Shakespeare.

Yet another young man, at least a man twenty years younger than Elizabeth, came to London in 1581, the repulsive Duke, and dupe, of Alençon, before whom the Queen had dangled the bait of marriage for the last ten years, thus cheaply keeping Philip of Spain at bay despite the depredations of her seamen and her unofficial intervention in the Netherlands. There were junketings at Court, Elizabeth kissed her Frog in the presence of Walsingham and the French ambassador, and swore she was going to marry him, then packed him off to the Netherlands, where he was accepted as nominal sovereign, on the understanding that Elizabeth would support him. Dissatisfied with his position as mere figurehead, his feeble mind turned to treachery, and after trying to seize Antwerp and the person of the Prince of Orange, he was returned ignominiously to France. Even Elizabeth could no longer pretend that he was a suitable partner for herself and the English throne; in any event he died a few months later, and the way was clear for another Catholic offensive.

Plans were made for the invasion of England by the Duke of Guise with French and Spanish forces, which, joining hands with what was imagined to be a large body of disaffected English Catholics, were to replace Elizabeth by Mary and restore the authority of the Pope. Philip, as usual, worked at his own perfectionist speed, and allowed Walsingham plenty of time for his underground activities. Francis Throckmorton, a Warwickshire Catholic, whose frequent visits to the Spanish ambassador, Mendoza, had aroused suspicion, was surprised in his house on Paul's wharf, where the constables found lists of English conspirators, plans of harbours for the use of the in-

A. F. Kersling

LONGLEAT
HOUSE

ROBERT DUDLEY, EARL OF LEICESTER
From *The Bishops' Bible*, 1568

vading forces, and other incriminating documents. He survived the first agony of the rack without confession, but the second broke him and he confessed all. Seminarists already under arrest were executed, Catholics of doubtful allegiance were thrown into prison and the rest placed under strict surveillance. Mendoza was ordered out of the country, and once again England prepared for war.

Two further attempts, unconnected with the Throckmorton conspiracy, were made on Elizabeth's life, and shortly afterwards the heroic leader of the Dutch resistance movement, William of Orange, was struck down by an assassin. Here was miching mallecho with a vengeance, and virtually the whole nation joined the Association formed to defend the Queen, and pledged to put to death any conspirator against her life, as well as anybody on whose behalf such an attempt should be made. With some modifications the Parliament of 1584 sanctioned the Association and its aims. Two newcomers to the Commons were the cousins Robert Cecil and Francis Bacon.

The Puritans, along with Anglicans and the great majority of Catholics, rallied to the defence of the Queen, and no body was more loyal than the City Corporation; but they were not prepared to defend the harlotry players and the public theatres, and Elizabeth's highhanded action in 1581 scarcely made for conciliation. On Christmas Eve, Elizabeth issued a patent empowering her Master of the Revels to summon all actors and dramatists to present their plays before him, presumably that he might select suitable material for Court performance. This was innocuous enough, but the sting lay in the almost parenthetic authority given to Tilney over 'all suche showes, plaies, plaiers and playmakers, together with their playing places, to order and reforme, auctorise and put downe as shalbe thought meete or unmeete unto himselfe', any previous statute or provision notwithstanding. The Privy Council now had the power to control the theatres if ever they chose to exercise it.

Having failed in their attempt to persuade the Council to close the theatres, having no authority over the suburb of Shoreditch where the Theatre and Curtain had with such forethought been built, and now that their powers were curtailed within the City itself, the Corporation changed their tactics. If they could not directly prohibit the performance of plays they would work obliquely and force the theatres to close for lack of patronage. The Lord Mayor, therefore, ordered all guildsmen to prevent, on pain of punishment, their servants, apprentices, journeymen and children from attending plays either in the City or suburbs, or 'without the same'. Of course it was impossible to enforce such a measure now that plays were firmly established as the most popular form of entertainment, and no guildsman could prevent his apprentices from spending their holiday afternoons at the theatre; besides, he was almost certainly an addict himself. Nothing more was heard of the matter, and the Corporation, following the lead of Elizabeth's imperious patent, unobtrusively inserted in a long Act of Common Council, dealing with the administration of the Poor Law, a clause prohibiting all 'enterludes in publique places' in the City. This was in the autumn of 1582, and as there was an unpleasant outbreak of plague the Council did not protest and the inn-theatres remained closed.

Early in the following year occurred an event that greatly strengthened the cause of the Puritans and the Corporation. On the afternoon of Sunday, January 13th, eight people were killed and hundreds injured in an accident at Paris Garden, the name still retained by the Beargarden, even though it had been moved to the Bankside from its original position in the liberty of Paris Garden farther west. The disaster was described in a hastily written pamphlet, *A Godly Exhortation*, by the Puritan preacher and organiser, John Field. According to him there were above a thousand people in the Beargarden, an amphitheatre resembling the public playhouses, when, 'being now amidest their jolity, when the dogs and Bear were in the chiefest Battel, Lo the mighty hand of God uppon them. This gallery that was double, and compassed the yeard round about, was so shaken at the foundation that it fell (as it were in a moment) flat to the ground'. We can sympathise with his exhortation to the Corporation, powerless to prevent Sunday performances on the Bankside, at least to try to prevent the citizens repairing to such unholy spectacles. But the disaster was only a pretext for an attack on the theatres with their summoning trumpets and flags of defiance against God, and Field concludes with an impassioned appeal that, as they have already so far prevailed that 'uppon Sabaoth dayes these Heathenishe Enterludes and Playes are banished, so it wyll please them to followe the matter still, that they may be utterly rid and taken away'. The closing of the Beargarden on Sundays was a very different matter from the permanent closing of the theatres.

Field's *Godly Exhortation* was followed close at heels by a much more elaborate treatise by Phillip Stubbes, a Puritan ballad writer and pamphleteer. His *Anatomy of Abuses* is an analysis of what he considers to be the evils of his rapidly changing and new-fangled age, among which evils the theatre figures prominently. Written in dialogue form, it anticipates *Erewhon* in its reversal of proper names—'a verie famous Ilande called Ailgna', 'Syrap Garden'—though his attack is not the oblique one of satire and laughter, but straightforward denunciation. After protesting that his censure is not indiscriminate, but aimed only at particular abuses, such as the profanation of the Sabbath and the beastliness of bear-baiting ('what christen heart can take pleasure to see one poore beast to rent, teare, and kill another?'), he warms to his work and denounces the players as idle lubbers, buzzing dronets, painted sepulchres and (delightful phrase) 'doble dealing ambo-dexters'. Some kinds of play, he admits, are very honest and commend-able exercises, yet if they be of profane matters they tend to the dis-honour of God and nourishing of vice, and if they be of divine matters, then are they most intolerable, being scoffingly, floutingly and gibingly treated, 'so that whither they be the one or the other, they are quite contrarie to the Word of grace, and sucked out of the Deuills teates to nourish us in ydolatrie, hethenrie, and sinne'. He has it both ways, and the subject-matter and treatment of plays would, if he could order affairs in 'Ailgna', be circumscribed indeed. The theatres are 'Venus pallace & sathans synagogue', nourishers of idleness, whoredom and all uncleanness, plain devourers of maidenly virginity and chastity, and he sketches incidentally a vivid picture of 'the flocking and running to Theaters & curtens, daylie and hourely, night and daye, tyme and tyde, to see Playes and Enterludes'. He concludes with a warning of God's wrath, as revealed in the earthquake of two years before and the Paris Garden disaster, which occurred, opportunely enough, just as he was finishing his book, and with the prayer that 'the Lord of his mercie open the eyes of the maiestrats to pluck down these places of abuse'.

The theatre was becoming a test of strength between the Puritans and the Privy Council, and though the Council agreed to the not unreasonable demand that the Beargarden and theatres, without as well as within the City, should be closed on Sundays, they remained quite firm that they should be free to open on any other day, except of course during Lent and periods of plague. Elizabeth, more anti-Puritan than her Council, was angry, and in March 1583 took the offensive by ordering Tilney to select a company of players for her own patronage; then let the Puritans try, if they dared, to close their City theatres to her servants. Tilney chose twelve men, three of them from Leicester's, who were grievously weakened as a result. Among the twelve were 'inimitable John Bentley', John Dutton, one of the chameleons from Oxford's, John Singer, a notable clown who later joined the Admiral's, and Richard Tarlton, playwright and the most famous comedian of his day, perhaps the original of Yorick in *Hamlet*, 'the king's jester' whose 'flashes of merriment were wont to set the table on a roar'. As members of the Queen's household, they wore her livery of a red coat and were sworn in by the Lord Chamberlain as Grooms of the Chamber, though without fee, their duties being merely nominal. They started badly, for at Norwich in June, playing at the Red Lion, a dispute arose between a spectator and Singer, who was acting as gatherer. Bentley, coming off stage, struck the man on the head with the handle of his sword; the wretch ran away, pursued by Singer with another sword, and in the scuffle was mortally hurt. The City authorities were not altogether perverse in wishing to be rid of the players.

The test came when the Queen's Men returned to London in November. The Privy Council wrote to the Lord Mayor, asking him to license Her Majesty's servants to play on weekdays within the City and liberties, 'so prayeng yowe that thereof there be no defaulte'. It was a royal command, which the Corporation could not very well disobey, though perhaps they might misinterpret, and their licence confined the company to 'the Bull in Bushoppesgate streete, and the Bell in Gratiousstreete', and performances to holy days. It was no use. In an acid note Walsingham replied on behalf of the Council, 'to explane more plainly' that the licence was to be for work days as well as holidays. He made the royal meaning transparently plain; the City theatres were opened, and the Queen's Men began their performances in preparation for the Revels, in which they appeared three times that winter. For the next seven years they were the dominant company at Court, giving altogether twenty-one performances, and quite eclipsing Leicester's, who made only one more appearance.

Elizabeth's hand had been strengthened by the death of the disgraced and ineffective Grindal in the summer, and by her translation of Whitgift from Worcester to Canterbury. Whitgift, her 'little black husband', was a man after her own heart; unmarried, as all good churchmen should be, he was the opponent of Cartwright, whom he had deprived of his Cambridge professorship and Trinity fellowship, and as violently anti-Puritan, vigorous and high-handed (some said tyrannical) as she could wish. Ably seconded by Richard Bancroft, the clerical counterpart of Walsingham as a detector of underground activities, he helped to counteract the puritanical element within her Council, Walsingham and, in a lesser degree, Burghley, and it was largely owing to him that in 1586 the Star Chamber issued an order whereby all books had to be licensed for printing either by the Archbishop of Canterbury or the Bishop of London, or their deputies. He was an invaluable ally in the struggle for the theatres, now coming to a climax.

When the Theatre and Curtain reopened after the austerities of Lent, 1584, they were the scene of further trouble, wittily described by the caustic pen of the puritanical Recorder of London, William Fleetwood, in a letter to Burghley:

Vpon Mondaye night I returned to London and found all the wardes full of watchers. The cause thereof was for that very nere the Theatre or Curten at the tyme of the Playes there laye a prentice sleping vpon the Grasse, and one Challes *al.* Grostock dyd turne vpon the Too vpon the belly of the same prentice, whervpon the apprentice start vp and after wordes they fell to playne bloues; the companie encressed of bothe sides to the nosmber of 500 at the least. This Challes exclaimed and said that he was a gentleman and that the apprentise was but a Rascall; and some there were little better than rooges that tooke vpon theym the name of gentilmen and said the prentizes were but the skomme of the worlde. Vpon these trobles the prentizes began the next daye, being Twesdaye, to make mutines and asembles, and dyd conspire to have broken the presones & to have taken furthe the prentizes that were imprisoned. . . .

Vpon Weddensdaye one Browne, a serving man in a blew coat, a shifting fellowe having a perrelous witt of his owne, entending a spoile if he cold have browght it to passe, did at Theatre doore querell with certen poore boyes, handicraft prentises. and strook some of theym, and lastlie he with his sword wondend and maymed one of the boyes vpon the left hand; where vpon there assembled nere a 1000 people. . . .

Brown turned out to be 'a common Cossiner, a thieff, & a horse stealer', and the upshot was that the magistrates did nothing from Wednesday to Saturday but examine these misdemeanours. On Sunday the Lord Mayor sent two aldermen to the Privy Council with a plea for 'the suppressing and pulling downe of the Theatre and Curten', to which all agreed except Lord Chamberlain Howard and the Vice-Chamberlain, and though the theatres were not literally pulled down, they were all closed for the time being. Even in the cause of humanism Elizabeth would not tolerate hooliganism. The Queen's Men were amenable, but the 'chiefestes' of them advised Fleetwood to send for the owner of the Theatre, 'who was a stubburne fellow'. Burbage, protesting that he was one of Lord Hunsdon's men, refused to come until Fleetwood showed him his master's signature as a Privy Councillor on the order of closure, and even then 'he stowted me out very hastie'. What happened when the Court met on the next day we do not know.

When the Queen's Men returned from their provincial tour at the approach of winter, they petitioned the Council to ask the Corporation for the renewal of their licence to play within the City as it was once again time to begin rehearsals for the Revels, and their 'poore lyvinge' was threatened by the closure. It was the central inn-theatres that they wanted opened, for apparently Shoreditch was too far afield to attract an audience in the depths of winter. The Council approached the Corporation, who of course had to acquiesce, though Fleetwood could not resist writing an ironical and highly informative preamble to their proposed terms of agreement. After pointing out that most of the Regulations of 1574 had been broken, he suggested that it was nobody's concern to consider the 'poore lyvinge' of the players, 'whoe if they were not her maiesties seruants shold by their profession be rogues'. Then, 'if in winter the dark do cary inconuenience, and the short time of day after euening prayer do leaue them no leysure, and fowlenesse of season do hinder the passage into the feldes to playes, the remedie is ill conceyued to bring them into London, but the true remedie is to leaue of that vnnecessarie expense of time, whereunto God himself geueth so many impediments'. If there must be plays, better have them in the suburbs than the City. One more dig and Fleetwood has done: 'It may please you to know that the last yere when such toleration was of the Quenes players only, all the places of playeing were filled with men calling themselues the Quenes players.' As a basis of agreement the Corporation suggested that the Regulations of 1574 should be revived and enforced, with the additional provisions that theatres should open only when weekly deaths *from all causes* had been less than fifty for a period of twenty weeks, that there should be no plays on the Sabbath, or in the dark, or before evening prayers on holy days, that the audience should not be admitted during prayer-time, and that the Queen's players only were to be tolerated.

We do not know exactly what agreement was arrived at. No doubt

the Council accepted some of the suggestions, though certainly not
the one about the weekly deaths in London; if they had, the theatres
would never have opened their doors, and a few years later they were
closed only when *plague* deaths exceeded thirty a week. Then, we may
be sure that the theatres were soon filled again with 'the Queen's
players', and that the attempt to limit performances to the royal company was a failure. Lord Chamberlain Howard and his successor,
Lord Hunsdon, would see to it that their companies got a fair share of
public playing. The Corporation had been defeated in their attempt to
close the theatres, and henceforth normally pursued a policy of co-
operation with the Council, advising and influencing them to their
own advantage as best they could. There can be no doubt that the
situation was relatively stable, for otherwise that astute man of business,
Philip Henslowe, would not, in March 1585, have taken a twenty
years' lease of a plot of land on the Bankside, 'the Little Rose with two
gardens'. The crisis was over, and the public theatres were firmly
established as part of the life of London just at the time when the
University Wits began to write for the stage. Unfortunately the same
could not be said about the private theatre at Blackfriars.

Sir William More had soon begun to regret having leased the room
in his Blackfriars property to Richard Farrant, Hunnis's deputy as
Master of the Chapel Children. He complained that Farrant had
rented it simply as a place where the boys could rehearse for their
Court performances, but had in fact turned it into a regular theatre,
thereby spoiling the amenities of the precinct, as well as disfiguring the
house itself. He had some cause for complaint if the Chapel boys
behaved like those in the dancing school next door, who 'cutt upp the
lead with knifes or boored yt through with bodkyns wherby the rayne
cometh throwghe'. Farrant died in 1580, leaving the house to his
widow, who sublet it to Hunnis, so that he might carry on the theatrical enterprise, but as subletting was contrary to the original lease
More claimed that it was forfeited, and tried to recover it. To frustrate him, Hunnis transferred the sublease to Henry Evans, a scrivener,
who transferred it to the Earl of Oxford, who passed it on to his
servant, John Lyly, so that the elusive title was 'posted over from one
to another' in a quite bewildering fashion. Meanwhile, in 1582,
Sebastian Westcott had died, leaving Evans as overseer of his will, and
the Paul's boys appear to have joined the Chapel Children at Blackfriars under the partners Hunnis, Evans and Lyly, with the Earl of

Oxford as their patron. Thus Lyly's first plays, *Campaspe* and *Sapho and Phao*, were performed before the Queen by 'her Maiesties Children and the Boyes of Paules' at the beginning of 1584, the payee being Lyly himself, and at the following Christmas Henry Evans was paid 'for one play by the children of Therle of Oxford'. The combination did not last long, for by this time More had recovered possession of his house, and the first Blackfriars theatre came to an end. A month later, Thomas Giles was appointed Master of the Paul's boys, with a royal commission similar to that given to the Masters of the Chapel, 'to take vpp suche apte and meete Children as are most fitt to be instructed and framed in the arte and science of musicke and singinge'. It was a temptation to take up, too, such apt children as were fit to be instructed in the art of acting.

When Lyly took Lord Oxford's boys to Court to present *Sapho and Phao*, the Earl of Worcester's players were at Leicester, where the mayor gave them an angel towards their dinner on condition they did not play, 'being Fryday the vjth of Marche, 1584, for that the tyme was not conveynyent'. However, having spent their angel and eaten their dinner, the actors, with many evil and contemptuous words, swore they would play in spite of the mayor, and went about the town proclaiming their intention with drum and trumpet. Their insolence seems to have spent itself in noise, and they apologised, the mayor magnanimously promising not to report them to their master, and licensing them to play, after all, that night at their inn. In the previous year they had been even more generously treated at Norwich, where they were paid 26s. 8d. not to play because of the plague, and having, nevertheless, given a performance were finally pardoned. One of Worcester's Men was Robert Browne, soon to be a populariser of English plays in Germany; another was Edward Alleyn, a boy of seventeen, who left the provincial Worcester's in the following year for the metropolitan Howard's, or Admiral's as they were called after 1585, when Lord Howard of Effingham became Lord High Admiral.

Young Alleyn's performance was probably seen, and possibly envied by Shakespeare, for Worcester's were regular visitors to Stratford, and were there shortly after the affair at Leicester. Shakespeare was then just twenty, a married man and a father. In September 1582 he had got Anne Hathaway with child, a Stratford girl eight years his senior, married her hurriedly in November after getting a special licence from Whitgift, then Bishop of Worcester, and in the following May his daughter Susanna was born. Perhaps he also envied Alleyn his liberty, yet if he did he only tethered himself the firmer, for Anne was soon pregnant again, and at the end of January 1585 gave birth to twins, Hamnet and Judith. Presumably Shakespeare was at the christening in the parish church on February 2nd; if so, it is the last we know of him for the next ten years. Tradition has it that he was driven from Stratford by Sir Thomas Lucy for poaching his deer, and was for a time a schoolmaster in the country, perhaps at Dursley in the south Cotswolds, perhaps as a tutor in some Shropshire household. Some say that he went off to the Netherlands with Leicester's expeditionary force, others that he joined one of the touring companies of actors when they came to Stratford. There is another possibility. When Thomas Vautrollier died in 1587, Richard Field married his widow and took over the business, and it is just possible that he gave Shakespeare an opening. Shakespeare was a good man of business, and his leaving Stratford might account for the further decline in his father's affairs. In 1586 John Shakespeare was replaced by another alderman for his failure to attend council meetings, and next year was sued for the debt of his shiftless brother Henry, which he had guaranteed. But what happened to his son we simply do not know, though we may be pretty sure that he was in London by Armada year.

Shortly after Shakespeare's entanglement with Anne Hathaway, Sidney was knighted and married Frances, the fifteen-year-old daughter of his friend and patron, Walsingham. At the same time the star of his rival, Raleigh, was rapidly rising. With his broad Devonshire accent, his rare wit and rarer learning, his dark handsome face, fine physique and splendid clothes, he was undeniably fascinating and ornamental, and, in the eyes of Elizabeth at least, a distinct acquisition to the Court. She showered honours and rewards upon him; £100 and the command of a company, Durham House in the Strand, the wine monopoly worth £2,000 a year, the monopoly for the export of woollen cloths, 40,000 acres in Ireland; she knighted him, made him Lord-Lieutenant of Cornwall and Warden of the Stannaries, Vice-Admiral and Captain of the Guard. When his half-brother, Sir Humphrey Gilbert, perished in the *Squirrel* on his way back from Newfoundland, he secured his colonising patent, and in 1585 sent out his first expedition under Richard Grenville in an attempt to found a settlement in Virginia. Meanwhile, in a less exalted sphere, Francis Beaumont was born in Leicestershire, Orlando Gibbons in Cambridge, where Thomas Nashe matriculated from St. John's College and Marlowe took his B.A. degree from Corpus, and shortly after the birth of Gibbons, last of the great Elizabethan composers, the first and greatest, Thomas Tallis died.

In the course of the early eighties a number of books were published, destined in some degree to influence the work of Shakespeare. To Arthur Hall, the obstreperous M.P. for his native Grantham, belongs the honour of first attempting to make an English version of Homer. Unfortunately he worked not from the Greek but from the French of Hugues Salel, and his *Ten Bookes of Homers Iliades*, written in rhyming fourteeners, is no more Homer than it is poetry, yet it may have furnished Shakespeare with material for *Troilus and Cressida*. *Riche his Farewell to Militarie Profession* appeared in the same year, 1581. Barnabe Rich was that strange yet characteristically Elizabethan compound of hard-headed adventurer and soft-hearted romantic, the soldier-author, of whom Sidney was the ideal type. His *Farewell* contains 'verie pleasaunt discourses fit for a peacable tyme', eight stories, most of them translations from the Italian, one being Bandello's *Apolonius and Silla*, the source of the main plot in *Twelfth Night*. Despite his *Farewell*, Rich had almost forty years of service before him, and was nearly eighty when he died, in Ireland of course, the oldest captain in the army. In 1582 Whetstone published his *Heptameron of Civil Discourses*, a collection of stories containing a translation of the Cinthio novel on which he had based his *Promos and Cassandra*. As a dramatist he was a failure, for he tells us in the *Heptameron* that his play was 'yet never presented upon stage', and, like Gosson, in his disappointment he turned upon the theatres in his *Touchstone for the Time*, condemning them as 'the springs of many vices, and the stumbling-blocks of godliness and virtue'. More important, and far more interesting, is *The Discovery of Witchcraft* by Reginald Scot, a Kentish gentleman who had already made a name for himself by writing the first English treatise on the culture of the hop. The *Discovery* is a jungle of a book, in part a defence of the wretched old women persecuted as witches, in part an untidy yet entertaining accumulation of anecdotes and spells, a curious mixture of scepticism and credulity, and a mine of information about Elizabethan superstitions. James I found it altogether too enlightened for his sombre philosophy, and ordered the book to be burned; but Shakespeare had a copy and made good use of it in *Macbeth* (as did Middleton in *The*

Witch), and in it he would find much about Robin Goodfellow and a story of transformation into an ass. Incidentally, William Adlington's delightful translation of *The Golden Ass* of Lucius Apuleius, first published in 1566, was reprinted in 1582, and this rather than the *Discovery* probably accounts for Bottom's metamorphosis. Finally, though it had little apparent influence on Shakespeare, mention must be made of one of the monumental books of the age, the *Britannia* of William Camden, the Westminster master of fourteen-year-old Ben Jonson. Written in elegant Latin and dedicated, as was most proper, to his old friend and patron Burghley, the book is an orderly and immensely erudite summary of all his reading and fieldwork in the new sciences of topography and archæology, a description not only of the surface of Britain, but also of its substrata and roots in the civilisation of Rome. It was at about this time, and largely owing to Camden and his pupil Sir Robert Cotton, that the Society of Antiquaries was formed, a select body of scholars who met at one another's houses to discuss all manner of antiquarian subjects: William Dethick, John Dodderidge, John Stow and, when they were in London, Henry Spelman of Norfolk, William Lambarde of Kent and Richard Carew of Cornwall. Although the Elizabethans eagerly looked forward, they had an uneasy feeling that they were losing something, as indeed they were, and nostalgically looked back at what they were leaving behind. They were the first Englishmen to live on three temporal planes at once, the unmistakable and by no means morbid symptom of a restless and violently transitional age. James I, having burned Scot's *Discovery* and snuffing conspiracy in this incomprehensible gathering of intelligence, dissolved the society.

Few of the plays of this period have survived, for the printing of such ephemeral matter scarcely began before the nineties, and even then only a trickle of the swelling stream reached the press. Of those performed in the public theatres at this time we know virtually nothing, and of the Court plays we generally know little more than the names as preserved in the Revels Accounts. Some of these are of more than common interest. The last mention of Westcott as payee for the Paul's boys is for a performance of *Pompey* on Twelfth Night, 1581, one of the many plays on the Cæsar theme before Shakespeare tried his hand at it. On Shrove Tuesday, 1583, the indefatigable Mulcaster took the boys of Merchant Taylors' to Court for the last time, to present *A historie of Ariodante and Geneuora*, presumably a dramatisation of the story in Ariosto's *Orlando Furioso*, and, therefore, a version of the Hero theme in *Much Ado*. Then on the first Sunday of 1585, for plays were not banned at Court on the Sabbath, the Queen's Men gave *Felix and Philiomena*, a story from Montemayor's *Diana Enamorada*, and the source of *The Two Gentlemen of Verona*. Again it was on a Sunday, at the end of 1582, that Lord Derby's gave the last of their three performances at Court, *Love and Fortune*. There can be little doubt that this is *The Rare Triumphs of Love and Fortune*, published anonymously in 1589 as 'plaide before the Queenes most excellent Maiestie', and it gives us a good idea of the nonsense that Elizabeth and her courtiers had to accept as entertainment just before the University Wits revolutionised the stage. Most of the Court plays given by the men's companies were rehearsed and performed in the public theatres, but if *Love and Fortune* is Court fare, one wonders what was served up to gratify the popular palate at the Shoreditch and City theatres. Yet the play is interesting historically, for Shakespeare may have borrowed the names of the hero and heroine, Hermione and Fidelia, for *A Winter's Tale* and *Cymbeline*. Then the Revels Office supplied the company with three 'houses', a city, a battlement and another unspecified canvas structure, the first and last of which represented the court and a cave respectively, while the battlement seems to have been a kind of gallery for the gods, whence Venus and Fortune, 'set sunning like a crow in the gutter', directed the proceedings. The plot is simple enough. Venus and Fortune squabble as to who is the more powerful, and to settle the matter Jupiter orders them to try out their strength on the lovers Hermione and Fidelia; Venus to strive to increase their joy, Fortune to defeat it. To begin with, Fortune has it all her own way and the lovers are separated (*Strike up Fortune's triumphs with drums and trumpets*). But enter Bomelio, a magician who, by a rare coincidence, proves to be Hermione's father, a wrongfully exiled duke (*Strike up a noise of viols: Venus' triumph*). With the best of intentions Hermione destroys the books of magic belonging to his father, who goes mad when he discovers the loss, and the lovers' plight is worse than ever (*Fortune's triumph: sound trumpets, drums, cornets, and guns*). We are now in what Dogberry would call a noncome, and the only solution is by way of direct Olympian intervention, *deæ ex machina*; the two goddesses reveal themselves and, severing the mortal complexities, finish their match all square. Light and rather vulgar relief is afforded by a Plautian parasite and runaway servant. Maybe it is little more foolish than the plot of *The Tempest*, but then the verse is no better than the plot, a gallimaufry of savour-less rhyming decasyllabics, hexameters and fourteeners. For a taste:

> In ransacking his cave these books I lighted on,
> And with his leave I'll be so bold, while he abroad is gone,
> To burn them all, for best that serveth for this stuff;
> I doubt not but at his return to please him well enough.

When Shakespeare wrote *A Midsummer Night's Dream* he had to go back only a dozen years to find any amount of matter little less silly than the tragical mirth of Pyramus and Thisbe. But then there might have been no *Midsummer Night's Dream* if he had not also found the comedies of Lyly.

How Tilney must have hugged himself when, on New Year's Day at night, in the Great Chamber at Whitehall, he presented the Chapel and Paul's boys in Lyly's first comedy, *Campaspe*. And how Elizabeth must have sat up and listened, all delight, to the delicious mockery of these pert boys playing Alexander, Diogenes, Aristotle and Plato, to the sophisticated Euphuism, purified and refined, of the prose dialogue, for Lyly is the only Elizabethan dramatist to write normally in prose, and to the songs, 'What bird so sings, yet so does wail?', 'Cupid and my Campaspe played'. Some say that Lyly did not write the songs, but it is no matter, the prose is enough; an exquisite, silvery prose, artificial and fragile as moonlight, the perfect medium for the fairy-like fantasy of his themes. No wonder that Elizabeth asked for more, and two months later Lyly brought her *Sapho and Phao*, the story of the love of a princess for a ferryman, whom she makes her gardener:

Sapho. What herbs have you brought, Phao?
Phao. Such as will make you sleep, madam; though they cannot make me slumber.
Sapho. Why, how can you cure me, when you cannot remedy yourself?
Phao. Indeed, I know no herb to make lovers sleep but heart's ease, which, because it groweth so high, I cannot reach, for——
Sapho. For whom?
Phao. For such as love.
Sapho. It stoopeth very low, and I can never stoop to it, that——
Phao. That what?
Sapho. That I may gather it. But why do you sigh so, Phao?
Phao. It is mine use, madam.
Sapho. It will do you harm, and me too; for I never hear one sigh, but I must sigh also.

Phao. It were best then that your ladyship give me leave to be gone; for I can but sigh.

Sapho. Nay, stay; for now I begin to sigh, I shall not leave though you be gone. But what do you think best for your sighing, to take it away?

Phao. Yew, madam.

Sapho. Me!

Phao. No, madam; yew of the tree.

Sapho. Then will I love yew the better. And, indeed, I think it would make me sleep too.

There had never been anything like it before; Elizabeth was enchanted, took Lyly into her service as Esquire of the Body, doubtless without fee, and hinted at the reversion of the Mastership of the Revels. But after the failure of the Blackfriars venture, Lyly had to be rescued from prison for debt, probably by Oxford, and for the next five or six years eked out his living by writing for the Paul's boys, possibly teaching them as well, for Gabriel Harvey, whose enmity he had inevitably incurred, gibes at him as 'Vicemaster of Paules and the Foolemaster of the Theatre'.

If, as is probable, one of the performances of the Chapel Children in the interval between the productions of Lyly's comedies was Peele's first play, *The Arraignment of Paris*, we can say with some accuracy that the theatrical renaissance came in with the year 1584, while Shakespeare was fretting at Stratford, just before his twentieth birthday. *The Arraignment of Paris* is a masque-like and uneven play, written in the old cantering fourteeners, blank verse and heroics, but the difference is that the verse is the verse of a poet, not that of a grocer measuring out beats to a line:

> The watery flowers and lilies on the banks
> Like blazing comets burgeon all in ranks;
> Under the hawthorn and the poplar tree,
> Where sacred Phoebe may delight to be,
> The primrose, and the purple hyacinth,
> The dainty violet, and the wholesome minth,
> The double daisy, and the cowslip, queen
> Of summer flowers, do overpeer the green;
> And round about the valley as ye pass,
> Ye may not see, for peeping flowers, the grass.

Milton remembered his Peele when he wrote *Lycidas*, as did Shakespeare when he wrote the masque in *The Tempest*. Then there is the

exquisite duet of Paris and Oenone, the music perhaps by Byrd, sung
by the pure treble voices of the Chapel boys, with its refrain:

> Fair, and fair, and twice so fair,
>   As fair as any may be,
> The fairest shepherd on our green,
>   A love for any lady.

The story of the Judgment of Paris is given a characteristically
Elizabethan twist. The gods insist on another verdict, and appoint
Diana arbitress, but instead of giving the apple to one of the three
competing goddesses, she offers it to the nymph Eliza. It is a variation
on the theme of Hans Eworth's allegorical painting of fifteen years
earlier. Before Peele's next play was published, Nashe wrote of him as
'the chief supporter of pleasance now living, the Atlas of poetry, whose
Arraignment of Paris goeth a step beyond all that write'. Though it
was not true when he wrote in 1589, it was true enough in 1584.
Peele inherited his father's position as pageant writer to the City
companies on the occasion of the Lord Mayor's installation, the
origin of our Lord Mayor's Show, his first venture in this kind apparently being the Skinner's pageant when Woolstan Dixie was installed.
That was in October 1585. By that time England was at war with
Spain.

The situation in the Netherlands had deteriorated. Parma, the
Spanish commander, had overrun the southern provinces, Antwerp
was invested, and sixty miles of coast opposite England afforded a base
from which to launch an invasion. To make matters worse, Henry III
of France threw in his lot with Guise and the Catholic League for the
exclusion of the Huguenot Henry of Navarre, the heir to the throne
now that Alençon was dead, and the last and fiercest phase of the civil
war began. This neutralised France, but though she could not help
Parma, she would do nothing to hinder a Spanish invasion of England.
Philip's opportunity had come, and in the summer of 1585 he ordered
the seizure of all English ships in Spanish waters. Swarms of privateers
were soon off the coast of Spain, and in September Drake sailed into
Vigo, demanded the release of the captured English crews, took some
prizes, and went on to sack San Domingo in the West Indies, and
Cartagena on the Spanish Main, before returning to England with his
spoils. Drake had no misgivings as to the result of a sea war with Spain,
but Philip, with impenetrable Podsnappery, brushed aside the idea

that his ships were vincible, and laboriously prepared his paper plans and his old-fashioned top-heavy galleons.

Meanwhile, the Netherlanders once again offered the sovereignty of their country to Elizabeth, who, after her customary indecision and hard haggling, sent a force of five thousand men, without pay and too late to save Antwerp, under the decorative and dilatory Leicester, supported by his nephew Sidney and his stepson Essex. Without any formal declaration, the twenty years' war with Spain had begun.

Leicester appears to have taken some of his players with him, for on St. George's Day, 1586, Shakespeare's twenty-second birthday, he entertained the citizens of Utrecht with an after-dinner show of 'dauncing, vauting, and tumbling, with *The Forces of Hercules*, which gave great delight to the strangers, for they had not seene it before'. One of the company was the dancing clown 'Mr Kemp, called Don Gulihelmo', to whom Sidney entrusted a letter to his wife, but 'Will, my lord of Lesters jesting plaier', delivered it to Lady Leicester. While Leicester revelled it in pageantry and shows, and Essex, as General of the Horse, distinguished himself in festive tournaments, Sidney constantly urged decisive action. In September came the heroic but futile affair at Zutphen; Essex behaved with great gallantry and was knighted by Leicester on the field of victory, but Sidney was mortally wounded by a bullet in the thigh, and died a month later at Arnhem. So perished 'the miracle of the age'. Spenser wrote a belated and wretchedly inadequate elegy, *Astrophel*, the pastoral make-believe of which is sickeningly inappropriate for such a theme; Fulke Greville wrote a *Life* of his dearest friend and an epitaph:

> Knowledge her light hath lost; Valour hath slain her knight;
> Sidney is dead; dead is my friend; dead is the world's delight.

He also wrote his own epitaph, engraved on his tomb in the church at Warwick: 'Folk Grevill Servant to Queene Elizabeth Concellor to King James Frend to Sir Philip Sidney.'

Walsingham knew that the prelude to a Spanish invasion would be another assassination plot in which Mary would be involved either wittingly or unwittingly, but he also knew that Elizabeth would never consent to her death unless convinced of her treasonable implication. In order to entangle her, he had her removed to less rigorous confinement at Chartley Manor, where she was able to begin a secret correspondence with one of her former pages, Anthony Babington,

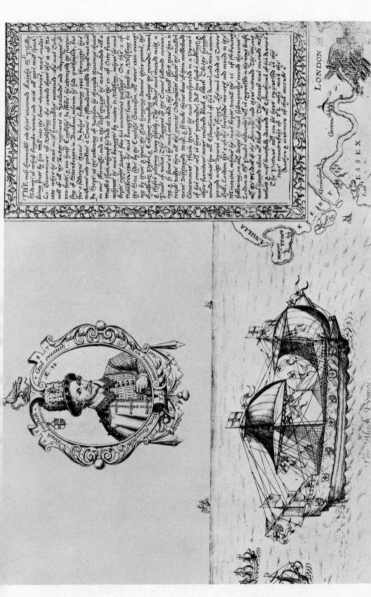

'THE BLACK PINNACE' IN WHICH SIR PHILIP SIDNEY'S BODY WAS BROUGHT
TO ENGLAND

By Thomas Lant

THE ARMADA
By Hendrick Cornelius Vroom

and John Ballard, a Jesuit priest, the leaders of a conspiracy to murder Elizabeth, organise a Catholic rising and a foreign invasion and put Mary on the throne. The correspondence was copied by one of Walsingham's spies, through whose hands it passed. Walsingham waited until August 1586 before he struck; Babington, Ballard and five others were arrested; under torture they confessed their guilt, and were duly executed with the customary barbarities. One of them was Charles Tilney, cousin of the Master of the Revels. Mary was moved to Fotheringay Castle, and tried before a special commission of nobles. She conducted her own defence, admitted that she had always made appeals for foreign aid, which, she contended, she was entitled to do, but denied any complicity in the Babington plot. The only evidence against her was the copies of the intercepted letters, which may or may not have been genuine, but the court found her guilty and Parliament ratified the verdict. For two months Elizabeth hesitated. She could have little doubt about Mary's guilt, and she was no longer the valuable pawn in foreign affairs that she had been; yet she was a queen, and the execution of queens was little to Elizabeth's liking. Even when she had signed the death-warrant at the beginning of February, she tried to shuffle off her responsibility by suggesting that Mary might be put to death before it arrived. Burghley and the other members of the Council took the matter into their own hands, and on the morning of Wednesday, February 8th, the sentence was carried out. Burghley himself described the scene: 'And then, turning to hir servants, she also required them to pray for hir, and hearyng hir women to weape and cry, she willed them to hold thir peace, and then she kissed them, and bad them depart from the scaffold. And so then she kneeled down, havyng a kyrcheff tyed about her eies, and received the strok of death by beheadyng.' It was well done, done with that startling Elizabethan courage and dramatic dignity, and fitting for a princess descended of so many royal kings.

There could no longer be any sort of pretence that England and Spain were not at war. So long as Mary lived, Philip had hesitated to attack England, persuading himself that the subjugation of the Netherlands must come first, for if he deposed Elizabeth he would have to make Mary queen in her stead, who, in all probability, would show her gratitude by making an alliance against him with France. But now she was gone and, what was more, had assigned to him, as a descendant of John of Gaunt, her claims to the English throne, to the exclusion of her son, James of Scotland. The way was now clear; the Netherlands must wait until England was subdued, and under the direction of his admiral, Santa Cruz, grandiose plans for invasion and an invincible armada were prepared. In April Drake received his orders and, slipping out of Plymouth before the Queen had time to send her customary countermand, on the 19th was off Cadiz, where he burned some ten thousand tons of Spanish shipping, then making for the Azores intercepted a great carrack, the *San Felipe*, and brought her back to Plymouth with all her East Indian treasure intact. Though the Armada was not destroyed, there was little chance of its sailing in 1587.

It must have been at about this time that Shakespeare arrived in London. Five companies of players, including Leicester's and the Queen's, visited Stratford that year, a powerful, maybe irresistible, enticement to an aspiring poet in an unprofitable environment; or perhaps he received an invitation from Field, now master of the Vautrollier printing presses. Whatever the reason, he arrived at one of the most thrilling moments in London's history when the great city was seething with rumours and excitement, alive, united and determined as never before, and clangorous with the warlike preparations described in *Hamlet*, that made the night joint-labourer with the day. That there was good reason for this sweaty haste was attested by the heads of Babington and his fellow-conspirators grimly grinning on their poles high above the Southwark gate on London Bridge. Marlowe, too, arrived that summer, having just been awarded his M.A. degree under circumstances that were distinctly mysterious. In puritanical Cambridge he had made an unsavoury reputation for himself as a papist, or worse, if scepticism really could be worse, and when at the beginning of the year he disappeared from his college, rumour had it that he had gone like so many other young men, to the English Catholic seminary at Rheims, and the authorities decided that he had forfeited his Master's degree. But Marlowe was joined with no foot land-rakers, but with nobility and great 'oneyers', and appealed to the Chancellor of the University, Burghley himself. The result was a Privy Council resolution and a letter to Cambridge:

Whereas it was reported that Christopher Morley was determined to haue gone beyond the seas to Reames and there to remaine, their Lordships thought good to certifie that he had no such intent, but that in all his accions he had behaued him selfe orderlie and discreetelie wherebie he had done her Majestie good seruice, and deserued to be rewarded for his faithfull dealinge. Their Lordships request was that the rumour thereof should be allaied by all possible meanes, and that he should be furthered in the degree he was to take this next Commencement; Because it was not her Majestes pleasure that anie one emploied as he had been in matters touching the benefitt of his Countrie should be defamed by those who are ignorant in thaffaires he went about.

There can be little doubt that Marlowe was in the secret service. His patron, Thomas Walsingham, must have recommended the brilliant young man to his cousin, Sir Francis, who in his turn employed him as a spy, possibly in Rheims, possibly in the unmasking of the Babington conspiracy. If so, the traitors' heads on London Bridge would have an even grimmer significance for Marlowe than for Shakespeare. It is strange to think of these two young men of twenty-three converging on London, the one fresh from the Warwickshire countryside, the other with a Cambridge degree and powerful friends at Court, but tainted by contact with the underworld of espionage, with creatures such as Ingram Frizer and Robert Poley, to whom the hunted Babington had written, 'ffarewell, sweet Robyn, if as I take thee, true to me', only to be betrayed.

Earlier in the year the Admiral's had been in Cambridge, where Marlowe may have met their recently recruited tragic actor, twenty-one-year-old Edward Alleyn. If so, it would not be long after their return to London that Alleyn introduced him to the stepfather of Joan Woodward. This was Philip Henslowe, once employed by Lord Montague's bailiff in managing property in Southwark, but for the last ten years more profitably employed in managing Woodward's own property, inherited when he married his widow. At this time he is described as 'citizen and dyer of London', but his main interest was in real estate, and in time he became a considerable owner of property on the Bankside, where he lived, including some of the notorious stews, or bawdy-houses, and the adjacent 'messuage or tennement called the little rose with twoe gardens'. There was no theatre on the south bank, and (here Henslowe agreed with the Puritans) stews and theatres being complementary, it was a gilt-edged investment rather than a speculation to lay out his wife's money in the building of a playhouse on the site of the Rose. The Privy Council had forced the City Corporation to accept the theatres as part of London's life, and in any event the site was outside the City jurisdiction, in the liberty of the Clink, only a few yards from the Beargarden and his own house. The work was begun early in 1587 and, Armada or no Armada, finished by the late autumn. Presumably Henslowe had made careful notes of any short-comings at the Theatre and Curtain, and incorporated correspond-ing improvements. If the players were not already protected by a canopy, one obvious improvement would be the addition of a 'shadow' over the stage, which would necessitate the raising of the 'heavens' to a hut above the top gallery, and perhaps it was Henslowe who con-ceived the idea of carrying it partly over the shadow, so that aerial ascents and descents could be made through trap-doors in its floor. There is no reason to think that there was any essential difference between the Rose and its predecessors, for the public theatres were functional buildings reflecting the kind of action performed in them, and the popular plays for which Henslowe was preparing to cater were much the same as those of a decade before.

It may have been in the Rose that the Admiral's were playing in November, when they met with the disaster described by Philip Gawdy in a letter to his father: 'My L. Admyrall his men and players having a devyse in ther playe to tye one of their fellowes to a poste and so to shoote him to deathe, having borrowed their callyvers one of the players hands swerved, his peece being charged with bullet missed the fellowe he aymed at and killed a chyld, and a woman great with chyld forthwith, and hurt an other man in the head very soore.' The play was the Second Part of *Tamburlaine*, in which the Governor of Babylon is hung in chains and shot to death. Evidently Marlowe had come down from Cambridge with at least the First Part already writ-ten, and probably having persuaded the Admiral's to produce it, with Alleyn as Tamburlaine, on their return to London. It is unlikely that Shakespeare missed the performance, perhaps the most momentous in the history of our theatre. Marlowe, as contemptuous of the buffoon-ery of the popular stage as of the pedantry of the university academic drama, at once proclaimed the manifesto of the new age:

> From jigging veins of rhyming mother wits,
> And such conceits as clownage keeps in pay,
> We'll lead you to the stately tent of war,
> Where you shall hear the Scythian Tamburlaine
> Threatening the world with high astounding terms,
> And scourging kingdoms with his conquering sword.

The normally restless, unruly and caterwauling audience, supplied with refreshments by Henslowe's temporary partner, must have for-

gotten their beer and apples, and listened as never before as the tor-
rential rhetoric, the thundering combers of the verse, the catalogues
of musical mysterious names, the astronomical imagery, swept over
them. The theme, too, was one of simple, elemental and universal
appeal—power, the scarcely secret desire of all mankind for self-
assertion:

> Nature that framed us of four elements,
> Warring within our breasts for regiment,
> Doth teach us all to have aspiring minds:
> Our souls, whose faculties can comprehend
> The wondrous architecture of the world,
> And measure every wandering planet's course,
> Still climbing after knowledge infinite,
> And always moving as the restless spheres,
> Will us to wear ourselves, and never rest
> Until we reach the ripest fruit of all.

And how the poets in the theatre, Peele, Greene, Lodge, Kyd,
Shakespeare, would strain to catch every syllable of Tamburlaine's
meditation on divine Zenocrate:

> If all the pens that ever poets held
> Had fed the feeling of their masters' thoughts,
> And every sweetness that inspired their hearts,
> Their minds, and muses on admired themes;
> If all the heavenly quintessence they still[1]
> From their immortal flowers of poesy,
> Wherein, as in a mirror, we perceive
> The highest reaches of a human wit;
> If these had made one poem's period,
> And all combined in beauty's worthiness,
> Yet should there hover in their restless heads
> One thought, one grace, one wonder, at the least,
> Which into words no virtue can digest.

The audience must have left the theatre in a state of dizzy exaltation,
resavouring such lines as 'Ride in triumph through Persepolis',
'To entertain divine Zenocrate', chanting again the high astounding
terms and eagerly anticipating more. Marlowe had made the fortunes
of Alleyn, Henslowe and the Admiral's, but that was of trivial significance; in a single afternoon he had demolished the clowns' and
grocers' drama and set up the drama of poets. Crude, rhetorical, inflated and nonsensical as much of *Tamburlaine* is, the rest is poetry,

[1] Distil.

and the play is the prototype of the matchless drama of the next twenty years, in which poetry and character replace the old acrobatics and horseplay. Marlowe had done for the public playhouses what Lyly had done for the private theatre. But the popular plays were incomparably more important than the esoteric entertainments at Black-friars and henceforth the full-blooded poetic drama of the adult companies and the public theatres was to be the staple fare at Court. The paltry plays that Shakespeare had seen at Stratford, indifferently acted on a makeshift stage, could have done little to fire him with the ambition to become a professional playwright, and on the whole it is improbable that he had gone up to London for such a purpose; but after that afternoon's performance he could have been in no doubt as to his true vocation.

'THAT ADMIRABLE YEAR EIGHTY-EIGHT'

FOR more than a century the year 1588 had loomed menacingly out
of the future as one of disaster, a year that betokened some great up-
heaval of the nations, possibly indeed the end of all things. The
astronomers were no more reassuring than the prophets; there were
to be two total eclipses of the moon, one of them within a few days of
an eclipse of the sun, a scarcely precedented portent, and as the world
swung helplessly into the beginning of the fatal orbit, it was evident
that the year of wonders was to witness the eclipse of one of the champions of the contending faiths, England or Spain. On July 19th the
Armada, a sombre crescent of nearly 150 ships, was sighted off the
Lizard; the next day it was engaged by Howard and Drake with the
main fleet from Plymouth, and for nearly a week there followed a
running fight up the Channel, the Spaniards being unable either to
board their nimble adversaries or to answer the broadsides poured into
their hulls. When at last they dropped anchor in Calais Roads, it was
only to be fired out like foxes. Cutting their cables to evade the drifting
fire-ships, they beat in panic out to sea, where some were sunk by the
English guns, others driven aground, while the remainder fled north-
wards to make their way as best they could round the gale-beaten
coasts of Scotland and Ireland. The English lost one ship; less than
half the Armada returned to Spain.

It was decisive; the incubus that had both oppressed and stimulated
the spirit of the nation for the last thirty years was lifted. England was
mistress of the seas, any immediate threat of invasion had vanished, all
the Americas and Indies lay open to her ships, and Spain itself, if
Drake and Walsingham could have their way. Though the war went
on for the rest of the reign, it changed its character, becoming a
desultory operation in which England assisted the Dutch, soon
virtually independent, and the Huguenots under Henry of Navarre,
who, after the murder of Henry III, fought for the throne to which
he was the legitimate heir.

It was the climax of the reign, the triumph to which all else had
been but prelude, and divided the first thirty years from the last

fifteen as neatly and incisively as any event in history. Elizabeth herself was fifty-five, though vigorous as ever, but some of her contemporaries were failing. Leicester, the red-faced Lieutenant-General of the army mustered to repel invasion, was the first to go, surviving the destruction of the Armada by only a few days. He was unimportant, a vain shallow man, yet Elizabeth could not but regret her first favourite and the lost delights and princely pleasures of Kenilworth, even though her people remembered other things: the sudden death of his first wife, his scraping from the church and commons, and rejoiced no less at his death than at the victory over Spain. Leicester was gone from Court, but then, his stepson had just arrived. The Earl of Essex, fresh from his triumphs in the Netherlands, was then just twenty-one; auburn-haired and graceful, becomingly ardent and dangerously impetuous, one of the greatest nobles of England, he was a man to flutter the hearts of queens, and his cousin Elizabeth wrote:

> When I was fair and young, and favour graced me,
> Of many was I sought, their mistress for to be;
> But I did scorn them all, and answered them therefore,
>   'Go, go, go, seek some otherwhere,
>   Importune me no more!'

> Then spake fair Venus' son, that proud victorious boy,
> And said, 'Fine dame, since that you be so coy
> I will go pluck your plumes that you shall say no more,
>   Go, go, go, seek some otherwhere,
>   Importune me no more!'

> When he had spake these words, such change grew in my breast
> That neither night nor day since that, I could take any rest.
> Then lo! I did repent that I had said before,
>   'Go, go, go, seek some otherwhere,
>   Importune me no more!'

It was fantastic, it was ridiculous; she was almost old enough to be his grandmother, yet, according to the mirror of her Court, time had had no power upon her beauty, and the young man appeared to be as fascinated as she. Within a few months he was installed in Leicester House in the Strand, now known as Essex House, Master of the Horse and Knight of the Garter. Raleigh, the upstart Captain of the Guard, was compelled to wait chafing outside the Privy Chamber door while the Queen and the Earl talked within. There was a challenge, which came to nothing, and Raleigh went off to Ireland to manage his estates, to visit Spenser at Kilkolman, and read the opening books of *The Faerie Queene.* He was back in time to take part in the Counter-Armada of 1589. Essex, too, was there, in spite of the Queen's express orders that he was to stay at home.

Drake was much the most popular man in England and, supported by Walsingham, the foremost exponent of the policy of carrying the war into Spain. Hawkins and Elizabeth favoured the less hazardous and more profitable course of looting the traffic on the sea-routes. Burghley disapproved of both; he had never wanted war, was ashamed of the buccaneering tactics of the seamen and now looked forward to the conclusion of an honourable and advantageous peace. The result was that, though Drake was given his chance, his expedition was crippled from the start: supplies were insufficient, there was no siege-train and no wholehearted, concerted support from home. With Sir John Norris in command of the land forces, the fleet set sail to the exhortations of the chauvinistic Peele:

> To arms, to arms, to glorious arms!
> With noble Norris and victorious Drake,
> Under the sanguine cross, brave England's badge,
> To propagate religious piety.

The plan was to detach Portugal from Spain by seizing Lisbon, raising the country in favour of the pretender Don Antonio and installing him on the throne. At least that was Drake's plan, but he was compelled to fritter away time and supplies on futile preliminary raids; then when Lisbon blankly refused to welcome Don Antonio, without the guns to reduce it, there was nothing for it but to return. There were heroic actions, some Spanish property was destroyed and a number of ships were taken; above all, Drake had shown that, with proper support, Spain could be defeated on her own soil. But the fact remained that the real object of the expedition had failed; Drake was discredited and, like Raleigh, fell back into the shadows.

Walsingham, Drake's best friend within the government, died shortly afterwards, and Sir Christopher Hatton, who long ago had danced himself into the Queen's favour, and recently into the Lord Chancellorship, followed within a few months. The year of wonders had swept away more than the ships of the Spanish Armada; the old favourites and counsellors were gone, and of the principal actors of the first thirty critical years of the reign Burghley alone remained. The favourite's place was already filled, and Burghley had long been carefully coaching an understudy for the post of Secretary, and his younger son, Robert Cecil, a delicate little hunchback of twenty-seven, stepped easily into Walsingham's room. Posts for his brilliant young nephews were not so easily found, and Anthony and Francis, sons of Lord Keeper Sir Nicholas Bacon, another of the old guard whom death had removed, were left to cool their ambitious heels. But they were not the sort of young men to wait for fortune's favour; if their uncle would not help them, perhaps the Earl of Essex would.

Armada year had completely transformed the political scene, and there was a similar transformation of the literary scene, as hard on the heels of Marlowe and Shakespeare the other poets of the last great phase of the reign, all of them young men in their early twenties, assembled in London. Tom Nashe came down from Cambridge to join his friends Greene and Marlowe, and was followed by his young contemporary at St. John's, the Earl of Southampton, who now entered Gray's Inn, and appointed the celebrated John Florio his tutor in Italian. Florio had married the sister of Samuel Daniel, tutor to the eight-year-old William Herbert at Wilton, where he was writing his sonnets to Delia, possibly the Countess of Pembroke herself. Both she and Daniel were celebrated by Spenser in his *Colin Clout's Come Home Again*, commemorating his visit to England with Raleigh, and his introduction to the Queen, 'Cynthia, the Lady of the Sea', who graciously inclined her ear to the mazy music of *The Faerie Queene*, which he read to her from his manuscript, though she failed to offer him the post he sought. Michael Drayton, a Warwickshire man, arrived in London at about the same time, and so in all probability did George Chapman, who must have known Marlowe at Cambridge, and soon became a member of the coterie that surrounded Raleigh at Durham House. This included Thomas Harriot, the mathematician and astronomer who discovered the construction of the telescope and observed the spots on the sun at about the same time as Galileo; the Earl of Northumberland, Raleigh's friend and Harriot's patron; Matthew Roydon, another mathematician, praised by Nashe as one of the 'most able men to revive poetry', and Marlowe himself, who had probably met Raleigh through his connection with the Walsinghams. It was a dangerous circle in which to move, for any meeting of inquiring minds to discuss science, philosophy and religion, amid the fumes of tobacco, was bound to be suspect in an age of bigotry and superstition; it became known as 'the school of atheism', and even the mild and harmless scholar Harriot was to be denounced at Raleigh's trial as 'that devil Harriot'.

In 1588 Byrd published his *Psalmes, Sonets and Songs of Sadnes and Pietie,* his three great *Masses* and contributed three pieces to Nicholas Yonge's *Musica Transalpina,* a collection of Italian madrigals, the words of which were translated into English. Although these were not the first madrigals to come into the country, it was Yonge's anthology that established and popularised the form, so that we can say with some precision that the beginning of Shakespeare's career coincided with the arrival of the music characteristic of Elizabethan England—which is all as it should be. Meanwhile, in the visual arts, Hilliard and Gower had acquired something like a monopoly of painting portraits of the Queen, and the break caused by Armada year was monumentally symbolised by the completion of Robert Smythson's greatest work, Wollaton Hall, and the beginning of Wimbledon House on the new H plan, much more severe than the early exuberant Elizabethan houses, and relying for its effect on receding masses of masonry or brick.

Even among the actors' companies 1588 was a year of significant change. Richard Tarlton died in September, an irreparable loss to the Queen's Men both as actor and dramatist. One of his last appearances was at the Bull Inn, where he doubled the parts of clown and justice in the anonymous *Famous Victories of Henry V,* a performance that may have been seen by young Ben Jonson, who was later to celebrate the great comedian in *Bartholomew Fair.* Symons from Strange's seems to have replaced Tarlton, and to have taken some of his tumblers with him, so that Lord Strange was left to recruit new men for his company. This was not so difficult, as Leicester's had been disbanded on the death of their patron, and Will Kempe was available, and possibly his companions in the Netherlands, Thomas Pope and George Bryan, who had recently returned from the Danish Court, where they had entertained King Frederick II. Henceforth Strange's were primarily players instead of acrobats, though all these early companies were capable of putting on a tumbling turn. In 1588, therefore, the Queen's Men began to lose ground, and their virtual monopoly of adult performances at Court, to two new rivals; one was the Admiral's with Edward Alleyn and the plays of Marlowe (there can be little doubt that their two performances at the Revels of 1588–9 were the two parts of *Tamburlaine*), the other Strange's, which, on their reorganisation, may have been joined by Shakespeare. But whatever company he was acting for, if any, he was living somewhere in London, probably near Bishopsgate and the Shoreditch theatres, writing his first play, and maybe a sonnet commemorating the destruction of the deadly moon-shaped Armada in that strange and memorable year 1588:

> The mortall Moone hath her eclipse indur'de,
> And the sad Augurs mock their owne presage,
> Incertenties now crowne them-selues assur'de,
> And peace proclaimes Oliues of endlesse age.

PART TWO
1588–1603

V

1588–1594

THE DRAMATIC REVOLUTION

AFTER the presentation of Lyly's first plays by 'Oxford's Boys' and the closing of the Blackfriars theatre in 1584, the Chapel Children gave no more Court performances until the turn of the century. For a time the Queen's Men were the favoured company, but in 1587 the Paul's boys reappeared under their master, Thomas Giles, and performed a series of new plays by Lyly, all in the same vein of delicate fantasy, the most delightful of which is the silver and gossamer *Endymion*, 'a tale of the Man in the Moon'. Then Lyly and the boys were caught up in the Marprelate controversy.

This was precipitated by Whitgift's resolute campaign against the Puritans, who were hauled up before his newly established Court of High Commission if they failed to subscribe to his minimum demands for orthodoxy, then prevented from publishing their protests by his Licensing Act. Even Burghley thought his methods savoured too rankly of the Inquisition. There was a truce during the critical period of threatened invasion, but soon after the defeat of the Armada there appeared a surreptitiously printed *Epistle* 'by the reverend and worthie Martin Marprelate, gentleman. Printed oversea, in Europe, within two furlongs of a Bounsing Priest'. In fact, it was printed no farther afield than Molesey in Surrey, where John Penry, a Welsh Puritan, had set up a secret press with the aid of the printer Robert Waldegrave. The tract, directed mainly against the bishops, was witty, scurrilous, abusively colloquial, and Bancroft went underground to discover the press and the real name of the author, but though Penry was eventually arrested and hanged on a charge of sedition, Martin was not found and his identity has never been discovered. The press was moved from place to place, and in the course of 1589 six more tracts were published, one of them being *Ha' ye any Worke for Cooper?* an annihilating reply to Thomas Cooper, Bishop of Winchester, who lucklessly intervened with a solemn *Admonition*. The bishops were no match for Martin, and enlisted the aid of professional writers, among them Lyly and Nashe, who quite outclassed Martin in his own manner, the one in *Pappe with an Hatchet*, the other in *An Almond for a Parrat*, and then produced him on the stage with a cock's comb, ape's face, wolf's belly, cat's claws, where he was wormed and lanced to let out the black blood and evil humours with which he was distended. Again, in the right Aristophanic vein, Divinity was brought forth 'wyth a scratcht face, holding of her hart as if she were sicke, because Martin would haue forced her, but myssing of his purpose, he left the print of his nayles vpon her cheekes, and poysoned her with a vomit which he ministred unto her, to make her cast vppe her dignities and promotions'. The playwrights and players were enjoying themselves at the expense of their old persecutors, but the affair was getting out of hand when the press was discovered, Waldegrave driven abroad and Martin silenced. Whitgift had won, but with characteristic cynicism the government found it expedient to sacrifice its own agents; the Paul's boys were suppressed, and there is no further record of them at Court for the next ten years. Lyly wrote only one more play, *The Woman in the Moon*, a comedy in blank verse presented by some adult company at Court about 1593, when the satire against women probably cost him the long-expected reversion of the Mastership of the Revels.

Another turn of the screw was given to the measures against unorthodoxy, Puritan and Catholic alike, one of the victims being the Jesuit poet Robert Southwell, arrested in 1592 and ten times tortured before his execution two years later. Much of his poetry was written in prison, including perhaps *The Burning Babe*, which Jonson would have given so much to have written, and *Saint Peter's Complaint*, in which some find echoes of *Venus and Adonis* and a deliberate attempt to raise the erotic theme to a spiritual level. It may be so, but it is possible that the influence was the other way round, and that *Romeo and Juliet* and the *Sonnets* owe something to Shakespeare's reading of such lines as:

> O sacred eyes, the springs of living light,
> Sweet volumes, stored with learning fit for saints.

Another sufferer under the new repressive measures appears to have been John Shakespeare, who in 1592 was included in a list of recusants 'for not comminge monethlie to the churche, it is said for feare of process for debt'.

While the contestants in the Marprelate controversy were happily engaged in the throwing about of brains, James VI of Scotland was awaiting the arrival of his bride, Anne of Denmark. He was twenty-three and she fifteen, a young lady much given to the more expensive pleasures of life, and already acquainted with the excitements of the English drama through the performances of Pope, Bryan and their fellows at her late father's Court, where her brother Christian IV now reigned. Although plays 'maid of ye cannonicall Scriptures' had long been forbidden by the Scottish General Assembly, profane plays were allowed, provided they were not acted on the Sabbath and were licensed by the local Kirk Session, a grim sort of censorship scarcely encouraging to companies of professional players, of which there was none in Scotland worthy of the name. Yet James was determined to celebrate his wedding with a play. It so happened that the Queen's Men were then 'in the furthest parte of Langkeshire', as far from the English Court as possible, where they were in disgrace for their part in the anti-Martinist plays, and at the request of James the English ambassador ordered them to wait in readiness at Carlisle. Unfortunately Anne was driven into a Norwegian port by the autumn storms, for the raising of which a number of Scottish and Danish witches were burned, and James had to undertake the one romantic adventure of his prosy life by going to fetch her. They were married in Christiania in November, and did not reach Scotland until the following spring, so that, after all, the royal couple had to forgo the pleasure of being entertained by the servants of their cousin of England.

Elizabeth herself did not forgo her entertainments. She revelled it at Christmas as in the old days, though it was no longer Leicester who stood beside her state as she watched the plays in the Great Chamber at Whitehall, nor were the players now the children of her Chapel or of Paul's. It is true that during the stormy decade of the eighties, when her life was constantly in danger, she had made a concession to prudence and curtailed her progresses, contenting herself with local holidays, at Theobalds with Burghley, or at her newly bought and favourite palace of Nonsuch, or at Oatlands on the fringe of Windsor Forest, where the hunting was so good; but with the return of more peaceful times she resumed the grand scale of the seventies, and in 1591 set out on a two-month tour of Surrey, Sussex and Hampshire. This was prefaced by a ten-days' visit to Theobalds, where she knighted Robert Cecil, while her 'Spirit', as she affectionately called Burghley, posed as 'the disconsolate and retired spryte, the

THE ELVETHAM ENTERTAINMENT, 1591

Heremite of Tybole'. In August she began her progress proper, and
after being entertained for a week at Cowdray by Lord Montague,
Southampton's grandfather, spent her fifty-eighth birthday with
Southampton himself at Titchfield, and on September 20th arrived at
Elvetham, the home of the Earl of Hertford. The visit was in the
nature of a reconciliation, for in the first year of her reign Hertford
had had the temerity to marry Lady Catherine Grey, sister of Lady
Jane Grey, with a claim therefore to the succession to her throne, and
though he had had two other wives since then, she had never forgiven
him. She stayed only three nights, but the entertainment was after the
princely model of the unforgettable occasion at Kenilworth. She was
received with a salute of guns, a Latin speech by a Poet and a song by
the Hours and Graces, and at night there was 'a notable consort of six
Musitions', who played, to the Queen's great gratification, a pavane
by Thomas Morley, recently admitted Mus.Bac. at Oxford. An
artificial lake had been constructed in the grounds, with three islands,
on one of which was a fort, on another a hill in the form of a snail
and by the third a ship, and here on the following afternoon Neptune
and the gods of the sea took part in a water-pageant. The next morning Elizabeth was awakened with a song by Phyllida and Corydon,

and after dinner ten of Lord Hertford's servants, in a square green court in front of her window, gave an exhibition of 'board and cord' a game that seems to have been a cross between fives and lawn-tennis, played five a side. That evening a banquet was given in the garden, followed by a firework display. On the last morning there was a dance of fairies, and Elizabeth left Elvetham to the laments of the sea-gods, the Hours and Graces, the Poet and all those who had helped to entertain her. Lord Hertford's players were not forgotten, and they made their one appearance at Court on the following Twelfth Night. They were an undistinguished provincial company, and it may have been their rustic performance that Shakespeare good-naturedly parodied in Bottom's interlude of Pyramus and Thisbe, and the water-pageants and fireworks of Elvetham and dimly remembered Kenil-worth that prompted Oberon's speech to Puck:

> Thou rememberest
> Since once I sat upon a promontory,
> And heard a mermaid, on a dolphin's back,
> Uttering such dulcet and harmonious breath,
> That the rude sea grew civil at her song,
> And certain stars shot madly from their spheres,
> To hear the sea-maid's music.

In September 1592, Elizabeth paid her second visit to Oxford— John Marston was a freshman at Brasenose—where she saw two Latin plays in Christ Church hall, one of them the *Rivales* of William Gager, then in the throes of a controversy with John Reynolds, who considered plays immoral and a waste of time, and players, even amateurs, no better than vagabonds. Twenty-six years before, on her first visit to Oxford, Elizabeth had congratulated the boy Reynolds on his performance as Hippolyta in Richard Edwards's *Palamon and Arcite*, now, with recent memories of Marprelate, she rated the man 'for his obstinate preciseness, willing him to follow her laws, and not run before them'. Despite this discord, she was well pleased with her entertainment, and invited both Oxford and Cambridge to present plays at Court that Christmas—in English. English, how-ever, was insufficiently academic, at least for Cambridge, who thought but meanly of the Oxford plays, and neither university attended.

But the future of the drama did not lie with dons, however talented and however much they might enjoy their cloistered squabbles and think they mattered. In London the bright and restless genius of

Marlowe was transfiguring the pedestrian blank verse of the old dramatists, creating new aspiring characters for Alleyn of the Admiral's to play, and staggering the groundlings with his rhetoric and sensational plots. Never before had audiences been gripped with such tense and pleasurable excitement as when they watched his ruthlessly fanatical figures striving with undivided aim for power, until inevitably they overreached themselves and fell. There was Barabas, the Jew of Malta, who murdered his own daughter and a convent-full of nuns, betrayed the Christians to the Turks and the Turks to the Christians, only to perish in a trap of his own devising. Even better, there was Faustus, who sold his soul to the devil in return for twenty-four years of all-voluptuous life, made Homer sing of Alexander's love and Œnone's death and, before being carried off to hell and an eternity of torment, had Helen of Troy for his paramour. Faustus's last frenzied monologue is still one of the most deeply moving speeches in our drama, and how fearfully it worked on the imagination of the age is attested by a number of lingering legends. When the play was produced at the Theatre, the very timbers creaked and cracked with terror; at the Bel Savage Inn the Devil himself appeared on the stage; at Exeter the players suddenly discovered a devil too many among them; and on another occasion Alleyn was surprised in the midst of the play by an apparition of the Devil, which so worked on his imagination that he made a vow and founded Dulwich College.

What with his interest in necromancy, his creation of fiendish mortals and equally realistic fiends, and his friendship with free-thinkers like Raleigh and Harriot, Marlowe had become one of the most notorious figures in the capital. Nor was his conduct calculated to allay mistrust. At least two Shoreditch constables went in such terror of him that he was bound over by the Lieutenant of the Tower to keep the peace, and before this he had been in much more serious trouble. One September afternoon in 1589, near his lodgings in the Liberty of Norton Folgate, he came to blows with William Bradley, an innkeeper's son. Swords were drawn, and while the duel was in progress Marlowe's friend and Bradley's particular enemy, the poet Thomas Watson, arrived on the scene. With a cry of, 'Art thowe nowe come? Then I will haue a boute with thee', Bradley took on Watson, and Marlowe withdrew. Watson was hard pressed, but eventually got inside his opponent's guard, ran him through the body, and killed him. This at least was the account given by Watson and

Marlowe after their arrest and confinement in Newgate prison on suspicion of murder. Marlowe was soon cleared, and so was Watson, who managed to persuade the jury that he had acted only in self-defence, though it was some months before he received the Queen's pardon and was released from Newgate.

At this time Marlowe was sharing a room with Thomas Kyd, who was in the service of a certain lord for whose company Marlowe, too, was writing, though which company is uncertain, the Admiral's perhaps, or Sussex's, or Strange's. Kyd was almost as well known as his companion, for he was the author of the recently produced and rapturously received *Spanish Tragedy*. It was Seneca modernised and popularised by discarding the drearier elements of pseudo-classical tragedy, and emphasising the themes of ghost, blood and revenge. It was brilliantly conceived and brilliantly done, and we can imagine the audience's gasp of delighted horror when the play opened with the appearance of a Ghost and the spirit of Revenge, before whom, as chorus, the sombre Spanish tragedy was unfolded. The plot is involved, but the essence of the play is the frantic grief and revenge of old Hieronimo for the murder of his son Horatio. After a series of minor murders and incidental insanities, Hieronimo and Bellimperia, Horatio's mistress, persuade the murderers to take part in a tragedy to be presented before their fathers, the Kings of Spain and Portugal. Bellimperia stabs one of the murderers before stabbing herself, Hieronimo accounts for the other, bites out his tongue and then kills himself. People never seemed to tire of the play; it was exported to Germany, where Jacob Ayrer made an adaptation, and in London it was revived time and again in the course of the next fifteen years; alterations and additions were made, and it became the model for innumerable tragedies of the 'revenge' type, of which *Hamlet* is only the most famous. There are, indeed, many points of resemblance to *Hamlet*: there is the hero Horatio; like Ophelia, Horatio's mother goes mad with grief and kills herself; there is a play within a play; and though the parts of father and son are reversed, Hieronimo resembles Hamlet when, with something of the pathos of Lear addressing Gloucester as blind Cupid, he mistakes an old man for young Horatio's ghost, and asks:

> And art thou come, Horatio, from the depth,
> To ask for justice in this upper earth,
> To tell thy father thou art unrevenged?

There is, moreover, some reason to think that Kyd was the author of the original play of *Hamlet*, now lost. Certainly such a play was in existence by 1594, when it was acted at Newington Butts, and that it was written by Kyd may punningly be implied by Nashe in his *Epistle* prefaced to Greene's romance, *Menaphon*, published in 1589. This *Epistle* is addressed *To the Gentlemen Students of Both Universities*, and is in the main directed against the players, whom he sees as parasites living on the playwrights, and against those playwrights without any university education, who artfully exploit the classics which they read surreptitiously in translation. A university degree meant much more in those days than it does to-day; for one thing, it gave a man the status of a gentleman, however humble his origin, and Gabriel Harvey was a ropemaker's son, Marlowe the son of a cobbler, and Greene, ever flourishing his twofold degree, the son of a small Norwich tradesman. Kyd's father was a scrivener, or noverint, a profession that Kyd himself probably adopted at the beginning of his career, which may account for Nashe's ill-natured and quite uncharacteristic gibe:

> It is a common practise now a dayes amongst a sort of shifting companions, that runne through euery Art and thriue by none, to leaue the trade of *Nouerint*, whereto they were borne, and busie themselues with the indeuours of Art, that could scarcely Latinize their neck verse if they should haue neede; yet English *Seneca* read by Candle-light yeelds many good sentences, as *Blood is a begger*, and so forth; and if you intreate him faire in a frostie morning, hee will affoord you whole *Hamlets*, I should say handfuls of Tragicall speeches. But O griefe! *Tempus edax rerum*, whats that will last alwayes? The Sea exhaled by droppes will in continuance bee drie, and *Seneca*, let blood line by line and page by page, at length must needes die to our Stage; which makes his famished followers to imitate the Kidde in *Aesop*, who, enamoured with the Foxes newfangles, forsooke all hopes of life to leape into a newe occupation.

The evidence is slender, but it looks as though there was a play of *Hamlet* as early as 1589, too early for Shakespeare to be the likely author and, if not Shakespeare, everything seems to point to Kyd. Perhaps Jonson was referring to this when he wrote of Shakespeare's far outshining 'sporting Kyd', meaning that the comic element in Shakespeare's *Hamlet* was far superior to Kyd's; otherwise, why he should call the apparently mirthless author of *The Spanish Tragedy* and *Cornelia*, a translation of Robert Garnier's *Cornélie*, 'sporting' is not at all clear. The original *Hamlet* was almost as popular as *The Spanish Tragedy*, and was humorously alluded to some years later by Lodge, when he wrote of 'the Visard of ye ghost which cried so miserably at ye Theator like an oister wife, Hamlet, reuenge', and again by Dekker in the next century: 'My name's Hamlet revenge: thou hast been at Paris Garden, hast not?' Kyd lacked the poetry of Marlowe, but he was a born dramatist, and when, after a decade, people still bandied phrases from his plays—'Hieronimo, go by, go by', 'Hamlet, revenge'—we may be sure that he was a successful one as well, which is by no means the same thing as an affluent one.

It was in his *Menaphon* epistle that Nashe called Peele 'the Atlas of poetry' whose *Arraignment of Paris* 'goeth a step beyond all that write'. This was the year in which Peele celebrated the sailing of Drake and Norris on their Lisbon expedition, in his fervidly patriotic *Farewell*, a poem that furnished Shakespeare with hints for the choruses of *Henry V*:

> Bid England's shore and Albion's chalky cliffs
> Farewell, bid stately Troynovant adieu . . .
> Bid theatres and proud tragedians,
> Bid Mahomet's Poo, and mighty Tamburlaine,
> King Charlemagne, Tom Stukeley and the rest,
> Adieu. To arms, to arms, to glorious arms!

'Mahomet's Poo' ('pow' or 'head') is probably a reference to his own lost play, *The Turkish Mahomet and Hiren the Fair Greek*, and by 'Tom Stukeley' he certainly means his *Battle of Alcazar*, a play that deals with the death of that Elizabethan adventurer in the battle between King Sebastian of Portugal and the Moors, a singularly appropriate theme in the year of Drake's attempt to put the pretender Don Antonio on the throne of Portugal. Peele, the pageant writer, could bombast out a blank verse with the best of his contemporaries, as when the defeated King of Morocco robs a lioness of her food to give to his wife Calipolis:

> Feed then, and faint not, fair Calipolis;
> For, rather than fierce famine shall prevail
> To gnaw thy entrails with her thorny teeth,
> The conquering lioness shall attend on thee,
> And lay huge heaps of slaughtered carcases
> As bulwarks in her way to keep her back . . .
> Feed then, and faint not, fair Calipolis.

His inflated poetry and patriotism seem to have made a deep impression, and Peele was Pistol's favourite dramatist, whose plays Shakespeare makes him constantly quote, misquote or parody: 'Then feed, and be fat, my fair Calipolis'; 'Have we not Hiren here?'

Peele's other plays all belong to the early nineties. *Edward I* is interesting as one of the first attempts to make a play out of a chronicle, a significant dramatic action from a series of dramatically unrelated historical episodes, and though the play is spoiled by the ludicrous 'sinking' and vilification of Queen Eleanor, a Spaniard, it may have prepared the way for Marlowe's *Edward II* and Shakespeare's *Henry VI*. *David and Bethsabe* is remarkable in being the only Elizabethan dramatisation of a Biblical story, but this is its only point of resemblance to the medieval miracles. The Prologue anticipates the opening of *Paradise Lost*, and the play is crammed with poetry, a compound of Spenserian sweetness and Marlovian rhetoric, much of it undeniably undramatic, as when the tree catches Absalon by the hair:

> O God, behold the glory of thy hand,
> And choicest fruit of nature's workmanship,
> Hang, like a rotten branch upon this tree,
> Fit for the axe and ready for the fire!
> Since thou withhold'st all ordinary help
> To loose my body from the hand of death,
> O, let my beauty fill these senseless plants
> With sense and power to loose me from this plague.

Dying men do not thus play nicely with conceits, though Romeo does, and so does John of Gaunt, and all the tragic figures in *King John*. There is scarcely a speech without some splendid line—'And brings my longings tangled in her hair'; 'Like golden wires of David's ivory lute'; 'Thou man of blood, thou sepulchre of death'—and there can be no doubt that the apprentice Shakespeare delighted in the fine excess of Peele, as Keats would have done had he come across his work. Lamb dismissed his poetry as 'stuff', but it was some years before Shakespeare wrote anything comparable to *David and Bethsabe*. *The Old Wives' Tale* is a light-hearted entertainment something in the manner of Lyly, a winter's tale begun by Madge, the smith's wife, that develops into an inconsequent and dream-like interlude of apparitions and magicians, which probably suggested the plot of *Comus* to Milton. The Induction is a little masterpiece, and incidentally Peele pokes some pretty fun at Gabriel Harvey and his hexameters:

> Dub dub-a-dub, bounce, quoth the guns, with a sulphurous huff-snuff;
> Wak'd with a wench, pretty peat, pretty love, and my sweet pretty pigsnie. . . .
> O, that I might—but I may not, woe to my destiny therefore!—
> Kiss that I clasp! but I cannot; tell me, my destiny, wherefore?

Peele was a pioneer in everything he wrote; one of the most considerable poets of his day, it was largely owing to his experiments that the
'drumming decasyllabon', the relentlessly beating and end-stopped
blank-verse line, began to be broken down to make the infinitely
varied music of which it is capable. He must have been a delightful
and lively, perhaps over-lively, companion, and after his early death
was celebrated in *The Merry Conceited Jests of George Peele*, a collection of apocryphal stories, one of which was dramatised in *The
Puritan*, a comedy at one time attributed to Shakespeare.

Peele's Oxford contemporary, the restless and improvident Thomas
Lodge, was one of those 'shifting companions that run through every
art and thrive by none', described by Nashe. After his early clash with
Gosson, developed in *An Alarum against Usurers*, he 'fell from books
to arms' and sailed with Captain Clarke on his expedition to Terceira
and the Canaries, beguiling the time by writing a romance, *Rosalynde*,
published in 1590. Its sub-title, *Euphues' Golden Legacy*, sufficiently
indicates its model, but though there are dreary patches of euphuism,
as when Alinda comforts Rosalind with, 'the fairer the rose is, the
sooner it is bitten with caterpillars; the more orient the pearl is, the
more apt to take a blemish', and so on, it is leavened with lyrics, of
which Rosalind's madrigal, 'Love in my bosom like a bee', is the best
known, and, despite the artifice of the pastoral convention, is altogether fresher and more wholesome than Lyly's *Euphues*. It is an
attractive work, but is read to-day mainly because it is the source of
As You Like It. In the previous year Lodge had published *Scilla's
Metamorphosis*, a melancholy and delicate poem that probably
furnished Shakespeare with hints for *Venus and Adonis*, and it must
have been at about this time that his one extant unaided play was
produced. *The Wounds of Civil War* is a disappointingly tedious and
confused tragedy inspired by *Tamburlaine*—'Enter Sylla in triumph
in his chair triumphant of gold, drawn by four Moors'—and based on
Plutarch's *Lives* of Marius and Sylla. But Lodge was no match for
Marlowe in tragedy, and is curiously heavy-handed in his verse, so
that the best he can do for the dying Sylla is:

> Pompey, Lord Flaccus, fellow-senators,
> In that I feel the faintful dews of death
> Steeping mine eyes within their chilly wet,
> The care I have of wife and daughter both,
> Must on your wisdom happily rely.

In August 1591, Lodge sailed on the dismally unsuccessful expedition to South America under the leadership of the extravagant adventurer Thomas Cavendish, who died on the way home. It was June 1593 before he returned to England, and by that time two of his London companions were dead.

We know more about Greene than the rest of his contemporaries, for his innate egotism, irritated by debauchery and poverty, frustration and jealousy, drove him to stimulate the sale of his wares by self-advertisement, and much of his later work is scarcely veiled autobiography. On his return from foreign travel in the early eighties, he married, but soon tiring of his wife, who tried to reform him, abandoned her and their child and went to London. There he lived a dissolute life with his mistress, the sister of a notorious thief known as Cutting Ball, who bore him a son, Fortunatus. He made some sort of a living by writing a series of 'love pamphlets', novelettes without a story, in the popular rhetorical euphuism of the period. Then in 1588, the year in which he added an Oxford M.A. to his Cambridge degree, he published *Pandosto*, a pastoral romance in which the sophisticated digressions are subordinated to the story of Fawnia and Dorastus, transformed by Shakespeare twenty years later into that of Perdita and Florizel in *The Winter's Tale. Menaphon*, which followed, is a similar sort of romance, but though the narrative is more convincing than *Pandosto*, its chief interest to-day lies in Nashe's prefatory *Epistle*, with its attack on ungrateful players and underbred playwrights, and its references to *Hamlet*. Like Lodge's *Rosalynde* and most of the other Elizabethan 'novels', Greene's romances are interspersed with poems, and few of his contemporaries had his technical skill and felicity in turning a lyric. The most famous is 'Weep not, my wanton', with its refrain 'Father's sorrow, father's joy'; though the almost metaphysical conclusion of the song to Fawnia,

> O glorious sun, imagine me the west,
> Shine in my arms, and set thou in my breast,

is as memorable as anything, except the burden of Infida's song in *Never too Late*:

> *Je vous en prie*, pity me:
> *N'oserez vous, mon bel, mon bel,*
> *N'oserez vous, mon bel ami?*

Never too Late (1590) is the first of those peculiar productions of Greene, a blend of realistic fiction, autobiography, confession, professed repentance and a moral. The hero, Francesco, the greater part Greene himself, tells how he fell in with a company of players who persuaded him to try his wit at writing a play, promising him large rewards if he could produce anything worthy of the stage. Francesco wrote so successful a play that the actors clamoured for more, yet in the preface to his *Perimedes* of 1588 Greene complained bitterly that Marlowe and another 'had it in derision for that I could not make my verses jet upon the stage in tragical buskins, every word filling the mouth like the fa-burden of Bo-Bell, daring God out of heaven with that Atheist *Tamburlan*'. The play was almost certainly *Alphonsus*, a history in which Greene attempted to out-Tamburlaine Tamburlaine in violence of verse and action, and evidently Francesco's success was Greene's compensation for his own failure. Perhaps there was a similar sort of fantasy in his boast that there was no one about London so famous a playwright as Robin Greene, though Nashe tells us how eager publishers were to pay him highly even for the very dregs of his wit. Certainly his next play, *Friar Bacon and Friar Bungay*, deserved any success and popularity it may have received. Although *Faustus* was the inspiration, this time Greene did not make the mistake of emulating Marlowe, but, by weaving an idyllic love-story into an entertaining legend of competitive conjuring, created one of the most charming of all Elizabethan comedies. There is a simplicity, ingenuousness almost, of language, and a lightness of rhythm in Greene's blank verse that gives it a peculiar distinction:

> Peggy, the lovely flower of all towns,
> Suffolk's fair Helen, and rich England's star,
> Whose beauty, tempered with her huswifery,
> Makes England talk of merry Fressingfield.

But this freshness and innocence are not without pathos when we remember the contrast of the conditions under which the play was written, and we see the nostalgic imaginary flight to his native countryside as another attempt to escape from the hideous reality of his surroundings in a London slum. The strange apologue, *A Looking Glass for London and England*, was written in collaboration with Lodge shortly before the Cavendish expedition, and *James IV*, an imaginary Scottish history, was probably Greene's last play, as it is also his best, largely because of Dorothea, a heroine of Shakespearean devotion comparable to Silvia in *The Two Gentlemen of Verona*, who may well be an idealised portrait of his wife, Doll. Incidentally, it was from this play that Shakespeare took Oberon, king of the fairies. Greene sank lower and lower until, surrounded by the riffraff of London, he took to the writing of pamphlets exposing the tricks of his companions, cut-purses, 'cony-catchers' and cheats of every kind, which brought upon him an exposure of his own method of swindling, as when he sold his play, *Orlando Furioso*, to the Queen's Men while they were on tour, and then again to the Admiral's in London. Greene defended himself on the grounds that there was no virtue in keeping faith with players, who themselves valued faith no more than a feather, and were always prepared to sacrifice their authors to their own profit. It was characteristic of the bitterness and cynicism to which he had been reduced by his excesses, and his morbid jealousy of more successful authors, and, financially at least, even more successful actors. In extenuation, it should be remembered that an actor's company bought a play outright for £5 or £6, and that it must have been galling in the extreme for an impecunious dramatist to see the players raking in the profits and pranking it in their finery. By this time the end was near, and in August 1592, after a supper of pickled herring and Rhenish wine with Nashe, he fell ill and died on September 3rd, in the house of a poor shoemaker, where he was tended by his landlady and his mistress. Shortly before his death he wrote a note to his wife: 'Doll, I charge thee, by the loue of our youth and by my soules rest, that thou wilte see this man paide; for if hee and his wife had not succoured me, I had died in the streetes.' Then he asked his landlady to lay a wreath of bays upon him. He was only thirty-four.

A few weeks later the last of Greene's autobiographical pamphlets was published, 'at his dying request', by Henry Chettle, a printer. This was *Greens Groats-worth of Wit, bought with a Million of Repentaunce*, in which Greene, in the character of Roberto, once again describes how he became an 'Arch-plaimaking-poet', whose 'purse like the sea sometime sweld, anon like the same sea fell to a low ebb'. Having described the extreme poverty to which he was reduced, and his companions, 'the lewdest persons in the land', he turns savagely on the parasitical players and warns his fellow *gentlemen* dramatists against the profession that 'gets by scholars their whole living', burs, puppets, antics, apes, buckram gentlemen, peasants, painted monsters.

This is the famous passage addressed to Marlowe, the 'famous gracer of Tragedians . . . who hath said . . . there is no God'; to Nashe, 'the young Juvenall, that byting Satyrist'; and to Peele, 'driuen (as my selfe) to extreame shifts'. One player is singled out for particular opprobrium, 'an vpstart Crow, beautified with our feathers, that with his *Tygers heart wrapt in a Players hide*, supposes he is as well able to bumbast out a blanke verse as the best of you: and being an absolute *Iohannes fac totum*, is in his owne conceit the onely Shake-scene in a countrie'. The reference to Shakespeare is unmistakable: a common player and no gentleman, who pranks and preens himself in their poetry, and even has the audacity to compete with university men in the writing of plays, more successful, it is legitimate to infer, than those of the envious Greene. It was bad enough when the actors merely sucked the playwright's blood, but there can be no future for gentlemen in the playwriting business if any upstart actor can capture their audiences with his illiterate fustian.

Evidently Shakespeare had already written, and successfully produced, his *Henry VI* trilogy, for Greene's quotation is a parody of a line in Part III, 'O tiger's heart wrapped in a woman's hide'; Henslowe records a performance of 'Harey the vj' in March 1592, and again, Part I seems to be referred to by Nashe in *Pierce Penilesse*, published at about the same time as *Greens Groats-worth*, when, after stating that the subject of most plays is borrowed out of our English Chronicles, he writes of how it would 'haue joyed brave Talbot (the terror of the French) to thinke that after he had lyne two hundred yeares in the tombe, hee should triumphe againe on the Stage'. Part I, or at least a first version of it, may have been written as early as 1589, and when Greene heard its opening lines, he must have admitted to himself that here was a man who really could rival Marlowe on his own ground:

> Hung be the heavens with black, yield day to night!
> Comets, importing change of times and states,
> Brandish your crystal tresses in the sky,
> And with them scourge the bad revolting stars
> That have consented unto Henry's death!

It should be added that Nashe no longer subscribed to Greene's jaundiced view of players, but now defended them as not being like 'the players beyond Sea, a sort of squirting baudie Comedians', maintaining that none of the admired tragedians of the past 'could ever performe more in action than famous Ned Allen', and in the second edition of *Pierce Penilesse* dismissed the *Groats-worth* as 'a scald trivial lying pamphlet'. Chettle, too, who had edited it and seen it through the press, disowned Greene's opinion of Shakespeare, and apologised handsomely for having left in the offending passage, protesting that he had not then met Shakespeare, whom he now found to be as civil in demeanour as excellent in the writing of plays, while 'diuers of worship haue reported his vprightnes of dealing'. As for Marlowe, who had also taken offence at the charge of atheism, he cared not if he were never acquainted with him. This was politic on the part of Chettle, for Marlowe was notoriously on the verge of serious trouble, though it should be noted that Greene's remarks were not an accusation but an exhortation: 'Why should thy excellent wit, his [God's] gift, be so blinded, that thou shouldst giue no glory to the giuer? Is it pestilent Machiuilian pollicie that thou hast studied? . . . The brother of this Diabolicall Atheisme is dead . . . and wilt thou, my friend, be his Disciple? Looke vnto me, by him perswaded to that libertie, and thou shalt finde it an infernall bondage.' The reference to Machiavelli was almost as dangerous as that to atheism, for 'murderous Machiavel', as Shakespeare had just called him in 3 *Henry VI*, was reputed to have been an arch-atheist and the principal exponent of 'policy', the doctrine that any means is justified in the attainment of a desired end. And had not Marlowe himself introduced Machiavel as Prologue to *The Jew of Malta*?

> Admired I am of those that hate me most . . .
> I count religion but a childish toy,
> And hold there is no sin but ignorance.

And was not Barabas the first of the now so popular villains who dealt in policy?

Chettle's apology comes in the prefatory epistle to his *Kind-Harts Dreame*, published late in 1592, in which the ghost of Greene, 'maister of Artes', appears, 'of face amible, of body well proportioned, his attire after the habite of a schollerlike Gentleman, onely his haire was somewhat long'. It is a sympathetic portrait, for Greene was not a vicious man, merely a weak and selfish one who, according to Nashe, was never guilty of any notorious crime. He was, at the last, generous to one rival, Marlowe, and if he had met Shakespeare might have been disarmed by his friendliness, civil demeanour and uprightness of dealing.

Greene's ghost was no mere literary titillation, but had come with Senecan intention and message; to complain that no sooner had he been laid in the grave than Envy had spat out her poison to disturb his rest, and to incite Pierce Penniless, *alias* Nashe, to vengeance: 'Awake (secure boy) reuenge thy wrongs, remember mine: thy aduersaries began the abuse, they continue it.' Their adversaries were the brothers Richard and Gabriel Harvey, and the squabble had begun when Richard had attacked Nashe and Lyly in the course of the Marprelate controversy, deriding them and their fellow poets as 'piperly make-plaies and makebates'. Greene had replied on behalf of his companions, and amongst other things taunted the Harveys with being sons of a ropemaker, which was as true as it was irrelevant, but an insult that at once promoted Greene to the top of Gabriel's list of enemies. As soon as he heard of his death, therefore, the gloating Gabriel visited the scene, extracted the details from his landlady and described his squalid end in *Foure Letters, Especially touching Robert Greene*. After righteously protesting that his own deadliest sins were the having been 'orderlie clapt in the Fleete' when certain satirical verses of his were piratically published, and the invention of the English hexameter, he proceeded to catalogue those of his silenced enemy: 'Green, vile Greene, the father of the misbegotten Infortunatus, the Ape of Euphues, the Vice of the Stage, an Inuentour of monstrous oaths, a derider of all religions', and so on. Then, less discreetly, he turned on Nashe: 'Loe, all on the suddaine, his sworne brother, M. Pierce Pennilesse, Loe his inwardest companion, that tasted of the fatal herringe, cruelly pinched with want, vexed with discredite, tormented with other mens felicitie, and ouerwhelmed with his owne misery; in a raving, and franticke moode, most desperately exhibiteth his supplication to the Diuell!' This was the poison spat by Envy that brought Greene's unquiet ghost into Chettle's dream, but it needed no ghost come from the grave to spur Nashe's revenge. He had already given Richard a drubbing in *Pierce Penilesse*, and now in *Strange News of the Intercepting of Certain Letters* he flayed and pilloried his brother, Gorboduc Huddleduddle as he delighted to call him, twitting him with his two confessed deadly sins:

> But eh! what news do you hear of that good Gabriel Huffe-Snuffe,
> Known to the worlde for a foole, and clapt in the Fleete for a Runner?

The tedious and bumbling Gabriel was no match for his Ariel-like opponent, whose lightnings flamed amazement from every side at once, but he retorted with an accusation that Nashe had aped Greene and shamefully misused all his friends—'Greene, Marlowe, Chettle, and what not?'. Nashe was now prepared to forget and forgive; but not so Harvey, and Nashe delivered the withering broadside of *Have With You to Saffron Walden*, in which he refuted the charge of abusing his friends and imitating Greene, 'hee subscribing to me in anything but plotting Plaies, wherein he was his crafts master'. And so the windy, and no doubt lucrative, warfare went on until it was suppressed by Whitgift at the close of the century.

Just a year after Greene's death, in September 1593, Nashe's *Unfortunate Traveller, or the Life of Jacke Wilton* was registered and soon afterwards published, with a dedication to the young dilettante and patron of poets, whom at the same time Shakespeare was wooing, the Earl of Southampton. It is an important book, for not only is it our first, albeit embryonic, picaresque and historical novel (the period is that of the early years of Henry VIII), but in it Nashe turns his back on euphuism and arcadian romance in favour of realism, of life as he knows it, thus doing for the novel much the same as Jonson was soon to do for the drama, and Donne for poetry. It is not uninstructive to compare the portrait of Tarquin that Shakespeare was then drawing in *Lucrece* with that of the ravisher Esdras listening to his victim's pleading: 'leaning his ouer-hanging gloomie ey-browes on the pommell of his vnsheathed sword, he neuer lookt vp or gaue hir a word'. Esdras had murdered the brother of 'one Cutwolfe, a wearish dwarfish writhen facde cobler', whose revenge was to shoot him in the throat as he was cursing God, and the book closes with Jack Wilton's description of Cutwolfe's execution:

The executioner needed no exhortation herevnto, for of his owne nature was he hackster good inough: olde excellent he was at a bone-ach. At the first chop with his wood-knife would he fish for a man's heart, and fetch it out as easily as a plum from the bottome of a porredge pot. He woulde cracke neckes as fast as a cooke cracks egges: a fidler cannot turn his pin so soone as he would turne a man off the ladder: brauely did he drum on this Cutwolfes bones, not breaking them outright, but like a sadler knocking in of tackes, iarring on them quaveringly with his hammer a great while together.

There was a glittering vein of cruelty in Nashe, as in Greene and Marlowe, and such stuff is not for all stomachs, but we must at least allow its vigour and vividness of violent and teeming imagery, and recognise it as a healthy, not a morbid, reaction from the polite make-believe and perfumed trimness of so much pseudo-euphuism. Much of Nashe's work may be little more than inspired journalism, but in spontaneous ingenuity and joyous invention his prose is rivalled by only one of his contemporaries, Shakespeare.

After thirty years of comparative immunity, severe plague had visited London in the summer of 1592; the theatres were closed, and after Greene's death Nashe stayed 'with my Lord in the Coun-trey', apparently with his patron, Archbishop Whitgift, at his palace of Croydon, where his one extant play, *Summer's Last Will and Testa-ment*, was performed in October. Nashe was a student of the early Tudor period, inspired perhaps by Skelton, and the Touchstone-like Will Summer, Henry VIII's celebrated jester, acts as chorus to the speeches of dying summer, the other seasons and various classical deities, in which Nashe shows that he can write blank verse with the best of his companions when he chooses to do so, and has a lyric gift equal to any of theirs. Indeed, if we did not know it to be Nashe's, there is no other poet but Shakespeare to whom we could attribute the crystalline purity of Ver's song, 'Spring, the sweet spring', and outside Shakespeare there is no more dramatically piercing lyric than 'Adieu, farewell, earth's bliss':

> Beauty is but a flower,
> Which wrinkles will devour;
> Brightness falls from the air,
> Queens have died young and fair,
> Dust hath closed Helen's eye.
> I am sick, I must die.
> Lord have mercy upon us!

To have heard that sung by a boy to a lute in a time of terror from plague must have been one of the great moments in Elizabethan drama. We could do with much more of Nashe's poetry, but all that remains is embedded in *Dido, Queen of Carthage*, which he seems to have finished for Marlowe, the only recognisable fragment of his work being the delightful footnote to Act IV, the irrelevant little comedy of the Nurse and Cupid.

While Nashe was at Croydon, Marlowe was putting the finishing touches to his tragedy of *Edward II*, the most carefully constructed, though not the noblest, of his plays, for after the unconfined splendour of *Tamburlaine* and *Faustus*, even of *Dido*, there is, in spite of the poetry, little more than pathos in the squalid end of the undesirable Edward. That winter the play was performed by a new company, the Earl of Pembroke's, and Marlowe turned to the more congenial theme and heroic couplets of *Hero and Leander*. A few months later, on May 12th, 1593, Kyd was arrested on the charge of composing handbills criticising the influx of Flemish immigrants, the posting of which on the walls of London had led to riots. His lodging was searched, and among his papers was found a manuscript copy of a unitarian heretic's creed, which he maintained belonged to Marlowe, who had, unknown to himself, left it in the room that they had shared together two years before. After Marlowe's death he had much to say about his former friend's monstrous religious opinions, and how he used to 'jest at the devine scriptures, gybe at praiers, and strive in argument to frustrate and confute what hath byn spoke or wrytt by prophets and such holie men'. It may have been so, but Marlowe was then beyond the reach of the law, and Kyd, charged with sedition, had a neck to save. In any event, on May 18th the Privy Council sent a warrant for Marlowe's arrest to the home of Thomas Walsingham, at Scadbury in Kent, where he was taking refuge from the plague. On the 20th he appeared before the Council, who ordered him to report daily until he should be licensed to the contrary.

Marlowe spent Wednesday, May 30th, at a tavern in Deptford, a few miles down the river. His companions were Robert Poley, jailbird and secret agent, Ingram Frizer, a notorious swindler, and Nicholas Skeres, his cutpurse accomplice. According to the account of these three, after supper they sat at the table to play backgammon, while Marlowe lay on a couch behind them. When the bill was brought there was some dispute as to who should pay, and Marlowe, snatching Frizer's dagger out of its sheath, struck and wounded him twice on the head. In the struggle Frizer tried in vain to disarm him, so, seizing his hand, he drove the dagger back upon him, two inches deep into his skull above the right eye, killing him instantly. At the inquest on June 1st, Frizer was found to have acted in self-defence and acquitted, and Marlowe was buried on the same day, probably in the churchyard of St. Nicholas, Deptford.

Gabriel Harvey was soon in print again with another *Newe Letter of Notable Contents*, celebrating the death of another enemy, though he was wrong as to the circumstances:

> He and the Plague contested for the game . . .
> The grand Dissease disdain'd his toade Conceit,
> And smiling at his tamberlaine contempt,
> Sternely struck home the peremptory stroke.

But Chapman mourned the loss of a poet 'Up to the chin in the Pierian flood', and Drayton wrote of one whose 'raptures were all air and fire'. With his death, brightness had indeed fallen from the air.

Marlowe was killed by a dagger in Deptford, though he might well have been killed by the plague in London, as Harvey assumed, for at least 11,000 died of it that year, and it raged, with some abatement in the winter months, from the summer of 1592 to that of 1594 during most of which time the theatres were closed. It played havoc with the organisation and finances of the actors' companies, and it is fortunate indeed that it did not begin until Marlowe and the other University Wits had carried through the first stage of the dramatic revolution, though, as a prelude to the plague, there had been the unfortunate consequences of the Marprelate campaign. The very success of the playwrights and players had been their undoing; Nashe complained that sly practice prevented the performance of a number of anti-Marprelate comedies, the Paul's boys were suppressed, and in November 1589 the Lord Mayor, acting on Burghley's authority, stayed all plays within the City because 'Mr Tilney did utterly mislike the same'. The Admiral's dutifully obeyed the order, but Strange's, 'in a very contemptuous manner', went to the Cross Keys and played on the afternoon of the prohibition, as a result of which some of them were very properly bundled into jail, and the Privy Council tightened up the licensing regulations and the penalties for non-observance.

A year later the Admiral's were at the Theatre, where stubborn James Burbage was making himself more than usually difficult. Mrs. Brayne, the widow of his late partner, claimed that she was entitled to half the gallery profits, but when she came with her supporters to collect the money, Burbage, his wife and elder son Cuthbert met them with a stream of abuse, while his younger son Richard laid about him, paying one of them his half share with a broom-handle, and 'scornfully and disdainfullye playing with the nose' of another. This is the first mention of the actor, then aged twenty-two, who was soon to dispute with famous Ned Alleyn himself the claim to be the greatest player of the age, and to do for Shakespeare's plays what Alleyn was already doing for Marlowe's. In the following May his father was equally indelicate in his dealings with the Admiral's Men in the tiring-house of the Theatre when there was a dispute about the division of the takings, swearing 'by a great oathe' that he cared not for them, nor for the Lord Admiral himself, nor 'for three of the best lordes of them all'. After that, presumably, the Admiral's and Burbage parted company.

It seems that there was at this time some sort of alliance, or even amalgamation, of the Admiral's with Strange's, for at Court that winter Strange's were paid for plays and 'activities' which, according to the Privy Council warrant, were performed by the Admiral's. If so, it was probably the combined company that was at the Theatre earlier in the year, where they revived Tarlton's *Second Part of the Seven Deadly Sins*, the 'plot' of which, though not the play itself, has been preserved. A plot is an abstract of a play scene by scene, made by the prompter, or bookholder as he was called, who, like the Cornish 'ordinary', was responsible for the conduct of the performance, for the correct timing of music and stage-effects; above all, for getting the actors on to the stage when their cues came. The plot was written legibly in a large hand, mounted on pasteboard, and hung on a peg in the tiring-house, where the bookholder stood. Thus the first episode of *The Seven Deadly Sins*, depicting Envy in the person of Porrex, begins:

Enter King Gorboduk with Counsailers: R. Burbadg, Mr. Brian, Th. Goodale.
The Queene with Ferrex and Porrex and som attendaunts follow: Saunder, W. Sly, Harry, J. Duke, Kitt, R. Pallant.

Apart from the light that it throws on Elizabethan methods of production, the plot is important for its first mention of some of the actors in the Strange-Admiral company, many of whom were soon to be colleagues of Shakespeare: in addition to Burbage, Bryan and Sly are Thomas Pope, Augustine Phillips and Richard Cowley.

After their rupture with Burbage, the company found quarters at the Rose, which, however, owing to some breach of the regulations by Henslowe, was closed by order of the Privy Council, and they had to perform at the remote and unprofitable playhouse at Newington Butts. As a result, Henslowe and the Bankside watermen, who were badly hit by the loss of passengers across the river, petitioned the Council for the reopening of the Rose, as did the evicted company, 'forasmuche our Companie is greate, and thearbie our chardge intollerable in travellinge the Countrie, and the Contynuance thereof wilbe a meane to bringe vs to division and seperacion'. Perhaps Henslowe's misdemeanour had been the opening of his theatre on forbidden days, not only Sundays, but Thursdays as well, the day traditionally assigned to bear-baiting, for in July the Privy Council had complained about the non-observance of the order, 'to the greate hurte and destruction of the game of beare baytinge and lyke pastymes, which are maynteyned for her Majesty's pleasure', and they strictly enjoined the Lord Mayor and the Middlesex and Surrey justices to see that the regulations were enforced. But whatever the reason for the Council's displeasure, their hearts were softened by the laments of the watermen and the thought of the 'tediousnes of the waie' to Newington Butts, and the company was allowed to return to the Rose. That winter, 1591–2, 'Strange's' gave six performances at Court to the Queen's one.

In February they were again at the Rose, and Henslowe began his invaluable *Diary*, in which, in his highly imaginative spelling, he recorded the companies who performed, the names of the plays, and the amount of his receipts, occasionally adding the cryptic 'ne', meaning apparently that the play was new to his theatre. 'Strange's' began their tenancy on a Saturday with a performance of Greene's *Friar Bacon and Friar Bungay*:

In the name of god Amen 1591 [1592] beginge the 19 of Febreary my lord Stranges mene as ffoloweth:

Feb. 19	Fryer Bacune	xvii^s iij^d
21	Mulomurco [1]	xxix^s
22	Orlando [2]	xvj^s vj^d
23	Spanes comodye: Donne Oracoe [3]	xiij^s vj^d
24	Syr John Mandevell [4]	xii^s vj^d
25	Harey of Cornwall [5]	xxxij^s
26	the Jewe of Malltuse	l^s

[1] Probably Peele's *Battle of Alcazar*.   [2] Greene's *Orlando Furioso*.   [3] A lost play, not *The Spanish Tragedy*, despite Don Horatio, and called in the next entry 'Doneoracio'.   [4, 5] Lost plays.

and so on until the end of the season on June 23rd, with a fine dis-
regard for the order about not playing on Thursdays, and a consequent
diversion of the audience from the neighbouring Beargarden. They
played every day except Sundays, Good Friday and two other days, a
hundred and five performances in all, the lowest receipts, 7*s*., being
for a revival of Greene's and Lodge's *Looking Glass for London* on
Wednesday, March 7th, the highest for Shakespeare's *Harey the VI*
('ne'), which brought in £3 16*s*. 8*d*. on the Friday of the previous
week. The average for the whole series was £1 14*s*. 0*d*. It should be
observed that there was no such thing as a continuous run in the
Elizabethan theatre; the same play was rarely given twice in one week,
and as the season progressed new plays were added to the repertory,
so that Strange's presented twenty-three plays altogether. Of these the
most popular were 'Jeronymo' (*The Spanish Tragedy*), played every
week but two, that is thirteen times; *The Jew of Malta* (ten), 'the
second parte of Tamber came' (*Tamburlaine*), inserted as 'ne' on
April 28th (five); *Henry VI*, such a success that it was acted three
times in eight days, and fifteen times altogether; and 'Tittus &
Vespacia' (probably *Titus Andronicus*), a 'ne' play on April 11th,
after which it was repeated six times. Shakespeare, Marlowe,
Kyd—and the rest nowhere. Their five plays account for fifty
performances to packed audiences, half the total number, whereas
Greene's three plays were given only nine times altogether, and
to a half-empty theatre, *Orlando Furioso* being scrapped after its
first performance. We can understand why he wrote his *Groatsworth
of Wit*.

Yet the history of *Orlando Furioso* is an interesting one. It will be
remembered that Greene sold it to the Queen's Men when they were
on tour, and then sold another copy to the Admiral's. Perhaps the
play was taken off because the Queen's, not unreasonably, protested,
leaving the Admiral's to seek redress from Greene. The only Elizabethan actor's part to have survived is that of Orlando, found at
Dulwich. It undoubtedly belonged to Alleyn, and was probably made
for rehearsals for this performance when he was leading the Strange-
Admiral company at the Rose. Later in the year he married Henslowe's stepdaughter, Joan Woodward, and thereby cemented a partnership that was to prove one of the most powerful factors in the world of
the theatre.

The successful opening of the season at the Rose, coupled with the swelling flood of plays turned out by the new phenomenon, a group of professional dramatists, fluttered the London Corporation and started something like a panic in their breasts. On February 25th the Lord Mayor wrote to Whitgift, rehearsing the evils of public playing in the old familiar phrases, and imploring him to confer with the Master of the Revels with a view to the reforming and banishing out of the city (apparently the same thing) so great an evil. Whitgift was unhelpful, and could only suggest that certain 'consideration and other capitulations' should be made over to Tilney: in less euphemistic language, that the Master of the Revels should be bribed. The Lord Mayor thanked the Archbishop for his advice, and a committee was formed to treat with Tilney; but when it came to the point, the guilds decided that the payment of an annuity was a dangerous 'president and enovacion', and too great a charge to be shouldered at such a troublesome time. The matter was dropped, but events were soon to play into their hands. On the evening of Sunday, June 11th, there was a disorderly assembly of apprentices in Southwark, 'by occassion and pretence of their meeting at a play', and the Privy Council, fearing a renewal of the disturbance on Midsummer Day, ordered the closing of the theatres until Michaelmas. This is why Strange's run at the Rose was cut short on June 23rd, but it was Christmas not Michaelmas, December 29th not September 29th, before they were able to resume.

Plague descended on London in August, and rapidly grew worse. At the beginning of October the Lord Mayor's feast was cancelled, the Michaelmas law term was postponed, the sittings eventually being transferred to Hertford, and Elizabeth, on her return from an extended progress, moved to Hampton Court (a palace she disliked after having had small-pox there in 1562), where access was forbidden to suitors. There was no question of reopening the theatres, and the companies had to refurbish their drums and trumpets and wagons and take to the road as their fathers had done in the days before the permanent theatres, as strolling players whose chief reward was the welcome they received in the provincial towns. The Strange-Admiral company travelled from east to west of England, from Ipswich and Cambridge, where the 'Mayor's play' brought in 20s., as compared with Oxford's paltry 6s. 8d., to Coventry and Gloucester, but they were home by Christmas, when they gave three performances at Hampton Court, and on December 29th began another season at the Rose. Their repertory was the same as before, with the addition of two new plays, 'the Gelyous comodey', possibly *The Comedy of Errors*, and 'the tragedy of the Guyes', almost certainly Marlowe's *Massacre at Paris*.

The theatre season was, however, desperately brief. Plague deaths mounted again, and on January 28th the Privy Council inhibited 'all plaies, baiting of beares, bulls, bowling and any other like occasions to assemble any nombers of people together (preacheing and Devyne service at churches excepted)'. Most of the players, rather than face another ruinous exile in the country, hung about for some time in the hope that the outbreak would subside, but there was to be no break that year. At the end of April Sussex's set off for the north of England, Pembroke's were already on their way towards the Welsh marches, and on May 6th the Privy Council issued a warrant to Strange's, authorising them to exercise their quality anywhere outside the seven-mile limit, 'that they maie be in the better readines hereafter for her Majesty's service', the actors named being, 'Edward Allen, servaunt to the right honorable the Lord Highe Admiral, William Kemp, Thomas Pope, John Heminges, Augustine Phillipes and Georg Brian, being al one companie, servauntes to our verie good Lord the Lord Strainge'. This leaves little doubt as to Alleyn's leadership of a company composed almost entirely of Strange's men, though presumably the six players named are the sharers, and we know that one of Alleyn's boy actors was with him, as well as Thomas Downton, later of the Admiral's. Though travelling companies were kept to a minimum, there would be two or three more boys and hired men with them, one of whom may have been Shakespeare, though it is unlikely, as by this time we should expect him to be mentioned as a sharer, and in any event he would be more profitably employed in writing plays for his company, and for his own gratification seeing *Venus and Adonis* through the press. Richard Cowley joined them at Bristol in July, bringing with him a letter for Alleyn from his wife. Alleyn, who had been ill at Bath, replied to his 'good sweete mouse', giving her sound advice on how to avoid infection, returning a troublesome white waistcoat, telling her they were ready to begin the play of *Harry of Cornwall*, and asking for news of his garden. Henslowe wrote to assure him that his garden was in prime condition, his beans hedge-high and well codded, and at the end of September sent him news of Pembroke's, about whom Alleyn had been inquiring: 'they ar all at home and haue ben this v or sixe weackes, for they cane not saue ther charges with trauell as I heare & were fayne to pawne ther parell'. 'As I heare' is delicious. There was only one pawnbroker in the theatrical business, and that was Philip Henslowe. Pembroke's were not the only company to be broken by the plague.

Elizabeth spent most of the year 1593 in the country, at Nonsuch, Oatlands, Windsor, retiring to Hampton Court again at the beginning of December. There was only one play in the Revels of that sombre winter, given by her own players on Twelfth Night for the entertainment of certain Germans, Essex standing as usual beside the high throne of the Queen, who talked to him 'in sweet and favourable manner'. It was the swan-song of the Queen's Men, their last performance at Court. Bankrupted by the plague and outclassed by the combination of Strange's and the Admiral's under Alleyn, Elizabeth took no further interest in them. At the beginning of April 1594, they gave three or four performances at the Rose, then in May Henslowe records that he lent £15 to his rascally nephew Francis Henslowe, whom he had employed in his pawnbroking business, 'to lay downe for his share to the Quenes players when they broke & went into the contrey to playe'. They never returned to London, and the once proud company, which had had it all its own way in the eighties, declined into a troupe of provincial players.

There was an easing of the plague at Christmas, 1593, and on December 26th Sussex's began to play at the Rose with a repertory that included *Buckingham* and *Titus & Ondronicous* ('ne'), both of which were given to packed houses, and so successfully that they were repeated two days after their first performance. 'Buckingham' is probably Shakespeare's *Richard III*, and the other certainly his *Titus Andronicus*, possibly a revision of the 'Tittus & Vespacia' already given by Strange's. But plague closed in again, and on February 6th their season came to an end with a third performance of *Titus Andronicus*. Two months later they shared the Rose with the Queen's for the week in which it was open, one or the other company giving the anonymous *King Leir*, and then, like the Queen's, possibly with them, Sussex's disappeared into the obscurity of the provinces. Alleyn's company remained, without a serious rival, in possession of the field.

In the middle of May 'my lord Admeralls men' got in three days' playing at the Rose; then, after a last flicker, the plague died down, at least one theatre reopened, and Henslowe made another heading in his *Diary*:

In the name of god Amen begininge at Newington my Lord Admeralle men & my Lorde Chamberlen men As ffolowethe 1594

June	5		Heaster & Asheweros	viij^s
	6		the Jewe of Malta	x^s
	7		Andronicous	xij^s
	8		Cutlacke	xj^s
	10	ne	Bellendon	xvij^s
	11		Hamlet	viij^s
	12		Heaster	v^s
	13		the Tamynge of a Shrowe	ix
	14		Andronicous	vij^s
	15		the Jewe	iiij^s

This calls for some explanation. Lord Strange had succeeded to the Earldom of Derby on his father's death in September 1593, and until he himself died seven months later Strange's were strictly Derby's. The loss of Strange was a severe blow, for he had been a kindly and conscientious patron, both of his players and of poets. He was himself a writer of verse, and before the publication of *Colin Clout's Come Home Again* Spenser added a few lines lamenting his death:

> Amyntas, flower of shepherds' pride forlorn:
> He whilst he lived was the noblest swain
> That ever piped in an oaten quill;
> Both did he other, which could pipe maintain,
> And eke could pipe himself with passing skill.

In April, therefore, Strange's company had to look round for another patron, and were fortunate in finding one in Henry Carey, Lord Hunsdon, bluff, merry, full of strange oaths and ribaldry. They could scarcely have found a more likely man, for not only was he a first cousin of the Queen, the son of Mary Boleyn, Anne Boleyn's sister, but for the last nine years he had been Lord Chamberlain, master, therefore, of the Master of the Revels, and ultimately responsible for the Queen's entertainment and the conduct of the theatres. The only disadvantage was his age, for he was seventy that year. Strange's, or Derby's, then, were 'my Lorde Chamberlen men' when they began to play at the wretchedly inadequate and remote Newington theatre, now apparently Henslowe's, where even *The Jew of Malta* brought in only 4s. on a Saturday afternoon.

Their repertory is interesting and, except for *The Jew of Malta*, quite different from that of eighteen months before. *Titus Andronicus* had last been played by Sussex's, and here is the first mention of the original *Hamlet*, apparently not new to Henslowe in 1594, and of *The Taming of A Shrew*, the anonymous play that Shakespeare transformed, at just about this time, into *The Taming of The Shrew*. Indeed, the anything but accurate Henslowe may easily have confused the two, and *A Shrew* may be a slip for Shakespeare's *The Shrew*. On the other hand, *A Shrew* had just been published as a 'Pleasant Conceited Historie, sundry times acted by the Earle of Pembrook his seruants', and though it is tempting to think that Henslowe himself had snapped it up along with the wardrobe of the bankrupt company, it is more likely that they had sold it to a publisher.

A company's stock of plays, each bought outright from a dramatist for anything up to £10, was the most valuable part of their capital, and as there was no law of copyright they took all precautions to prevent the manuscripts getting into the hands of other companies or of the printer, rarely making more than one copy of a play, which was in the charge of the bookholder. But during the two disastrous years of plague there was much interchange of stock when companies combined and played together, as did Sussex's and the Queen's, Strange's and the Admiral's. This, of course, gave scope for much sharp-practice; one company might memorise and make a more or less accurate copy of a play that belonged to another, or even a single hired actor might do the same thing, with far less accuracy, and sell his mangled version to another company or to a publisher. Plays were not treated as serious literature, and on the whole it was the less reputable stationers who dealt in them. It is just possible that this is what happened to *The Shrew*; that the very inferior *A Shrew* issued in 1594 is a memorised, mangled and pirated version of Shakespeare's *The Shrew*, the correct text of which remained unpublished until the Folio of 1623. It is certainly what happened to *Henry VI*, Part 2, published in March 1594 by Thomas Millington, a stationer of very dubious reputation, as 'The First part of the Contention betwixt the two famous Houses of Yorke and Lancaster'. The text of this is so bad that it used to be considered the work of an inferior hand, which Shakespeare rewrote as 2 *Henry VI*, but it is now recognised as being a mutilated version of Shakespeare's play, memorised probably by an actor who had doubled the parts of Suffolk and

Cade, whose lines are relatively accurate. The same thing happened to 3 *Henry VI*, published by Millington in the following year as 'The true Tragedie of Richard Duke of Yorke'. As plays were normally printed in quarto form, these pirated editions are known as Bad Quartos, and four other plays of Shakespeare first appeared as Bad Quartos: *Romeo and Juliet, Henry V, The Merry Wives of Windsor* and *Hamlet*.

Of course, a company could always realise capital by selling a play, but as this was tantamount to giving it to their rivals, few plays were sold in normal times. But the plague years of 1592–4 were not normal times; the companies were driven to raise money by selling their stock, and in 1594 at least eighteen plays were published and ten more registered to be issued later. The Queen's sold seven, many of them Greene's; Sussex's and Pembroke's each sold three or four, and even Strange's and the Admiral's parted with one or two, but as plays had sometimes changed hands in a bewildering fashion, it is not always easy to tell who were the ultimate vendors. When, for example, *Titus Andronicus* was published early in 1594, it had already been played by 'the Earle of Darbie, Earle of Pembrooke, and Earle of Sussex their Seruants', and now, in June, it was being played at Newington by the Admiral's and Chamberlain's, the quondam Strange's-Derby's.

It is probable, however, that the two companies were now re-organised and virtually independent, and sharing the Newington theatre only because it was the first to be reopened on account of its isolation, for after June 15th all restrictions seem to have been lifted, and Henslowe, drawing a line across the page of his *Diary*, transported the Admiral's to the Rose, where receipts went up to the usual level, and *Titus Andronicus, Hamlet* and *The Taming of A Shrew* dropped out of their repertory, presumably because they belonged to the Chamberlain's. They, no doubt, went to the Theatre, where James Burbage would welcome them on account of his son Richard, now their leading tragedian, though in October Lord Hunsdon applied for more central winter-quarters for his company. Elizabeth was at Nonsuch, and it was from there that the Lord Chamberlain wrote to the Lord Mayor on October 8th:

Where my nowe companie of Players haue byn accustomed for the better exercise of their qualitie, & for the seruice of her Maiestie if need soe requier, to plaie this winter time within the Citye at the Crosse kayes in Gracious street. These are to requier & praye your Lo. (the time beinge such as, thankes be to god, there is nowe no danger of the sickness) to permitt & suffer them soe to doe; The which I praie you the rather to doe for that they haue vndertaken to me that, where heretofore they began not their Plaies till towardes fower a clock, they will now begin at two, & haue done betwene fower and fiue, and will not vse anie Drumes or trumpettes att all for the callinge of peopell together, and shalbe contributories to the poore of the parishe where they plaie accordinge to their habilities.

There can be no doubt that the request was granted, and for the next two untroubled years we must imagine the Chamberlain's playing at Burbage's Theatre in the spring and summer, and at the Cross Keys in winter, while the Admiral's, in no need of alternative winter-quarters, played under Alleyn at his father-in-law's Rose on the other side of the river. To our infinite loss, Burbage did not keep a diary like Henslowe, or if he did it has never been found, and we know comparatively little about the plays acted by the Chamberlain's. That winter, 1594–5, there were six performances at Court, three by the Chamberlain's, three by the Admiral's. The great rivalry had begun, and so far honours were even.

There is no evidence to show that Shakespeare was a member of Strange's before their reorganisation as the Chamberlain's; indeed, the fact that he is not mentioned in their licence to travel suggests that he was not. We know that he was an actor in the summer of 1592, when Greene wrote so bitterly of his tiger's heart and player's hide, and the gibe would have far more point, as well as pathos, if he were then an actor (an excellent one, too, according to Chettle) with the company to which Greene sold most of his plays, the Queen's. To the impecunious playwright the sight of the prosperous player stealing the plaudits of the audience, and making unlimited profits out of the lines that he himself had written, must have been gall indeed. There is, in fact, a fair case to be made for Shakespeare's having joined the Queen's as early as 1587. In that year they visited Stratford, and at least four of their early plays were rewritten, or used as sources, by Shakespeare: *The Famous Victories of Henry V*, *The Troublesome Reign of King John*, *The True Tragedy of Richard III* and *King Leir*. Though all is little more than surmise, the most likely reconstruction of these years seems to be that Shakespeare joined the Queen's before the death of Tarlton, to whom he paid tribute as Yorick in *Hamlet*— 'I knew him, Horatio: a fellow of infinite jest, of most excellent fancy'—then, being well established as a dramatist by 1592, spent the two plague years writing, perhaps in Stratford, and when the theatres reopened joined the newly constituted Chamberlain's company, to whom he sold his most recently written plays, *A* or *The Shrew*, recorded by Henslowe, possibly being one of them.

In any event, by the middle of 1594 Shakespeare was the author of at least half a dozen successful plays, most of them, as we should expect, resembling the work of his predecessors and masters, the University Wits. *Henry VI*, at least Parts 2 and 3, is full of the arrogant and furious rhetoric, humourless hyperbole and arid imagery of Marlowe, and written in verse dominated by a comparatively inflexible end-stopped line, indistinguishable from his. Gloucester in *Richard III* is a characteristically overreaching and overweening Marlovian villain, though with a most unMarlovian and quite Shakespearean sense of humour. Aaron in *Titus Andronicus* is less subtle, and the play owes more to *The Spanish Tragedy*, while some of the lush poetry might be mistaken for Peele's. Again, there is a good deal of Marlovian verse in *The Taming of the Shrew*, and more than a touch of Greene in the other early comedies, *The Comedy of Errors* and *The Two Gentlemen of Verona*. But the authentic Shakespearean note becomes progressively more assertive, from the Temple Garden scene in 1 *Henry VI* to the adorable Julia and the poetry of the unspeakable Proteus in *The Two Gentlemen*:

> For Orpheus' lute was strung with poets' sinews,
> Whose golden touch could soften steel and stones,
> Make tigers tame, and huge leviathans
> Forsake unsounded deeps to dance on sands.

The plague years had given Shakespeare time to write his two long poems, *Venus and Adonis* and *The Rape of Lucrece*, both of them carefully printed by Richard Field, the one in 1593, the other in 1594, and both of them dedicated to the Earl of Southampton, then aged twenty-one, and eager as Elizabeth for the flattering attention of poets. He was doubtless one of the 'divers of worship' known to Shakespeare, for the raw young man from Stratford must soon have been transformed by the company he kept in London; as an actor he would be acquainted with the Court and courtiers, as well as with the gallants and scholars of the Inns of Court; as a poet his friends and acquaintances would be among his peers and such patrons as Southampton, on the look-out for a cheaply earned immortality. There can have been few more liberal forms of education in the latter half of

Elizabeth's reign than the life of a successful actor-dramatist, and the poems reflect the social and literary sophistication that he had acquired. Yet, loaded as they are with all manner of fashionable devices, humanity and nature constantly break the surface of the wanton narrative and interminable competitive rhetoric; they are, we feel, the poems of a young man healthy both in mind and body. The same cannot be said of the work that presumably inspired them, the unfinished *Hero and Leander* of Marlowe. Here there is neither humanity nor nature; love is no more than a conquest, an assertion of power, and the couplets are even more heartless than the blank verse of the plays. Yet it is a splendid fragment, hard and bright and resonant as the best of Marlowe's poetry always is.

No doubt both Shakespeare and Marlowe were influenced by Harington's *Orlando Furioso*, one of the first Elizabethan translations of the Italian poets, published in 1591. John Harington was Elizabeth's godson, a young spark about Court, who obviously delighted in the romance and naughtiness of Ariosto's epic, and went to work with such gusto that his version is very unequal, and the *ottava rima*, which he was the first to use in English, sometimes sounds far more like *Don Juan* than a sixteenth-century Italian epic:

> Rogero at the first had surely thought
>   She was some image made of alabaster,
> Or of white marble, curiously wrought,
>   To show the skilful hand of some great master.
> But viewing nearer he was quickly taught
>   She had some parts that were not made of plaster;
>   Both that her eyes did shed such woeful tears,
>   And that the wind did wave her golden hairs.

But the work that set the fashion and the standard for all these narrative poems was *The Faerie Queene*, the first three books of which Spenser published in 1590, when on a visit to England. The poem was dedicated to Elizabeth, preceded by a cloud of sonnets to the most influential men in the country, and prefaced with a letter to Raleigh in which he explained the dark conceit of his continued allegory. His purpose was to fashion a gentleman in the twelve private moral virtues expounded by Aristotle, and to this end, like Homer, Virgil, Ariosto and Tasso, he chose a worthy hero, Prince Arthur, or Magnificence, whose quest was the Faery Queen, or Glory, and at the same time quite frankly the most excellent and glorious person of Elizabeth.

The second Booke
of the Faerie Queene.

Contayning

The Legend of Sir Guyon.
O R
Of Temperaunce.

Ight well I wote moſt mighty Soueraine,
That all this famous antique hiſtory,
Of ſome th'aboundance of an ydle braine
Will iudged be, and painted forgery,
Rather then matter of iuſt memory,
Sith none, that breatheth liuing aire, does know,
Where is that happy land of Faery,
Which I ſo much doe vaunt, yet no where ſhow,
But vouch antiquities, which no body can know.

But let that man with better ſence aduize,
That of the world leaſt part to vs is red:
And daily how through hardy enterprize,
Many great Regions are diſcouered,

Which

Each of the proposed twelve books was to be devoted to the adventures of a hero or heroine symbolising one of the Virtues, as, in the first three, the Red Cross knight is Holiness, Sir Guyon is Temperance and Britomartis Chastity. On this unpromising medieval foundation Spenser patiently constructed his moral epic, investing it, however, with all the trappings of romance, and adorning it with all the opulence of the Renaissance, a Hardwick Hall or Wollaton in verse. And what verse! The unit is the nine-lined stanza of Spenser's invention, formal yet infinitely adaptable, turning sinuously on itself in the middle, and falling or soaring at will in the extended, and always surprising, cadence of the last line. Within this framework Spenser weaves his grave incantatory music; there is little variation of the majestic planetary pace, no crisis, no tension; it is the least dramatic of poems, but it is the most musical long poem in our language. With such a stanza and such harmonies it is not surprising that the best episodes, ostensibly monitory, are those descriptive of a languorous and voluptuous beauty, and it was these that particularly enchanted young and amorous poets like Harington, Marlowe and Shakespeare. Gabriel Harvey dismissed his friend's epic as a fantastic trifle, but Spenser knew better; he retired again to Ireland to recapture his dreams, and three years later celebrated his marriage with Elizabeth Boyle in the magnificent *Epithalamion*, published in 1595 with the *Amoretti*, a sequence of sonnets addressed to his wife before their marriage.

Wyatt and Surrey had brought the sonnet form from Italy some forty years before, but the sonnet sequence, the record of a poet's meditation on love and life, a dreamlike fragment of autobiography, highly selective and distorted by enigmatic emphasis, omission and symbolism, was something new to England, but the first, Sidney's *Astrophel and Stella*, corruptly printed in 1591, was the forerunner of a score of sequences written or published in the course of the nineties. Shakespeare's was one of them, though it remained unpublished till 1609, and we can imagine him in his temporary retirement from the stage during the plague years, discarding the brazen line of Marlowe and evolving his own princely lyrical measure, traces of which are to be found even among the wastes of 3 *Henry VI*:

> See how the morning opes her golden gates,
> And takes her farewell of the glorious sun!
> How well resembles it the prime of youth,
> Trimm'd like a vounker, prancing to his love!

It is possible that the young man to whom the sonnets were addressed
was the Earl of Southampton, for whom he was then writing *Venus
and Adonis*; we should like to know, but it is no great matter in
comparison with the sonnets themselves, in which each phrase seems
to enter to a flourish and even an elegiac theme is transformed by the
triumphant labials into something in the nature of a pæan. Drayton
occasionally achieves an almost comparable splendour in his sonnets to
Idea, as in the passionate, 'Since there's no help, come let us kiss and
part', but next to Shakespeare's the finest sequence is Daniel's *Delia*,
dedicated to Sidney's sister, the Countess of Pembroke, to whose twelve-
year-old son, William Herbert, he was then tutor. No praise could be
too high for the sonnet beginning, 'My cares draw on my everlasting
night', and 'Shakespearean' is not too proud a boast for number forty-
six, with its opening reference to *The Faerie Queene* and its archaic
diction:

> Let others sing of knights and paladins
> In aged accents and untimely words;
> Paint shadows in imaginary lines,
> Which well the reach of their high wits records . . .

Henry Constable's *Diana* (1592) is good average work, but the gulf
between the average and Shakespeare may be judged by comparing a
sonnet of Constable's with what Shakespeare made of the same theme:

> Miracle of the world! I never will deny
>   That former poets praise the beauty of their days;
>   But all those beauties were but figures of thy praise,
> And all those poets did of thee but prophesy.
> Thy coming to the world hath taught us to descry
>   What Petrarch's Laura meant, for truth the lip bewrays.
>   Lo! why th' Italians, yet which never saw thy rays,
> To find out Petrarch's sense such forged glosses try.
> The beauties, which he in a veil enclosed beheld,
>   But revelations were within his secret heart,
> By which in parables thy coming he foretold;
>   His songs were hymns of thee, which only now before
>   Thy image should be sung; for thou that goddess art,
>   Which only we without idolatry adore.

> When in the chronicle of wasted time
> I see descriptions of the fairest wights,
> And beauty making beautiful old rhyme
> In praise of ladies dead, and lovely knights;
> Then, in the blazon of sweet beauty's best,

Of hand, of foot, of lip, of eye, of brow,
I see their antique pen would have express'd
Even such a beauty as you master now.
So all their praises were but prophecies
Of this our time, all you prefiguring;
And, for they look'd but with divining eyes,
They had not skill enough your worth to sing:
    For we, which now behold these present days,
    Have eyes to wonder, but lack tongues to praise.

One of the most influential and noble prose works of the reign was published at this time, the first four books of *The Laws of Ecclesiastical Polity*, by Richard Hooker, sometime Master of the Temple, an eminent scholar, but the least pedantic of humanists. Wearied by the incessant jars and janglings in religion, he sympathetically reviews the Puritan position, without a trace of rancour demolishes their defences, and then, basing his argument on natural law and the Aristotelian doctrine that different circumstances demand different kinds of organisation, develops his great apologia for the Anglican Church. After the thin and tinkling euphuism of the period, it is a joy to read his sonorous and adult prose, which has just enough artifice of manner to enforce and emphasise the matter: 'If the frame of that heavenly arch erected over our heads should loosen and dissolve itself; if celestial spheres should forget their wonted motions, and by irregular volubility turn themselves any way as it might happen . . . what would become of man himself, whom these things now do all serve? See we not plainly that obedience of creatures unto the law of nature is the stay of the whole world?' Shakespeare must have read this passage with delight, and Exeter in *Henry V*, Hamlet and Odysseus all say much the same thing.

But 'the most influential writer in the age of Shakespeare, if it were not Foxe the Martyrologist, was Hakluyt, author of *The Principall Navigations, Voiages and Discoveries of the English Nation*'. The words are G. M. Trevelyan's, yet they are in one way misleading, for Hakluyt was primarily editor and compiler of the book, rightly preferring to let the seamen tell their own stories, however badly at times. It was published at exactly the right moment, in the year after the Armada, and we have only to read the dedicatory epistle to Walsingham to recapture something of the unalloyed excitement felt by the Elizabethans at the prospect of unlimited adventure and expansion after the defeat of Spain: 'Which of the kings of this land before her Majesty, had their banners ever seen in the Caspian Sea? Which of them hath ever dealt with the Emperor of Persia?', and there follows a recital of seas and cities, high-sounding and enchanting as those in *Tamburlaine*, where liegers now represented Elizabeth, English merchants traded and their ships repassed and anchored. The book was so much in demand that in 1598 Hakluyt reissued it in three volumes, containing much new matter, including James Lancaster's account of his voyage to the East Indies, whence he returned in the spring of 1594 with only twenty-five of his original company. Lancaster was the first English captain to reach the Indies by the Cape route, and his expedition, despite his desperate losses, was the prelude to the East India Company, founded a few years later. Another narrative in the second edition was Raleigh's *Report* of the last fight of the *Revenge*, when in August 1591, Sir Richard Grenville engaged a Spanish fleet of fifty-three sail for fifteen hours, until the masts were 'all beaten overboard, all her tackle cut asunder, her upperwork altogether razed, and in effect evened she was with the water, but the very foundation or bottom of a ship, nothing being left overhead either for flight or defence'. Grenville was a proud and grasping man, but his last heroic action transformed him into the sea-counterpart of Sidney, a legendary figure who finding 'none other to compare withal in his life, strived through a virtuous envy to exceed it in his death'.

Raleigh wrote his *Report* soon after the news was received in England, but a few months later he was in disgrace. The Queen discovered that he had committed the unpardonable offence of seducing Elizabeth Throckmorton, one of her Maids of Honour, for whose safety and good name she was personally responsible. John Aubrey relates an amusing, though apocryphal story that the blue-eyed maid surrendered to the imperious Captain of the Guard to a twitter of 'Nay, sweet Sir Walter! Sweet Sir Walter! Switter Swatter! Switter Swatter!' However that may be, surrender she did, and both were confined in the Tower, where they were married, a union that was to prove a singularly happy one. Raleigh appealed to the Queen for pardon, comparing her not only to Diana and Venus, but also, despite her sixty years and her sex, to Alexander and Orpheus, but though he was released to superintend the distribution of plunder from a Portuguese carrack that he had captured, he had to retire from Court to his estate at Sherborne. Raleigh's disgrace and Marlowe's

death ended the fellowship of the School of Atheism, or School of
Night, which may be referred to by Chapman, one of the coterie, in
his first published poem, the cryptic and cloudy *Shadow of Night*, and
glanced at by Shakespeare in *Love's Labour's Lost*:

> Black is the badge of hell,
> The hue of dungeons and the school of night.

And Raleigh's disgrace removed the most dangerous of Essex's rivals
from Court.

There remained tall, brown-haired, sweet-faced and bashful
Charles Blount, with whom Essex had once quarrelled. Elizabeth had
given him a queen from her golden chessmen, and next day he appeared with it bound to his sleeve with a crimson ribbon. 'Now I
perceive', Essex scoffed, 'that every fool must have a favour'. There
was a duel in which Essex was disarmed and wounded. 'By God's
death', exclaimed Elizabeth, 'it was fit that someone or other should
take him down, and teach him better manners; otherwise there will
be no rule with him'. She was right. But the rivals were soon reconciled, for Blount became the lover of Essex's sister Penelope, Lady
Rich, Sidney's Stella, and at about the same time Essex married
Sidney's widow, Frances Walsingham. Elizabeth was very angry at
this defection, and even angrier when he sailed, against her express
command, with Drake and Norris on the Portugal expedition. However, the quarrel was made up, the hot-headed earl restored to favour,
and after earnest entreaties Elizabeth at last succumbed, though not
without profound misgivings, to his entreaty to be given the command of a force sent to help Henry IV of France. A Spanish army had
landed in Brittany and overrun Normandy in support of the Catholic
League, and Elizabeth could not afford to let northern France become another Netherlands, a base for another Armada and attempted
invasion of England. She agreed to help the shifty, penniless and plau-
sible Henry to capture Rouen, and in August 1591 Essex landed in
France with a force of four thousand men. There he played at soldiers, took part in a leaping match with Henry and his nobles, had to be
rescued by his men from one escapade, lost his brother in another and
fatuously challenged the governor of Rouen to single combat. Henry
could no more pay the English army than his own mutinous troops,
and in January Elizabeth recalled Essex, leaving the command to a
less romantic and impetuous head, and more competent hands.

Before he left his ruinous enterprise Essex had the audacity to abuse his commander's privilege by knighting twenty-four of his officers, a useful nucleus if ever he should stand in need of support in England. In the following year, to the disgust of Elizabeth, Henry IV decided that Paris was worth a Mass, and embraced the Catholic faith. She had spent £300,000 in helping a renegade to the throne of France.

When Essex returned he found Raleigh on his way to the Tower, but Robert Cecil he found on the way to the highest office of all. While he had been abroad Elizabeth had advanced the thirty-year-old hunchback to the Privy Council, and though she had not yet given her 'Pigmy' the title of Secretary, he filled Walsingham's place, and it could only be a matter of time, and no very long time, before he stepped into his father's shoes. Raleigh had been a rival for the position of first favourite, but the upstart courtier could never have been a rival for the position of first subject, perhaps of an even higher place than that; for if Burghley was over seventy, Elizabeth was only ten years younger, and there was still no acknowledged heir to the throne. Cecil, however, was a different matter; he was both a rival and an obstacle. And this, on a rather lower level of aspiration, was what Cecil's cousins, Anthony and Francis Bacon, found him to be. It was not long before the brilliant brothers, the delicate Anthony, with an unrivalled knowledge of foreign affairs, and Francis, all intellect, were installed in Essex House in the Strand—still called Leicester House in Norden's exquisite map of Westminster issued in this year—organising an unofficial intelligence service that would rival the Queen's. The Cecils were to be challenged on their own ground. Elizabeth was impressed by Essex's knowledge of foreign affairs, and in 1593 admitted him to the Privy Council, where, with the Bacons and their fine-spun network of intelligence behind him, he became almost another Foreign Secretary, courted by ambassadors. Anthony was content to be the power behind the earl, the spider at the centre of the web, but the frigid Francis coveted a more outward honour. The Attorney-Generalship opportunely fell vacant and Essex vehemently pressed the claims of his supporter, while Burghley counselled the appointment of the Solicitor-General, Edward Coke. It was an open struggle for power between the rival factions, and Essex threatened Cecil, 'whosoever getteth this office out of my hands for any other, before he have it, it shall cost him the coming by'. Elizabeth appointed Coke. It was a bitter blow, but the Solicitor-Generalship remained, and she could scarcely refuse Bacon that office. Again Essex pressed his suit, and Elizabeth appointed Thomas Fleming, Recorder of London. Essex could be in no doubt as to how it was. Much as she liked him, the Queen was not going to pack her offices with Essex's supporters. Bacon, too, saw how matters stood, and when Essex generously consoled him with a gift of land, warned him that he could be no more his than he was already, for his first duty was to the Queen. It was a discreet acceptance, for Elizabeth was still mistress in her own house, however much the Commons might be muttering about liberty of speech, as she had just proved by sending to the Tower old indomitable Peter Wentworth, who had dared to raise the question of the succession in Parliament, and had even considered approaching Essex on the subject.

So matters stood in the summer of 1594, after two years of plague; the arrogant, impulsive Essex, competing for power with the urbane and submissive Burghley and his hunchback son; the ageing Gloriana's spoiled Adonis ranged against her old and gouty Sprite and her puny Pigmy. In the world of the theatre there was rivalry, too, though of a more friendly and less dangerous nature; the Admiral's company under Alleyn, comfortably quartered at Henslowe's renovated Rose on the Bankside, competing for the favour of London's citizens and of the Queen with the Lord Chamberlain's servants at James Burbage's antiquated Theatre in Shoreditch, where his son Richard was playing the lead in Shakespeare's histories. There were no other rivals, for they were the only London companies of any importance to survive the plague, and even the boys at Blackfriars were silenced. Nor, by 1594, was there any serious rival left to Shakespeare. Of the *Pléiade* of poets who had carried through the first stage of the dramatic revolution in the six wonderful years after the defeat of the Armada, Greene and Marlowe were dead; Kyd died in destitution and disgrace before the end of the year; Lyly had written his last play; so too had Peele, a sick man, who died two years later; and so had Lodge, back from South America, to turn Catholic and physician and write no more for the stage. Nashe, not really a dramatist, was to have one last fling.

Shakespeare, aged thirty, and by now almost certainly one of the Chamberlain's Men, had no immediate rival. But Ben Jonson, recently returned from conscript service in the Netherlands, was out of his bricklayer's apprenticeship, and married in November. He was twenty-two.

VI

1594–1597

THE CHAMBERLAIN'S AND ADMIRAL'S

SURFEITED at last by its 20,000 victims, the plague lay dormant, and there were no further visitations during Elizabeth's reign. But plague was followed by dearth, and continued dearth meant something approaching famine in days when there were no appreciable reserves of food and few facilities for importation. The summer of 1594 was cold and wet, and those of the two following years little better, so that the green corn 'rotted ere his youth attained a beard, and the fold stood empty in the drowned field'. Prices rose, and those who had escaped death by plague at home and by battle abroad were threatened with starvation. The war with Spain, now ten years old, had lost its popularity, and Burghley was ready to make an honourable peace. Not so Essex, however, who knew that peace would reduce him to relative insignificance. War was his province, or so he thought; on war depended his fortunes and his favours, and he cast about to re-inflame the smouldering passions of his countrymen. His eye fell on the unfortunate Dr. Lopez, and he wrote to Anthony Bacon: 'I have discovered a most dangerous and desperate treason. The point of conspiracy was her Majesty's death. The executioner should have been Dr. Lopez; the manner poison.'

Dr. Lopez was a distinguished Portuguese Jew, naturalised and a Christian, who had been physician to Leicester and Walsingham, and for the last ten years chief physician to the Queen herself. But he had offended Essex by speaking indiscreetly of his ailments, and of 'some other things that did disparage his honour'. Cecil questioned him, but could find no grounds for suspicion, and, eager to discredit his rival, told the Queen that Essex was mistaken. Angered by his apparently malicious attack, she rated Essex soundly in Sir Robert's presence. Essex, too, was angry, and shut himself in his room. After two days of brooding he emerged; it was to be another struggle between him and the Cecils, the prize Dr. Lopez. This time Essex won. There can be little doubt that Lopez was innocent of any plot against the Queen, though, bribed by Philip of Spain, he may have been implicated in some conspiracy against the Portuguese pretender, Don Antonio. Witnesses under torture informed against him, and after weeks of questioning the old man broke down and agreed to anything his tormentors cared to accuse him of. On June 7th he was taken to Tyburn, where his dying speech, that he loved his Queen as he loved Christ, was drowned in laughter, and he was hanged, disembowelled and quartered to the mockery of the assembled mob. Essex had won; he had vindicated his honour, defeated his rivals and roused a new frenzy of hatred against Spain, and incidentally against the Jews. That week Henslowe put on two performances of *The Jew of Malta*; but Shakespeare was more merciful, and gently satirised his countrymen by treating Shylock more sympathetically than the priggish Portia and the rest of the Christian Jew-baiters.

It was, then, in the middle of a dreary English June, when passions were newly inflamed against Spain, that the reorganised Chamberlain's company assembled at the Theatre, where they were welcomed with open arms by old James Burbage, himself one of Lord Hunsdon's men in the old days, and by his elder son Cuthbert, now virtually in charge of the business, for two years without tenants had hit them hard. But now the plague was over, and with it the lean days of playing in the provinces, a wet summer might well mean good business in London, and there can be no doubt that all were in jubilant mood, both theatre managers and players.

There were eight partners, or 'sharers', in the company; sharers, that is, of the profits after half the gallery takings had been paid to the Burbages as rent. Of these, at least six had been with Strange's under Alleyn's leadership on the tour from which they had just returned. There was Will Kempe, Tarlton's pupil, or as Nashe inimitably has it, 'that most Comicall and conceited Caualeire Monsieur du Kempe, Jester monger and Vice-gerent generall to the Ghost of Dicke Tarlton'. After entertaining Leicester in the Netherlands, he had made his way to Denmark, and then joined Strange's, with whom in June 1592, just before plague closed the theatres, he performed in the immensely popular *A Knack to Know a Knave*. It was one of the plays published in 1594, and contains a scene of 'Kemps applauded Merrimentes of the men of Goteham', a dull anticipation of Dogberry, whose part he later took, as well as Peter in *Romeo and Juliet*. Kempe's comedy was broad and crude, but he excelled at a jig, the song and dance, often bawdy, with which comedies and even tragedies were generally brought to a riotous conclusion. Probably the most popular actor of the day, even Elizabeth delighted in his foolery. Thomas Pope and George Bryan had also been in Denmark. Pope was another comedian and an acrobat, coupled with John Singer of the Admiral's in the lines:

> what meanes Singer then,
> And Pope, the clowne, to speak so borish, when
> They counterfaite the clownes upon the stage?

Bryan, like Pope, had played in *The Seven Deadly Sins*, apparently more serious parts, but there is no record of his performances with the Chamberlain's, whom he soon left for a post at Court as Groom of the Chamber. Richard Cowley seems to have been an actor of no great distinction, for, although he stayed with the company for twenty-five years, little is known of him beyond his playing Verges to Kempe's Dogberry in *Much Ado*. We should like to know more about Augustine Phillips, apparently the most loyal of colleagues, and a particular friend of Shakespeare, to whom no doubt he was endeared by being a musician, a useful accomplishment for an actor in those days. Not above writing jigs, he published 'Phillips his gygg of the slyppers', but it is as a player of graver and more stately parts than Kempe that we imagine him. The business manager of the company was John Heminge, a Droitwich man aged about thirty-five, with a formidably proliferating family, one member of which was to cause him trouble in later years. If Malone is correct in saying that he created the part of Falstaff, we have some idea of the kind of part he played. He, too, was a friend of Shakespeare, perhaps quite an old friend in 1594, for there is some reason to think that he also began his acting career with the Queen's.

The other two sharers, neither of whom appears to have travelled with the Alleyn company, were acquisitions beyond price, the two who transformed an ordinary troupe of players into a legendary fellowship. The Admiral's had lost Richard Burbage after their quarrel with his father, and now, aged twenty-six, he was the most accomplished tragedian of his day, for whereas Alleyn's greatest parts were Marlowe's ranting heroes, who could have no successors, he was interpreting far subtler characters whose line was just beginning, the characters of Shakespeare, the eighth member of the company.

There were two or three boys, such as Samuel Gilburne, apprenticed to Phillips, carefully trained to play women's parts, and a number of 'hirelings', adult actors employed by the sharers. John Sincler was one of these, a wafer of a man for whom Shakespeare created a number of small parts: the diminutive Beadle in 2 *Henry IV*, Shadow in the same play, thin as the edge of a penknife, and the Apothecary in *Romeo and Juliet*. More important were William Sly and Henry Condell. Sly, whose portrait is preserved at Dulwich College, seems to have been an actor of more than common merit and became a sharer when Bryan left the company. Shortly afterwards Condell succeeded Pope. He is imperishably associated with Heminge, for not only were they neighbours in St. Mary Alderman-bury, friendly rivals in philoprogenitiveness and fellow officers in the parish church, but they were the longest lived of the original fellow-ship, the only two who remained to edit the collected edition of Shake-speare's plays. Shakespeare, Burbage, Heminge and Condell were the four cornerstones on which were founded the fortunes of the company that assembled at the Theatre on that June day of 1594.

What sort of an actor Shakespeare was we do not know, though it is difficult to imagine that accomplished man being an indifferent one. But it was not as an actor that the Chamberlain's Men so eagerly welcomed him. He arrived with a great reputation, as the author of half a dozen very successful plays and, now that Marlowe, Greene and Kyd were gone, a dramatist without a rival in the country. During the plague years he had had time to write his two poems for Southampton: *Venus and Adonis* had just been reprinted, and to the recently published *Lucrece* there was a flattering reference in *Willobie his Avisa*, a strangely cryptic poem in which Henry Willobie's 'familiar friend W. S.' might be Shakespeare himself. In a period when the public theatres were closed, it was only natural that he should write for his patron, and it is possible that *Love's Labour's Lost* was commissioned for private performance at Titchfield, Southampton's Hampshire home. *The Comedy of Errors*, too, had been written for the private stage, so that he had at least two plays new to the public theatre to offer the Chamberlain's, possibly four, for *Richard III* might still have been unperformed, and *The Two Gentlemen of Verona* recently written.

The Comedy of Errors may have been one of the two plays presented at Court by the Chamberlain's on December 26th and 27th. It was certainly the play that they performed on the following night at

Gray's Inn, a particularly riotous Grand Night, when the Lord of Misrule lost all control over his subjects, who so offended their guests from the Inner Temple that they withdrew. It is tempting to try to reconstruct the performance; the hall thronged with disorderly revellers; the stage set with three 'houses'; the cast: Shakespeare as Solinus, Heminge as Aegeon, Burbage and Phillips as the Antipholus twins, Kempe and Pope clowning the Dromios, a part for Sincler as Pinch, 'a mere anatomy, a living dead man', and so on, late into the night that was ever afterwards called 'The Night of Errors'. In March the Chamberlain's were paid for their Court performances, the payees being 'Willm Kempe, Willm Shakespeare & Richarde Burbage'. On the same day 'Edwarde Allen, Richarde Jones & John Synger' received payment for the plays that the Admiral's had presented.

It had been an astute move on the part of Heminge to persuade Shakespeare to join their company. They now had their own dramatist on whom they could rely to produce at least two popular and profitable plays a year, which, as they accumulated, would very nearly fill their repertory. Moreover, they would almost certainly be acceptable to the Master of the Revels and the Queen, and a Court performance was worth four or five full houses in a public theatre. Shakespeare did not disappoint them. After joining the fellowship he wrote for no other company, and in the course of the next sixteen years gave them more than thirty plays. But if they were expecting him to repeat his former triumphs in the manner of Marlowe and Kyd, they were, if not disappointed, at least surprised. *Venus and Adonis* and *Lucrece* had opened up a fabulous lyrical vein, further developed in the sonnets that he was then writing under a compulsive excitement, and it was this precious lyrical poetry, peculiarly his and owing nothing to Marlowe and the rest of the University Wits, that he poured prodigally into the plays of this period. Rhyme, too, flows over into the plays, not only couplets, but the formal stanza of *Venus and Adonis*, and even the sonnet is curiously carved into dramatic dialogue. Then, the first of the matchless lyrics, 'Who is Silvia?' appears in *The Two Gentlemen of Verona*.

Perhaps Shakespeare was inspired partly by the music of his friend Thomas Morley, who published a number of madrigals, canzonets and ballets at this period, following them up with his invaluable *Plaine and Easie Introduction to Practicall Musicke*. The nineties were the great decade of Elizabethan secular music, particularly of vocal music, since the recent introduction of the madrigal, and to be able to sing a part at sight was now a necessary social accomplishment, at least according to the not disinterested Morley, who describes the plight of the wretched Philomathes at a party: 'Supper being ended, and Musicke bookes, according to the custome being brought to the table, the mistresse of the house presented mee with a part, earnestly requesting mee to sing. But when, after manie excuses, I protested unfainedly that I could not, everie one began to wonder. Yea some whispered to others, demaunding how I was brought up.' In the same year as Morley's *Introduction*, Dowland published his *First Book of Songs*, and Weelkes his *Madrigals*, one of which was his setting of Richard Barnfield's 'My flocks feed not', attributed to Shakespeare in *The Passionate Pilgrim*, two years later. Barnfield was an ardent young poet of chameleon-like quality, whose three books of verse were all published in the middle nineties. He was the first to imitate the stanza of *The Faerie Queene*, and his sonnet 'To his friend Maister R. L.' is a confession of his love for Spenser, as well as an admirable illustration of the Elizabethan view that poetry and music are inseparably linked, a relationship that was for so long to be forgotten:

> If Musique and sweet Poetrie agree,
> As they must needes (the Sister and the Brother),
> Then must the Love be great twixt thee and me,
> Because thou lov'st the one, and I the other.
> Dowland to thee is deare; whose heavenly tuch
> Upon the Lute doeth ravish humaine sense;
> Spenser to mee; whose deep Conceit is such,
> As, passing all Conceit, needs no defence.
> Thou lov'st to heare the sweete melodious sound,
> That Phœbus Lute (the Queen of Musique) makes:
> And I in deepe Delight am chiefly drownd,
> When as himselfe to singing he betakes.
>   One God is God of Both (as Poets faigne),
>   One Knight loves Both, and Both in thee remaine.

There is a Shakespearean quality about that, and after Spenser, Barnfield's next love was Shakespeare. *The Affectionate Shepherd*, the preposterous and sugary 'complaint of Daphnis for the love of Ganymede', was inspired by *Venus and Adonis*, and in his last work he celebrates the poet whose *Venus* and *Lucrece* had placed his name in Fame's immortal book, a statement of doubtful validity, for if

Shakespeare had written only those two poems he would to-day be scarcely more remembered than Barnfield himself. He makes no mention of the plays that had followed in the course of the next three years: *The Two Gentlemen of Verona, Love's Labour's Lost, Romeo and Juliet, Richard II, A Midsummer Night's Dream, King John, The Merchant of Venice.* There indeed was immortality. And there indeed was a challenge to the Admiral's!

If we look at Henslowe's list of new plays at the Rose during the same period, 1594–7, we shall find scarcely one that has escaped oblivion; *Galiaso, Philipo and Hippolito, The Merchant of Emden* and the rest, where are they now? Virtually the only plays in their repertory to have survived are the five tragedies of Marlowe, revived again and again in a vain attempt to compete in quality with the Chamberlain's. But if they could not emulate their quality, they could at least outrival them in quantity, and fifty-five new plays were added to their stock at the rate of one a fortnight, a big strain on their finances, which they were able to bear only by a modification of their organisation. Gradually Henslowe, in partnership presumably with Alleyn, began to take over the management of the Admiral's, financing the buying of their properties and plays, advancing loans to the actors, both corporately and individually, eventually even binding them to himself by contract. He made desperate attempts to find new and promising dramatists from whom he commissioned work, needy hack-writers were pressed into service to refurbish or 'dress' old and dated plays, and again he got them into his clutches by advancing money and making them sign away their freedom. His fully developed system was one of mass production with carefully planned division of labour, whereby as many as five dramatists worked at one play, each concentrating on the part at which he excelled. It was sweated labour in the Henslowe workshop, for he was a hard, though not a heartless, taskmaster; but at least it meant a certain market and prompt and regular payment, with an occasional bonus, for impecunious playwrights. And the system worked. Plays were turned out with factory-like precision, a little loose in the joints perhaps, and because of this rapid and efficient production they were cheap, highly competitive commodities, good enough for the groundlings, that could be retitivated or discarded when they failed to fill the theatre. The Admiral's was Henslowe's company in all but name.

One of Henslowe's first recruits was Thomas Heywood, a young

Lincolnshire man recently down from Cambridge, and, like Shakespeare, an actor-dramatist. In October 1596 Henslowe made a payment 'for Hawodes booke', perhaps the first of the two hundred and twenty plays in which, forty years later, Heywood claimed to 'have had either an entire hand, or at the least a maine finger'. Chapman, deprived of Raleigh's patronage and finding little profit in the writing of obscure and windy poems, also entered Henslowe's service, and in February 1596 the Admiral's produced his *Blind Beggar of Alexandria*, a worthless but nevertheless successful piece, which he followed up with *A Humorous Day's Mirth.* This again was well received, but the delicate and fastidious scholar John Chamberlain wrote to young Dudley Carleton: 'We have here a new play of humors in very great request, and I was drawne along to it by the common applause, but my opinion of it is (as the fellow saide of the shearing of hogges) that there was a great crie for so little wolle.' Chapman was better employed at this time in completing Marlowe's fragmentary *Hero and Leander*, a splendid and sympathetic piece of narrative writing in which his recently acquired dramatic experience stood him in good stead. A less distinguished member of the Henslowe workshop was the egregious Anthony Munday, who had been rewarded for his political services as anti-Catholic spy and informer with the post of Messenger of the Chamber, a perennial source of merriment and derision to his fellow dramatists. His *John a Kent*, written perhaps as early as 1590 and produced by the Admiral's in December 1594, is important, not for any literary merit, but because it is one of the few extant manuscript plays in the hand of its author. Moreover, its wrapper is one of the leaves of a medieval breviary used also as a cover for *Sir Thomas More.*

This is another manuscript play, apparently a typical product of the Henslowe workshop, written by Munday, Chettle and Heywood, censored by the Master of the Revels, and returned for alteration. One of the additions made in the revision, 147 lines in which More pacifies the anti-alien riots of 1517, is written in a hand and in a style that are claimed as Shakespeare's. But the evidence is slight—the only known writing of Shakespeare for comparison is his six signatures made towards the end of his life—and if the verse is his, the technique seems later than 1594. In any event, it is most improbable that the play was written earlier than 1594, for Henslowe's organised collaboration developed only in the settled period succeeding the plague, and it is even more improbable that Shakespeare helped to revise an Admiral's play once he was a member of the Chamberlain's. *Sir Thomas More* is invaluable as an example of one of Henslowe's plays in the making, but unfortunately it is most unlikely that Shakespeare had anything to do with it.

Munday was scarcely a match for Shakespeare and, despite the acquisition of Chapman and Heywood, the Admiral's lost ground to their rivals. In the winter of 1595–6 they gave four Court performances to the Chamberlain's five, but in the following year they were completely eclipsed, the Chamberlain's giving all six plays presented in the course of the Revels. To make matters worse, Henslowe was threatened with a rival on the south bank. Some years before, Francis Langley, a London goldsmith, had bought the Manor of Paris Garden, at the western end of the Bankside, and soon after the reopening of the theatres decided to build a playhouse of his own. Of course the London Corporation protested, and in November 1594 the Lord Mayor wrote to Burghley, 'I vnderstand that one Francis Langley intendeth to erect a niew stage or Theater (as they call it) for thexercising of plays vpon the Banck side. And forasmuch as wee fynd by daily experience the great inconuenience that groweth to this Citie & the government thearof by the sayed playes', and so on and so on, 'vnchast fables, lascivious divises, shifts of cozenage . . . theeues horsestealers, whoremoongers, coozeners, connycatching persones, practizers of treason . . .'; all the old arguments and terms of abuse were there. Burghley however refused to intervene, Langley prepared to build, and Henslowe hastened to make improvements to the Rose, so that it might compete with the projected Swan and its new devices. It was only three years since, just before plague closed the theatres, that he had spent over £100 in repairs, painting the stage, ceiling of 'my lords rome' and 'the rome ouer the tyerhowsse', and making a 'penthowsse shed at the tyeringe howsse doore'; now he spent as much again in painting, 'doinge it abowt with ealme bordes', and, a month or two later, 'mackinge the throne in the heuenes'. Perhaps he had got wind of this projected contrivance at the Swan, and anticipated Langley's plan, so ridding the stage of that cumbersome traditional property, which could now be lowered and raised at will, though according to the impatient realist Jonson it was a clumsy, creaking and childish procedure, as we may well believe.

This opportune assumption of the throne and removal of its steps, at least as a permanent feature, made room for considerable refinements of staging. It has generally been assumed that the Elizabethan theatre had an 'inner' stage, a curtained alcove in the tiring-house wall, with a similar recessed 'upper' stage above it on the level of the middle gallery. There is no evidence for this; besides, players and properties within such recesses would be invisible to an appreciable proportion of the audience. It has already been suggested that in the early theatres action 'above' took place either on the pulpit where the throne stood *in front* of the upper entry, in which case the apron stage would be 'below', or on the apron when 'below' was in the yard, as when in 1 *Henry VI* the French 'leap over the walls', jumping into the yard from one side of the stage while the English scale the other. This was admirable for scenes of violent action and in keeping with the circus-like tradition of the theatre, but the convention was a somewhat primitive one for the subtler and quieter action of the plays of the middle nineties. It was now, perhaps, that Henslowe supported the pulpit, on to which the throne could be lowered, by pillars about which curtains could be drawn to form an inner stage below, and *in front* of the tiring-house. He would thus have a small open 'upper' stage or terrace, railed for safety, and a lower one in which the scene could be 'discovered' by drawing the curtains, as in the medieval 'houses', of which it was merely an ingenious elaboration.

These important changes made possible another revolutionary innovation. There was no longer the same need for action in the yard, for with the large open apron and small supplementary stages action 'above' and 'within' could more easily and effectively be represented than by the old conventions, and most of the medieval houses could be dispensed with. Moreover, after the recent dramatic revolution, plays were no longer half circus and acrobatics demanding an arena, and if the yard was not needed for the actors it could be filled with spectators, which would mean a very substantial increase in receipts, a consideration that would not be lost upon Henslowe, and it was probably at about the time of the building of the Swan that the groundlings were let into the yard, so severing the main link with the traditional staging of medieval times. That this was so is supported by the fact that we now hear for the first time of spectators sitting on the apron stage, which would have been an uncommonly uncomfortable position for them when the yard was in use and players leaping up and down its sides.

One change led to another. The raising of the heavens meant that musicians could be moved to the level of the upper gallery, and spectators put into the old music-rooms on either side of the pulpit, 'over the stage', as these boxes were described in the nineties. Other good seats appear to have been those in the bottom gallery adjoining the tiring-house, where the groundlings once stood. These, now raised above the level of the yard, are marked 'orchestra' in the sketch of the Swan made soon after its completion, about 1596, though it should be remembered that the sketch is only a copy made by the Dutchman Arend van Buchel from a memory drawing by his friend Johannes de Witt, who saw a performance there. But he never saw this view, and would not have drawn it thus had he been sitting in the theatre: a bird's-eye view from well above roof-level. Though it gives a good general impression of the theatre, it is undoubtedly inaccurate and misleading in many of its details. The people in the boxes at the back appear to be spectators 'over the stage'; if so, there is no upper stage, nor is there any inner stage built into the tiring-house (*mimorum ædes*) below. But such a scaffolding as that already described—a pulpit supported by pillars forming a curtained stage below—could be a movable structure and unnecessary in the play depicted. On the other hand, Langley may have gone only as far as getting rid of the throne and its steps, while Henslowe went one better at the Rose, or it may be that these developments had to wait for the building of the Globe two years later.

No doubt there was a transitional period of experiment, and methods of production would vary from theatre to theatre. *Romeo and Juliet*, for example, a Curtain play, seems to have needed some action in the yard, for the vexed question of Romeo's leap into the Capulet garden is easily solved, without the ludicrous hypothesis that a property wall was trundled in for the occasion, by a simple vault from the yard on to the stage. And if the position of the gallery entrances (*ingressus*) in de Witt's sketch is correct, it looks as if even the Swan was built with no very certain idea of always accommodating spectators in the yard, for gallery patrons would scarcely relish pushing to their seats through 'stinkards glewed together in crowdes with the steames of strong breath', as Dekker was unflatteringly to describe the groundlings. Then, it is significant that de Witt labels the yard 'planities sive arena' (plain or arena), for he is thinking in terms of the Roman and neo-Roman stage of Serlio where some of the action took place in the arena.

THE SWAN THEATRE
From the drawing of J. de Witt, c. 1596

But the staging of plays could end only in one way; the yard was no longer an essential part of the playing-place, whereas groundlings were distinctly desirable, and by the turn of the century action in the yard would be exceptional. Exceptional, but not quite at an end. Some of Shakespeare's later plays simply demand its employment; *Hamlet* for example, and *Antony and Cleopatra*, and if we interpret literally the opening chorus of *Henry V*, it assumes a new and startling significance:

> Can this cockpit hold
> The vasty fields of France? or may we cram
> Within this wooden O the very casques
> That did affright the air at Agincourt? . . .
> Suppose within the girdle of these walls
> Are now confined two mighty monarchies . . .

Once the revolutionary proposal has been accepted that there were not always groundlings in the yard, and the action of the more spacious plays is conceived as flowing over platform and arena alike, our understanding and enjoyment of the Elizabethan drama will be enriched.

If Henslowe could not command plays comparable to those of the Chamberlain's, he was at least the owner of a better theatre. But then, in the autumn of 1596, the Chamberlain's moved into the Swan, according to de Witt the finest and biggest in London, built of a concrete of flints, with wooden pillars painted to resemble marble, and a seating capacity of 3,000. It was fortunate that the Swan was there to receive them, for they had nowhere else to go that winter. In July the Lord Chamberlain had died, and though they secured his son, the second Lord Hunsdon, as their new patron, he was not the new Lord Chamberlain. This was William Brooke, Lord Cobham, a man who had little sympathy for the players and little inclination to defend them against the attacks of the City Corporation, who naturally took advantage of this weakening in the Privy Council. 'The players', Nashe wrote in September, 'ar piteously persecuted by the L. Maior & the aldermen, & howeuer in there old Lords tyme they thought ther state setled, it is now so vncertayne they cannot build vpon it'. Shortly afterwards the Corporation succeeded in what they had been trying to do for twenty years and more, ejecting the players from the City and dismantling the stages of the inn-theatres. The Chamberlain's, therefore, who made their winter-quarters at the Cross Keys, would have had to stay at the remote and antiquated Theatre if Langley had not been able to offer them the Swan.

There had been an outbreak of plague that summer, severe enough to close the theatres for a time, and Shakespeare may already have been in Stratford when his only son, Hamnet, aged eleven, died. On his return to London he moved from the parish of St. Helen's, Bishops-gate, near the Theatre, to somewhere on the Bankside, where he would be conveniently close to the Swan, and it was then that the curious Gardiner affair occurred. In November, Langley sought legal protection from one William Gardiner and William Wayte, and a few days later Wayte replied by seeking similar protection from Langley, Dorothy Soer, Anne Lee—and 'William Shakspere'. Nothing is known of the women in the business, but Gardiner was a rascally Surrey magistrate who defrauded his good-for-nothing stepson Wayte, and was sturdily called by Langley, 'a false knave, a false forsworn knave, and a perjured knave'. More to the point, he was one of the magistrates who would have liked to see the closing of the theatres on the Surrey side of the river, and it seems that Shakespeare, perhaps as representative of the Chamberlain's (or 'Hunsdon's' as they now were), vigorously supported Langley in his protest.[1]

Before Hunsdon's returned to the Theatre in the following spring, James Burbage was dead, disappointed in his last venture. For £600 he had bought part of the Blackfriars buildings, where the Chapel Children used to perform, and in the course of 1596 con-verted it into a private theatre some seventy feet long and forty-five feet wide, with a stage at one end, galleries and seats. But, encouraged by the banishing of the players from the City, some of the inhabitants of the liberty petitioned the Privy Council that no playhouse 'be used or kept there', as it would destroy the amenities of the precinct, encourage lawlessness and breed plague, while 'the noyse of the drummes and trumpetts will greatly disturbe and hinder both the ministers and parishioners in tyme of devine service and sermons'. Lord Hunsdon, who had a house in the precinct, was one of the signatories. Perhaps Burbage had made the playhouse to serve as winter-quarters for Hunsdon's, where Shakespeare's courtly lyrical comedies might be seen to better advantage than at the Theatre, or perhaps he had a scheme for promoting another children's company, which might account for Lord Hunsdon's curious action. The

[1] Cf. Leslie Hotson, *Shakespeare versus Shallow.*

petition, backed by Cobham, was successful; Burbage was forbidden to open his new playhouse, and in his will left it to his son Richard.

Burbage died in February 1597. A month later, to the ill-concealed delight of the players, Cobham died, and within a few days the second Lord Hunsdon was installed as Lord Chamberlain, so that, after a break of seven months, Shakespeare's company was once again officially the Chamberlain's. They were now back at the Theatre and Langley, therefore, on the look-out for new tenants at the Swan, but as there was no other company that could compete with the Chamberlain's and Admiral's, he had somehow or other to form one. By offering the bait of £300's worth of apparel and properties, he persuaded three of the Chamberlain's hirelings, Robert Shaw, Gabriel Spencer and William Bird, to join him, and even enticed two of the sharers in the Admiral's, Richard Jones and Thomas Downton, a shrewd blow to Henslowe, who had to suspend performances at the Rose. These five became sharers in a new, or revived, company under the patronage of the Earl of Pembroke, contracting under bond with Langley to play at the Swan for twelve months, and nowhere else within five miles of London. Langley was setting up as another Henslowe. He was soon to find that the theatre business was not all profits and roses.

In July Pembroke's presented a new play at the Swan, Nashe's *Isle of Dogs*, and the Privy Council, scenting a 'lewd plaie contanynge very seditious and sclanderous matter', at once ordered the closing of all the theatres for a season, and the imprisonment of the author and some of the actors. Henslowe's version of the title, *Jeylle of Dooges*, was not inappropriate. Shaw, Spencer and Ben Jonson were sent to the Marshalsea, but Nashe fled to Yarmouth where he consoled himself with writing *Lenten Stuff*, a dazzling *tour de force* in praise of red herrings, and one of the best things he ever did. Soon afterwards he died, and the last but one and all-but-brightest star of the pioneering *Pléiade* was extinguished.

Unfortunately the *Isle of Dogs* has been lost. No doubt it was sauced with satire, the Isle probably England, but the government were acutely sensitive to political criticism, and in *Lenten Stuff* Nashe complains that 'a deepe politique state meaning' was wrested from his most innocent remarks, adding that, in any event, he wrote only the induction and the first act, 'the other foure acts without my consent, or the least guesse of my drift or scope, by the players were supplied, which bred both their trouble and mine too'. This may be an exaggeration, but there can be no doubt that Ben Jonson was part author of the play, and it is peculiarly fitting that the rising revolutionary playwright should have been associated with the last play of the revolutionary University Wits. He may have acted in it as well—for he was certainly an actor, though apparently a very bad one—but if so it is odd that on the very day that the Council closed the theatres Henslowe lent £4 to 'Bengemen Johnson player, to be payd yt agayne when so euer ether I or any for me shall demande yt'. Probably Henslowe had his eye on him as a promising playwright, put him in his debt by financing his imprisonment, for prisoners had to pay for their entertainment in the Marshalsea, and then offered to accept repayment of the loan in the form of a play. Jonson, with Shaw and Spencer, was released in October, when he borrowed another 5s. from Henslowe, and wrote for him, though not exclusively, for the next few years.

Henslowe worked hard while the theatres were closed, and it was not long before he had his seceding players back at the Rose, Jones and Downton, bringing with them Shaw, Spencer and Bird, all of them bound by contracts for two or three years to play for the Admiral's, or 'my company', as he now with some justification called it. On October 11th, three weeks before the lifting of the official inhibition—one is constantly struck by the laxity of enforcement of the laws—the Rose reopened its doors, but a few weeks later the reconstituted company suffered an irreparable loss by the retirement of Alleyn, which, however, proved to be only temporary, though for a period of three years. After all, he was only just over thirty.

The unfortunate Langley was unable to reopen the Swan when the restraint was lifted, as Tilney for a time refused to renew his licence, and although he brought an action for breach of contract against the five deserters, he did not get them back. Pembroke's were broken for the second time, the rump again returning to the provinces, and Langley never succeeded in forming another company, largely owing to the opposition of the Council, who considered two companies quite enough for the capital. He died in 1601, after being reduced to letting his theatre for various sorts of non-dramatic entertainment, such as fencing matches and feats of activity. The Chamberlain's did not occupy the Theatre much longer, for after travelling during

the summer of the inhibition, from Rye and Dover to Bristol and
Bath, they found Cuthbert Burbage quarrelling with his ground
landlord, Giles Allen, about the renewal of the lease. Negotiations
broke down, and they had probably moved to the Curtain by
the end of the year, the original twenty-one-year lease having
expired.

Meanwhile, after the Lopez affair and despite the poverty and
distress caused by the bad harvests, the embers of the Spanish war
flared up again. Spanish sea-power was recovering, and when, in July
1595, four galleys put in to Mount's Bay, landed a force of two hundred men, and burned part of Penzance, Elizabeth reluctantly, for she
was at her wit's end for money, accepted the challenge. Drake was
recalled to favour, and, after the customary hesitations and delays, sent
off with Hawkins, now well over sixty and grown cautious with age,
to repeat his classic raids on the Spanish Main and Panama. Raleigh
was already engaged on a more peaceful expedition to the Orinoco, in
search of the fabled land of El Dorado where the ground was strewn
with precious stones and gold, whence he unprofitably returned to
write his *Discovery of Guiana*, the most entrancing of the stories added
by Hakluyt to his second edition of the *Principal Navigations*. He was
back in time to take part in the Cadiz expedition.

Philip II was preparing another Armada, and Elizabeth, stimulated by the distant roar of Spanish guns besieging Calais, agreed to a
repetition of the raid that had prevented the sailing of the first Armada.
Lord Admiral Howard and Essex were appointed joint commanders,
and Raleigh, once again in some favour with the Queen, was given an
important command. It was a perilous combination, and there were
bitter struggles for precedence between the leaders. The peremptory
Essex stood firmly by his title: he was an earl; but Howard was old
enough to be his father, and had commanded the fleet in '88.
When a letter to the Queen was brought for their signature, Essex
seized a pen and so wrote his name that Howard was obliged to sign
below. But Howard was not to be beaten and, when Essex had gone,
cut out his rival's name and dispatched the mutilated missive to
Elizabeth. And so the confused and hectic preparations at Plymouth
went forward until, just before they were ready to sail, Drake's
expedition returned—without either of its commanders.

Elizabeth's vacillation had given the Spaniards time to prepare for
'El Draque', the dragon whose breath had so often singed their beards.

Porto Rico in the West Indies was fortified and proof against attack, and there Hawkins died, more than thirty years after his first raid in those waters. His death, however, was not altogether loss, for it relieved the enterprise of divided counsels, and Drake went on to sack the towns along the Spanish Main. But when he came to Nombre de Dios and tried to force his way across the Darien isthmus to the beckoning Pacific he found the passes securely held and had to abandon the attempt. Distressed by his failure and exhausted by his exertions, he died on board his ship in January 1596, and was buried at sea.

It was a melancholy recital and of unpromising augury for the joint-commanders who were to attempt a repetition of Drake's raid on Cadiz. Yet the venture was a triumphant, or at least a spectacular, success. In June the English fleet sailed into Cadiz Bay, and within a few hours the action was over. Howard and Raleigh destroyed the incipient armada, while Essex led the land forces that scaled the walls and took the town. Such gallant rivalry had become co-operation, and Essex was all chivalry as well, treating nuns and priests with elaborate courtesy, and sparing their convents and their churches. But, victory achieved, co-operation was at an end. The sailors joined the soldiers in pillaging the town, and the greatest spoil of all, a fleet of more than forty merchantmen crammed with treasure, was over-looked as it lay within an inner harbour. The Duke of Medina Sidonia, doomed to watch the destruction of Spanish fleets, ordered them to be burned rather than fall into English hands, and Philip, or Elizabeth, lost twelve million ducats. After a fortnight the victorious forces sailed for home, pausing on the way to sack the town of Faro. Essex, a lover of books, found room among the plunder for the famous library of Jeronymo Osorio, which he presented to his supporter, Sir Thomas Bodley, by whose munificence it became the nucleus of the great Bodleian Library at Oxford.

Essex was the hero of the hour, the symbol of England triumphant, though if the truth had been known the success of the venture had been due in the first place to the counsels of Raleigh. To one of his noblest poems Spenser added a stanza in praise of

> Great England's glory and the world's wide wonder,
> Whose dreadful name late through all Spain did thunder
> And Hercules' two pillars standing near
> Did make to quake and fear.

And Shakespeare, having lowered his beloved Hamnet into the grave, wrote *King John* as a tribute to the Protestant triumph:

> This England never did, nor never shall,
> Lie at the proud foot of a conqueror,
> But when it first did help to wound itself.

Yet Elizabeth was dissatisfied. The expedition had cost her £50,000, and all that she received in return was a paltry £13,000 of plunder, and further demands for money to pay her sailors' wages, while rumour had it that London was flooded with the illicit booty of the soldiers. Essex, too, was dissatisfied, for he now found Cecil officially installed as Secretary. Against the advice of Bacon, who coldly counselled the assumption of less spectacular and invidious offices, he pressed, as compensation, for the post of Master of the Ordnance. At last he received it, but only after threatening to leave the Court when, on the death of Lord Chamberlain Cobham, Elizabeth gave the Wardenship of the Cinque Ports, for which he asked, to the new Lord Cobham. Bacon was writing his *Essays* as well as letters of advice to his patron: 'If ambitious men be checked in their desires, they become secretly discontent, and look upon men and matters with an evil eye'; and when, from his chamber at Gray's Inn on that January day of 1597, he penned the dedication of his slender volume, it was addressed, not to Essex, but to his 'loving and beloved brother', Anthony.

News arrived that the indefatigable Philip was preparing a third Armada, and Elizabeth consented to yet another raid. This time Essex was to have the sole command, and with Raleigh as rear-admiral was to destroy the Spanish fleet in the harbour of Ferrol. Essex was jubilant, Cecil polite and Raleigh restored to favour as Captain of the Guard, returning to his post outside the Presence Chamber in a suit of silver armour. In July, while the Privy Council were persecuting the authors of the 'seditious and sclanderous' *Isle of Dogs*, the fleet left Plymouth, only to be struck by a fearful south-westerly gale that forced it back to port. Rumours arrived that Essex was dead, and Elizabeth was almost frantic with grief. He was safe, however, and soon repairing his ships for a second attempt. With a depleted fleet he sailed again, but on reaching Ferrol an easterly gale held him off the harbour, so, abandoning the attack, he made for the Azores, on the so-called Islands Voyage, to intercept the Spanish treasure fleet on its way back from America. The central island and stronghold of

Terceira proving too formidable to be attacked, he wisely decided to occupy the western island of Fayal. The ships were separated as they approached, and after waiting four days for Essex, Raleigh landed and sacked the town. Essex was furious; some of his friends, among whom was the devoted Southampton, advised him to court-martial and execute his rival. 'I would do it, if he were my friend' was Essex's ominous reply, then with incredible fatuity set off to emulate Raleigh by attacking San Miguel, the most *easterly* of the islands. No sooner was he gone than the Spanish treasure fleet arrived and sailed unmolested into Terceira. Even San Miguel proved unassailable, and Essex turned for home having achieved precisely nothing.

Meanwhile England had been virtually defenceless. Philip's chance had come at last, and he frantically ordered the Armada to leave Ferrol, seize the forts of Falmouth, destroy the English ships on their return from the Azores, after which their ten thousand men were to march on Plymouth and London. In October, reluctantly and all-unprepared, the Spanish fleet put out to sea, but near Land's End it was caught and scattered by the autumn gales, and the remains of the third Armada slunk back to Ferrol. On the whole, Philip had to admit, the winds had favoured the heretic cause rather than that of the true faith—and he began the preparation of a fourth Armada. It had been a near thing, and when the English fleet returned Raleigh at once went to work upon the shore defences, while Essex romantically wrote, 'Though we eat ropes' ends and drink nothing but rain-water, we will make a final end of this proud nation'.

But Elizabeth had had enough, and vowed that there should be no more raids. Her reception of Essex was frigid, and all the more so because he still remained the idol of the people, who blamed the unpopular Raleigh, whose successful action at Fayal had been omitted from the official report. Essex sullenly retired to his house at Wanstead, even refusing to attend the customary tilt and celebrations of November 17th, Queen's Day, the anniversary of Elizabeth's accession. He had, so he thought, good reason to be offended, for in his absence Cecil had been made Chancellor of the Duchy of Lancaster, and, worse still, Howard created Earl of Nottingham, which title, with his office of Lord Admiral, gave him precedence over all other earls except the Lord Chamberlain, Lord Steward and Earl Marshal. Moreover, Nottingham's patent said that the honour was a reward for his capture of Cadiz. It was intolerable, and he would not return to Court until the insult had been amended. At last Elizabeth relented and created him Earl Marshal.

Among the adventurers who took part in the Islands Voyage was young John Donne, a brilliant and wealthy young man of twenty-four, who had recently rejected the Catholic for the Anglican faith. He was already known as a poet with a mordant wit, and his satires, like (yet so very unlike) Shakespeare's sonnets, were eagerly passed round among his private friends. Perhaps he was thinking of Shakespeare and his dedicatory epistles to Southampton when he wrote:

> And they who write to Lords, rewards to get,
> Are they not like fingers at doores for meat?

And perhaps of Shakespeare the player and Greene the playwright, who:

> gives ideot actors meanes
> (Starving himselfe) to live by his labor'd sceanes;
> As in some Organ, Puppits dance above
> And bellows pant below, which them do move.

But that was only an exercise in vituperation, written three or four years before, and while waiting for the fleet to refit he wrote a verse epistle to his friend Christopher Brooke, describing the storm that had driven them back to Plymouth:

> *Ionas*, I pitty thee, and curse those men,
> Who when the storm rag'd most, did wake thee then;
> Sleepe is paines easiest salve, and doth fulfill
> All offices of death, except to kill.
> But when I wakt, I saw, that I saw not;
> Aye, and the Sunne, which should teach mee, had forgot
> East, West, Day, Night, and I could onely say,
> If the world had lasted, now it had beene day . . .
> Then note they the ships sicknesses, the Mast
> Shak'd with this ague, and the Hold and Wast
> With a salt dropsie clog'd, and all our tacklings
> Snapping, like too-high-stretched treble strings.
> And from our totterd sailes, ragges drop downe so,
> As from one hang'd in chaines, a yeare agoe.

Here was something new, something very different from the smooth music and conventional imagery of the normal run of Elizabethan verse. Realistic, witty, grotesque, deliberately harsh, with images fetched from the most unlikely sources (we cannot imagine Spenser describing a battered ship as clogged with dropsy), by its fusion of intellect and emotion, ugliness and beauty, an extension of the frontiers of art, a pioneering and civilising poetry. Twenty years later Jonson told William Drummond that he esteemed 'John Done the first poet in the world in some things', adding, however, that he would perish for not being understood. But there he was wrong.

It is in the opening lines of *The Storm* that Donne praises the painting of Nicholas Hilliard, a man whose graceful, lyrical, unimpassioned style was so unlike his own, except for its emphasis on line, for Donne's poetry is essentially linear, nervously and tortuously etched, and we rarely think in terms of colour when we read it, as we do, for example, when reading Milton. It was at about this time that Hilliard wrote his *Arte of Limning*, in which he described his method: 'Shadowing in Lymning must not be driuen with the flat of the pensel as in oyle worke, distemper, or washing, but with the pointe of the pencell by little light touches with cullor very thin, and like hatches as wee call it with the pen; though the shadowe be neuer so great it must be all done by littel touches.' Line, not chiaroscuro, was, and is, the secret of miniature painting, 'for the lyne without shadowe showeth all to a good jugment, but the shadowe without lyne showeth nothing'. Hilliard's colour is transparent and luminous as medieval glass, his painting the perfect counterpart of the Elizabethan lyric. But his pupil, the Huguenot refugee Isaac Oliver, was now his rival, winning favour and corrupting taste by exploiting an opaque oil-painting technique that was destroying the art of limning as surely as the paintings of the High Renaissance had destroyed the art of designing stained glass windows.

George Gower died in 1596. In some verses written in the corner of a self-portrait, he somewhat apologetically explains why he, a gentleman, had become a painter; at the same time symbolising the victory of art over birth by drawing a pair of scales in which his coat-of-arms is outweighed by a pair of dividers. As Serjeant Painter he would have been responsible for work commissioned by Tilney and the Office of Revels, and no doubt painted or designed scenery and properties required for Court performances, including some of Shakespeare's. Another gentlemanly painter of the period, but one who always insisted on his amateur status, was Henry Peacham. He was a very young man when Gower died, but at Longleat there is a drawing attributed to him, made apparently as early as 1595. It illustrates, not quite accurately, an episode from the first scene of *Titus Andronicus*,

'Tamora pleadinge for her sonnes going to execution', and beneath are written, probably by a later hand, speeches taken from Acts I and V. It is by far the earliest illustration to Shakespeare, and important in showing that the Moor Aaron, and presumably therefore Othello, was conceived as a coal-black negro, and that, while minor parts were played in 'modern' dress, there was some attempt at historical accuracy in the costumes of the principal, or at any rate princely, characters.

Donne's poems were not printed until long after this time, and much the most important poetry published in these years was Spenser's. As Clerk of the Council of Munster in the troubled nineties, Spenser can have had little time to spare for literature, and it was five years after the publication of the first three books of *The Faerie Queene* that he returned to England, in 1595, bringing with him Books IV–VI, and *Prothalamion*, the marriage ode with the refrain, 'Sweet Thames, run softly, till I end my song', the stanza in praise of Essex, and the complaint of disappointed hopes after 'long fruitless stay in prince's court'. *The Faerie Queene* dragged its slow and lovely length along another 16,000 lines of bewildering allegory; yet there was no mistaking the part played by false chameleon-like Duessa, the Roman Catholic Church of Book I, but now 'untitled Queen, brought to her sad doom' by Zeal:

> Then brought he forth with grisly grim aspect
> Abhorred Murder, who with bloody knife
> Yet dropping fresh in hand did her detect,
> And there with guilty bloodshed charged rife:
> Then brought he forth Sedition, breeding strife
> In troublous wits and mutinous uproar;
> Then brought he forth Incontinence of life,
> Even foul Adultery her face before,
> And lewd Impiety, that her accused sore.

No wonder that James VI of Scotland protested, not against the very proper execution of a witch—was he not himself engaged in writing *Dæmonologie*, a treatise denouncing witchcraft and advocating its merciless suppression?—but when the witch was his own mother it was another matter.

One of James's more laudable and innocent ambitions was to excel as an author, and he had already published a competent essay on prosody and two small volumes of verse, remarkable chiefly for the acquaintance they show with the work of du Bartas, whose metaphysical poems Donne was now so avidly reading. Impelled by his giddy young wife, Anne of Denmark, James was also anxious to acclimatise the drama in the unpromisingly bleak air of Presbyterian Scotland. His first child, Henry, was born in 1594, and to celebrate his christening 'Inglis comedianis' were invited to perform at Court, for which they received the princely reward of £333 6s. 8d. Who the players were we do not know, but their leader was almost certainly Lawrence Fletcher, who became a great favourite of James, and it was probably he who received the frosty answer from St. Andrews kirk session: 'Ane Jnglishman haveing desyrit libertie of the session to mak ane publik play in this citie, it was voted and concludit that he suld nocht be permitted to do the samin.' In the following year James gave Fletcher a warrant and money 'to by timber for ye prepartioun of ane house to thair pastyme', and soon afterwards the players marched through the streets of Edinburgh with trumpets and drums, calling all people to come and see the acting of their comedies. This was too much, and the ministers, fearing the profanity that was to ensue, hastily convoked the four sessions of the Kirk, who passed an ordinance forbidding the performances. Their little sally was ill received by James, who summoned them to meet him within three hours to rescind their decree countermanding his warrant. But they protested that they had done no such thing, the warrant being only for the building of the theatre, whereas they had merely ordered that there should be no plays in it. According to the twenty-year-old ordinance of the General Assembly, they were within their rights, but James told them that he was the interpreter of the laws of Scotland, and ordered them to meet the next day and publicly repeal their act, 'or ellis to passe to the horne immediately'. There was nothing for it; plays were legalised in Edinburgh, and when James came to London on his accession to the throne of England, he was accompanied by Fletcher, who became an honorary member of Shakespeare's company.

It would not take Shakespeare long to read the ten *Essays* published by Bacon early in 1597, nor is he likely to have been greatly impressed by the worldly advice of this climber's guide delivered in platitudinous and sententious broadsides. He knew from current experience that 'in all negotiations of difficulty, a man may not look to sow and reap at once, but must prepare business, and so ripen it by degrees'. At that very moment he was engaged in an abortive attempt to recover his mother's Wilmcote property, mortgaged by his father

seventeen years before, and, again on behalf of his father, involved
in seemingly endless negotiations with the Office of Heralds for the
grant of a coat-of-arms, with which he hoped to impale the arms of his
mother's family, the Ardens. As if that were not enough, he had no
sooner signed the agreement to buy New Place, a fine old house in
Stratford, than the vendor was poisoned by his eldest son, and he was
involved in further negotiations with the trustees of the estate. By
1597 Shakespeare was a very busy man, as well as a very successful
one, and it seems as if the death of Hamnet had strengthened his ties
with Stratford. After certain necessary repairs, he established his wife
in New Place, and re-established the self-respect and fortunes of his
father, who may have suffered from the disastrous fires of 1594 and
1595, when most of the buildings in the north part of the town were
gutted.

Bacon's apophthegm that 'reading maketh a full man' he would
receive as axiomatic, and turn from the *Essays* to the greater delights
of *The Faerie Queene* and the other recently published poetry. There
were the *Spiritual Sonnets* of Barnabe Barnes, a rival for the favour of
Southampton, and one of the select friends of Gabriel Harvey. Then
there was Richard Carew's *Godfrey of Bulloigne*, a translation of Tasso's
Gerusalemme Liberata, and, more important, the couplets of Drayton's
England's Heroical Epistles, in which the new metaphysical quality of
curious conceit was so happily wedded to the old familiar lyricism:

> Canst thou by sickness banish beauty so?
> Which if put from thee knows not where to go,
> To make her shift and for her succour seek
> To every rivelled face, each bankrupt cheek.

He would read with peculiar pleasure the *Orchestra* of John Davies,
a poem in which Antinous tries to persuade Penelope to dance, by
arguing that nature herself moves to the orderly measure of a dance, a
view that particularly appealed to Shakespeare, who conceived all forms
of government, human and divine, in terms of harmony and music:

> Dancing, bright lady, then began to be,
> When the first seeds whereof the world did spring,
> The fire, air, earth, and water, did agree
> By Love's persuasion, nature's mighty king,
> To leave their first disordered combating,
> And in a dance such measure to observe,
> As all the world their motion should preserve.

GEORGE
2nd BARON HUNSDON

By Nicholas Hilliard

ROBERT DEVEREUX
2nd EARL OF ESSEX

By Isaac Oliver

Reproduced by gracious permission of
H.M. the Queen

NICHOLAS HILLIARD. Self-portrait, aged 30, 1577 (enlarged)

The Bull by force
In field doth Raigne
But Bull by skill
Good will doth Cayne

AN ATATIS SVÆ 27
1 5 8 9

Music Schools, Oxford

JOHN BULL

Davies, a barrister of the Middle Temple, dedicated the poem to his, and probably Shakespeare's, friend Richard Martin, the witty and hilarious Prince d'Amour of the Christmas revels at the Inn. Soon afterwards the excitable young men quarrelled; Davies struck Martin in the hall of the Middle Temple, for which breach of decorum he was expelled from the society, and spent his temporary retirement in writing the didactic poem, *Nosce Teipsum*.

Then there was the most recent work of Daniel to be read. A few years earlier the Countess of Pembroke had published her *Antony*, a translation of a neo-classical tragedy by the French poet and dramatist, Robert Garnier. Daniel, as a tribute to his patron, for he was still tutor to her son at Wilton, replied with the complementary *Cleopatra*, equally Senecan in form and complete with a chorus of Egyptians. The play was never acted and probably was never intended to be, but Shakespeare read and remembered it when he wrote his own *Antony and Cleopatra*. He would be even more interested in *The Civil Wars between Lancaster and York*, the first four books of which were published in 1595, for here Daniel was attempting in epic form, though it turned out to be little more than a verse chronicle, the theme that he himself had already dramatised, and was at that very moment expanding in *Richard II*. Daniel would get very little help from Shakespeare's histories, as the only two published by 1595 were the hopelessly mutilated 'bad' quartos of *Henry VI*, Parts 2 and 3, but Shakespeare may have taken a hint or two from Daniel for his *Richard II* and *Henry IV*.

A third 'bad' quarto appeared in 1597, from the press of John Danter, a printer of poor quality and dubious repute. Apparently an actor in a shortened version of *Romeo and Juliet* reproduced the play as best he could from memory, and sold the script to Danter, who published it without registration. The title-page is interesting, as it states that the tragedy had 'been often (with great applause) plaid publiquely, by the right Honourable L. of Hunsdon his Seruants'. It is the only Shakespearean quarto to have been published during the seven disastrous months that Cobham was Lord Chamberlain. Hunsdon's, or the Chamberlain's as they were once more by the middle of March, had no redress, but two years later they sold the correct version to a reputable publisher, who issued another quarto, 'newly corrected, augmented and amended'. Two more Shakespearean quartos were legitimately published in 1597. It was probably owing to the loss incurred by the closing of the theatres after the *Isle of Dogs* affair that the Chamberlain's raised money by selling *Richard III* and *Richard II* to Andrew Wise, for whom they were printed by Valentine Simmes. Then, early in the following year, Wise bought and published the First Part of *Henry IV*.

Richard II and *Henry IV*! The one is the sequel of the other, but Shakespeare had travelled a long way as a dramatist in the two years that separated their writing. Here is Bolingbroke when Richard surrenders to him at Flint Castle:

> See, see, King Richard doth himself appear,
> As doth the blushing discontented sun
> From out the fiery portal of the east,
> When he perceives the envious clouds are bent
> To dim his glory and to stain the track
> Of his bright passage to the occident.

It is sheer lyric, the extension of an image through a series of subordinate clauses and qualifying phrases, with little or no relevance to the action or to character, almost indeed a falsification of the ruthless and bustling Bolingbroke with his contempt for Richard and his poetry. But here is Bolingbroke on the same subject, now that Richard is dead, and he is Henry IV:

> The skipping king, he ambled up and down,
> With shallow jesters and rash bavin wits,
> Soon kindled and soon burnt; carded his state,
> Mingled his royalty with capering fools,
> Had his great name profaned with their scorns.
> And gave his countenance, against his name,
> To laugh at gibing boys, and stand the push
> Of every beardless vain comparative.

This is dramatic poetry, verse that keeps the action going, is creative of character, and, while still remaining unmistakably and unequivocally verse, by its vigour, impetus, rhythmical freedom and commonplace imagery approximating to the naturalness and colloquialism of prose. And prose seems to be the secret of the development.

Up till this time Shakespeare had used prose only for low comedy, and as, with one exception, there is no low comedy in the early histories, there is no prose. Yet prose was the medium out of which his most memorable characters had been created: Juliet's nurse, Launce and Bottom are characters in the round, whereas the verse-speaking Romeo, Valentine and Theseus are little more than paste-board figures. Then, after *King John* came *The Merchant of Venice*, the play in which Shakespeare's lyrical, quasi-dramatic poetry reached its full perfection; yet in it was a development of the profoundest significance: the principal character, Shylock, speaks prose as well as verse. It is one of the major landmarks in Shakespeare's development, for in the plays of the next few years, the genial historical and romantic comedies from *Henry IV* to *Twelfth Night*, there is twice as much prose as verse, and no longer is it only the humbler characters who speak prose: Orlando and Rosalind make love in prose, Benedick and Beatrice speak scarcely anything else, Prince Henry talks the same language as Falstaff, and even when king woos Katharine in prose, and *The Merry Wives of Windsor* has only two hundred lines of verse altogether.

It was not that the lyrical vein was worked out, but stimulated perhaps by the early work of Jonson, who claimed that dramatic dialogue should be 'language such as men do use', Shakespeare abandoned, or almost abandoned, his splendid but diffuse and un-dramatic poetry, and the language of the next plays is a much closer approximation to that really spoken by men. Rhyming dialogue almost disappears, lyric is confined virtually to the songs, prose becomes the staple medium, the blank verse itself is chastened, and in place of the artificial lyrical drama there emerges the comedy of character, of Falstaff and Prince Hal, Benedick and Beatrice, Rosalind and Jaques, Viola and Malvolio. *Henry IV*, Part 1, the first of these plays, was probably written in the early part of 1597, when Shakespeare and his company were performing at the Swan.

VII

1597–1599

JONSON AND HIS CONTEMPORARIES

THE *Isle of Dogs* affair had further repercussions. It was twenty-five years since the Act regulating the position of players, and in those two and a half decades the great theatrical revolution had taken place; permanent theatres had been built in London, the University Wits had written and died, plays were now being poured out by an ever-increasing band of professional dramatists, playwriting was even an organised business and the drama by far the most popular form of entertainment. It was high time that the regulations were brought up to date, and the recent disturbances goaded the government into vigorous action. By the statute of 1572 players not in the service of a peer of the realm had been allowed to 'wander abroad' provided they were licensed by two Justices of the Peace, but by the Act of 1598 all strolling players who were not members of some peer's company were adjudged rogues, vagabonds and sturdy beggars, and liable to whipping till the 'body be bloudye' and to transportation. At the same time, by an order in Star Chamber, the Privy Council and their agent, the Master of the Revels, took over the control of the London theatres; the number of companies was limited to two, the Admiral's and the Chamberlain's, and the Master of the Revels and the Middlesex and Surrey magistrates were ordered to suppress a third intrusive company, presumably the unfortunate Pembroke's organised by Langley, who were not retained for playing before the Queen. The fiction still held good that public performances were only exercises and rehearsals for performance at Court, where in the winters of 1597 and 1598 the Chamberlain's outpointed the Admiral's by seven plays to five. Provided, then, the players behaved themselves and produced no more *Isles of Dogs*, they could now feel secure in the support of the Privy Council. It was a heavy defeat for the City authorities, who had failed to gain control of the suburban theatres.

The opportunity was also taken to tighten up the regulations governing the publication of plays. According to the Star Chamber decree of 1586, all books had to be licensed for printing by the Archbishop of Canterbury or the Bishop of London, or their deputies, most of whom were London clergymen. But the spate of pamphlets and plays was more than they could cope with, and with characteristic laxity these flimsy productions had been allowed to slip through with no more authority than that of a Warden of the Stationers' Company. Thus, when Andrew Wise registered *Richard II* for publication, he 'entred for his Copie by appoyntment from master Warden Man'. This was not good enough; it would never do for such things as the *Isle of Dogs* to get into print, and Archbishop Whitgift sharply checked the practice by warning the Wardens that 'noe playes be printed except they be allowed by suche as haue authority'. When, therefore, Thomas Fisher registered *A Midsummer Night's Dream* in October 1600, it was 'vnder the handes of master Rodes and the Wardens'. The flood of pamphlets was checked in the same way and the protracted skirmishings of Nashe and Gabriel Harvey brought to an end.

Elizabeth had more important things than plays and players to think about in 1598. First there was France. In May that 'antichrist of ingratitude', Henry IV, having gained what he wanted from his alliance with England and the Netherlands, cynically broke with his allies and made a separate peace with Spain. The Privy Council was divided: Burghley was in favour of ending the war, provided the Netherlands could be persuaded to accept the Spanish terms, but Essex would have none of it and proposed a more vigorous offensive. Essex carried the day, and the aged Burghley, opening a prayer-book, pointed prophetically to the last verse in the fifty-fifth psalm: 'Bloody and deceitful men shall not live out half their days.'

Then there was Ireland, where Tyrone had once again raised the ugly head of rebellion. At a Council meeting in the July dog days, when nerves were strained, Elizabeth announced that she was going to send Sir William Knollys as the new Lord Deputy. But Knollys was Essex's uncle, a valuable ally, and Essex at once suggested sending Sir George Carew, a supporter of the Cecils, whom he could well afford to see lost in the bogs of Ireland. Elizabeth was firm, and Essex persistent, until she declared that whatever he might say Knollys should be Lord Deputy. Essex turned his back on her, and the infuriated Queen boxed his ears, telling him to be gone and be hanged. Putting his hand to his sword, and shouting, 'This is an outrage that I will not put up with', he made towards her, but when Nottingham interposed he turned and fled from the room. It was perilously near treason, yet Elizabeth allowed him to sulk at Wanstead undisturbed. Her wounded feelings were overwhelmed by a greater sorrow.

Burghley, worn out by the years, by illness and by overwork, was dying. Elizabeth visited and even nursed him, the counsellor who had never failed her and had helped to guide the fortunes of the country ever since she had been Queen, for just on forty years. On August 4th he died, leaving his son Robert to serve her as he had done. Yet the son could be no substitute for the father, the friend who had been Robert's age when she had ascended the throne as a young woman of twenty-five. He was the last of those, the great ones, who remembered her when she was young and fair—all but one. But Philip of Spain was dying, too. For days he lay deliriously planning yet another Armada, tormented by the putrefying and stinking sores with which his body was covered. He died in the middle of September, and Elizabeth could not help but weep, not for her old enemy but for herself.

It happened that just at this time an observant German traveller, Paul Hentzner, was in England, and wrote an account of his visit, including a description of Elizabeth as she came from the Privy Chamber into the Presence Chamber at Greenwich on her way to a service in the chapel. 'Next came the Queen, in the sixty-fifth year of her age (as we were told), very majestic; her face oblong, fair but wrinkled; her eyes small, yet black and pleasant; her nose a little hooked, her lips narrow, and her teeth black; her hair was of an auburn colour, but false; her bosom was uncovered, as all the English ladies have it till they marry; her hands were slender, her fingers rather long, and her stature neither tall nor low; her air was stately, her manner of speaking mild and obliging.' A black-toothed, be-wigged Gloriana, magnificently dressed in white silk and smothered in jewels, who had yet to play another important scene before she went to join Burghley and Philip of Spain.

While Hentzner was making his notes on England and the musical, freedom-loving, bell-ringing and piratical English, the stationer Cuthbert Burby published two books. One was 'A Pleasant Conceited Comedie Called, Loues labors lost', the first of Shakespeare's plays to be issued with his name, and one of the plays presented before the Queen at the last Christmas Revels. The other was *Palladis Tamia: Wits Treasury*, by Francis Meres, a parson in his early thirties, and

Master of Arts at both universities. The book is a collection of apophthegms, as fantastic as pedantic, on philosophy and the arts, set out after the pattern of *Euphues*: 'As Mandrake growing neare Vines, doth make the wine more mild: so philosophie bordering vppon poetrie dooth make the knowledge of it more moderate.' It is for the most part quite worthless, but the short 'Comparative discourse of our English Poets, with the Greeke, Latine, and Italian Poets' is valuable as an account of what the Elizabethans themselves thought of their literature.

'As the Greeke tongue is made famous and eloquent by Homer', etc., etc., 'and the Latine tongue by Virgill', and so on, and so on, 'so the English tongue is mightily enriched, and gorgeouslie inuested in rare ornaments and resplendent abiliments by Sir Philip Sidney, Spencer, Daniel, Drayton, Warner, Shakespeare, Marlow and Chapman'. Except for the inclusion of William Warner, author of the tedious *Albion's England*, nobody to-day could take exception to that list. Having stated his theme, Meres begins to elaborate. Sidney is our rarest poet, Spenser the most divine and Drayton, 'now in penning a poem called *Polu-olbion*', is singled out for special notice as 'a man of vertuous disposition, honest conversation, and wel gouerned cariage, which is almost miraculous among good wits in these declining and corrupt times, when there is nothing but rogery in villanous man'. The last phrase is a quotation from *Henry IV*, and is followed by the famous panegyric of 'mellifluous & hony-tongued Shakespeare', of his *Venus and Adonis* and *Lucrece*, and 'sugred Sonnets among his priuate friends'. Not only is he a poet comparable to Ovid, but also the Plautus and Seneca of the day, the most excellent writer of both comedy and tragedy, and Meres adds a list of most of the plays he had already written. Even 'the Muses would speak with Shakespeares fine filed phrase, if they would speake English'. Among the other dramatists mentioned are George Peele, who died 'by the pox', and Anthony Munday, quaintly described as 'our best plotter', as indeed, in one sense at least, he was. Meres has a tilt at Gabriel Harvey and his 'inhumanitie to Greene', and an endearingly genial word for Nashe: 'As Actaeon was wooried of his owne hounds: so is Tom Nash of his *Isle of Dogs*. Yet God forbid that so braue a witte should so basely perish; thine are but paper dogges, neither is thy banishment like Ouids, eternally to conuerse with the barbarous Getes. Therefore comfort thy selfe sweete Tom with Ciceros glorious return to Rome.' Such a catalogue would be incomplete without a reference to the poetry of James of Scotland, and to the 'learned, delicate and noble Muse' of Elizabeth. But it is Shakespeare who steals the limelight.

After characteristic prolegomena concerning Apelles and load-stones, Meres adds perfunctory lists of contemporary painters and musicians: Hilliard and Oliver; Tallis, Byrd, Bull, Dowland and Morley.

Among the best writers of comedy Meres noted 'eloquent and wittie Iohn Lilly'. But Lyly was a disappointed man. George Buck, Tilney's nephew, with the weight therefore of the Lord Admiral and the Howard family behind him, had recently been all but promised the reversion to the Mastership of the Revels, the office that Lyly for so long had been led to expect would one day be his, and he was now vehemently petitioning Cecil, even upbraiding the Queen for her ingratitude: 'Thirteen yeares, your Highnes Servant, butt yett nothing.' While the last of the old generation of dramatists was thus living on dead hopes, the foremost member of the new generation was thriving on lively expectations, for September 1598 was the month in which Ben Jonson produced his first memorable play.

Meres had mentioned 'Beniamin Iohnson' as an after-thought in his list of dramatists, curiously enough as one of 'our best for Tragedie', presumably because the young man was no more to him than a name, which anyway he got wrong. Perhaps he had heard of him as hack-writer for Henslowe, or as the author of *The Case is Altered*, a comedy, not a tragedy, with amusing digs at Anthony Munday, or Antonio Balladino, 'pageant poet to the city of Milan, when a worse cannot be had', one who used 'as much stale stuff as any man does in that kind'. The play was probably given by Pembroke's at the Swan shortly before the *Isle of Dogs*. Jonson was a man with a passion for learning, and ever since he had been driven by poverty to leave Westminster School as a bricklayer instead of an undergraduate, he had pursued the classical studies to which his revered master, Camden, had introduced him. His heart was in the theatre, and from his reading of Aristotle's *Poetics* and Horace's *Art of Poetry*, reinforced by the moderns, Scaliger and Castelvetro, with their sterilising precepts and petrifying rules, he formulated his ideas of what comedy and tragedy should be. He had far too much good sense and independence of mind to be a pedant, yet he was convinced that Marlowe and his followers had set the course of the drama in the wrong direction. Contemporary tragedy was chaotic, altogether too comprehensive in its action, where all should be concentrated, unified and controlled; and comedy was even worse, either contemptible farce or sentimental romance, improbable fictions of fairies and girls masquerading as boys. Comedy should be realistic, not romantic, the mirror of the times, the portrayal of prevalent types of affectation and folly, by ridiculing which the minor errors of the age would be purged away. If Shakespeare chose to write comedies 'all for your delight', he would write them to reform the world, or at least to make it a less silly place to live in. This defiant neo-classical manifesto he put into the mouth of the Prologue to *Every Man in his Humour*, versifying Sidney's urbane mockery of the sprawling drama of the early eighties: 'In the meantime two armies fly in, represented with four swords and bucklers, and then what hard heart will not receive it for a pitched field? . . . Ordinary it is that two young Princes fall in love: after many traverses, she is got with child, delivered of a fair boy; he is lost, groweth a man, falls in love, and is ready to get another child, and all this in two hours' space.' Thus Sidney in his *Apology for Poetry*, and Jonson barbs the censure by its application to Shakespeare's *Henry VI*:

> To make a child now swaddled, to proceed
> Man, and then shoot up, in one beard and weed,
> Past threescore years; or, with three rusty swords,
> And help of some few foot and half-foot words,
> Fight over York and Lancaster's long jars,
> And in the tiring-house bring wounds to scars.
> He rather prays you will be pleased to see
> One such to-day as other plays should be;
> . . . deeds, and language, such as men do use,
> And persons such as comedy would choose,
> When she would show an image of the times,
> And sport with human follies, not with crimes.

It was a courageous gesture for a virtually unknown playwright of twenty-five; but then, whatever Jonson's failings, and they were many, lack of courage was not one of them.[1]

Every Man in his Humour was performed by the Chamberlain's probably at the Curtain, about the middle of September. There is a tradition that Shakespeare was responsible for his company's acceptance of the play, but however that may be, we know that he acted in it, for when Jonson made a collected edition of his works and published them in folio in 1616, he recorded the names of the actors in

---

[1] Part of the Prologue may have been written for a later revival, since there are lines that seem to refer to *Henry V*, others even perhaps to *The Tempest*.

the original productions; the pity is that he did not add the parts they played. The list for *Every Man in his Humour* reads, 'The principall Comœdians were, Will. Shakespeare, Ric. Burbadge, Aug. Philips, Ioh. Hemings, Hen. Condel, Tho. Pope, Will. Slye, Chr. Beeston, Will. Kempe, Ioh. Duke'. This is the first actor-list of the Chamberlain's that has been preserved. Bryan had gone, and been replaced by Sly as a sharer, or 'full adventurer'; Beeston and Duke were hired men who, like Kempe, were soon to join the reorganised Worcester's.

The England of 1598 was very different in temper from that of ten years before, the heroic age when the war with Spain was new and popular, the Armada shattered, Drake the hero of the hour and Alleyn thundering Marlowe's verses to astonished and delighted citizens, a symbol of the nation's confidence and vigour. Since then plague and all but famine had swept the land, the war dragged expensively and inconclusively along. Ireland was now in rebellion, and there was a paralysing feeling of anxiety as to what would happen when the aged Queen died. Men were waiting helplessly for the end of an epoch; disillusion and cynicism were in the air, and the most popular reading was the flyting and scurrilous pamphlets with which the booksellers' stalls were loaded. Jonson's satirical comedies, though bracing and astringent, reflected the disenchanted spirit of the late nineties as accurately as Marlowe's tragedies had reflected the energy of the eighties, and London laughed at his 'humorous' types, who spoke not in inflated verse but in prose approximating to its own, at the melancholy gulls Mathew and Stephen, and the cowardly braggart Bobadill.

The word 'humour' had been used in medieval times to denote the four kinds of moisture in man's body: blood, phlegm, yellow bile and black bile. Since then it had come to mean the temperament produced by the combination of these humours, particularly a temperament determined by the morbid excess of any one, as when a disproportionate excess of yellow bile produced a choleric man. It is in this sense that Jonson uses it in his comedies, as he explains in the Induction to *Every Man out of his Humour*:

> As when some one peculiar quality
> Doth so possess a man, that it doth draw
> All his affects, his spirits, and his powers,
> In their confluctions, all to run one way,
> This may be truly said to be a humour.

Such one-sided, unbalanced characters are inevitably flat and stagey creatures, types rather than individuals, but Jonson managed his puppets with such assurance and dexterity that *Every Man in his Humour* at once made his reputation. Shakespeare laughingly replied to the new comedy by creating the taciturn, quarrelsome and darkly hinting Corporal Nym, with his meaningless refrain, 'that's the humour of it'.

Jonson himself was a 'humorous' man, choleric and quarrelsome, proud of his exploits as a soldier, when he had, 'in the face of both the camps', killed an enemy and stripped him of his arms, and his humour led to a real tragedy in the fields a few days after the production of his comedy at the Curtain. A quarrel with Gabriel Spencer, his fellow-prisoner after the *Isle of Dogs* disaster and now one of the leading actors of the Admiral's, was followed by a duel. According to Jonson, Spencer wounded him in the arm with a sword ten inches longer than his own, but in spite of this disadvantage he outfenced his opponent and killed him. Spencer was a dangerous adversary, for he had himself killed a man two years before in a brawl in a barber's shop. After lying for a fortnight in the noisome Newgate prison Jonson was brought to trial at the beginning of October, when the jury found him guilty of murder: 'the aforesaid Benjamin Johnson feloniously and wilfully slew and killed the aforesaid Gabriel Spencer at Shoreditch'. The penalty was hanging, but clerks in holy orders could not be punished by a lay court for a first criminal offence, and as in medieval times clerks were virtually the only literate people, they proved their right to immunity, or 'benefit of clergy', by showing that they could read. Illiterate men and all women were hanged for a first offence, but Jonson was able to plead benefit of clergy, read his 'neck verse' from the psalter, and escape with nothing worse than a branding on the base of his left thumb. He left prison a branded felon who would not a second time escape hanging—and a Papist. While in Newgate he had been visited by, or more probably imprisoned with, a priest who converted him to the Roman Catholic faith, to which he remained loyal for the next twelve years. Despite the success of *Every Man in his Humour*, the young playwright had not made life any easier for himself by his exploits in the autumn of 1598.

Henslowe was in great distress, and wrote to Alleyn in Sussex: 'Now to leat you vnderstand newes I will teall you some but yt is for me harde & heavey. Sence you weare with me I hau loste one of my company which hurteth me greatley; that is Gabrell, for he is slayen in Hogesden fylldes by the handes of Bengemen Jonson bricklayer.' It was not only the loss of Spencer that hurt him—he had died more than £3 in his debt.

By this time the entries that Henslowe made in his *Diary* had changed their character. Instead of a list of plays performed and profits received, there are inventories of properties and costumes, records of advances made to 'his' company for the purchase of plays, and of loans made to the players themselves. Henslowe had, in fact, become the banker of the Admiral's, both corporately and individually, and after July 1598 he secured his loans by taking the profits of 'the wholle gallereys', instead of the half share to which he was entitled as rent. Players and poets alike were in his hands, or, less charitably, in his clutches, for as he himself wrote later, 'Should these fellowes come out of my debt I should have noe rule over them'. The play-workshop was now in full production, and at a pinch a play could be turned out within a fortnight by a squad of five or six collaborators, who would receive £1 or so apiece for their work: not a very high return even for mass-produced potboilers. A dramatist would submit the plot of a play, with a sample scene, to one of the sharers in the company, who, if he liked it, would recommend Henslowe to commission it by paying a first instalment towards the finished product. Thus Samuel Rowley, himself a playwright as well as a player, wrote: 'Mr. Hinchloe, I haue harde fyue shetes of a playe of the Conqueste of the Indes & I dow not doute but it wyll be a verye good playe; tharefore I praye ye delyuer them fortye shyllynges in earneste of it & take the papers into your one handes & on Easter eue thaye promyse to make an ende of all the reste.' The authors, John Day, William Haughton and Wentworth Smith (whose initials, to our confusion, are the same as Shakespeare's), were duly paid their earnest money, various advances and the balance when the play was finished, six months after the promised time. Just before the fatal duel, Jonson had written *Hot Anger Soon Cold* with Chettle and Henry Porter, and Henslowe had then lent him 20s. 'vpon a boocke which he showed the plotte vnto the company'. He does not seem to have finished his assignment, for a month after the duel Henslowe advanced Chapman £3 'one his playe boocke & ij ectes of a tragedie of Bengemenes plotte'. But by 1599 Jonson was back in the fold, writing *The Page of Plymouth* with Dekker, and Henslowe records payments in earnest of

Robert II to 'Thomas Deckers, Bengemen Johnson, Hary Chettell & other Jentellman'.

One of the 'other Jentellman' was John Marston, a young Oxford man destined for the law but turned professional writer. Under the pseudonym of W. Kinsayder, he had already published *Pygmalion*, a slightly salacious parody of *Venus and Adonis*, and *The Scourge of Villanie*, eleven satires dedicated to 'his most esteemed and best beloved Self', in which, like an inferior Donne, he lashes himself into a fury over the real or imagined vices of the world. Both books were burned when Whitgift ordered the strict enforcement of the licensing laws. Marston was as arrogant and vain as Jonson, but gloomy, professedly at least, and wildly melodramatic, and the two young men were made to quarrel with one another. His first unaided play, the two parts of *Antonio and Mellida*, produced in 1599, might almost have been written at the time of *Tamburlaine*, and was the kind of extravaganza against which Jonson's ordered classical mind revolted. A revenge play, inspired by *The Spanish Tragedy*, the characteristic scene is a churchyard at midnight, a ghost in the cellarage crying for revenge and the 'putry mould' groaning when the murder is committed. Yet the play is by no means devoid of poetry and pathos, as in the description of the death of Mellida, whose 'cheek changed earth, her senses slept in rest'.

Thomas Dekker, another of the gentlemen-collaborators in *Robert II*, was a very different character, a genial happy-go-lucky romantic who could turn his hand to anything, and one of the last writers of the true Elizabethan lyric, with its poignant purity of tone, silver-voiced as the boys who played Viola and Marina:

> Art thou poor, yet hast thou golden slumbers?
>   O sweet content!
> Art thou rich, yet is thy mind perplexed?
>   O punishment!
> Dost thou laugh to see how fools are vexed
> To add to golden numbers, golden numbers?
> O sweet content! O sweet content!

Like Chettle and most of the men who worked for Henslowe, Dekker was chronically impecunious and embarrassed with troubles, but none of his misfortunes soured the sweetness of his disposition or shook his faith in his fellow men. His first entry into history is ominous enough, the record of £2 lent by Henslowe in February

1598, 'to dise charge Mr. Dicker owt of the cownter in the Powl-trey'. And a year later Henslowe found another £3 10s. 'to descarge Thomas Dickers frome the a reaste of my lord Chamberlens men'. This may have been charity on Henslowe's part, but from his other entries it seems clear that the loans were treated as instalments on the plays that Dekker was then writing. One of these was *Old Fortunatus*, a tale of magic reminiscent of *Friar Bacon*, and indeed it is probable that he dressed an old work, half morality, by Greene, who called his unfortunate son Fortunatus. Its incoherent romanticism must have made Jonson writhe, and perhaps he was referring to its Chorus, so like that of *Henry V*, when in *Every Man in his Humour* he pillories the, to him, clumsy device of the Chorus that 'wafts you o'er the seas'. Even worse were the Peter Pan-like paraphernalia of ropes and pulleys let down from the heavens to transport Fortunatus through the air in his magic hat. But it is a delightful entertainment, if only for its innocence and freshness, and Fortunatus himself, who chooses gold rather than wisdom when offered the gifts of Fortune, for 'If that lean tawny face tobacconist Death, that turns all into smoke, must turn me so quickly into ashes, yet I will not mourn in ashes, but in music. Hey, old lad, be merry'. It might almost be Simon Eyre speaking, the jovial cobbler of *The Shoemaker's Holiday*, which Dekker wrote soon afterwards, perhaps inspiring Henry V's great speech before Agincourt on Crispin Crispian, the patron saints of cob-blers. *Old Fortunatus* and *The Shoemaker's Holiday* were the only plays presented by the Admiral's at the Revels of 1599.

All the dramatists of this period, save Shakespeare, seem to have gone through the Henslowe mill; Chapman and Drayton were there, and of the newer generation, besides those already mentioned, Richard Hathway, Thomas Heywood, Thomas Middleton, John Day, William Haughton (released 'owt of the Clyncke' by Henslowe), Robert Wilson, Henry Porter and of course 'our best plotter', Anthony Munday. Like Shakespeare and Jonson, Heywood was actor as well as dramatist, in March 1598 hiring 'him seallfe' to Henslowe 'as a covenante searvante for ij yeares & not to playe any wher publicke a bowt London but in my howsse', on penalty of £40. Porter, too, was securely bound, for when, in February 1599, Henslowe advanced him £2 for his *Two Angry Women of Abingdon*, it was on condition that he should have 'alle the bookes which he writte ether him sellfe or with any other'. It was an astute move, for Porter's rural comedy has something of the quality of *The Merry Wives of Windsor*. But it came to nothing; at the end of May Porter borrowed 10s. from Henslowe, and on June 7th he was dead. He had quarrelled with his fellow dramatist, John Day, who mortally wounded him with a rapier near the heart. Day pleaded self-defence, the old story that he was cornered before he turned to fight, and after being found guilty of manslaughter was acquitted, presumably by a royal pardon. More fortunate than Jonson, he escaped without even a branding. Young Henry Porter was a real loss to the English drama, but it was something that Day survived to write the golden *Parliament of Bees*, a dramatic allegory inspired by *A Midsummer Night's Dream*, the fairy octosyllabics of which it closely resembles. But there is an appropriate satirical sting among the honey, directed generally at the parasitic players, and very directly at Henslowe:

> Most of the timber that his state repairs
> He hews out o' the bones of foundered players:
> They feed on poet's brains, he eats their breath.

Jonson called Day a base fellow—but then he called Dekker a rogue.

Anthony Munday was in tremendous fettle. Early in 1598 Henslowe paid him £5 for 'the firste parte of Robyne Hoode', and as much again to him and Chettle for a second part. These were the two parts of *The Downfall of Robert Earl of Huntingdon*, probably the two plays given by the Admiral's at the Revels of 1598, since in November Chettle received another 10s. 'for mendinge of Roben Hood for the corte'. To this tragic romance of Sherwood Forest Shakespeare replied for the Chamberlain's with a romantic comedy of the Forest of Arden. Not to be outdone and elated by his success, Munday planned a counterblast to the two parts of *Henry IV*. Shakespeare had been in trouble over these plays. His original name for Falstaff had been Sir John Oldcastle, an historical character and the friend of Henry V, who reluctantly had to agree to his execution for his treasonable Lollardism. Whatever his faults, Oldcastle did not lack courage, and his descendants, Lord Chamberlain Cobham and his son, not unnaturally resented his portrayal as a cowardly corrupter of the Prince of Wales. Shakespeare therefore changed his name to Sir John Falstaff, a variation of Fastolfe, whom he had already depicted in 1 *Henry VI* as a knight with a kind of alacrity in running away, though again the historical Fastolfe was anything but a poltroon.

Munday, therefore, set out to confound Shakespeare, and at the same
time win the approval of the new Lord Cobham, by writing 'the true
and honorable historie' of Oldcastle and his martrydom, for, as he
wrote in his prologue:

> It is no pampered glutton we present,
> Nor aged Councellor to youthfull sinne.
> . . . Let fair Truth be grac'te,
> Since forg'de inuention former time defac'te.

He enlisted the help of Drayton, Wilson and Hathway, and in
October 1599 Henslowe paid the collaborators £10 for the first part
of *Sir John Oldcastle* and in earnest of the second part. Evidently the
play was the success that it deserved to be, for Henslowe distributed
unwonted largesse to 'Mr. Munday and the reste of the poets, at the
playinge of Sir John Oldcastell, the firste tyme, x*s*. as a gefte'. Ironically enough, the first part (the second has been lost) was published
twenty years later as 'Written by William Shakespeare'. And although
Munday got his money, he also got a drubbing from Marston in
Histriomastix, a recension of an old play, in which Munday figures as
Posthaste, the frothy poet of an incompetent and arrogant company of
players who call themselves Sir Oliver Owlet's men, strutting, in
Marstonian phrase, 'in shreds of nitty brogetie'. The healthy rivalry
of the Admiral's and Chamberlain's was working up towards a fiercer
form of warfare among the playwrights themselves.

While Shakespeare was acting in *Every Man in his Humour*, writing
Much Ado about Nothing and planning *Henry V*, he was also doing a
good turn for his old Stratford friend Richard Quiney, who was then in
London. From the Bell in Carter Lane, Quiney wrote to his 'loveinge
good ffrend & contreyman' asking for a loan of £30 to help him out
of his London debts. Richard, his father Adrian, and their friend
Abraham Sturley were all financially embarrassed after the disastrous
Stratford fires, and it seems that Shakespeare helped them by investing
in some enterprise of theirs. It must have been at about this time that
his only surviving sister, Joan, married William Hart, a shadowy
character about whom nothing is known save that he was a hatter.
Their first son, and Shakespeare's first nephew, was born in 1600.

Shakespeare's fortunes continued to prosper. For some time the
Theatre had stood unfrequented 'in dark silence and vast solitude',
and Giles Allen, the owner of the land on which it stood, was threaten-

ing to pull it down. But his move was anticipated by Cuthbert Burbage. Exercising the right contained in the original lease, he had it dismantled shortly after Christmas, 1598, and then sent a dozen men— according to Allen, 'in verye outragious, violent and riotous sort'— to cart away the timbers to the Bankside, where he had secured the lease of a plot of land on the other side of the road that ran past Henslowe's Rose. Here in the course of 1599, among the brothels, the smells of the Beargarden, the taverns and the prisons—Clink, Marshalsea and King's Bench—the old Theatre was resurrected in the form of the new Globe. The Burbage brothers supplied half of the capital, the other half being supplied by Shakespeare, Phillips, Pope, Heminge and Kempe, so that the theatre itself now became part of the joint-stock of the company, or at least of most of the sharers. Each member of this syndicate of housekeepers, as they were called, was entitled to his share of the profits, and liable for his proportion of the ground-rent and other expenses. This free association of players, with an important stake in the success of their common venture, was a very different sort of enterprise from that across the way, where Henslowe owned the theatre and almost everything in it, including, it might almost be said, the players and playwrights themselves.

In spite of all that has been written and the innumerable attempted reconstructions, we really know very little about the construction of the Globe, even though the Fortune of the following year, for which the contract has been preserved, had some features in common. The auditorium must have resembled that of the Swan, a circular or polygonal building with three galleries surrounding the yard, but we are left distressingly in the dark about the stage, for the Fortune contract, after making certain specifications, simply states that its stage is to be 'contryved and fashioned' like that of the Globe. No doubt all the latest devices were installed in the heavens for the production of the spectacular effects that Jonson derided and disdained to use in his plays, in which he boasted that

> Nor creaking throne comes down the boys to please;
> Nor nimble squib is seen to make afeard
> The gentlewomen; nor rolled bullet heard
> To say, it thunders; nor tempestuous drum
> Rumbles, to tell you when the storm doth come.

But such apparatus was by now a standard part of theatrical equipment to entertain the groundlings; Shakespeare and the Burbages were concerned with more important things, and we may be sure that they embodied in the Globe all the improvements that they had devised for the ideal theatre of which they must have dreamed for years while playing at the antiquated Theatre and Curtain. Much the most important of these would be a fully developed upper and lower stage in front of the tiring-house, perhaps so constructed that steps could be placed against the pulpit as an alternative, or even as an addition, to the curtained lower stage, so retaining the eminently desirable medieval entry from 'above'. It seems probable that Henslowe had already been experimenting along these lines, but his theatre was now sadly out of date, his stage but a makeshift affair; no wonder he coveted one like that at the Globe—an even bigger and better one if possible.

It may have been the newly opened Globe that a Basle doctor, Thomas Platter, visited late in September, when he saw a tragedy of Julius Cæsar, conceivably Shakespeare's. He also saw a comedy at the Curtain, where one of the characters went 'into the tent', which is suggestive of a projecting curtained stage at the back of the apron. Then he describes how every day at two o'clock two or three plays are presented at different theatres, how they perform on a raised platform surrounded by galleries, how anybody who stands below pays a penny, a seat costing another penny at a farther door, and a seat with a cushion yet another penny at another door. No doubt the groundlings were by now usually in the yard, though Platter does not say so, and the normal interpretation of his account would be that they stood in the lowest gallery. Apparently there were intervals when refreshments were carried round for sale, and the play was concluded with an elegant dance.

One of the first plays to be given at the Globe was *Every Man out of his Humour*. Jonson had never lacked confidence, but now confidence was swollen into something perilously like insolence. In the Induction, in the character of Asper, 'an ingenious and free spirit, eager and contant in reproof', he lectured the audience in the 'thronged round', arrogantly proclaiming his mission to 'strip the ragged follies of the time', then left 'his friend' Cordatus to act as chorus, apologist and panegyrist ('Have you heard a better drunken dialogue?' he asks) throughout the play. Jonson is his own hero, Macilente, a scholar of uncommon, though insufficiently recognised, talents, whose envy of his unworthy rivals is purged and turned to pity by their well-

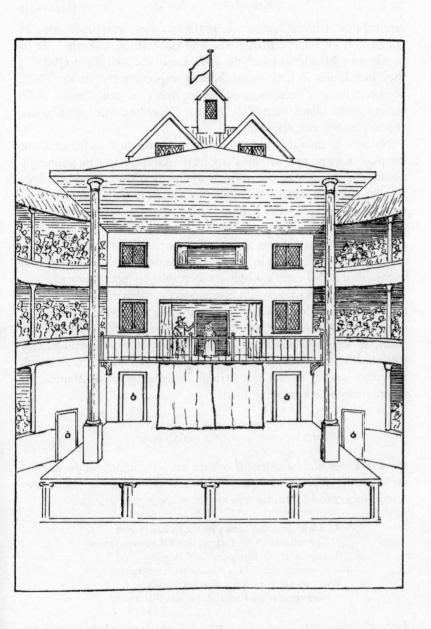

THE GLOBE

merited misfortunes. The play lacks the freshness of its predecessor, of which it is little more than a laboured elaboration, and when, at its conclusion, Macilente asked the audience in the 'fair-filled Globe' if they had found it tedious, confidently expecting the answer 'No', Jonson must have been disappointed, for in his dedication of the Folio version to the Gentlemen of the Inns of Court he wrote that of them, at least, 'it was not despised'.

Neither Kempe nor Shakespeare acted in the first performance of the play. Kempe had sold his share in the Globe, or, as he punningly put it, 'daunst my selfe out of the world', and in the following February, for a wager, danced his celebrated morris from London to Norwich. He was replaced as a sharer in the company by Robert Armin, a writer, whose fooling was more subtle and sensitive than Kempe's, and for whom Shakespeare seems to have written the parts of Touchstone, Feste and the Fool in *Lear*. Shakespeare himself may have been in Stratford at his sister's wedding when the play was produced.

They were busy years, and Shakespeare can have had little leisure for reading; but he would find time to taste and even to chew and digest, some of the rarer books. One of these was *Musophilus*, a discourse in which Daniel makes a general defence of all learning and a special plea for the sacred art of poetry. This is the poem in which we come nearest to the earnest and dedicated spirit of Daniel, for whom no good was equal to this:

> To do worthy the writing, and to write
> Worthy the reading, and the world's delight.

He concludes with a splendid tribute to the English language, and prophetically foreshadows the day when it will spread from 'this scarce discerned isle' to the new world of the west:

> And who, in time, knows whither we may vent
>   The treasure of our tongue, to what strange shores
> This gain of our best glory shall be sent,
>   T' enrich unknowing nations with our stores?
> What worlds in th' yet unformed Occident
>   May come refined with th' accents that are ours?

Daniel's passionate love of poetry, his absolute integrity and his agonising struggle with the shadowy champions of doubt advanced by his Philistine opponent, 'Now when this busy world cannot attend

Th' untimely music of neglected lays', make *Musophilus* one of the most moving poems of the whole Elizabethan Age.

Another book to be lingered over was Chapman's *Seven Books of the Iliads*, published at about the same time as his conclusion to *Hero and Leander*. No doubt Chapman's version of Homer came to Shakespeare, with his little Greek, much as it came to Keats, as a revelation, and it may have been the spark, conflagration rather, that inspired him to write *Troilus and Cressida*, not that the story of Cressida is Homeric, but he could scarcely have written the Greek scenes without its aid. If the rival poet of Sonnet 86 was a real character and not a fiction, he may well have been Chapman, for to no other poem of the period can Shakespeare's description of his style, 'the proud full sail of his great verse', be so appropriately applied. Sometimes the swinging fourteeners develop a surge and momentum comparable almost to the original:

> Cranes, geese, or long-necked swans, here, there, proud of their pinions fly,
> And in their falls lay out such throats, that with their spiritful cry
> The meadow shrieks again; so here, these many-nationed men
> Flowed over the Scamandrian field, from tents and ships; the din
> Was dreadful that the feet of men and horse beat out of earth . . .

But sometimes the combers collapse or shatter themselves in a flurry of froth and spray. Chapman always strove to write above a mortal pitch, and his intrusive glosses, hyperbole, rodomontade and general attempt to out-Homer Homer are often destructive of the poetry. Jonson called it prose, yet had at least one passage by heart, and despite its blemishes it still remains one of the noblest renderings of Homer into English.

Another translation that would interest Shakespeare appeared at the end of 1598. This was Bartholomew Yonge's version of Jorge de Montemayor's *Diana Enamorada*, a Spanish romance containing the story that he had already dramatised, with some variations, in *The Two Gentlemen of Verona*. If he had used Yonge's version, he must have seen it in manuscript, for it was written by 1582, but more probably he had worked from the lost play of *Felix and Philiomena*, presented by the Queen's Men at the Revels of 1585.

Hakluyt's second edition of the *Principal Navigations*, containing Molyneux's *Hydrographical Description*, 'the new map with the augmentation of the Indies', so like Malvolio's multilinear smile, was

issued in three volumes between 1598 and 1600. In 1598 came the
Italian-English dictionary of Daniel's brother-in-law, John Florio,
A World of Words from which Jonson culled the names of the characters in *Every Man out of his Humour*—Fungoso, Sogliardo and the
rest. And in the same year merry old John Stow published his homely,
unpretentious and so much the more endearing therefore *Survey of
London*. A tailor and antiquary, almost it might be said by birth, he
had met the great Camden, who encouraged him to publish his edition
of Chaucer, to write the *Annals of England*, and to do for London
what Camden himself had done for England as a whole—describe the
city that he had known for seventy years. His eccentric antiquarian
activities and detestation of the iconoclasm of the Reformation
brought him into disfavour with the authorities, but he went his way
—literally on foot, for he could never manage to sit a horse—
impoverishing himself to record the old Tudor London that he so
passionately loved, and the so rapidly expanding late-Elizabethan city
that he could love only with reservations. One entry at least must
have moved the Burbages and the rest of the Chamberlain's Men as
they made their plans for the dismantling of the Theatre: 'Near
thereunto are builded two public houses for the acting and show of
comedies, tragedies, and histories, for recreation. Whereof the one is
called the Curtain, the other the Theater, both standing on the
south-west side towards the field.'

It was at this time that Shakespeare's name was first associated
with that of the not over-scrupulous printer William Jaggard. In
1599, seeing a chance to profit from the reputation of the most popular
poet and dramatist of the day, Jaggard issued *The Passionate Pilgrim*
without so much as registration, and impudently ascribed it to Shakespeare. Of the twenty-one poems in the miscellany only five are
certainly Shakespeare's: versions of sonnets filched from one of the
manuscripts in circulation, and from the recently published *Love's
Labour's Lost*. A number of the others are by his admirer, Richard
Barnfield, and include the sonnet 'If music and sweet poetry agree',
with its tributes to Dowland and Spenser. Dowland, now approaching
the zenith of his career, had just published his first *Book of Songs*, 'so
made that all the parts together, or either of them severally, may be
sung to the lute', an important anticipation of the solo-song, which
was soon to rival the madrigal in popularity. But Spenser had written
his last. Shortly after his appointment as Sheriff of Cork in 1598, his

castle at Kilcolman was set on fire and destroyed by the Irish rebels. On Christmas Eve he arrived in London, where he died a month later, and was buried beside Chaucer in Westminster Abbey. Twenty years later Jonson told Drummond that 'he died for lack of bread, and refused twenty pieces sent to him by my Lord of Essex, and said he was sorry he had no time to spend them'. It may be so, yet it seems improbable that the poet accorded such a funeral should have died in destitution, a funeral in which his coffin was carried by his peers— Shakespeare among them, perhaps—who threw their elegies into his grave, along with the pens that had written them.

Ireland was Spenser's undoing, and Ireland had become the most pressing problem of the hour. The situation had deteriorated so rapidly in the summer of 1598 that Elizabeth had made of it an excuse for a reconciliation with Essex, who was recalled to the deliberations of the Council. Lord Knollys, after all, had not been appointed Deputy, but it was essential that somebody should be sent as soon as possible. The Queen now favoured Charles Blount, Lord Mountjoy, the lover of Essex's sister Penelope, Lady Rich. Essex again demurred at the loss of one of his supporters, and, when pressed as to whom he would send, sketched such a one as he was himself. As no one else seemed eager for the office, Elizabeth at length allowed herself to be persuaded, and Cecil had no objection to his rival's going to what foreign diplomats called 'the Englishman's grave'. 'I have beaten Knollys and Mountjoy in the Council,' Essex wrote jubilantly to Harington, 'and by God I will beat Tyrone in the field.'

Brave words! If ever a man had taken upon himself complete responsibility for a task it was Essex. Jubilation began to give way to foreboding, but after months of hard bargaining with the Queen an army was collected, and in March 1599 London poured out her citizens to cheer their hero as he set out for Chester at the head of a force of 17,000 men. Bacon gave him encouraging words, but quite plainly, as in a glass, foresaw his patron's overthrow.

Among the many friends of Essex, for he saw to it that he was surrounded by his supporters, were his stepfather, Sir Christopher Blount (for his mother had married a third time), whom he made Marshal of the Army, and the young Earl of Southampton, whom he wished to make his General of the Horse. But Southampton was out of favour. In the previous year he had seduced one of the Queen's maids of honour, and, though he had married his mistress, a short period of imprisonment was followed by a long disgrace. The lady was Elizabeth Vernon, Essex's cousin. Jealous of his own honour, Essex was strangely insensitive to its loss by his female relations, whose dishonour seemed only to gain him friends, and, once in Ireland, out of immediate reach of the Queen's displeasure, he gave Southampton his command. As soon as she heard, Elizabeth ordered his dismissal, but Essex refused, and even began the indiscriminate creation of knights, a privilege that he had been expressly ordered not to abuse. He was piqued by the appointment of Cecil to the Mastership of the Wards, the lucrative post for which he had himself pleaded in vain. It seemed as though, as soon as his back was turned, Elizabeth deliberately insulted him by rewarding his rival with the offices that he particularly desired. And not only Cecil, but his other rivals, Raleigh and Cobham, he complained, were favoured, though they only wished the ill success of his great venture. He had been the first to taunt Cobham with the name of Falstaff, no doubt because of the fuss he had made over Shakespeare's unflattering portrayal of his ancestor, and now the new Countess of Southampton wrote a charming and cheerful letter to her husband, describing the arrival of a counterfeit young Cobham: 'Al the nues I can send you that I thinke wil make you mery is that Sir John Falstaf is by his Mrs Dame Pintpot made father of a goodly milers thum, a boye that's all heade and veri litel body, but this is a secrit.' 'Peace, good pint-pot; peace, good ticklebrain,' says Falstaff to Mistress Quickly. Evidently *Henry IV* was well known among the Essex circle.

Another history of Henry IV was equally well known. A Cambridge scholar, John Hayward, had just published *The Life and Reign of King Henry IV*, containing a detailed account of the deposition of Richard II by his cousin Bolingbroke, a theme abhorrent to Elizabeth Tudor, whose grandfather had seized the crown from another Richard. Then, the book was dedicated in adulatory language to Essex, and Essex was her cousin. It was treason, or something very near treason. She ordered Hayward's arrest, and the wretched man spent the remainder of her reign in the Tower.

'By God, I will beat Tyrone in the field', Essex had boasted, and the proper course for any commander, he had told the Council, was to attack the Irish rebels without delay. Yet, instead of attacking Tyrone in Ulster, he frittered away his forces in a futile march through Leinster and the south. The summer was slipping away with nothing accomplished, and Elizabeth wrote a withering letter ordering him to march at once against Tyrone. By now Essex was a broken man, sick in body and mind, all his confidence gone as well as most of his men, uselessly dispersed in garrisoning castles, the very policy that he had deplored in others. To extricate himself, he desperately thought of sailing for England with a force of a few thousand men to 'rescue' the Queen from her evil counsellors. But Blount and Southampton would have none of that, and advised his returning with just sufficient men to save him from danger should he be arrested.

Meanwhile England was hopefully awaiting news of his success, and Shakespeare writing the last act of *Henry V*, in the Chorus of which he compared the king's victorious return from the Agincourt campaign to the anticipated triumph of Essex:

> As by a lower but loving likelihood,
> Were now the general of our gracious empress,
> As in good time he may, from Ireland coming,
> Bringing rebellion broached on his sword,
> How many would the peaceful city quit,
> To welcome him!

But Essex, too, was beginning the last act of a history. Early in September he made a show of attacking Tyrone, but, after a skirmish, secretly met and parleyed with him. What passed between them is unknown, possibly some wild talk of England for the one and Ireland for the other, but the immediate outcome was a truce, and Essex retired to Dublin. The campaign that had cost Elizabeth £300,000, and more men than she could well spare, was at an end.

Early on the morning of September 28th Essex arrived in London with a number of his devoted followers, still with a vague idea of affecting some sort of *coup d'état*. But the Court was at Nonsuch, and Essex, leaving all but six of his supporters in London, galloped south to see the Queen. Bursting through the Presence and Privy Chambers, he found her in her bedroom, where she was being dressed by her ladies. She kept her head, welcomed him and laughingly told him to change his muddy clothes while she completed her toilet. Essex's spirits revived, but in the afternoon she demanded an explanation before the Council. She had had time to consult Cecil and to gauge the strength of the Earl's support. That night he was ordered to keep to his chamber. Two days later he was committed to the custody of Lord Keeper Egerton, at York House in the Strand. For the moment

Essex was accounted for, yet London was seething with discontent. Elizabeth proposed vindicating her action by bringing him to public trial in the Star Chamber, but Cecil and Bacon, who now saw on which side his interests lay, advised her against inflaming the passions of the people, whose darling Essex was. Then he fell ill, his popularity rose still higher and ugly slogans against Cecil and his faction appeared on the walls of the palace. There was nothing for it but to wait and allow passions to cool. That winter, when *Henry V* was produced at the Globe, it was without the Chorus and its reference to the 'general of our gracious empress'.

VIII

1600–1601

NEW THEATRES AND NEW COMPANIES

THE building of the Globe was an expensive enterprise, and to help pay for their new theatre the Chamberlain's Men sold a number of plays in the course of 1600. In August, *Much Ado* and *2 Henry IV* were registered together by two reputable publishers as 'Wrytten by master Shakespere'—the first appearance of Shakespeare's name in the Stationers' Register—and soon afterwards the quartos appeared on their bookstalls. It was either the first or the second part of *Henry IV* that the Chamberlain's had presented before their patron at Hunsdon House when he entertained the Flemish ambassador, 'to his great contentment', one afternoon in March. Though the play was described as 'Sir John Old Castell', this was the popular name for *Henry IV* (much to Cobham's annoyance) just as *Twelfth Night* came to be known as 'Malvolio'. The *Much Ado* quarto is interesting, as it was printed from the manuscript prompt-copy in which the book-holder had substituted for Dogberry and Verges the names of Kempe and Cowley, who played the parts, and the compositor did not always remember to alter them. But by the time *Much Ado* appeared, Kempe had left the Chamberlain's, published an account of his 'morris to Norwich', hung up his buskins in the Guildhall and set off for Italy and Germany. *A Midsummer Night's Dream* came out in October, and was followed a few weeks later by *The Merchant of Venice*, though this had first been conditionally registered as early as 1598. *Henry V* is a different matter, for it is a 'bad' quarto. Evidently the company suspected that one of their hired men had made a memorial version of the play, and they tried to prevent its piratical publication. However, a shockingly mutilated text was issued by Thomas Millington, the stationer who had already published the 'bad' quartos of *Henry VI*, Parts 1 and 2. Shakespeare's were not the only plays that helped to pay for the Globe, and Jonson, who was as careful as Shakespeare was careless about the publication of his dramatic work, had the satisfaction of seeing *Every Man in his Humour* and *Every*

Man out of his Humour in print by the beginning of the new century.

Henslowe watched uneasily as the fine new playhouse went up opposite his Rose, and when it was completed his worst fears were realised. The London citizens thronged to the Globe with its splendid stage to see the plays of Shakespeare, leaving his own theatre half empty. He consulted his son-in-law, and Alleyn, who had retired some three years before, agreed to help. The moment was propitious; the Queen herself had expressed the wish that he would resume his playing, and to signalise his return it should be to a new theatre and not to the obsolescent Rose in the swamps of Bankside. He looked about for a suitable position on the north bank of the river and picked on a site just to the north of Cripplegate, in the liberty of Finsbury, an expanding and prosperous suburb within easy reach of the Inns of Court. On December 22nd, 1599, he bought the lease of a plot of land between Golden Lane and Whitecross Street, and a fortnight later he and Henslowe signed an agreement with Peter Street for the building of a playhouse. Street was the carpenter who had built the Globe, but the Fortune was to be even finer than the Globe, though its best features were to be incorporated.

Opposition to the project was only to be expected. In March a few of the more influential inhabitants of Finsbury protested, and the Council were stampeded into ordering the Middlesex magistrates to stay the building. But in April a counter-petition was presented by the humbler denizens of the liberty, urging the Council to allow the work to go forward, on the grounds that the site was too remote to cause annoyance and, more to the point, Alleyn had agreed to give 'a very liberall porcion of money' towards the relief of the poor of the parish. He had also taken the precaution of securing a letter of commendation from the Lord Admiral. The Council thought again, and, reversing their former decision, ordered the justices to do all they could to assist Alleyn in his enterprise. The site, they wrote, was 'a verie remote and exempt place', and the Rose had become impossible, 'scituate vppon the Bancke, verie noysome for the resorte of people in the wynter tyme'. Then, the old Curtain was to be pulled down in compensation, and, finally and conclusively, 'her Maiestie hath sondrye tymes signified her pleasuer' that Alleyn should revive his service. Alleyn and Henslowe had gone round to work, and no doubt underground as well. The combination was a formidable one.

Their contract with Street has been preserved. From it we learn that the frame of the theatre was made of timber, 'lardger and bigger in assize' than the timbers of the Globe. The plan was revolutionary (or, if we choose, a reversion to the inn-yard design), a square, the outer walls of which were eighty feet, enclosing a yard of fifty-five feet each way. There were three galleries, twelve, eleven and nine feet high, all of which were provided with seats. This, too, may have been revolutionary, for there was now no standing room for the groundlings save in the yard. Four 'gentlemens roomes' were partitioned off, as well as an unspecified number of 'Twoe pennie roomes'. The stage, forty-three feet broad, projected as far as the middle of the yard, and was backed by a tiring-house within the frame, and roofed with 'a shadowe or cover'. There is no mention of supplementary upper and lower stages, and though we know that the stage was 'in all other proporcions' like that of the Globe, with glazed windows to the tiring-house, the plan attached to the contract has perished, and with it the possibility of reconstructing with any certainty the most vital features of an Elizabethan playhouse. Alleyn found the money for the building, £520, but Henslowe soon joined him as partner, and seems to have directed operations, occasionally advancing small sums to Street, 'to pasify him'.

By the autumn of 1600 all was ready. The theatre was occupied by the Admiral's, once again with Alleyn in the lead, and its opening celebrated probably with a performance of Dekker's appropriately named *Fortune's Tennis*. So, at the turn of the century, there was a complete reversal of the situation. The Chamberlain's had moved from Shoreditch to Bankside and driven the Admiral's from Bankside to Finsbury. The Theatre and the Rose had been superseded by the Globe and the Fortune.

The new situation was recognised by the Council, and in June, before the completion of the Fortune, they issued an order to the Lord Mayor and magistrates of Middlesex and Surrey, 'to the end that bothe the greatest abuses of the plaies and plaienge houses maye be redressed, and the vse and moderacon of them retained', for plays are not evil in themselves, and 'yeald hir Maiestie recreacion and delight'. There were to be no plays in any of the City inns, and only two houses were to be allowed 'about the Cittie', one in Middlesex and one in Surrey: the Fortune for the Admiral's, the Globe for the Chamberlain's. As for the Curtain, and presumably the Rose, they were to be 'ruinated', or applied to some other good use. Moreover, the two licensed companies were strictly forbidden to play on the Sabbath, in Lent and in time of infection, and were to give no more than two performances a week. It was a crippling injunction, but, in spite of a rider almost pathetically pointing out that their orders would be of little force unless the magistrates played their parts, it was as ineffective as much of the rest of Elizabethan legislation. We may be quite sure that the Admiral's and Chamberlain's did not confine themselves to two days' playing. Then, by October Pembroke's were playing at the Rose, which remained in Henslowe's hands until his lease expired in 1605. In the following May the Council complained, not that the Curtain was still open, but that a particularly offensive play was being given there, and in the spring of 1602 they themselves licensed a combined company of the Earls of Oxford and Worcester to play at the Boar's Head, within the City. Their Lordships were scarcely justified in complaining that there was such a 'multitude of play howses within and about the cittie of London'; but then, perhaps they did not expect to be taken too seriously.

Francis Langley's Swan, too, was still open, though not as a regular playhouse, but as a sort of circus or variety theatre. In May 1600, the Queen was so enchanted by the performance of the French acrobat, Peter Bromvill, and his 'feates upon a rope', that she made the Council grant him licence to perform publicly at the Swan a few days later. Langley died in the following year, but the business was carried on, and in the winter of 1602 the house was the scene of a celebrated hoax by Richard Venner, an impudent and shiftless lawyer who ended his life in a debtor's prison. The story is told in an amusing letter of John Chamberlain to his friend Dudley Carleton:

And, now we are in mirth, I must not forget to tell you of a cousening prancke of one Venner, of Lincolns Inne, that gave out bills of a famous play on Satterday was sevenight on the Banckeside, to be acted only by certain gentlemen and gentlewomen of account. The price at cumming in was two shillings or eighteen pence at least; and when he had gotten most part of the mony into his hands, he would have shewed them a faire paire of heeles, but he was not so nimble to get up on horsebacke, but that he was faine to forsake that course, and betake himselfe to the water, where he was pursued and taken . . . In the meane time the common people, when they saw themselves deluded, revenged themselves upon the hangings, curtains, chairs, stooles, walles, and whatsoever came in their way, very outragiously, and made great spoile. There was great store of good companie, and many noblemen.

The building of the Globe and Fortune were not the only major theatrical events at the turn of the century. The competition from the boys' companies was revived. By 1600 Edward Pearce, a Gentleman of the Chapel Royal, had been appointed Master of the Children of Paul's, where Mulcaster, the enthusiastic believer in the drama as a means of teaching boys good behaviour and audacity, was now headmaster. The last Court performance by the Paul's boys had been in 1590, when they were suppressed, apparently for the part they had played in the Marprelate controversy, but on January 1st, 1601, Pearce brought them once again to Whitehall. They must have begun dramatic operations in their old singing school some time before this, and Marston's *Antonio and Mellida* of 1599 seems to have been one of their first plays. Another play that Marston wrote for them was *Jack Drum's Entertainment*, in which he gave the boys a humorous puff:

> *Sir Edward Fortune.* I saw the Children of Paul's last night,
> And troth, they pleased me pretty, pretty well;
> The apes in time will do it handsomely.
> *Planet.* I' faith, I like the audience that frequenteth there
> With much applause. A man shall not be choked
> With the stench of garlic, nor be pasted
> To the barmy jacket of a beer-brewer.
> *Brabant Junior.* 'Tis a good audience, and I hope the boys
> Will come one day into the Court of Requests.
> *Brabant Senior.* Ay, an they had good plays. But they produce
> Such musty fopperies of antiquity,
> And do not suit the humorous age's back
> With suits in fashion.

Sir Edward Fortune is probably meant to be Edward Alleyn, then engaged in building the Fortune, and the churlish and censorious Brabant Senior, with his insistence on 'humorous' plays, is almost certainly Jonson. The 'musty foppery' to which he alludes seems to be *Histriomastix*, the old play new 'dressed' by Marston, whose turgid style Jonson had parodied in *Every Man out of his Humour*: 'The ecliptic line being optic, doth demonstrate to us the ventosity of the tropics, and whereas our intellectual, or mincing capreal, as you may read in Plato's Histriomastix—You conceive me, sir?' Marston did, and the inevitable quarrel between the two arrogant young dramatists was on the point of breaking out into their plays. Jonson was never to forget that Marston had 'represented him in the stage' as a querulous cuckold, and if Marston chose to satirise him on the Paul's stage, he would reply on that of the Chapel Children.

The Children of the Chapel Royal had been silent, dramatically at least, even longer than the Paul's boys. It was sixteen years since their Blackfriars theatre had been closed, and their Court performances had come, for lack of a place for rehearsal, inevitably to an end. That was some years before the Armada, and since then the great dramatic revolution had been carried through; the University Wits had written and first the Queen's Men, and then the Admiral's and Chamberlain's with the plays of Marlowe and Shakespeare, had usurped the early popularity of the boys, and the once bright comedies of Lyly were dusty and forgotten. The Rose, the Swan and now the Globe and Fortune had been built, and the little private theatre at Blackfriars was scarcely more than a legend.

Yet there was another private theatre at Blackfriars. This was the hall converted by James Burbage in 1596, which, owing to the protests of the neighbouring inhabitants, he had been unable to open as a playhouse. In 1600, however, his son Richard, who had inherited the property, leased the building to Henry Evans, an enterprising business-man who had been associated with Hunnis in the first Blackfriars venture. Having taken a few of his friends into partnership, Evans approached the recently appointed Master of the Chapel Children, Nathaniel Giles, most erudite of musicians and most unworldly of men, and an arrangement was come to whereby the choir-boys should perform at Blackfriars as in the old days. To begin with they revived the comedies of Lyly, 'the ghosts of three or four plays departed a dozen years since', but something new was called for; the syndicate commissioned a play from Jonson, and he wrote *Cynthia's Revels* for the boys.

'By God, 'tis good', Jonson modestly assured the audience in his Epilogue. It may have been good in 1600, but even then it was far too long, and to-day it makes but wearisome reading. To the mythological apparatus that Lyly had so exquisitely manipulated Jonson grafts a 'comical satire' directed against self-love. As in *Every Man out of his Humour* he is Asper, so in *Cynthia's Revels* he is Criticus, 'a creature of a most perfect and divine temper', who virtuously castigates the 'rhymer', Hedon, and 'Impudence itself', Anaides:

> The one a light voluptuous reveller,
> The other, a strange arrogating puff,
> Both impudent, and ignorant enough.

Rightly or wrongly, Marston and Dekker assumed that it was they who were thus held up to ridicule, and prepared their revenge. The best parts of the play are the lyrics—'Queen and huntress, chaste and fair', is one of them—and the Induction, in which three of the boys squabble as to who shall speak the Prologue, and imitate an ignorant critic: 'They do act like so many wrens, and their music is abominable, able to stretch a man's ears worse than ten pillories.' Two of the boys were Solomon Pavy and John Underwood, and the third was probably Nathan Field. Pavy died three years later, when he was thirteen, and Jonson immortalised him in his epitaph. Underwood was to become one of the 'principal actors' in Shakespeare's plays, and Field to succeed Shakespeare himself as one of the sharers in the company. Nid Field was Jonson's favourite, 'his scholar', for, when he was pressed for service with the Chapel, Jonson took his education in hand, and read him the satires of Horace and some of the epigrams of Martial—not, perhaps, reading that we should choose to-day for a boy of nine. Whether Field and the others could sing as well as they could act is another matter.

While the Chamberlain's and Admiral's Men, and the Paul's and Chapel's boys were settling into their new theatres, while Jonson was writing *Cynthia's Revels*, with an eye on the Court Revels of the following winter, and Shakespeare drafting *Twelfth Night*, Essex remained in confinement. Yet Elizabeth appeared to be relenting; the Star Chamber trial was dropped, and in March she allowed him to go to Essex House in charge of a keeper. She herself seemed to be in the best of health and spirits, despite the slump in her popularity and the abuse directed at her advisers and other favourites, at Cecil, Bacon and Raleigh. She entered into the Revels of 1599–1600 with even more than usual gusto, visiting the Presence Chamber almost every night to watch the ladies perform the old and new country dances to pipe and tabor. It could be only a matter of time before Essex was released and restored to favour, and Raleigh wrote to Cecil warning him of the danger: 'If you take it for a good counsel to relent towards this tyrant, you will repent it when it shall be too late.' Cecil did nothing. In June Essex made a full confession of his faults before the Queen and Council, and by the end of August was free to go where he wished, except to Court.

But the real test of his restoration to favour was yet to come. In September the ten-year monopoly of the sweet wines would come to

an end. It was the main source of his income, and if it were not renewed he would be a ruined man. He wrote dutiful, passionate and
persuasive letters to the Queen, and even contrived to see her. For
some weeks she hesitated, and then announced that she herself would
retain the profit on the wines. It was the one fatal policy; she had disgraced and impoverished the most popular man in England, and yet
allowed him to go free. It was a classical example, as it was the last,
of her passion for compromise. Essex completely lost his head; though
he still wrote pitiful and cajoling letters to the Queen, he raved
against the 'old woman, as crooked in her mind as in her carcase',
and when Harington visited him he talked so wildly, 'bordering on
such strange designs', that he escaped from his presence as soon as he
could. As the year drew towards its close, strange faces began to appear
in the streets, and in the neighbourhood of Essex House and Drury
House, Southampton's London home, reckless-looking men loitered
and passed by.

And so the winter Revels of 1600 came round. The Court was at
Whitehall, and on December 26th the Chamberlain's presented the
first play of the season, followed two days later by the Admiral's,
once again, to the Queen's delight with Edward Alleyn. On January
1st Edward Pearce brought the Paul's boys to make their bow, and on
the same night the Earl of Derby's gave a performance. William
Stanley, 6th Earl of Derby, was the son of the Lord Strange, for a
few months the 5th Earl, who had been the patron of the company
that had become the Chamberlain's on his death in 1594. Now a man
of forty, he had a company of provincial players, for whom, it was
said in 1599, he was 'busy penning comedies'. None of his plays can
be identified, yet because he wrote plays and his initials were W. S.,
some people have persuaded themselves that the comedies he penned
were those that most of us attribute to Shakespeare. After their two
performances in 1601, Derby's retired into the provinces, and the
Earl into the obscurity of history.

On January 6th, Twelfth Night, the climax of the Revels, there
were four performances at the palace, which was full of important
visitors and their retainers. The Queen dined in state in the Great
Chamber with the Russian ambassador, and in the course of the dinner
Nathaniel Giles presented the newly formed company of Chapel
Children in 'a showe with musycke and speciall songes prepared for
the purpose'. To Jonson's mortification, *Cynthia's Revels*, despite its

alluring and apposite title, had been rejected as unsuitable by Tilney and the Lord Chamberlain. After supper, in one chamber Derby's gave their second performance, and in another the Admiral's presented *Phæthon*, a new play by Dekker, whom Henslowe had paid £2 for 'alterynge' for the Court. But the play of the evening, the play that the Queen graced with her presence, was given in the Great Hall, and there can be little doubt that it was here that the servants of the Lord Chamberlain, himself responsible for the proceedings, presented *Twelfth Night*.[1]

Shakespeare had probably written *Twelfth Night* in the autumn of 1600, a play with 'greate variety and change of Musicke', such as the Queen loved. Sir Toby's song, 'Farewell, dear heart', he had taken from Robert Jones's newly published *First Book of Songs*, and Thomas Morley's air, 'O mistress mine', in his *First Book of Consort Lessons*, had inspired the writing of the lyric for Robert Armin, who played Feste. John Bull, the Chapel organist, was in charge of the music, and it may be that Robert Hales, the Queen's lutenist and 'the Orpheus of the Court', sang 'Come away, come away, death' that night. What was the original name that Shakespeare gave to the Duke of Illyria we may never know, but when, about a week before the performance, it was learned that Don Virginio Orsino, Duke of Bracciano, was about to visit Elizabeth, he changed it, as a pretty compliment, to Orsino. Don Virginio was only twenty-eight, but he was the nephew of the Grand Duke of Tuscany, a valuable friend in time of war with Spain; moreover, he was the kind of handsome courtier that Elizabeth liked to have about her, and if she, despite her sixty-eight years, cared to identify herself with Olivia, so much the better. So it was Don Virginio, in place of Essex, who stood beside the Queen's state in the Great Hall, to watch Shakespeare and his fellows perform *Twelfth Night* on Twelfth Night of the year 1601.

According to the note added to the Lord Chamberlain's memoranda, Wolsey's vast banqueting-hall, nearly a hundred feet long and almost half as wide, 'was richly hanged, and degrees placed rownd about it', and Don Virginio himself, in a tantalisingly elusive letter to his wife describes it as being *atorno atorno . . . gradi*, 'surrounded on all sides with tiers of seats'. Apparently, then, the play was produced in

---

[1] In this section I am, of course, indebted to Dr. Leslie Hotson, whose brilliant discoveries have recently been revealed in his *First Night of Twelfth Night*. I do not, however, always accept his inferences.

the medieval manner in the centre of the playing-place, with painted canvas 'houses' as the only scenery, one for Olivia's house, the other for the palace of Orsino. As the performance was preceded by a dance, there was no stage, but when there was no preliminary dancing a stage was sometimes erected in the middle, instead of at the end, of the hall; indeed, the Office of Works framed and set up 'a broad Stage in the middle of the Haull' for the Revels of the following year.

And so the last and loveliest of Shakespeare's romantic comedies was played that night while Don Virginio stood beside the Queen, who acted as interpreter and talked to him continually. But the loquacious old lady must have fallen silent as she listened to the poetry of Viola:

> 'Tis beauty truly blent, whose red and white
> Nature's own sweet and cunning hand laid on:
> Lady, you are the cruell'st she alive,
> If you will lead these graces to the grave
> And leave the world no copy.

It is no longer the linear lyricism of the early plays, but the perfected, dramatic and contrapuntal poetry of Shakespeare's middle years, in which rhythm and assonance are complementary and interdependent, the one setting off and emphasising the other throughout passages of intricate harmony in which almost every syllable is involved.

When all was over and Armin had sung his last bawdy and melancholy song, Don Orsino escorted the Queen to her lodgings, where a collation was awaiting them, and it was past two o'clock in the morning before he, and no doubt the Chamberlain's Men as well, set out for home. A month later they were to play a part in a more sombre scene.

Despite his protestations and professed submission, Essex had never abandoned his treasonable designs, and while still a prisoner in York House was in secret communication with his friends, Mountjoy and Southampton. Elizabeth had forced the reluctant Mountjoy to take over the command in Ireland, but before setting out he wrote to James of Scotland, telling him that his best hope of succeeding to the English throne lay in Essex, and that if he would help to restore him he would bring an army from Ireland to overthrow the Cecil faction and rescue the Earl. James showed little enthusiasm, and Mountjoy sailed for Ireland. In April he was joined by Southampton, who brought a letter from Essex urging him to lead his army into England, with or without James. But Mountjoy was now a different man, no longer a philandering courtier, but a competent commander whose mission was to subdue Tyrone. He had found himself at last. Essex's cause, which had once seemed so important, was now no more than 'private ambition', and he refused to have anything more to do with such an enterprise. In July Essex appealed to him again, when James was on the Border with a strong power. But Mountjoy had other things to think of. So, too, had James.

A few days later, according to his own account, James was lured into the castle of John Gowrie, Earl of Ruthven, where an attempt was made to assassinate him. Calling for help, he was rescued by his followers, and in the struggle Gowrie and his brother were killed. It was, on the whole, a not unhappy occasion for James, for Gowrie had claims to the English throne, and ever afterwards he celebrated August 5th as a day of delivery from death.

Deserted by Mountjoy, in January Essex made a direct appeal to James, whose reply was so encouraging that it nerved him to action. On February 3rd five of the conspirators met at Drury House, where plans were laid for seizing the Court and raising the City. Cecil was well aware of what was happening, and on Saturday, the 7th, Essex was summoned to attend the Council. There could be no wavering now. Some of the Earl's followers had already persuaded the Chamberlain's Men to play Shakespeare's *Richard II* that afternoon. They were determined that the London citizens should see that it was possible to dethrone a monarch, even, if need be, to kill one. The players protested that it was such an old play that 'they should have small or no Company at yt', but, when Sir Christopher Blount and his friends offered them forty shillings more than their ordinary takings, they agreed. And on that Saturday afternoon at the Globe, a bewildered audience saw, instead of the play they had expected, 'the kyllyng of Kyng Richard the second' played by the Lord Chamberlain's servants.

On Sunday morning three hundred excited men were gathered in the courtyard of Essex House when four of the Queen's Councillors arrived. They were made prisoners, and, as the Court was forewarned and prepared, Essex and his three hundred made for the City, brandishing their swords and calling on others to join them. But a herald was already proclaiming him a traitor, and as he rushed up Ludgate Hill and along Cheapside the citizens shut their doors. Though Essex was their hero, Elizabeth was their queen, and not a man joined him. Even his original followers were melting away, and he turned desperately for home. After a skirmish at Lud Gate he reached the river, and slipped into Essex House by the water-gate. It was all over, and after destroying incriminating papers, the wretched man surrendered.

Ten days later Essex and Southampton were brought to trial before their peers. On the previous day, February 18th, a deposition had been extracted from Augustine Phillips, the player who had accepted the forty shillings on behalf of the Chamberlain's for the performance of *Richard II.* The affair was taken seriously, as another proof of Essex's admiration for Bolingbroke, evidenced by Hayward's 'treasonous book' with its notorious dedication to the Earl, whose favourite plays, it was well known, were *Richard II* and *Henry IV.* 'I protest upon my soul and conscience', thundered the hectoring Attorney-General, Edward Coke, 'I doe beleeve she should not have long lived after she had been in your power. Note but the precedents of former ages, how long lived Richard the Second after he was surprised in the same manner? The pretence was alike for the removing of certain counsellors, but yet shortly after it cost him his life.' Bacon, who had no scruples about appearing as one of the counsel for the prosecution of his patron, benefactor and friend, drew a more recent and more deadly parallel, the overthrow of Elizabeth's former suitor, Henry III of France, by the Duke of Guise, who, 'attended only with eight gentlemen, found that help in the city, which, God be thanked, you failed of here. And what followed? The King was forced to put himself into a pilgrim's weeds, and in that disguise to steal away to escape their fury. Even such was my Lord's confidence too, and his pretence the same— an all-hail and a kiss to the City. But the end was treason, as hath been sufficiently proved.'

The two earls were found guilty, and condemned to the barbarous death reserved for traitors. Essex had borne himself proudly at the trial, but in the Tower he collapsed, denouncing himself and the friends, including his sister Penelope, who had led him astray. Elizabeth relented only so far as to change his form of death to beheading, but she allowed Cecil to persuade her to commute Southampton's sentence to life imprisonment, on the grounds that 'the poor young earl, merely for the love of Essex, had been drawn into this action'. Essex himself was only thirty-four.

The execution was to be on the 25th. On the 23rd the Queen

ordered its postponement; on the 24th she countermanded her order. That night the Chamberlain's performed at Whitehall, but, whatever else the play may have been, it was not *Richard II*. On the following morning Essex was led to the block in Tower yard. Raleigh, as Captain of the Guard, was there, but had the grace to withdraw into the White Tower to witness the scene. And then the executioner did his office.

IX

1601–1603

THE END OF THE REIGN

ELIZABETH's policy was one of forget and forgive, and only five of the other conspirators were executed. To appease the people, Bacon was commissioned to write an official account of the revolt justifying the Council's action, and his deftly edited narrative was published as 'The Declaration of the Practices and Treasons of Robert, late Earl of Essex and his Complices'. Shakespeare voluntarily added his contribution, for, when Laertes burst into the Privy chamber at Elsinore, none could fail to identify him with the earl who had burst into Elizabeth's bedchamber at Nonsuch, or fail to think of his Queen when the King of Denmark said:

> There's such divinity doth hedge a king,
> That treason can but peep to what it would,
> Acts little of his will.

Though there had never been any great danger, the Council's nerves were still a little on edge; after all, the insurrection might be said to have begun at the Globe, and for some months they addressed a series of unusually tart notes to the magistrates, directing them to enforce the recent Order regulating the theatres.

The people could forgive their Queen, yet neither the regulations and official publications of the Council nor the sermons that they ordered to be preached in the City could make them forget their hero. Popular feeling inevitably found its expression in ballads; 'Our Jewel is from us gone, the valiant Knight of Chivalry', they sang in *Essex's Last Good Night*; and again, 'Sweet England's pride is gone! Welladay! Welladay!' Broadsides hawked about the streets lampooned his envious and malicious enemies, 'little Cecil', his elder brother Burghley, 'the clown', and Raleigh with 'his bloody pride', polling the poor to the skin.

Nor indeed, whatever her policy, could the Queen herself forget. One day in August, the antiquary William Lambarde brought her a digest of the records in the Tower, of which he was the recently appointed Keeper. Receiving him in the Privy Chamber at Greenwich, she learnedly discussed the meaning of various legal terms. At length she came to the pages relating to the reign of Richard II, and said sharply, 'I am Richard II. Know ye not that?' 'Such a wicked imagination', the loyal old man replied, 'was determined and attempted by a most unkind gentleman, the most adorned creature that ever your Majesty made.' She continued, 'He that will forget God will also forget his benefactors. This tragedy was played forty times in open streets and houses.' At Westminster, she told him, she had a picture of Richard, which she would let him see. And then, 'In those days force and arms did prevail; but now the wit of the fox is everywhere on foot, so as hardly a faithful or virtuous man may be found.' A fortnight later the old antiquary was dead.

'Sweet England's pride is gone.' With the Earl of Essex something indeed had gone from England, as well as from Elizabeth's heart. The old chivalry, gaiety and delight in impetuous adventure had given place to a moody disillusion, cynicism and boredom. Where the lion once had walked, the fox was now afoot. Cecil was in secret correspondence with the King of Scotland, whose mind he delicately poisoned against his one remaining rival, Raleigh. Even Shakespeare seems to have been infected, and embarked on his most enigmatic series of plays: *Troilus and Cressida, Hamlet, All's Well that Ends Well* and *Measure for Measure*.

To dispel her settled melancholy, the Queen set out on what was to be the last of her extended progresses. The air of Berkshire raised her spirits, and when, at the beginning of September, she visited Sir William Knollys at Caversham, he made 'great chere, and entertained her with many devises of singing, dauncing, and playing wenches, and such like'. Sir William was her cousin, and Comptroller of her Household; he was also a slightly ridiculous figure. A man of fifty-four, with a wife older than himself, a dyed beard and puritanical pretensions, he was, nevertheless, notoriously known to have been a suitor of the flighty Mary Fitton, one of the Queen's Maids of Honour. Perhaps it was he whom Shakespeare ridiculed as Malvolio,[1] the puritanical steward who, according to Feste, talked nothing 'but of ladies'. Knollys, however, was beaten in the chase. In the previous year,

[1] Dr. Hotson ingeniously suggests that his name stands for *Mal-voglio*, 'I want Moll', i.e. Mary Fitton.

Daniel's former pupil at Wilton, the philandering William Herbert, had captivated Mary, who surrendered to his amorous advances and bore him a son in March 1601, shortly after his succession to the Earldom of Pembroke and shortly before his coming of age. Raleigh and Southampton had married their mistresses, culled from the ranks of Elizabeth's attendant virgins, but Pembroke flatly refused to marry his, and was packed off to the Fleet Prison to reflect on his follies. If 'Mr. W. H.' of the *Sonnets* was either Henry Wriothesley, Earl of Southampton, or William Herbert, Earl of Pembroke, he was now in disgrace.

Shakespeare himself at this time was presumably in Stratford, where his father was buried on September 8th. No doubt he took the opportunity of opening negotiations with his friends, the Combes, for the purchase of some 130 acres of land on the outskirts of the town. The price was a stiff one, £320, a measure of the popularity and prosperous fortunes of the Globe. He would receive little enough from the work published at this period in his name. His friend, Richard Field, had recently printed Robert Chester's poem, *Love's Martyr*, for Edward Blount, who had added a number of 'Poeticall Essaies . . . done by the best and chiefest of our moderne writers'. All were on the same allegorical theme, the love of the Phœnix for the Turtledove, and among the authors commissioned were Jonson, Marston, Chapman and Shakespeare. He would profit not at all from the sale of copies of *Thomas Lord Cromwell*, a Chamberlain's play published as being written by 'W. S.', possibly Wentworth Smith (or, if the Derbyites wish to claim it, William Stanley), but probably the now famous initials were no more than a bait to attract buyers. Nor would he receive anything for the pirated edition of *The Merry Wives of Windsor*, the mangled memorial script of which was then in the unscrupulous hands of John Busby, the publisher of the 'bad' quarto of *Henry V. The Merry Wives* had been presented at Court, and, if Sir Thomas Lucy of Charlecote was the original of Justice Shallow, presumably before his death in the summer of 1600. 'Death is certain; all shall die', Shallow murmurs sadly in his Cotswold orchard, and it would have been unlike Shakespeare to have pursued him beyond the grave.

While Shakespeare was busy with his affairs at Stratford, and Elizabeth enjoying the hospitality of the gentlemen of Hampshire, news arrived that a Spanish force had landed at Kinsale in the south of Ireland to help Tyrone. But when they were both back in London in December, the joyful tidings came that Mountjoy had completely routed the rebels and their Spanish supporters. The Irish rebellion was broken.

Despite the victory, the Revels were unusually subdued, the Court being so small that the guard were not troubled to keep the doors at the plays and pastimes. The Chamberlain's gave four performances, and on February 2nd the barrister John Manningham recorded in his diary that a play called 'Twelue Night, or What You Will' was given at the Middle Temple. The performance would be in the Great Hall, with its Elizabethan double hammer-beam roof; the occasion the Inn's Candlemas Revel, their Grand Day. The Middle Temple was the favourite inn of the West Country gentry, and many of Shakespeare's Warwickshire friends and neighbours went there, the Combes for example, but it was probably the famous wit, Richard Martin, leader of their frolics and Prince d'Amour, who invited Shakespeare and his fellows to bring *Twelfth Night* for their festivities.

The Admiral's seem to have had little to offer in the way of plays acceptable for Court performance, for they were called upon for only one appearance, and even then the chief attraction was the tumbling of one 'Nycke'. No doubt the rebuff accounts for Henslowe's vigorous search for new authors who could supply him with plays that would compete with the Chamberlain's. One of these was Thomas Middleton of Gray's Inn, a man of about thirty, who was soon put to work on a play in collaboration with Dekker, Drayton, Munday and— another find—John Webster. Little or nothing is known of Webster's life, though it is possible that he was one of the actors who had toured Germany in the nineties. The full range of his great genius was not to be displayed for some years yet, though there is a foretaste in the 'new additions of the Painters part' made to the 1602 quarto of the ever popular *Spanish Tragedy*. It is true that in June, Henslowe paid 'Bengemy Johnsone for new adicyons for Jeronymo', but Jonson is the last man we should credit with Hieronimo's description to the Painter of how he found his murdered son: 'Let the clouds scowl, make the moon dark, the stars extinct, the winds blowing, the bells tolling, the owls shrieking, the toads croaking, the minutes jarring, and the clock striking twelve. And then at last, sir, starting, behold a man hanging and tottering, as you know the wind will wave a man, and I with a trice to cut him down.' Jonson may have written other 'adicyons', but this is surely Webster.

A new competitor at Court this year was the company under the patronage of the Earl of Worcester, Master of the Horse. For the time being, however, as far as Henslowe was concerned, they were not rivals of the Admiral's, for after entertaining them to a nine-shilling supper at the Mermaid 'we weare at owre a grement'. In other words, although the theatre was supposed to be closed, Worcester's moved into the Rose, and Henslowe arranged to finance the buying of their plays and apparel. Instead of 'my company', he could now talk about 'my companies'. Thomas Heywood, Will Kempe, back from Italy, and John Lowin were three of their principal actors, and all of them, of course, were soon in Henslowe's debt; Heywood, indeed, who had bound himself to Henslowe four years before, would scarcely remember the time when he was not. It was a strong combination, with Heywood as actor-dramatist playing the part of Shakespeare in the Chamberlain's, and he and Kempe were payees for their Court performance on January 3rd. Their position was further strengthened when, in March, they absorbed the company of the Earl of Oxford. This was Edward de Vere, 17th Earl, Elizabeth's testy favourite, who had once picked a quarrel with Philip Sidney, and since then wasted his fortune on his extravagant whims. He was a writer of conventional lyrics and, according to Meres, 'one of the best for Comedy amongst us'. Presumably he wrote for his own company, but little is known of their plays, and nothing of his, for none can definitely be assigned to him. He died in 1604, yet there are those who believe that he (and not Marlowe, or Bacon, or William Stanley, or Roger Manners, or Elizabeth Tudor) was 'the real Shakespeare'. After their absorption of Oxford's, Worcester's were admitted by Order of the Council as a third company authorised to play in London, curiously enough at the Boar's Head Inn, which, like the Rose, should have been closed. But by the end of the year they were back at Henslowe's old theatre on the Bankside.

Ever since the formation of the Chamberlain's and reorganisation of the Admiral's after the plague years, in 1594, the two companies had had a virtual monopoly of playing at Court and in London, a monopoly that had been confirmed by the Council's Order of June 1600. Now Worcester's had broken into the charmed circle, and more serious for all the adult companies was the reappearance of the choir-boys in their comfortable little private theatres. They could offer far better musical fare than the men, and their pert mimicry of their elders was a welcome innovation, deliciously piquant to the more literate Londoners restlessly awaiting the end of an epoch. The Queen herself may have patronised the Chapel boys' theatre, for after dining with the Lord Chamberlain on December 29th, she was seen by Dudley Carleton 'at the play' at 'the blackfriers'. Though the performance could have been merely one given by the Chamberlain's servants in his Blackfriars house, it is significant that the Chapel Children made three appearances at Court shortly afterwards. Possibly, though not very probably, one of their plays was Jonson's *Poetaster*.

About the time of the Essex rebellion the quarrel between Jonson and Marston had developed into a regular war of the theatres, or, more strictly, of the private theatres, another reason for the immense popularity of the boys at this time. It was the Paul's boys who had played *Jack Drum's Entertainment*, in which Marston ridiculed Jonson, and the Chapel boys who had replied with *Cynthia's Revels*, where Dekker was coupled with Marston as the object of Jonson's satire. By the beginning of 1601 the Paul's boys were aping Jonson as Lampatho Doria in Marston's *What You Will*, and Dekker was preparing his revenge, the addition of a satirical sub-plot to a half-finished tragi-comedy. Jonson, hearing of this, and of Marston's collaboration in the fun, wrote his *Poetaster* with all speed, and within a few months the Chapel Children were playing it at Blackfriars. Three of the boys were Pavy, Field and Underwood, a newcomer being William Ostler, also destined to become a fellow of Shakespeare's.

The scene is ancient Rome, and Asper-Criticus-Jonson of the earlier comedies is now the meritorious Horace, baited and traduced by the envious versifiers Crispinus and Demetrius, that is, the poetaster Marston, 'new turned poet, and a satirist too', and Dekker, 'a dresser of plays about the town'. Evidently Jonson knew that the Chamberlain's, as well as the Paul's boys, were to produce Dekker's projected satire, for he introduces the actor, Histrio, who says that his company has hired Demetrius 'to abuse Horace, and bring him in, in a play'. Histrio must be Augustine Phillips, who received the famous forty shillings for the unfortunate production of *Richard II*, for he has 'forty–*forty* shillings' to hire Crispinus to help Demetrius, and Jonson has some good fun at the expense of the players 'on the other side of Tiber'. The scheme goes forward but is discovered by Cæsar, and the poetaster and the play-dresser are accused of maliciously calumniating the person and writings of Horace, poet and priest to the Muses. Examples of their work are read aloud. First Crispinus:

> Ramp up, my genius, be not retrograde,
> But boldly nominate a spade a spade.
> What, shall thy lubrical and glibbery muse
> Live, as she were defunct, like punk in stews?
> Alas! that were no modern consequence,
> To have cothurnal buskins frightened hence.
> No, teach thy incubus to poetise,
> And throw abroad thy spurious snotteries
> Upon that puft-up lump of barmy froth.

Then Demetrius:

> Our Muse is in mind for th'untrussing a poet;
> I slip by his name, for most men do know it:
> A critic that all the world bescumbers
> With satirical humours and lyrical numbers;
> And for the most part himself doth advance
> With much self-love, and more arrogance.
> And, but that I would not be thought a prater,
> I could tell you he were a translator.
> I know the authors from whence he has stole,
> And could trace him too, but that I understand them not full and whole.

They plead guilty, and confess that their only motive was envy, whereupon the magnanimous Horace freely forgives them, but not before administering pills to Crispinus, to purge his brain and stomach of their tumorous heats. The poetaster hastily calls for a basin, into which he vomits his windy words: *retrograde*, *oblatrant*, *furibund*, *prorumped*, and at last after much retching, *obstupefact* comes up. The prisoners are dismissed, having sworn a solemn oath never again to malign Horace or any other eminent man transcending them in merit, or at any time to affect the title of 'Untrussers or Whippers of the age'.

The conclusion was an ingenious attempt to forestall Dekker, whose play, which followed close on the heels of *Poetaster*, was called *Satiromastix* (that is, 'The Satirist Whipped'), *or The Untrussing of the Humorous Poet*. It is a strange production, for the untrussing is slipped into a play on the subject of Walter Tyrrell and William Rufus, the central scene of which is one of the best things that Dekker ever wrote. The king has made Tyrrell swear that on his wedding night he will send his wife to the palace. Rather than she should be thus dis-

Satiro--maſtix.

OR

The vntruſſing of the Humo-
rous Poet.

As it hath bin preſented publikely,
by the Right Honorable, the Lord Cham-
berlaine his Seruants; and priuately, by the
Children of Paules.

By *Thomas Dekker.*

Non recito cuiquam niſi Amicis *idq; coactus.*

LONDON,
Printed for Edward VVhite, and are to bee
ſolde at his ſhop, neere the little North doore of Paules
Church, at the ſigne of the Gun. 1602.

TITLE PAGE OF *SATIROMASTIX*, 1602

honoured, her father makes her drink a cup of poison, and Tyrrell
turns on him with:

> Thou winter of a man, thou walking grave,
> Whose life is like a dying taper; how
> Canst thou define a lover's labouring thoughts? . . .
> Because thou'rt travelling to the land of graves,
> Thou covet'st company, and hither bring'st
> A health of poison to pledge death.

The writing is worthy of great tragedy, but they poison merely in
jest; the drink is only a sleeping-draught, and all ends happily. Into
this tragi-comedy of Norman England Dekker and Marston incon-
gruously inserted their satirical comedy of Augustan Rome, and
Horace even composes a wedding-ode for Tyrrell. He is discovered
ponderously toiling over this trifle—Jonson was a notoriously slow
and laborious writer:

> O me, thy priest, inspire!
> For I to thee and thine immortall name,
> In—in—in golden tunes,
> For I to thee and thine immortall name—
> In—sacred raptures flowing, flowing, swimming, swimming:
> In sacred raptures swimming,
> Immortall name—game, dame, tame, lame, lame, lame,
> Pux ha' it, shame, proclaime, oh—
> In sacred raptures flowing, will proclaime, not—
> O me, thy priest, inspyre!
> For I to thee and thine immortall name,
> In flowing numbers fild with spright and flame—
> Good, good—in flowing numbers fild with spright and flame.

Jonson's own magnificent creation in *Poetaster*, swaggering Captain
Tucca, joins in the baiting, and eventually Horace is arraigned before
King William as Demetrius and Crispinus had been impeached before
Cæsar. It is only poetic justice that Crispinus should be appointed judge:

> Or should we minister strong pilles to thee,
> What lumpes of hard and indigested stuffe,
> Of bitter *Satirisme*, of *Arrogance*,
> Of *Self-love*, or *Detraction*, of a blacke
> And stinking *Insolence* should we fetch up?
> But none of these, we give thee what's more fit,
> With stinging nettles crown his stinging wit.

Finally, the unfortunate Horace is made to swear never again to sit
in a gallery while his plays are being performed, and there pull vile

faces at every line to make gentlemen have an eye to him; never again to venture on the stage when his play is ended, and exchange compliments and courtesies with gallants in the lords' room, to make all the house rise up and cry, 'That's Horace, that's he, that's he, that's he, that pens and purges humours and diseases'; and never again, when his plays are misliked at Court, to cry mew like a puss-cat and say he is glad he writes out of the courtiers' element. Jonson got as much as he had given.

In his epilogue Dekker assured his audience that 'Horace will write against it, and you may have more sport'. But Jonson did not reply; he had been in trouble with the authorities. Not only had he attacked playwrights and players, he had satirised soldiers and lawyers as well, and after the Essex rebellion the government was particularly sensitive to criticism of its institutions. It was only the good offices of his friend Richard Martin, to whom he dedicated the play, that saved him from trouble more serious than censure, and he had to confine himself to the writing of an Apologetical Dialogue. In this, Horace is visited by two friends who wish to see 'how he looks after these libels'. He tells them that he is in excellent form, 'unhurt of envy, as unhit', protests that he has merely attacked vices and not persons, and complains that he has had enough of a world that does not appreciate its disinterested reformers:

> and, since the Comic Muse
> Hath proved so ominous to me, I will try
> If Tragedy have a more kind aspect.

The Apologetical Dialogue was only once spoken upon the stage; it, too, was suppressed, and Jonson turned to the writing of *Sejanus*.

That Christmas, 1601–2, the undergraduates of St. John's College, Cambridge, performed an anonymous play, *The Return from Parnassus*, the theme of which was the disillusionment of students who set out to make their living in the capital. As we might expect, there is some discussion of contemporary authors: of Marston, 'lifting up his leg and pissing against the world'; Jonson is 'a bold whoreson, the wittiest fellow of a bricklayer in England'; Shakespeare, whose *Adonis* and *Lucrece* everybody admires, is gently censured for not undertaking some graver subject than love's foolish languishment; and Tom Nashe, a John's man, is mourned for a mother-wit such as few have ever seen. In desperation, two of the students seek employment with the Chamberlain's company, and are interviewed by Burbage and Kempe, who criticise the amateurish acting and pedantic play-writing at the universities:

Few of the university men pen plays well; they smell too much of that writer Ovid, and that writer Metamorphosis, and talk too much of Proserpina and Jupiter. Why, here's our fellow Shakespeare puts them all down, ay, and Ben Jonson too. O that Ben Jonson is a pestilent fellow; he brought up Horace giving the poets a pill, but our fellow Shakespeare hath given him a purge that made him bewray his credit.

What was the purge that Shakespeare gave Jonson has been the subject of endless discussion, for there is no patent satire of Jonson anywhere in the work of that generous and easy-going man, and the simplest and most probable solution is that the author of *Parnassus* assumed that *Satiromastix* was his. After all, the play was given by the Chamberlain's, who had been attacked by Jonson, and it was only natural that their own dramatist should reply with an appropriate cathartic. Cambridge had followed the war of the theatres with donnish delight; they knew the outline of events, but were shaky as to the details. Kempe, for example, was then playing at Court with Worcester's.

It is worth noting that the author of *Parnassus* was as bitterly critical and envious of the players as many of the professional playwrights, as Greene and Nashe had been, as Marston in *Histriomastix*, and now Jonson. The students refuse to be apprenticed to 'the basest trade', either as hireling actors or as hack dramatists, for:

> Better it is 'mongst fiddlers to be chief,
> Than at a player's trencher beg relief.
> But is't not strange these mimic apes should prize
> Unhappy scholars at a hireling rate?
> Vile world, that lifts them up to high degree,
> And treads us down in grovelling misery.
> England affords those glorious vagabonds,
> That carried erst their fardels on their backs,
> Coursers to ride on through the gazing streets,
> And pages to attend their masterships.
> With mouthing words that better wits have framed,
> They purchase lands, and now esquires are made.

No doubt Shakespeare is glanced at in the last lines, though Alleyn and Burbage would be the fairer targets, for after all Shakespeare framed many of the words that he and his fellows mouthed.

We cannot say what purge, if any, Shakespeare gave Jonson, and it is quite possible that the role of physician and patient was reversed, that the bitter pill administered to Marston served as a salutary warning to Shakespeare, persuading him to submit to a similar, though less violent and a voluntary, purgation. *Troilus and Cressida*, probably written at about the same time as *Poetaster*, is remarkable for the number of its ponderous latinisms, incompletely assimilated, and protruding somewhat rawly from the text. Such words as *tortive, protractive, persistive, propension, propugnation, assubjugate* remind one irresistibly of the windy stuff vomited up by Marston, and Shakespeare may well have profited from the satire and laughed at his own extravagance. In any event, the grotesque excesses of *Troilus and Cressida* were purged away, and the enrichment of his vocabulary with new latinisms in *Hamlet* and the subsequent plays was also an enrichment of his poetry.

Even if Shakespeare took no active part in the war of the theatres, it affected him financially. Except for a few performances of *Satiromastix* at the Globe, the war had been waged in the private theatres, and the competition of the boys was a real threat to the fortunes of the Chamberlain's and the other adult companies. Apart from the novelty and the popularity of the Jonson-Marston feud, the private playhouses were much snugger than the open public theatres, and Jonson had alluded to the winter of 1600–1 as a season that made all the men actors 'poorer than so many starved snakes', forcing them 'to travel with their pumps full of gravel, after a blind jade and a hamper, and stalk upon boards and barrel heads to an old cracked trumpet'. This of course is only part of his satire, but Shakespeare genially develops the theme in the famous passage in *Hamlet*, where Rosencrantz describes how 'the tragedians of the city' were compelled to go on tour because of the popularity of the children, whose authors so belaboured the public theatres that people were afraid to patronise them. No play was worth producing unless it took part in the controversy, and even the Globe was affected. The corresponding passage in the first, the 'bad', quarto is even more explicit:

> Yfaith my Lord, noueltie carries it away,
> For the principall publike audience that
> Came to them, are turned to private playes,
> And to the humour of children.

By the time *Hamlet* was written the war of the theatres was over, though not the competition of the boys, for whom many of the dramatists now began to write, Chapman and Middleton for example, as well as Jonson and Marston. But the Chapel boys, or at least their managers, were in trouble. As Master of the Children, Nathaniel Giles was empowered to press any boy with a good voice into the service of the Chapel Royal, which was precisely why Henry Evans had gone into partnership with him and taken a lease of the Black-friars theatre. Acting as Giles's deputy, he had, like Falstaff, misused the Queen's press damnably, by exceeding the statutory number of twelve and pressing boys not for their vocal but for their histrionic ability. In December 1601, not long after their presentation of *Poetaster*, a certain Henry Clifton complained to the Star Chamber that the syndicate had seized a number of boys for their private profit at Blackfriars, 'noe way able or fitt for singing, nor by anie the sayd confederates endevoured to be taught to sing'. One of these was his thirteen-year-old son Thomas, who had been abducted on his way to school and carried off to Blackfriars 'to exercyse the base trade of a mercynary enterlude player, to his vtter losse of tyme, ruyne and disparagment'. He had found him at the theatre 'amongste a companie of lewde and dissolute mercenary players', and when he protested, Evans, 'in moste scornefull disdaynfull and dispightfull manner', had given Thomas a paper containing part of one of their plays, threaten-ing to beat him unless he learned it by heart. Two of the other boys 'noe way able or fitt for singing' were Nathan Field and Solomon Pavy. Clifton recovered his son, and Evans was ordered to surrender the lease of the theatre and leave the country. He went abroad, but had already taken the precaution of assigning the lease to four of his partners, and the Blackfriars theatre remained flourishingly open, though without the assistance of Giles and his commission to take up boys.

The last performance of the Chapel Children seen by Elizabeth was at the beginning of 1602. After the tension of events leading up to Essex's final treachery and death, came the inevitable reaction, and she began to age rapidly. When she opened Parliament in October 1601, she faltered and almost fell, and in the following May confided to the French ambassador that she was tired of a life that no longer gave her any pleasure. But those were moments of weakness, and her indomitable spirit refused to accept defeat. She paid a round of visits, two to her favourite cousin, Lord Hunsdon, and in the summer went on a fortnight's progress, hunting and sometimes riding as much as ten miles in a day. On September 7th she celebrated her sixty-ninth birthday, and there was the customary tilt on Queen's Day, November 17th, the forty-fourth anniversary of her accession. On December 6th she dined with Sir Robert at Cecil House, the fine new house that he had just built in the Strand. He entertained her with 'a pretty dialogue 'twixt a Maide, a widow, and a wife', each commending her own state, the virgin, as ever on these occasions, getting the best of the dispute. Yet when Sir John Harington came to Court for Christmas, he found her changed, and wrote sorrowfully to his wife, 'Our dear Queen doth now bear show of human infirmity; too fast for that evil which we shall get by her death, and too slow for that good which she shall get by her releasement from pains and misery'.

She had, however, regained her popularity. When the question of monopolies—Elizabeth's way of rewarding her favourites by granting them the sole right of selling some commodity—was being angrily debated by a restive Parliament, she graciously sent word that the wrong should immediately be redressed. The members were so enraptured that all asked permission to go to Whitehall to express their gratitude and loyalty. And there the Queen addressed her kneeling Commons for the last time: 'Mr. Speaker, we perceive your coming is to present thanks to us. Know I accept them with no less joy than your loves can have desire to offer such a present, and do more esteem it than any treasure or riches; for those we know how to prize, but loyalty, love and thanks I account them invaluable; and, though God hath raised me high, yet this I account the glory of my crown, that I have reigned with your loves.' Then bidding them stand, for she had more to say, she continued, 'Of myself, I must say this: I never was any greedy scraping grasper, nor a strict fast-holding prince, nor yet a waster; my heart was never set upon any worldly goods, but only for my subjects' good. And for my own part, it is not my desire to live nor to reign longer than my life and reign shall be for your good. And, though you have had, and may have, many mightier and wiser princes sitting in this seat, yet you never had, nor shall have, any love you better.'

At about the same time as she made this, her Golden Speech, Thomas Morley prepared a trophy for the Queen. Ten years before, twenty-nine madrigals by Palestrina and other Italian composers had been published in Venice as *Il Trionfo di Dori*, each madrigal ending with the refrain 'Viva la bella Dori'. Dori was probably the symbol of Italy or of Italian womanhood, and it was this symposium that inspired Morley to assemble twenty-nine English madrigals, each with the refrain 'Long live fair Oriana', Oriana being the heroine of the romance of *Amadis de Gaul*. All the leading composers of the day, including John Milton, father of the poet, but with the notable exception of Byrd, contributed to the book, which was published in 1601 as *The Triumphs of Oriana*.

A few more triumphs yet remained for song, a final flare of the Elizabethan spirit before the decades that were to have so little valid cause for celebration. There was Mountjoy's great victory in Ireland. Tyrone surrendered on his knees, and Spain, too, had been brought to her knees. The twenty years' war was almost over. But not quite. In June 1602, Sir Richard Leveson attacked and captured a great treasure-ship as it lay at anchor near Lisbon, protected by four hundred volunteers, eleven galleys, the guns of the harbour and ten thousand men on shore. It was a return to the days of Drake and the great decade of the eighties. The galleon was a Portuguese, and Portugal shared the rapid decline of Spain, as English and Dutch merchants thrust into their trading preserves in the East. Sir James Lancaster had led the way, and it was he who was given command of the first fleet of the East India Company, incorporated by royal charter on the last day of 1600. From such a small beginning sprang the great British Empire in the East, the Empire of which Carlyle was prophetically to write, 'Indian Empire will go, at any rate some day; but this Shakespeare does not go, he lasts forever with us'.

It was only fitting that a momentous English contribution to physical science should be made within the Elizabethan Age. In 1601 William Gilbert was appointed one of the Queen's physicians, the year in which he published his great work, *De Magnete*. The book, which was the result of years of patient research, describes his experiments on magnets, magnetic bodies and electrical attractions, and advances the epoch-making hypothesis that the earth itself is merely a huge magnet, which accounts for the direction and variation of the magnetic needle. Gilbert has never had the popular recognition of Newton or even of William Harvey, yet his book is the foundation of the sciences of electricity and magnetism. Moreover, he was the first English scientist to champion the theory of Copernicus, that the sun and not the earth is the centre of our universe. For Shakespeare and his contemporaries the sun, as anybody could see, revolved about the earth, and though they might not really believe in the celestial music of the crystal spheres, the stars and planets moved in enviable harmony about the home of man. Bacon was as impatient of the new Copernican theory as he was of the ancient Ptolemaic system, and arrogantly erected an astronomical mechanism of his own. Donne, with his ranging and inquiring mind, was the first English poet to incorporate the new scientific perplexities and theories in his verse, though not yet awhile.

The arts, too, had their latter triumphs. The Cecil brothers, great builders like their father, finished their London houses: Cecil House, the work of Sir Robert, and influential Wimbledon, the project of his worthless brother, Thomas, 2nd Lord Burghley. And down in Somerset, out of the noble Ham Hill stone, Edward Phelips of the Middle Temple completed Montacute. All, in a sense, were trophies erected to Elizabeth, houses in which the sovereign could worthily be entertained. A little farther west, the medieval Guildhall in Exeter, where the goldsmith Richard Hilliard had once been Sheriff, was brought up to date with a startling Elizabethan frontage in which no neo-classical detail had been overlooked. At about the same time, 1600, Richard's son Nicholas wrote his *Art of Limning*. His contemporaries compared him to 'the late worldes-wonder Raphaell Vrbine', yet it has ever been the fault of the English to honour foreign artists before their own. In 1601 Hilliard wrote to Cecil that he had 'taught divers, both strangers and English, which now, and of a long time, have pleased the common sort exceeding well, so that I am myself unable by my art any longer to keep house in London without some further help of her Majesty'. One of the 'strangers' was Isaac Oliver, whose 'smutted and darkned' likenesses pleased the common sort, but the old master went his own way, projecting his tiny beam of Elizabethan delicacy and brightness into the gathering gloom of the Jacobean Age.

Like the miniature, the madrigal was about to suffer change. *The Triumphs of Oriana* is one of the most important, but it is also one of the last books of English madrigals. The form had reached its full perfection, and was on the point of being reduced to solo song. The age of polyphonic music was drawing to a close, yet there was to be a short and brilliant period of transition. The development was inevitable, for when a voice was lacking for the singing of a madrigal, it was often possible to replace it by an instrument, and sometimes the performers would deliberately select one part for the voice and play the rest on lute or cittern. The tendency was, therefore, to emphasise and elaborate the singing part, and to simplify the accompaniment. Dowland's *First Book of Songs* (1597) was so arranged that all the parts together, or any one of them alone, could be sung to the lute. Although not strictly solo songs, they pointed the way, and the first books of airs for a single voice with lute accompaniment appeared in 1601, the year of *The Triumphs of Oriana*. One was *The First Book of Songs* by Robert Jones, who claimed that his were the first of their kind, the other *A Book of Airs* by Thomas Campion and his friend Philip Rosseter. They are very beautiful, very simple and the perfect counterpart of the fragile and artificial Elizabethan lyric; another of the minor triumphs of Oriana's reign.

Campion wrote the words as well as the music in *A Book of Airs*, and almost certainly the words for Rosseter's settings, too. All are exquisite of their kind, graceful as the poems of Horace and Catullus, though without their passion; indeed, the first song in the book, 'My sweetest Lesbia, let us live and love', is a version of Catullus's 'Vivamus, mea Lesbia', the line 'nox est perpetua una dormienda' being rendered, 'Then must we sleep one ever-during night', and repeated with variations as a refrain in the Elizabethan manner. In his earlier poems Campion had affected classical measures, as in 'What fair pomp have I spied of glittering ladies', but he had never eschewed rhyme until, in 1602, he followed up his *Book of Airs* with *Observations in the Art of English Poesy*. It is a perverse little book, though not a return to the absurdities of Gabriel Harvey's cacophonous hexameters, which he admits are 'altogether against the nature of our language'; but rhyme, he concludes, is 'vulgar and inartificial', the invention of a barbarous age. This is humanism at its worst, for if rhyme is barbarous, so are the madrigal, medieval architecture (indeed it was soon to be called 'Gothic'), stained glass and, for the matter of that, Christianity. He wrote some rhymeless lyrics to make his point, admittedly almost as lovely as his rhyming ones:

> Rose-cheeked Laura, come;
> Sing thou smoothly with thy beauty's
> Silent music, either other
> Sweetly gracing.

But Campion was not really deeply engaged; for him his songs were only 'the superfluous blossoms of his deeper studies'—he was a lawyer turned physician—and he contented himself with throwing off another century or so of faultless—and rhyming—lyrics.

The chivalrous Daniel at once assumed the championship of rhyme, and wrote a long letter to 'a learned Gentleman', his Wilton pupil, young William Herbert, Earl of Pembroke, now back at Court after the Mary Fitton affair. This letter he expanded and published in the following year as *A Defence of Rhyme*. He treats Campion, whom he does not name, with characteristic courtesy, as a man of fair parts and good reputation, whose commendable rhymes have given the world the best notice of his worth. Then, taking his stand on Custom and Nature, he proceeds to demolish 'our Adversary's' argument. Custom is before all law, nature above all art, and it is ludicrous to impose on a language laws that are contrary to its nature. Call rhyme a barbarous device if you will, yet it 'sways the affections of the barbarian', it pleases him, and the object of poetry is to please. The most that Daniel will concede is that 'tragedy would indeed best comport with a blank verse'. This is humanism at its best, and there is really no more to be said. Though the essay was published after the accession of James I, it belongs to the last year of Elizabeth's reign, and is one of the sanest, as it is one of the best, pieces of critical writing of the Elizabethan Age, a worthy pendant to Sidney's *Defence of Poesy*.

Nobody would rejoice more than Daniel when, while he was writing his *Defence*, the Bodleian Library at Oxford was formally opened by the Vice-Chancellor in November 1602. He was himself an Oxford graduate, a Magdalen man like Bodley, and when he presented a copy of his *Works* to the Library it was with a specially printed dedication:

> Heere in this goodly Magazine of witte,
> This Storehouse of the choicest furniture
> The world doth yeelde, heere in this exquisite,
> And most rare monument, that dooth immure
> The glorious reliques of the best of men;
> Thou, part imperfect worke, voutsafed art
> A little roome, by him whose care hath beene
> To gather all whatever might impart
> Delight or Profite to Posteritie.

Appropriately enough, one of the pleasantest anthologies of Elizabethan verse, *England's Helicon*, belongs to these last years. There, gathered together, are selections from the poetry of the reign, poems, primarily pastoral, by Sidney, Drayton, Barnfield, the best of

Nicholas Breton, Marlowe's 'Come live with me and be my love', Raleigh's reply, 'If all the world and love were young', and Shakespeare's 'On a day, alack the day!' from *Love's Labour's Lost*. One major poet was missing from this, and from all the other miscellanies —Donne, who, according to Jonson, 'wrote all his best pieces ere he was twenty-five years old', that is, before the end of the century. The pity is that he did not publish, and that Elizabeth never read, unless she saw the manuscripts, some of the very finest, and certainly the most original, poetry of her reign. At this time Donne's fortunes were at a low ebb; having dissipated his inheritance, he secretly married the niece of his patron, Lord Keeper Egerton, for which indiscretion he was thrown into the Fleet prison in 1601.

Two other prose books of the period, besides Daniel's *Defence of Rhyme*, deserve mention. In 1601 Philemon Holland, the indefatigable 'translator-general in his age', published his version of Pliny's *Natural History*. Much more important was Florio's translation of the *Essays* of Montaigne, which appeared in 1603, though it had been registered some years earlier. Shakespeare was to make good use of both these books. For the moment he had his own contribution to add to the triumphs of Oriana—*Hamlet*.

It may be that *Hamlet* was the last play that Elizabeth saw. The Revels of 1602 'flourished more than ordinary', and there were plays by the Chamberlain's, Admiral's and Paul's boys, though there was nothing from the eyrie of children at Blackfriars, that 'nest of boys able to ravish a man', as their author, Middleton, called them. The Court moved to Richmond on January 21st, 1603, and on February 2nd Shakespeare and his company travelled the ten miles up-river in bitterly cold weather to entertain the Queen. The Admiral's followed at the beginning of March, but by that time Elizabeth's strength had failed her. Unable any longer to stand, she lay listlessly on cushions with her finger in her mouth, refusing food and physic. Cecil told her that to please her people she must go to bed. 'Little man, little man,' she murmured, 'the word *must* is not used to princes.' But at length she had to submit. On the 19th the Council issued an order restraining all stage-plays until further notice, and on the next day Cecil wrote to James of Scotland that the Queen had named him her successor. Then, having performed her last royal duty and listened to the prayers of her 'little black husband', the aged Archbishop Whitgift, in the early hours of March 24th, she died.

PART THREE

1603–1616

JAMES I

THE England that Elizabeth bequeathed to James was both internally and externally, absolutely and relatively, far more powerful than the England that she had inherited from Mary forty-five years before. The process of integration and centralisation had been completed; power was in the hands of the sovereign and the Privy Council, though the system was sufficiently liberal and flexible to allow the safeguard of a reasonable degree of local autonomy. The social malaise of poor and unemployed, the 'displaced persons' of that transitional period following the collapse of the guild and manorial systems, had been cured, partly by the natural restorative of prosperity, partly by the administered physic of a labour code. It is true that the code was harsh, as was that which had imposed the Anglican form of Protestantism as the established religion, but a harsh order was infinitely preferable to a harsher anarchy, as the overwhelming majority of the people recognised. Feudalism had died a natural death, hastened a little perhaps by those interested in its demise, while the entry of the younger sons of the nobility into trade and inter-marriage among the gentry and merchant class had eased the transition from a medieval to a capitalist economy. Then, the finances were once again in order and the country solvent, in spite of the twenty years' war that had sapped the power of her enemies as it forged the English into a nation, strong and confident to endure.

These, however, were for the most part abstract and invisible changes, and the apparent differences between the England of 1603 and that of 1558 were primarily those of degree rather than of quality. Without any really revolutionary change, by a process of healthy and organic growth, most things were now on a rather larger scale. The population was increasing, ships were bigger, and the enclosure of land led to better farming and a greater product, as it wove the tapestry of field-wall and hedgerow over valley and down, the man-made magic of the English countryside. Thanks largely to the influx of German engineers, the mining of iron, tin and coal had made rapid advances, and Protestant refugees had not only helped to swell the volume of manufactured goods, but had established new industries, particularly in London and the eastern counties. As a consequence, trade was growing apace, ports were expanding and London had almost doubled its population. Now a city of some 200,000 inhabitants, despite its narrow streets and labyrinthine alleys, it was still sufficiently close to the fields and open to the winds of the country to remain a comparatively healthy centre. Foreign trade was taking the place of exploration and adventure, not easily always to be distinguished from piracy, and trade was inevitably followed by colonisation. When Elizabeth died there were no English settlements abroad, and though the foundations of empire were laid in her reign, the early imperial structure was the work of the Jacobeans. In 1583 Sir Humphrey Gilbert had taken possession of Newfoundland in the Queen's name, but it was another thirty years before any settlement was established, and, in spite of the efforts of Raleigh, the name Virginia, given to an unsettled strip of coast, was the only claim to empire on the American mainland.

The Elizabethans and the Dutch had drained the strength of Spain and Portugal, and it was the rapid decline of these two imperial powers that made colonial expansion relatively easy in the seventeenth century. France, exhausted by the long internecine wars of religion, brought to an end by the Edict of Nantes of 1598, was too busy reorganising itself under Henry IV and Sully to enter yet into the colonial race, but the Netherlanders were soon to become England's most formidable rivals. In 1609 their independence was formally recognised, and the little republic of Holland entered on the brilliant period when it led the world in the arts of war and peace, when it was the mistress of the seas, the school of agriculture, commerce and finance, and the academy of painting, the period of Hals, Rembrandt, Ruysdael and Vermeer. Moreover, England had something to learn from its recent history: the possibility of successful revolt against a legitimate sovereign.

For the social and economic development of Elizabeth's reign had been sufficient to bring about a change of temper in the upper and literate classes. The gentry and merchants had begun to chafe at the restrictions of Tudor despotism, however benevolent and velvet-gloved, and were determined to exact an extension of their privileges and liberties from the House of Stuart. Indeed, all parties, sects and factions, having acquiesced in the order imposed by the legendary Queen, eagerly anticipated some amelioration or advancement under the new King. Politicians, Puritans, Catholics, authors and even actors, all had something to hope for. 'Now,' wrote Daniel in the Preface to his *Defence of Rhyme*, 'seeing the times to promise a more regard to the present condition of our writings, in respect of our Sovereign's happy inclination this way, we are rather to expect an encouragement to go on with what we do, than that any innovation should check us.' But, though James gloried in the name of author and was, within limits, quite prepared to play the patron, he was the last man to surrender any of his privileges to Parliament or to fulfil the aspirations of rival religious minorities.

The progress of the arts, like that of so many other things, had, with one exception, been evolutionary rather than revolutionary. The Elizabethans had preserved the delicate linear form of the Middle Ages, into which they had worked, with miraculous effect, quasi-classical detail derived mainly from France and the Netherlands. The original purity, simplicity and brightness had been wonderfully sustained, but by the end of the epoch the time had come for the inevitable plunge into a greater complexity of mass, depth, orchestration and chiaroscuro. The builders of the great Elizabethan houses, from Longleat to Hardwick Hall and Montacute, relied for their effect on their façades, but Audley End, begun in 1603, was to be a dramatic—and brilliantly successful—exploitation of receding masses. In painting, the heavier realism and oil-painting technique of Isaac Oliver was preferred to the linear fancy of Hilliard. In music, sacred motet and secular madrigal were being superseded by accompanied solo song, which was soon to be merged in the elaborate confusions of opera. But the golden age of English music was not yet over. Byrd, aged sixty, was at the height of his powers; John Bull, professor of music at Gresham College, Dowland, lutenist to Christian IV of Denmark who paid him a fabulous salary, and Campion were all about forty; Rosseter, Tomkins, Wilbye and Weelkes were barely thirty; and Orlando Gibbons, organist of the Chapel Royal, was only twenty. Morley, however, had been in failing health for some time, and died shortly after the Queen whose triumphs he had so recently sung.

The one major revolution of the Elizabethan Age had been in

literature. At the beginning of the reign little or nothing of any consequence was being written, by the end the literature of England was the greatest of the modern world. Then there had been neither theatres nor even plays in the true sense of the word, but by 1603 the only drama that could compare with the English was that of ancient Greece. And the greatest was yet to come. The oldest practising playwright was Anthony Munday, aged fifty, who was soon to turn his talents to devising entertainments for the City, and pageants for its liveried companies. Lyly was about the same age, but had long since ceased to write anything of significance; a member of the last parliaments of Elizabeth, he enjoyed some sort of compensation for his frustrated hopes of the Office of Revels, and died in 1606. Lodge, too, the last of the University Wits, was no longer a serious writer, but had turned physician as well as Catholic. Marlowe, had he lived, would have been forty, the same age as the other four great poets born in the early sixties, Chapman, Daniel, Drayton and Shakespeare. Heywood, Dekker, Jonson, Marston, Middleton, and perhaps Webster as well, were ten years younger. Donne, too, was just turned thirty. Of the men who were yet to make their mark, John Fletcher was twenty-four, Philip Massinger twenty, Francis Beaumont nineteen, John Ford seventeen and James Shirley, last of the great line, seven. Robert Burton, busy writing a Latin comedy as a prelude to *The Anatomy of Melancholy*, was twenty-five, and Thomas Hobbes, Robert Herrick, Izaac Walton, Francis Quarles, Henry King and George Herbert were all boys of about ten.

Of all these Shakespeare was the undisputed leader, the major poet and dramatist of his day, the author of more than twenty plays, from *Henry VI* and *Richard III*, *Romeo and Juliet* and *A Midsummer Night's Dream*, *Henry IV* and *Twelfth Night* to *Julius Cæsar* and *Hamlet*. There was no other dramatist who could claim such princely progeny. Ben Jonson was a noisy and quarrelsome young fellow who had attracted some attention by his comical satires, but most of the rest were driven by necessity to work for Henslowe as dressers of old plays and collaborators in new, with comparatively little original or unaided dramatic work to their credit. Shakespeare, neither noisy nor quarrelsome, attracted attention by his merit, and was as popular with the wits and gallants of the Inns of Court as with the groundlings and stinkards of the Globe, if we may judge from the diary of John Manningham of the Middle Temple, where naughty anecdotes about

JAMES I AND VI
By John De Critz (?)

THE
SOMERSET HOUSE
CONFERENCE, 1604

Attributed to

M. Gheeraerts II

playwrights and players circulated among the students. He was now engaged in writing his greatest series of plays, which, starting with *Hamlet*, was continued in *Othello, Macbeth, Lear, Timon, Coriolanus* and—most splendid of all—*Antony and Cleopatra*. The dramatic poetry which he had mastered in the romantic comedies that culminated in *Twelfth Night* he now applied to tragedy, though with a difference. The more obvious poetry of line and phrase had already given place to one more natural, yet more elusive, because of the extended compass of its verbal harmonies and rhythms, but in the tragedies the texture of the verse becomes increasingly complex, its colour at once richer and more sombre, with a greater range of tone, of light and shade, its music deeper and more sonorous. In a word, Shakespeare's Jacobean poetry shares the qualities characteristic of the other arts, but here there is no decline; though much of the Elizabethan lightness and elation has gone, the medium was the only one possible for the portrayal of the great tragic characters.

At this time Shakespeare was lodging with Christopher Mountjoy, in Silver Street, near Cripplegate. Mountjoy was a Huguenot craftsman, a maker of ladies' tires, cunningly wrought headdresses of gold thread set with precious stones. His wife was in the business as well, and in the first year of the new reign supplied Queen Anne with tires worth £59, more than £1,500 of our money. They had a daughter whom, for some reason or other, they wished to marry to their apprentice, Stephen Belott, and at their request Shakespeare helped to further the marriage, which took place in November 1604, a few days after the Court production of *Othello* at Whitehall.

The peaceful transition from the House of Tudor to the House of Stuart was primarily the work of Cecil. While the Queen lay dying her subjects stood to arms, but when they learned that the Council unanimously endorsed Cecil's policy, and that there was to be no civil war, they laid them down and cheered with thankful hearts. King James was duly grateful, and retained Cecil as his chief minister, creating him Viscount Cranborne, and in the spring of 1605, Earl of Salisbury. Bacon, too, had done some service, and was rewarded, rather meanly as he thought, with a knighthood. The Lord Steward was the veteran Earl of Nottingham, commander of the fleet that had destroyed the Armada and patron of the Admiral's company at the Fortune. One of the most attractive characters of the age, he was to live another twenty years, spanning the lives of both Elizabeth and

James, and dying shortly before his ninetieth year. Lord Hunsdon was less fortunate. He had been a sick man for some time, and, after surrendering the office of Lord Chamberlain to the Earl of Suffolk, died a few months after his cousin, the Queen. But of far greater moment than a change in the office of Lord Chamberlain was the death of Archbishop Whitgift, and the elevation to the see of Canterbury of Richard Bancroft, Bishop of London, the most implacable opponent of the Puritans. He was grimly supported by his ex-chaplain, Samuel Harsnett, Master of Pembroke Hall, Cambridge, and Vice-Chancellor of the University, who published his *Declaration of Egregious Popish Impostors* in 1603, the book from which Shakespeare culled the names for the spirits in *King Lear*.

While Elizabeth was being solemnly interred in Westminster Abbey, and London, in equal scale weighing delight and dole, was singing 'A mournefull Dittie entituled *Elizabeths losse* (together with a welcome for King Iames)', in which brave Shakespeare, Jonson—and Greene!—were called upon to lament in elegies, the new King was making his royal progress from Scotland. Apple and pear were breaking into blossom, the air quivered with the peal of bells, towns and villages poured forth their cheering people, addresses of welcome were read and lavish entertainments were prepared. Theobalds was reached by the beginning of May, and there James stayed with Cecil for a few days, to his great content, before entering London on the 11th. A not altogether unprepossessing man of thirty-seven—two years younger than Shakespeare—the wonder is that he had so many good qualities. The son of the vicious young Darnley and the flighty Queen of Scots, he had been abominably brought up by a drunken nurse and a bullying tutor, so that physically he suffered from weak legs, and mentally from a mass of ill-digested learning. But, though he was no walker, he was a mighty hunter, and after the chase a great drinker, though one who carried his cups lightly. His heart was warm and generous, even to extravagance, but his mind was cold, narrow and illiberal. An obstinate pedant with an exalted notion of his own capacity and the divine authority of kings, he conceived himself confusedly as a sort of benign mother and schoolmaster, whose business it was to cherish and lecture his children and pupils. With a long experience of affairs, but little knowledge of men and no capacity for discerning merit, he was quite ignorant of English customs and traditional liberties, at Newark summarily ordering a thief to be hanged without trial. Fate could scarcely have found a less competent monarch to cope with the problems left by Elizabeth.

Queen Anne followed in June with the two elder children, Henry and Elizabeth, aged nine and seven. On the 25th she stayed at Holdenby in Northamptonshire, the splendid country house built by Sir Christopher Hatton, and on the next day passed to the neighbouring Althorp, the seat of Sir Robert Spencer. There she was most agreeably greeted by an entertainment devised by Jonson, in which Shakespearean fairies gracefully transferred their allegiance from 'our late Diana' to the new Oriana. The next day, being Sunday, the Queen rested, and Jonson wrote a speech to be delivered by Nobody, attired in a pair of breeches that were made to come up to his neck, with his arms out at his pockets, and a cap drowning his face. Unfortunately the hubbub made by the great company of wondering countryfolk prevented its being heard, as also a parting speech addressed primarily to Prince Henry:

> And you, dear lord, on whom my covetous eye
> Doth feed itself, but cannot satisfy,
> O shoot up fast in spirit, as in years
> That when upon her head proud Europe wears
> Her stateliest tire, you may appear thereon
> The richest gem, without a paragon.

The young Queen—she was only twenty-eight—was flattered and enchanted. There had never been the like in Denmark or in Scotland and, when she discovered the six thousand dresses that Elizabeth had left her, soon succumbed to the pleasures of such entertainments, and abandoned herself to their delights. It was owing to her extravagance and passion for spectacle that the masque flowered as never before. But she was not merely a frivolous spendthrift. Intelligent, affectionate and loyal, she was a devoted mother and one of the few friends of Raleigh in his misfortunes. Sometimes she joined her husband in the chase, but her most remarkable exploit in that sphere was to shoot his 'most principal and special hound'.

London was overflowing with visitors come up to see the coronation, with its processions, fireworks and other attendant festivities, but the Privy Council was anxiously watching the weekly returns of deaths in the City and suburbs. Signs of plague had appeared in April; there were thirty plague deaths at the end of May, forty in the following week and then the figures soared rapidly into hundreds. The

Court moved up the river to Hampton Court, whence James and Anne emerged to be hurriedly crowned in Westminster Abbey on July 25th. All who could had left the capital, where the weekly death-roll was now nearly two thousand, and the royal couple went on progress, reaching Winchester towards the end of September, and a month later settling with the Court at Wilton House as the guests of the young Earl of Pembroke, who was rewarded with the Order of the Garter. One of the first acts of James had been to liberate the Earl of Southampton, so that the two main claimants for the honour of being Shakespeare's young friend and rival for the love of the dark lady, 'Mr. W. H.' of the *Sonnets*, were both again in royal favour.

But if Essex's friend was in favour again, his enemies were in disgrace. James was persuaded that Raleigh stood for everything that he himself abhorred; the leader of the party that favoured the war with Spain, with an unsavoury reputation for atheism, he was even responsible for bringing the 'filthy stinking custom' of smoking tobacco from Virginia. Expelled from Durham House, dismissed from the Captaincy of the Guard and deprived of most of his other offices, Raleigh listened to the proposals of his friend Cobham—the 'Falstaff' of the Essex circle—for placing James's Catholic cousin, Arabella Stuart, on the throne. The plot, if such a wild and harebrained scheme might so be called, was discovered. Cobham tried to wriggle out of his complicity by accusing Raleigh, who was savagely attacked by the Attorney-General, Coke, as a viper of hell with a Spanish heart— Raleigh, who had dedicated his life to the struggle with Spain! Deserted by the servile Court, friendless and misunderstood, he was committed to the Tower, where he spent the thirteen years of his imprisonment writing *A History of the World*. Released at length on the impossible condition of finding gold for James in Guiana without offending Spain, he sailed on his last hopeless expedition, in which his son was killed in a skirmish with the Spaniards. 'Comfort your heart, dear Bess,' he wrote to his wife, 'I shall sorrow for us both, and I shall sorrow the less because I have not long to sorrow, because I have not long to live.' He was executed on his return, as James had promised the Spanish ambassador. Cobham died in prison in the same year.

The theatres had been closed shortly before Elizabeth's death, and as her funeral coincided with the beginning of plague, it is probable that they were not opened again until the epidemic, a particularly severe one in which 30,000 people perished, was over in the following spring. Nevertheless, James found time to give some attention to theatrical affairs, and only a week after his arrival in London issued letters patent appointing the ex-Chamberlain's Men his own servants. The names of the players are given as, 'Lawrence Fletcher, William Shakespeare, Richard Burbage, Augustyne Phillippes, Iohn Heninges, Henrie Condell, William Sly, Robert Armyn, Richard Cowly'. Thomas Pope, one of the original members of the fellowship, was missing, for he was then on his death-bed. Fletcher had been 'comedian to his Majesty' in Scotland, and was already therefore one of the King's Servants, but as he does not appear in any of the company's actor-lists or in the Folio list of principal actors in Shakespeare's plays, it looks as though he was merely an honorary member.

The exaltation from Chamberlain's to King's Players did not directly mean any change of fortune, for patrons did not retain their companies. Like the royal players of Elizabeth in the eighties, they were sworn in as Grooms of the Chamber, ranking between the Gentlemen and Yeomen, but, though forming part of the ordinary household establishment, they were unpaid, as they were not normally in attendance. Their one perquisite was a 'watching' livery for the winter, and a summer livery of scarlet, renewed every two years. In 1604 the Master of the Great Wardrobe supplied Shakespeare and each of his fellows with four and a half yards of red cloth for their office. But indirectly they were in a way to profit considerably. James intended spending money on his pleasures rather than on a fruitless Spanish war, and this meant mainly on hunting, drinking and various forms of spectacular and dramatic entertainment. In the last ten years the Chamberlain's had given thirty-two Court performances; in the next ten the King's were to give four times as many. As the reward for a Court performance was £10, this meant an increase in their annual revenue of something like £3,000 of our money, about £300 a year for each sharer. Then, James was a more generous, or at least more prodigal, spender than Elizabeth, and as earnest of his bounty paid his new company £30 for their 'mayntenaunce and releife, being prohibited to presente any playes publiquelie in or neere London by reason of the plague'. Before the end of 1603, Edward Alleyn and the Admiral's had been taken under the patronage of Prince Henry, and Thomas Heywood and Worcester's, now playing at the Curtain and Boar's Head, under that of Queen Anne. All three companies were authorised by the King to play anywhere within the realm, so that they were no longer subject to mayors and magistrates, at one remove from rogues and vagabonds, but privileged members of the royal household.

During the year of plague and closing of the theatres, the players were obliged to travel, the King's striking west and east, to Oxford and Shrewsbury, Cambridge and Ipswich. They took *Hamlet* with them as part of their repertory, so that when the pirated first quarto appeared that year, its title-page read, 'The Tragicall Historie of Hamlet Prince of Denmarke. By William Shake-speare. As it hath beene diuerse times acted by his Highnesse seruants in the Cittie of London: as also in the Vniuersities of Cambridge and Oxford, and else-where'. A corrected quarto, 'enlarged to almost as much againe', was issued in the following year, though, in deference to the Queen, Hamlet's unfortunate allusion to Denmark as a prison was omitted. More to the point, perhaps, would have been the omission of his ironical greeting of Horatio, 'We'll teach you to drink deep ere you depart'. Less easily accountable is the cutting of the passage about the eyrie of children and war of the theatres. But perhaps this was because the Blackfriars boys were also under the Queen's protection. With a new King and a new Lord Chamberlain, Henry Evans had thought it safe to return to England, and, after refurbishing their theatre, he and his partners managed to secure royal patronage by a patent author-ising them to 'bring vppe a convenient number of Children, and them to practize and exercise in the quality of playinge by the name of Children of the Revells to the Queene'. Now that Nathaniel Giles had withdrawn, there was no question of pressing boys into service; but 'convenient nomber' is good, and it no longer mattered if some of the boys were 'noe way able or fitt for singing'. The Children of the Queen's Revels were to have their own official censor, and Samuel Daniel was appointed to license all plays that they presented both at Court and at Blackfriars. Like Giles, he was soon to have his fingers burned.

At the end of November the King's Men were rehearsing at Mortlake, a few miles west of London, where Augustine Phillips lived, when they received a summons to go to Wilton. There is a tradition that 'Sidney's sister, Pembroke's mother', wishing to inter-cede on Raleigh's behalf, wrote to her son telling him to bring the King, who was on a visit to Salisbury, to see *As You Like It*, for 'we have the man Shakespeare with us'. In any event, the King's Men gave

a performance at Wilton on December 2nd, and were paid £30 for
their 'paynes and expences in comming from Mortelake unto the
courte and there presenting before his majestie one playe'. Perhaps
the players accompanied the King and Court when they set out a few
days later for Hampton Court, where, according to Dudley Carleton,
they were to have 'a merry Christmas, for both male and female
masques are already bespoken, whereof the Duke of Lennox is *rector
chori* of th' one side, and the Lady Bedford of the other'.

James's first Revels began with five plays by his own company, that
on New Year's Day being 'a play of Robin goode-fellow', presumably *A Midsummer Night's Dream*. On the same night the Duke of
Lennox, the King's cousin, presented the first masque of the reign.
Out of a heaven built at the lower end of the hall descended a Chinese
magician, who drew a curtain revealing eight Indian and Chinese
knights sitting in a 'vaulty place' with their torchbearers. There was a
song by two boys and two musicians while the masquers presented
sonnets and scutcheons to the King. Then they danced a measure and
took out the most important ladies, including the Queen, Penelope
Rich and the Countess of Bedford, patroness of poets. The younger
ladies were led out for corantos, and after a final song the magician
dissolved his enchantment, revealing the masquers to be the Duke,
the Earl of Pembroke, his brother Philip, and five of their companions. On Twelfth Night there was a masque of Scottish sword-
dancers, from which Jonson, who had tried to gain admission, was
ejected by Lord Chamberlain Suffolk with his white staff. And then,
on the night of Sunday, January 8th, came the long-expected 'Queen's
Masque', *The Vision of the Twelve Goddesses*. This was the work of
Daniel, who had been preferred to the Queen by Lady Bedford, to
whom the printed version was dedicated. It was an elaborate but conventional and visually distracting affair, with a mountain at one end
of the hall, in which were cornet players in the guise of satyrs, the
cave of Sleep at the other end, a temple of Peace on the left, containing
the consort music, while viols and lutes were ranged down one of the
side walls. The masquers were led by the Queen, as Pallas, whose
clothes, wrote Carleton, 'were not so much below the knee but that
we might see a woman had both feet and legs, which I never knew
before'. They presented their emblems to Sibylla, who placed them
on the temple altar, then danced their own measures, led out the lords
for galliards and corantos, and after a short departing dance reascended

the mountain from which they had appeared. Queen Elizabeth's wardrobe had been rifled for the occasion, but even then the spectacle cost between £2,000 and £3,000, and Anne is said to have worn jewellery worth £100,000. The French and Spanish ambassadors, between whom there was some nice diplomatic manœuvring for precedence, were appropriately impressed.

One of the four plays presented by the King's Men before the New Year may have been the tragedy that Jonson had retired to sing 'high and aloof' after the flutter he had caused by his *Poetaster*. This was *Sejanus*, a play in which he conscientiously tried to establish a classical form approximating to the Senecan, as a counterblast to the lawless and negligent romanticism of Shakespeare in *Julius Cæsar* and, worse still, in *Hamlet*. Though the unities could not absolutely be enforced, one of the characters acts as chorus, and violent action, including the death of Sejanus, is reported by messengers. When it came to the printing of the quarto, Jonson even quoted his authorities in the margin to show his 'integrity in the story', and to save himself from the attacks of those 'whose noses are ever like swine spoiling and rooting up the Muses' gardens'. He did not go out of his way to avoid trouble. No doubt the play was received politely enough at Court, but the Globe audience was another matter. Accustomed to tragedies like the perennial *Spanish Tragedy*, and other revenge plays such as the new and overwhelmingly popular *Hamlet*, in which the stage is prodigally strewn with corpses, they had no patience with fine rhetoric devoid of action, and

> screwed their scurvy jaws, and looked awry,
> Like hissing snakes adjudging it to die.

Even Jonson admitted that his play suffered no less violence from the Londoners than Sejanus himself from the people of Rome, who tore the aspiring tyrant in pieces.

Sejanus was another failure, even though it deserved a better fate and was given every chance, the principal actors being Burbage, Shakespeare, Phillips, Heminge, Sly, Condell, and the newcomers John Lowin and Alexander Cooke, two of the men who at this time raised the number of sharers in the King's company from eight to twelve. Cooke, as an apprentice, had been taught his acting by Heminge, and then been employed as a hireling before becoming a sharer. Lowin was a youngster of twenty who had come from

Worcester's. He remained with the King's until the closing of the theatres at the beginning of the Civil War, dying 'very old, and his poverty was as great as his age'. He played Falstaff 'with mighty applause', and tradition has it that Shakespeare coached him in the part of Henry VIII. It may well be so, for *Sejanus* is the last actor-list in which Shakespeare is mentioned, and it seems probable that, like Alleyn, he retired from acting and concentrated on the writing and production of plays for his company.

The Queen's Men (Worcester's) gave two performances in January, and it is more than likely that one of them was Heywood's recent tragedy, *A Woman Killed With Kindness*, for which Henslowe had paid £6 in the previous March. It is Heywood's masterpiece, written with an almost Shakespearean breadth of sympathy, partly in prose, partly in verse, which is never false, never strained. One of the first of the domestic tragedies that were to become so popular—*Othello*, which Shakespeare was then writing, was another—there is a certain decline into bourgeois realism and sentiment, more pathos than tragedy, but at least the pathos rings true, unlike the meretricious prettiness that Fletcher was to exploit. Then, the play is in the nature of a protest against the growing popularity of tragedies of revenge and blood, an anti-revenge play, or at least a refinement of the revenge motif, in which the futility of the pursuit of vengeance is implicit.

Heywood's gentle and tolerant philosophy was lost on James. In January a conference was called at Hampton Court to consider a petition of the Puritan clergy for some modification of the Anglican ritual and liturgy, and a legalised tolerance of, and security for, Puritanism within the Established Church. John Reynolds, President of Corpus Christi, Oxford, and one of the principal denouncers of stage-plays, in which Elizabeth had seen him act as an undergraduate, led the Puritan party, while Bancroft, exponent of the divine right of bishops, represented the orthodox right-wing view. James, who liked nothing better than an argument, assumed the role of genial, loquacious and impartial chairman, checking the arrogance of Bancroft, but at the same time rejecting one after the other the proposals advanced by Reynolds. Finally, when Reynolds suggested that the lower clergy might form synods that should be consulted by their bishops, James, remembering how the Presbyterians had treated his mother and himself in his minority, lost all control and shouted, 'If you aim at a Scottish Presbytery, it agreeth as well with a monarchy as God with the Devil. I thus apply it: no Bishop, no King. If this be all your party hath to say, I will make them conform themselves, or else will harry them out of the land'. They were the words that were to bring his son to the scaffold forty-five years later.

In February the Court returned to Whitehall, for the plague was almost over, and on March 15th James, accompanied by the Queen and Prince Henry, made his belated progress through London, a triumphant passage from the Tower, through the City, back to Whitehall. At the time of the coronation, triumphal arches made of wood had been erected at appropriate sites along the route, but some of these were 'such small timbered gentlemen' that they had to be replaced. These arches were elaborately carved and painted, adorned with symbolic devices and verses, with niches and pedestals to be filled with allegorical figures who would make appropriate speeches when the King passed through. Dekker, Jonson and Middleton were commissioned by the City to design their five pageants and to write the eulogies. At Fenchurch, near the Tower, was Jonson's first formidably allegorical structure, tricked with apposite quotations from Virgil, Horace and Ovid. He made no concessions to the multitude, who were there only to gaze and admire; the Latin was for the 'sharp and learned', for scholars like the King. There were twelve figures on the pageant, the chief of whom were the Genius of London and the Thames, impersonated by Edward Alleyn and one of the Blackfriars boys 'in a skin-coat made like flesh, naked and blue'. He leaned his arm upon an earthen pot, out of which ran water with live fishes that played about him. Alleyn delivered a hundred lines of rhyming gratulation 'with excellent action, and a well-tuned, audible voice', and James passed on to the arches erected by the Dutch and Italian merchants at the Exchange. At Soper Lane he was greeted by Dekker's 'Arabia Britannica', a speech by one of the Paul's boys, and the song, 'Troynovant is now no more a city'. Dekker was also responsible for 'The Garden of Eirene and Euporia' at the Cross in Cheapside. There was Middleton's 'Globe of the World' at Fleet conduit, where one of Alleyn's colleagues delivered a speech as Zeal. Jonson concluded, as he had begun, the City's tributes. At Temple Bar was a temple, the walls and gates of which were brass, the pillars silver, their capitals and bases gold. At the highest point of all was a Janus' head, signifying that James filled all parts of the world with majesty, as the Genius of the City was at pains to explain. Jonson, too, had the satisfaction of designing the last pageant, that in the Strand, contributed by the City of Westminster. The invention was a rainbow, the moon, sun and Pleiades, advanced between two magnificent pyramids seventy feet in height, on which were drawn the King's pedigrees, English and Scottish. Electra, hanging in the air, in figure of a comet, was to have delivered the final century of hyperbolic and admonitory couplets. But James was bored and the speech was cut. He had been persuaded to endure the day's proceedings patiently only by the assurance that he should never have such another. No doubt Shakespeare, in his new scarlet livery, derived more amusement from the entertainment.

A few months later Shakespeare and his eleven colleagues were called upon for more than nominal duties as Grooms of the Chamber. For eighteen days in August they were in attendance at Somerset House, where the Spanish ambassador, the Constable of Castile, was lodged, and were paid altogether £21 12s. for their services. The occasion was the negotiations for peace with Spain, brilliantly carried through by Cecil. England insisted on her right to trade with Spanish America, and, as neutrals, to carry goods for the Dutch and to supply them with volunteers. It was peace with honour; the one great triumph of James's reign. The twenty years' war was over and the way open for English expansion beyond the seas.

XI

1604–1605

MASQUE AND PLOT

ON March 19th, 1604, four days after his progress through London, James opened his first Parliament. Jonson, who was now assuming the role of unofficial Laureate, made up for the eulogies that the King had so unfortunately missed as he hurried under his allegorical arches, by writing a 'Panegyre' on the happy event. Kings, he assured him,

> by heaven are placed upon his throne,
> To rule like heaven,

adding, however, the salutary warning,

> That kings by their example more do sway
> Than by their power; and men do more obey
> When they are led, than when they are compelled.

Finally he congratulated his delirious countrymen on 'How dear a father they did now enjoy'. That, in a large measure, was the trouble. James's paternal instincts were almost morbidly over-developed. The Commons, on the other hand, considered that they had come of age under the Tudors, and assembled to demand the privileges of their majority. When, therefore, James informed them that kings were not only God's lieutenants upon earth but even by God himself called gods, they grew restive, and when he added that it is seditious in subjects to dispute what a king may do, they recorded their unanimous and emphatic dissent. Most of them had Puritan sympathies, or at least, like Bacon, favoured a policy of tolerant comprehension within the Church, but James, obstinately convinced that Puritanism was only the thin end of the wedge of Presbyterianism and democratic Church government, lectured them on the essential authority of bishops, and assured them that he would fulfil his threat to expel any Puritan clergy who refused to conform. He was as good as his word. When Parliament rose in July, the zealous Bancroft ejected 300 non-conforming and conscientious clergy from their livings. James's first session of Parliament could scarcely be called a success.

Nor were James's dealings with the Catholics any more successful. It was not that he was intolerant, in theory at least. On the contrary, his most cherished ideal was peace at home as well as abroad, and this involved a fair measure of religious toleration. Despite a bungled Catholic plot soon after his arrival in London, the fines for recusancy were remitted, on the understanding that all Catholics would acknowledge the King instead of the Pope, and that there should be no increase in their numbers. This was real altruism on James's part, for recusants were a valuable source of revenue, as well as a convenient means of clandestine payment. By granting, as it were, one or more to a creditor or a favourite, James could by-pass the Exchequer, an important consideration for a needy king anxious to dispense with Parliament, though admittedly the method was something of a gamble, for there was always the danger that the recusant would come to an untimely end, or, just as bad, turn Protestant. The result of the remission was, of course, that secret as well as professed Catholics absented themselves from Anglican Church services, and this was fearfully interpreted as a vast proselytising movement by the priests. James now flew to the other extreme. In February 1604 all priests were ordered to leave the country, in August some of them were hanged, in November the fines for recusancy were reimposed. On December 11th Robert Catesby and four of his followers began to tunnel their way towards the foundations of Parliament House.

A year of plague, religious persecution and parliamentary bickerings had rubbed the bloom off the new reign. Nor did James sway, as Jonson had implied that he would, by his example. In spite of her whims and her parsimony, the people had revered their dead Queen; they could not even respect their new King. He was, indeed, almost a figure of fun, with his weak legs, slobbering tongue, outlandish northern accent, pedantic loquacity, gross manners, petulance, intemperance and passion for the chase. Then, his strained relations with his wife were an embarrassment even to the corrupt and frivolous Court, swollen with rapacious and expectant Scots. As early as the summer of 1604 the French ambassador wrote that the King was represented on the stage to the great amusement of the Queen, who enjoyed the laugh against her husband. And a few months later we learn that 'the players do not forbear to represent upon their stage the whole course of this present time, not sparing either King, state or religion, in so great absurdity, and with such liberty, that any would be afraid to hear them'.

One of the offending plays was the, now lost, tragedy of the Gowrie conspiracy, produced by the King's own company, for John Chamberlain wrote in December: 'The tragedy of *Gowry*, with all the action and actors hath been twice represented by the King's Players, with exceeding concourse of all sorts of people. But whether the matter or manner be not well handled, or that it be thought unfit that Princes should be played on the stage in their life-time, I hear that some great Councillors are much displeased with it, and so 'tis thought shall be forbidden.'

Apparently no punitive action was taken, but poor Samuel Daniel got into trouble at about this time, though for a somewhat different kind of offence. 'Overmastered by necessity', he took advantage of his position as censor of the Queen's Revels' plays to license an old closet-drama of his own for their performance at Blackfriars. This was *Philotas*, a tragedy in the classical manner, on the subject of Alexander the Great's favourite, who was put to death on the charge of conspiring against his prince's life. The story was too like that of Essex, and Daniel was called before the Council, severely reprimanded and made to apologise. The serious and conscientious poet—one instinctively wants to call him 'old', though he was only forty—took it very hard, and when he dedicated the printed version to Prince Henry, called himself 'the remnant of another time', a man who had 'outlived the date of former grace, acceptance and delight'. In a sense it was true, for he was essentially an Elizabethan, and the *Philotas* affair drove him into a more dedicated seclusion than ever. 'As the *Tortoise* burieth himself all the winter in the ground', wrote Fuller, 'so Mr. Daniel would lye hid at his Garden-house in Oldstreet, nigh London, for some Months together (the more retiredly to enjoy the Company of the Muses), and then would appear in publick to converse with his Friends.' However, he was still to write two pastoral plays and another masque for the Jacobean Court.

In Elizabeth's reign, an average of about seven plays had been given during the season of the Revels, all of them within the Twelve Days of Christmas, except for a few sporadic performances between Twelfth Night and the beginning of Lent. Under James and Anne the period of plays was considerably extended, normally beginning on November 1st and sometimes going on until well after Easter; 'It seems that we shall have Christmas all the year', wrote a bewildered Elizabethan in the middle of January 1605. There were rarely fewer than twenty performances, though the King was by no means always present.

Whenever possible he slipped away to his stables, leaving Prince Henry and the Queen to enjoy the entertainments, and sometimes to pay for them as well. Fortunately the Revels Accounts for 1604–5 are much more detailed than usual. The season began on November 1st with a performance of *Othello* by the King's Men in the banqueting house erected by Elizabeth in the early eighties. Between then and February 12th they gave a series of six more plays by 'Shaxberd', as he is called in the Accounts, some of them old ones revived for the benefit of the new sovereigns: *The Merry Wives, Measure for Measure, The Comedy of Errors, Henry V, Love's Labour's Lost* and, on Shrove Sunday, *The Merchant of Venice*, which 'so did take our James' that he called for a second performance on the following Tuesday. The Chamberlain of the Exchequer, Sir Walter Cope, then planning the building of Holland House, was at his wit's end for suitable plays that the Queen had not already seen, and wrote to Cecil: 'I have sent and bene all thys morning hunting for players Juglers & Suche kinde of Creaturs, but fynde them hard to find, wherfore Leavinge notes for them to seeke me, Burbage ys come, & Sayes ther ys no new playe that the quene hath not seene, but they have Revyved an olde one Cawled *Loves Labore lost* which for wytt & mirthe he sayes will please her exceedingly. And thys ys apointed to be playd to Morowe night at my lord of Sowthamptons, unless you send a wrytt to Remove the Corpus Cum Causa to your Howse in Strande.' So the Revels overflowed into the houses of the nobility, and *Loves' Labour's Lost* was played either at Southampton's or at Cecil House in the Strand. Altogether the King's gave eleven performances, including revivals of *Every Man in his Humour* and *Every Man out of his Humour*. Jonson's labours, at least, had not been lost.

The Prince's, the former Admiral's, made eight appearances. There is no record of their plays, though two of them would almost certainly be the two parts of *The Honest Whore*, or 'the onest hore', as Henslowe preferred to write it when making his payment to Dekker and Middleton. Like *Othello*, which it echoes, it is Jacobean, not Elizabethan, drama, tinged with a new melancholy, and as in *Hamlet* and so many Jacobean plays—and prose and funeral monuments for that matter—there is a fanciful dallying with death and preoccupation with physical dissolution:

> What but fair sand-dust are earth's purest forms?
> Queens' bodies are but trunks to put in worms.

For the rest it is characteristic Dekkerian compassion, caricature and good-natured farce, the kind of thing that so offended Jonson.

It had been at the special request of Elizabeth that Alleyn had returned to the stage after his first retirement, and now, having welcomed the new sovereign from the top of Jonson's Fenchurch pageant, he finally and positively, as we should say to-day, retired, though he always retained an interest in his old company who were his tenants at the Fortune. The playhouse was well named, for it had made his fortune. Though still only thirty-eight, he was a very wealthy man. Apart from his theatre, he owned considerable property in London and Sussex, and for the last ten years had had a financial interest in Paris Garden, that is, the Beargarden, next to the Rose, and not much further from the Globe. Then, on his retirement he and Henslowe jointly bought the Mastership of the Game at Paris Garden for £450. This was a lucrative monopoly, for the Master received £5 whenever the sovereign was a spectator, in addition to the profits made out of public baiting and the sale of licences; Alleyn and Henslowe themselves had paid £40 a year to the former Master for licence to bait. Thursdays were reserved for public baiting, and one of their posters gives a good idea of the 'sport' enjoyed by these sensitive-insensitive Elizabethans and Jacobeans, whose civilised delight in motet and madrigal, poetry and play, merely skinned and filmed their desire for grosser pleasures. The orthography has the authentic Henslowe touch:

Tomorrowe beinge Thursdaie shalbe seen at the Beargardin on the banckside a greate mach plaid by the gamstirs of Essex who hath chalenged all comers what soeuer to plaie five dogges at the single beare for five pounds and also wearie a bull dead at the stake and for your better content shall haue plasant sport with the horse and ape and whipping of the blind beare.

The whipping of the blind bear, Harry Hunks, 'till the blood ran down his old shoulders', was a humorous interlude, as was also the baiting by dogs of a horse with an ape tied to its back. The sport was so profitable that within a year Alleyn was able to take the first steps towards buying the manor of Dulwich, though, like his father-in-law, he preferred to live on Bankside near the Beargarden.

Shortly after his Dulwich transaction, an anonymous pamphlet called *Ratseis Ghost* was published. Gamaliel Ratsey was a highwayman who had been hanged in March 1605, and the tract purports to give some account of his life. One chapter describes 'a pretty Prancke passed by Ratsey upon certain Players that he met by chance in an

THE CIVILE WARES
betweene the Howses of Lancaster
and Yorke corrected and continued
by Samuel Daniel one of the Groomes
of hir Maiesties most honorable
Priuie Chamber.

Ætas prima canat veneres
postrema tumultus.

PRINTED
AT LONDON
by Simon Waterfonne.
1609;

SAMUEL DANIEL

OBERON'S PALACE

Design by Inigo Jones for *The Masque of Oberon*

Inne'. Like Hamlet, Ratsey criticises them for 'striving to over-doe and go beyond' themselves, so marring all, and then asks them to give him a 'private play'. He professes to be so pleased with their performance that he rewards them with forty shillings, twice as much as they had ever received for playing 'in the countrey'. The next day Ratsey pursues them in his professional capacity, forces them to hand back the forty shillings—with interest—then good-humouredly advises their leader to quit the provinces and seek his fortune in London:

Get thee to London, for, if one man were dead, they will have much neede of such a one as thou art. There would be none in my opinion fitter than thyself to play his parts. My conceipt is such of thee, that I durst venture all the mony in my purse on thy head to play Hamlet with him for a wager. There thou shalt learn to be frugall—for players were never so thriftie as they are now about London— and to feed upon all men, to let none feede upon thee, to make thy hand a stranger to thy pocket, thy hart slow to performe thy tongues promise; and when thou feelest thy purse well lined, buy thee some place or lordship in the country, that, growing weary of playing, thy mony may there bring thee to dignitie and reputation; then thou needest care for no man, nor for them that before made thee prowd with speaking their words upon the stage.

The reference is almost certainly to Alleyn, though Shakespeare, a 'gentleman' and the owner of New Place, may be glanced at. The 'one man' who played Hamlet is undoubtedly Burbage. The prejudice against players, who made their money out of speaking what other men wrote, died hard.

The Queen's gave only one Court performance that season, a play by Heywood, who was then writing the first part of *If You Know Not Me, You Know Nobody*. This was published in 1605, but in a later Prologue Heywood complained that, though it had no merit—so like Heywood!—it

Did throng the Seates, the Boxes, and the Stage
So much, that some by Stenography drew
The plot, put it in print (scarce one word trew).

This was something new. Pirated editions of plays were normally memorial reconstructions by actors who had played in them, but now apparently there was a system of shorthand sufficiently developed to make it possible for a member of the audience, or more probably two or three in collusion, to take down roughly what the actors said. The publisher of *If You Know Not Me* was Nathaniel Butter, who in 1608 issued the quarto of *King Lear*, which was probably put together in the same way. Butter's record is not a good one. Heywood's play was soon joined on his stall 'in Pauls Church-yard at the signe of the Pide Bull' by '*The London Prodigal. As it was plaide by the Kings Maiesties seruants. By William Shakespeare.*' The name was one to conjure with, or at least one with which to sell books.

Butter had made his Pied Bull notorious, but the Queen's were to make their Red Bull famous. This was a new theatre in Clerkenwell, not far from the Fortune, which they occupied at about the time of the 1604–5 Revels, abandoning their old houses of the Curtain and the Boar's Head. One of the first plays they gave there was Heywood's *Rape of Lucrece.* The long-suffering author insured himself against further rape by Butter by selling it to him.

The fourth company of royal players made their bow on New Year's Day, when Samuel Daniel and Henry Evans presented the Queen's Revels in *All Fools,* one of the first of a series of plays written, or revised, by Chapman for the Blackfriars boys. It is a comedy of intrigue and of humours, something in the manner of his friend Jonson, with a taut and complex plot worked out through a sequence of ingenious situations. In this it is quite uncharacteristic, for Chapman's plots are generally flaccid and chaotic, overwhelmed by a great sea of rhetoric and poetry, alternating between turgidity and splendour. In his tragedies the characters address one another, or more frequently the audience, in speeches of epic proportions, for he was essentially an epic poet driven to make a living by writing for the stage. The wonder is that his plays were so popular, when he worked from the thesis that 'material instruction, elegant and sententious excitation to virtue, and deflection from the contrary, are the soul, limbs, and limits of authentical tragedy'. But then, like Juliet's nurse, the Jacobeans loved to hear good counsel almost as much as they liked to see it disregarded, and, after all, they could ever be sure of plenty of blood and horror at the end of a Chapman tragedy. Even Dryden was astonished at the brilliance of *Bussy D'Ambois* when he saw it on the stage, though in his study he found that he had been cozened with a jelly, a cold, dull mass of hyperbole, false poetry and true nonsense. *Bussy D'Ambois,* the first of the famous group of tragedies dealing with contemporary French history, was written at about the same time as *All Fools,* though for the Paul's boys, and the second Court performance by the Queen's Revels may well have been the recently published *Malcontent.*

The Malcontent is an interesting play for a variety of reasons, not the least being its dedication to the most elegant and learned of poets, Ben Jonson, by his dear friend the author, John Marston. The war of the theatres had been forgotten, for the moment at least, and Marston's 'reformed Muse' inspires a play with the Jonsonian purpose of curing such vices as stand not accountable to law, by casting ink upon them. It was originally written for the Queen's Revels, who had somehow got hold of one of the King's plays, *Jeronimo* (not to be confused with *The Spanish Tragedy*), and performed it at Blackfriars, to which impertinence the King's replied by producing *The Malcontent* at the Globe. Webster wrote an Induction for the occasion, in which Burbage, Condell and Lowin appear in person and explain to Sly, in character of a gallant sitting on the stage, how it is they have come by the play of the malcontented Malevole:

Condell. Faith, sir, the book was lost; and because 'twas pity so good a play should be lost, we found it and play it.

Sly. I wonder you would play it, another company having interest in it.

Condell. Why not Malevole in folio with us, as Jeronimo in decimosexto with them? They taught us a name for our play; we call it *One for Another*.

Sly. What are your additions?

Burbage. Sooth, not greatly needful; only as your salad to your great feast, to entertain a little more time, and to abridge the not-received custom of music in our theatre.

The shortened version played by the boys at Blackfriars, where the intervals for music were so popular, had been lengthened to suit conditions at the Globe, where there were no choirboys to hale souls out of men's bodies with their song.

Altogether there were twenty-three plays during the Christmas festivities of 1604–5, some of them in honour of that lusty visitor and reveller, the Queen's brother, the Duke of Holst, but the great occasion was Twelfth Night when the five-year-old Prince Charles was created Duke of York. Inspired perhaps by having seen *Othello*, the Queen decided that in her next masque she and her companions must be blackamoors, and Jonson had so pressed himself on the royal attention that he was commissioned to write it. To write, not to design it, for 'the bodily part', the scenery and costumes, were to be the work of a new man. Exactly the same age as Jonson, thirty-two, Inigo Jones had recently been in the service of the Queen's elder brother, Christian IV of Denmark, but more important, he had been to Italy, where he had studied classical and Renaissance architecture at first hand, and, moreover, like Italian architects, learned to draw. With their geometrical instruments, English architects were admirable at a plan or an elevation, but Jones could draw in the tradition of Michelangelo and Leonardo, bold and sweeping designs that were to revolutionise the art in England. His conception of the masque, therefore, was something very different from the glorified charades of Tudor times. They were amateurish toys; his were to be the work of a highly trained professional, architectural and scenic splendours to be set off by poetry and music. Such, however, was not the conception of Jonson, for whom poetry was the soul of masque, and spectacle no more than than the outward flourish. Jones was as arrogant as Jonson, and their emulative collaboration led inevitably to an open quarrel, in which the poet assailed the architect and his 'carpentry' in his ironical *Expostulation*, and *Inigo Marquis Would-be*. But all this was in the future, and in the course of the next ten years the two men collaborated in the production of almost as many masques.

Jones's great innovation was the concentration of the spectacle within a proscenium arch in the Italian manner. *The Masque of Blackness* was presented in the old wooden banqueting-house, at the lower end of which Jones set up a stage on wheels, forty feet square and four feet high; underneath was the machinery for his effects, and framing it a Renaissance proscenium with a curtain to conceal the scene, another important innovation. On it was painted, not very appropriately, but to the great content of the expectant James, a landscape with hunting scenes. The hall was crowded; some of the ladies complained that they were shut up in heaps between doors, where they had to stay till all was over, and there was the usual comic ambassadorial scramble for precedence, in which the Frenchman was worsted by his Spanish and Venetian rivals, who sat by the King in his state at the upper end. When the curtain was lowered, for these early curtains were rolled down in the Roman manner, the scene was disclosed. According to Jonson, 'an artificial sea was seen to shoot forth, as if it flowed to the land, raised with waves which seemed to move, and in some places the billows to break'. In front of this sea were six blue-haired tritons with wreathed conches, two singing sea-maids, and two great sea-horses as large as life, ridden by blue-skinned Oceanus and Ethiopian Niger. The masquers were twelve negro nymphs attired in azure and silver, seated in a great concave shell like mother of

pearl, moving on the waters and rising with the billow. Six sea-
monsters swam beside it, bearing the twelve torch-bearers on their
backs. 'The scene', wrote Jonson admiringly, 'caught the eye afar
off with a wandering beauty'. 'All fish and no water', commented the
caustic Carleton. As for the masquers, 'their apparel was rich, but too
light and curtizan-like for such great ones. Their faces and arms, up
to the elbows, were painted black, and you cannot imagine a more
ugly sight than a troop of lean-cheeked Moors.' Three of the negro
nymphs had fallen out during rehearsals: one because she was sick,
another had the measles and the third a polypus in her nostril. But
there had been no lack of understudies, and the Queen led her eleven
aristocratic Ethiopians through their dumb-show and dancing.

After a song by one of the tritons and the two sea-maids, Niger
explained to Oceanus how his twelve daughters were visiting the west
to find the country of a temperate sun, where they could recover their
original fair-skinned beauty. 'At this the moon was discovered in the
upper part of the house, triumphant in a silver throne, made in figure
of a pyramid', and the goddess Ethiopia spoke. This country, she
explained, was Britannia, the longed-for landfall:

> Ruled by a sun, that to this height doth grace it:
> Whose beams shine day and night, and are of force
> To blanch an Ethiop and revive a corse.

Here the tritons sounded, the masquers danced ashore, presenting
their fans adorned with erudite symbolic devices, danced their own
single measure, and were about to choose their men when one of the
tritons sang:

> Come away, come away,
> We grow jealous of your stay:
> If you do not stop your ear,
> We shall have more cause to fear
> Sirens of the land, than they
> To doubt the sirens of the sea.

Nevertheless, they danced several measures and corantos with their
men before they were called again by the sea-maids, with a song whose
cadences were repeated by a double echo from different parts of the
land. Ethiopia assured the nymphs that they should remain the guests
of western Ocean for a year, by which time their former fairness
would be restored. At this, in a dance they returned to sea, took their

places in the shell and went out with a full song. The night's entertainment cost about £3,000, almost £100,000 to-day, probably more than Elizabeth had spent in masques in the whole of her reign.

It was a triumph for Jonson. He was now a well-known figure at Court and on friendly terms with some of the great ones of the land. Perhaps too well known, and certainly too sure of himself, for he was soon to learn how fickle Fortune could be to the aspiring courtier. Dekker and Webster had just finished a comedy, *Westward Ho!*, for the Paul's boys, and after the strain and labours of rehearsing his masque, Jonson joined Chapman and Marston in writing a reply for the Queen's Revels, *Eastward Ho!* Not that they claimed to do better, but,

> Only that eastward, westward still excels;
> Honour the sun's fair rising, not his setting.

'Eastward Ho!' was the cry of the watermen taking passengers down the river, and the play is a comedy of the City, one of the most amusing —and bawdy—pieces of the period, tilting at and parodying all manner of things in its progress. *The History of Richard Whittington* had recently been produced by the Prince's, and *Eastward Ho!* is a burlesque of a similar success story, in which the virtuous and industrious apprentice marries the virtuous daughter of his virtuous master, while the other daughter comes to grief by marrying a penniless knight. Even *Hamlet* does not escape parody:

> *Enter Hamlet, a footman, in haste.*
> *Ham.* What coachman! my lady's coach, for shame! Her ladyship's ready to come down.
> *Enter Potkin, a tankard bearer.*
> *Pot.* 'Sfoot, Hamlet, are you mad?

And again, the equivocal aside of her ladyship to the unvirtuous apprentice:

> *His head as white as milk, all flaxen was his hair;*
> *But now he is dead, and laid in his bed,*
> *And never will come again.* God be at your labour.

Such stuff as this, of course, was innocent enough as far as the Master of the Revels was concerned, although it had not been shown to him, as it should have been, for his allowance. But it was another matter when there were jocular references to 'Scotch knights', and to 'the knighthood nowadays being nothing like the knighthood of old times'.

The crowning impertinence, however, was when one of the Revels children, affecting a Scottish accent, parodied the King himself: 'I ken the man weel; he's one of my thirty pound knights.' James's prodigal creation of knights was one of the stock jokes of London—Bacon himself, to his disgust, was only one of three hundred mass-manufactured at the same time—but this was more than a joke, and one of the Scottish knights complained. Marston, apparently the real culprit, fled, but Chapman and Jonson were thrown summarily into prison, under threat of having their ears and noses cut off. On 'prison-polluted paper' they wrote innumerable letters to their influential friends, protesting that the 'chief offences are but two clawses, and both of them not our owne', and asking them to intercede on their behalf. The King relented, and they were released in October, when Jonson feasted his friends, including Camden and his old mother, who flourished the poison she would have mixed for her son and herself had the sentence been carried out. It was a frightening experience, and the Blackfriars syndicate might have been expected to become more circumspect, especially as James withdrew the patronage of the Queen, who had been to their theatre 'to enjoy the laugh against her husband'. Instead of the Children of the Queen's Revels, they were now simply the Children of the Revels.

Meanwhile James had been on progress, and at the end of August put in a few days at Oxford, where he was rigorously entertained with a series of Latin plays in Christ Church hall, during which, however, he had an unfortunate disposition to sleep. But if the evidence of a Cambridge man, John Chamberlain, is to be trusted, they were dull enough, and James missed the best, and last, performance, put in for the benefit of the ladies, Daniel's pastoral *Queen's Arcadia*, 'which made amends for all, being indeed very excellent'. The Oxford men had engaged one 'Mr. Jones, a great traveller' to supply scenery and machinery for the plays. The stage was slightly raked, and, in a specially constructed tiring-house wall at the back, revolving prism-shaped pillars were fixed. Each of the three sides of these was painted, so that when they were turned a new scene was presented to the audience, and in this way, 'with the help of other painted cloths', there could be two changes of scene during a performance. The device was one that may have been employed in the classical Greek theatre, and Inigo Jones had learned of it while he was in Italy.

A month later the King's Players themselves were in Oxford.

London was rarely quite free from plague; at the beginning of October there was 'a sudden rising of the sickness' to more than thirty deaths a week, and on the 5th the Council issued instructions 'to forbidde Stage plaies and to take order that the infectede bee kept in their howses'. By the 9th the King's Men were at Oxford, where they received the customary ten shillings for their official performance before the mayor, a sad declension after a full house at the Globe. They were without Augustine Phillips, who had died in May. Most loyal of colleagues, he had left legacies to nearly all his fellows, including a thirty-shilling piece in gold to Shakespeare, and to his late apprentice, Samuel Gilburne, who took his place as a sharer, forty shillings, much of his wardrobe and his bass viol. His then apprentice, James Sands, received another forty shillings, his cittern, his bandore and his lute. The company could ill afford to lose such a musician and such a friend. On his return to London after making the sad journey to Mortlake for the funeral, Shakespeare, then engaged on *Timon of Athens*, wrote of the shame experienced on abandoning a comrade to the grave:

> As we do turn our backs
> From our companion thrown into his grave,
> So his familiars to his buried fortunes
> Slink all away.

If Shakespeare had then retired from acting, it is improbable that he went on tour with the company; he would be more profitably employed in writing for them, and having thrown aside the intractable *Timon*, with its foolish and essentially untragic hero, he resumed the theme of ingratitude in the story of *King Lear*.

It was probably his reading of Camden's recently published *Remaines of a greater Worke concerning Britaine* that led him to do this, for though he knew the story of Lear from various sources, including the anonymous old, though newly published, play of *King Leir*, Camden gave a new and stimulating version of the legend. He also gave a more detailed account than Plutarch of the fable of the belly and the members, which Shakespeare was soon to incorporate in *Coriolanus*. There, too, Shakespeare would read a suggested derivation of his name 'from that which they commonly carried, as Longsword, Broad-speare, Fortescue, that is, Shake-Speare, Shotbolt, Wagstaffe', as well as an appreciation of his work: 'If I would come to our time, what a world could I present to you out of Sir Philip

Sidney, Ed. Spencer, Samuel Daniel, Hugh Holland, Ben Johnson, Th. Campion, Mich. Drayton, George Chapman, John Marston, William Shakespeare, and other most pregnant wits of these our times, whom succeeding ages may justly admire.' The order of mention is amusing; like Jonson, Holland was an old pupil of Camden's at Westminster. Now a Fellow of Trinity, Cambridge, he had just published a volume of undistinguished poems, and was to write the equally mediocre elegiac sonnet on Shakespeare, prefaced to the Folio. Another new book to be read was Bacon's *Advancement of Learning*, fulsomely addressed to the King, the phœnix of learning, for it was intended to be the advancement of Bacon as well as of learning. His reward was not long delayed: the Solicitor-Generalship, the coveted office that Essex had tried in vain to get for him. Nevertheless, *The Advancement of Learning* was an immensely important book. In it Bacon surveyed the whole field of knowledge, and by distinguishing the province of science from that of philosophy, prepared the way for the exact experimental science of the new century. 'This writing seemeth to me', he eloquently and modestly concludes, 'not much better than that noise or sound which musicians make while they are tuning their instruments: which is nothing pleasant to hear, but yet is a cause why the music is sweeter afterwards. So have I been content to tune the instruments of the Muses, that they may play that have better hands.'

Shakespeare may have taken the opportunity of the closing of the theatres to visit Stratford, accompanying his fellows as far as Oxford, where, tradition has it, he used to lodge at the Crown Tavern. The hostess was the beautiful Mrs. Davenant, whose fourth child, William, born in the following spring, was reputed to be Shakespeare's godson, if not indeed even more intimately related. It may be so, but in Stratford, another forty miles on, he had a wife, two marriageable daughters and a considerable property to look after. He had just added to this by investing several hundred pounds in the tithes of the open fields adjoining his estate on the outskirts of the town. His friend, Thomas Russell, had been negotiating for the purchase of the neighbouring Clopton House and park, but a new tenant was now moving in, a wealthy young Catholic dandy with a passion for horses, Ambrose Rookwood.

Although there was still plague in London and the theatres remained closed, the King's Men must have returned to the Globe

before the end of October to rehearse for the Revels. By this time
Jonson had been released from prison, and shortly afterwards was
invited to a select little party by Rookwood's friend, Robert Catesby,
a man of his own age and of great charm and beauty, 'above two yards
high, and as well proportioned to his height as any man should see'.
Other guests were Thomas Winter and Francis Tresham, all of them,
like Jonson, Catholics. But Jonson did not know that these men had
placed thirty-six barrels of gunpowder in a vault beneath the House of
Lords, where James was to open Parliament on November 5th.
Another of their colleagues was Guy Fawkes, a Yorkshire gentleman,
and a professional soldier versed in the sieger's craft of sapping. He
had directed operations against the nine-foot foundation wall of
Parliament House until they found that there was a cellar to be hired
on the other side, and it was here that their two tons of gunpowder
now lay hidden under piles of coal and faggots. Tresham and Rookwood were two of those who had stocked the country-houses of
Warwickshire with arms that were to be used in the great Catholic
rising when King, Lords and Commons had been blown at the moon.
The moon, indeed, portended no good. There was an eclipse on the
27th, and only a fortnight before there had been a total eclipse of the
sun.

But despite eclipses and plague, life went on much as usual as winter
closed in on London. The King was back at Whitehall preparing for
another round with Parliament, Shakespeare working at *King Lear*,
Jonson finishing *Volpone*, and Munday putting the final touches to his
Lord Mayor's pageant, called, ironically enough, *The Triumphs of
Reunited Britannia*. On the 26th Lord Monteagle, Tresham's
brother-in-law, was handed an anonymous letter imploring him not
to attend the opening of Parliament, 'for God and man hath concurred
to punish the wickedness of this time, and they shall receive a terrible
blow, and they shall not see who hurts them'. Monteagle at once
showed the letter to Cecil, now Earl of Salisbury, but there was no
clue as to the conspirators, and only a vague hint as to the nature of
the conspiracy, if there really was one. Salisbury made inquiries, and
then waited until the last moment. On the afternoon of November
4th, Lord Chamberlain Suffolk visited the cellar beneath the House
of Lords where Fawkes was keeping watch, and after making a few
inquiries about the tenant and his fuel, left. Fawkes, knowing that
the Council had got wind of the plot and that the chances were that

he would be seized, resolutely kept to his post. Towards midnight his vigil was broken by the arrival of a magistrate and his men. They searched the chamber, knocked him down, and carried him to the King's bedchamber, where he remained scornfully defiant, regretting merely that the plot had miscarried.

The next morning the rest of the conspirators made for Warwickshire to raise the now hopeless rebellion, but not a single person joined the little band of thirty-six desperate men. On the 8th they were trapped at Holbeche House in Staffordshire. The sheriff and his men opened fire. Catesby and two others were killed, and the rest taken as prisoners to London. Jonson was questioned, but obviously knew nothing of the plot, while in the Tower, on the King's authority, Fawkes was subjected to tortures unrecognised by the law of England. Yet it was only after he knew that nothing now could save his friends that a confession was wrung from him. A few weeks later he and Rookwood were executed with the traditional barbarities opposite Parliament House. New penal laws were clamped upon the Catholics, making it a capital offence to convert anybody to their faith. So ended James's attempt to unite Englishmen of every creed in loyalty to their sovereign. And Shakespeare wrote: 'These late eclipses in the sun and moon portend no good to us: though the wisdom of nature can reason it thus and thus, yet nature finds itself scourged by the sequent effects: love cools, friendship falls off, brothers divide: in cities, mutinies; in countries, discord; in palaces, treason.'

XII

1605–1608

TRAGEDY AND SATIRE

PARLIAMENT met in a highly emotional mood, and as a thank-offering for their escape voted James a substantial subsidy. But such an uneasy and fortuitous accord could not last long. James was spending more on peace than Elizabeth had spent on war and running into debt at the rate of £100,000 a year. Prices, too, were soaring, and to meet his mounting expenses without becoming dependent on Parliament, James strained the prerogative rights of the crown, the imposition of customs duties and sale of monopolies, as far as they would go. John Bate, a merchant of the Levant Company, refused to pay an additional duty imposed by the King on the ground that the tax was illegal without the consent of Parliament, but the judges unanimously upheld the King's prerogative. Parliament saw the danger. Trade was increasing rapidly, and if the King had power to regulate it and pocket the proceeds, he would become independent of their control. Salisbury did his best to bring about an agreement, but financial and constitutional questions were so bedevilled by religious squabbles that nothing came of it, and James angrily dismissed the Commons, determined to rule the country without their support and without their interference. That was at the beginning of 1611, but by the end of 1608 tension was mounting and the struggle approaching a critical stage.

These years were also a period of plague, not as severe as that of 1603, but more than 2,000 died of the sickness each year from 1605 to 1608. The worst time was the summer and autumn, when deaths were so high that the theatres were closed and the London companies had to go on tour. In the autumn of 1607 the King's visited Cambridge as well as Oxford, and at the end of 1608 James paid them £40 by way of reward 'for their private practise in the time of infection, that thereby they might be inhabled to performe their service before his Majesty in Christmas hollidaies'.

Neither constitutional quarrels nor plague account for Shake-

speare's concentration on tragedy at this time. There is no reason to
suppose that he took any great interest in politics, and even if he did
they had not yet reached a tragic stage, and he could always escape
from infection by retiring to Stratford or merely into the countryside
that still lapped London so closely. It is true that his youngest brother,
Edmund, a player, died in December 1607, probably of the plague—
he was buried in the church of St. Saviour's, a few hundred yards from
the Globe—but a man does not write tragedies because his brother
dies, and in any event they were all written by the beginning of 1608.
Of course, it may be that some emotional disturbance of which we
know nothing led to the writing of the great series of tragedies in the
first five years of James's reign, but it is not necessary to assume such
an anguished insurrection. Tragedies are not necessarily the product
of a tragic mood induced by spiritual distress, and it may well be that
Shakespeare turned to sombre themes merely because after the Elizabethan brightness the Jacobean scene *was* sombre, life less of a struggle
for glory than a scramble for riches. Romantic comedies and histories
had lost their charm, heroes like Orlando and Hotspur their popularity; the public demanded dramas of wealth, sex and violence, and
Shakespeare gave them *Timon*, *Othello* and *Lear*. He was by no means
the only one to turn to tragedy at this time; Jonson had tried his hand
at it in *Sejanus*, only to be deflected by its failure; Chapman was
writing his series of tragic French histories; Marston's last two plays,
Sophonisba for the Paul's boys, and the unfinished *Insatiate Countess*,
were tragedies; in 1602 Henslowe paid Chettle for his tragedy of
Hoffman, or 'howghman', and a year or two later came *The Atheist's
Tragedy* by a new man, Cyril Tourneur. Very little is known about
Tourneur, though he is credited, on the very doubtful authority of
the Restoration booksellers,[1] with the authorship of *The Revenger's
Tragedy*, a King's play of about 1606. Both are tragedies of revenge,
of violent and perverted passions, but whereas *The Atheist's Tragedy*
is crude and even laughable melodrama, almost devoid of poetry, at
times almost of verse, which crumbles into fragments at the extremi-
ties, *The Revenger's Tragedy* is both dramatic and tragic in its reve-

[1] If we are to believe their play-lists of 1656–71, Shakespeare wrote the anony-
mous *Edward III*, *Edward IV*, *King Leir*, *Merry Devil of Edmonton* and *Mucedorus*,
Peele's *Arraignment of Paris*, Marlowe's *Edward II*, Chettle's *Hoffman*,
Middleton's *Trick to Catch the Old One*, Massinger's *Roman Actor*, as well as the
Chances of Beaumont and Fletcher, and even *The Spanish Tragedy*.

lation of human baseness, its verse firm, its poetry among the very finest of the period, and overwhelmingly Jacobean in tone. It opens with Vindice, the Revenger, addressing the skull of his mistress, murdered by the Duke because she would not consent to his palsied lust:

> Thou sallow picture of my poisoned love,
> My study's ornament, thou shell of death,
> Once the bright face of my betrothed lady;

and again, before he confronts the murderer 'with the skull dressed up in tires':

> Does the silkworm expend her yellow labours
> For thee? For thee does she undo herself?
> Are lordships sold to maintain ladyships,
> For the poor benefit of a bewildering minute?

His jesting is of Hamlet's grim variety: 'Brother, fall back a little with the bony lady', and, 'She has somewhat of a grave look with her'. Disguised as a pander, he kills the Duke, and then his son, who had tried to seduce his sister, whispering in the ear of the dying man surrounded by his courtiers:

> Now thou'lt not prate on't, 'twas Vindice murdered thee.
> Murdered thy father.
> And I am he—tell nobody.

The play is full of splendid lines. Spurio, the bastard, describes the time of his begetting as 'such a whispering and withdrawing hour', and Vindice makes trial of his sister's chastity with:

> Who'd sit at home in a neglected room,
> Dealing her short-lived beauty to the pictures?

If Tourneur wrote *The Atheist's Tragedy*, and it was published with his name, it is scarcely conceivable that he wrote *The Revenger's Tragedy* as well. There was only one poet who could have written such a play—Webster.

Having finished *King Lear*, which was produced at Whitehall on St. Stephen's Night, 1606, Shakespeare was free to write a play that would flatter his patron's vanity, and perhaps the 'amicable letter' that James is said to have written to him with his own hand was to ask for a play on a Scottish theme. In any event, 1606 seems the most likely year for the writing of *Macbeth*. The witches and their apparitions would have a professional interest for the royal author of the *Dæmon-ologie*, who maintained that his mother's execution was foretokened by a bloody head dancing in the air. He would be delighted by the masque-like show of eight kings, the last of whom was James himself, holding a mirror in which his descendants stretched almost to the crack of doom. Then the drunken porter's equivocator and farmer struck a delicately congratulatory note, referring to the execution for complicity in the Gunpowder Plot of the Jesuit, Henry Garnet *alias* Farmer, whose equivocating defence James had overheard when he visited Guildhall incognito. Best of all, perhaps, he would enjoy the blatant because dramatically quite irrelevant, compliment to his 'heavenly gift of prophecy', and to his power of curing scrofula by the heavenly benediction of his hands. The surgeon William Clowes had just written a book on the subject, and it was his son, Serjeant-Surgeon to James, who helped to expose an interloping quack who, being a seventh son, professed to cure 'the evil' by his touch, until it was revealed that his father had had only six children. Having made a masterpiece out of a compliment, Shakespeare turned again to North's *Plutarch*, an enlarged edition of whose *Lives* had recently been published, and wrote *Coriolanus* and *Antony and Cleopatra*.

We do not know what were the ten plays presented by the King's at the Revels of 1605–6, but we may be sure that most of them were Shakespeare's and one of them at least Jonson's. The dramatist who had been taunted for taking a year to write a play had, in the course of five strenuous weeks, penned *Volpone*, one of the great comedies of all time. It is, as Jonson claimed, 'comedy refined', purged of his former fault of tortuous prolixity, and because of its observance of the unities, as simple, as smoothly moving and as powerful as the piston of some well-oiled machine. Volpone himself is a sort of Jacobean Faustus, one who glories in his wealth, but glories more in the cunning process of its getting, and Jonson's poetry of gold soars to the pitch of Marlowe's, which, to change the figure, it links to Milton's:

> Hail the world's soul, and mine! more glad than is
> The teeming earth to see the longed-for sun
> Peep through the horns of the celestial Ram,
> Am I, to view thy splendour darkening his,
> That lying here, amongst my other hoards,
> Show'st like a flame by night, or like the day
> Struck out of chaos, when all darkness fled
> Unto the centre.

Satire is the complement of tragedy, Aristophanes the contemporary of Sophocles, and as Jonson's genius did not run to tragedy, he lashed the vices of the age in satire as savage and scarifying as the vituperation of Timon or King Lear. *Volpone* is a terrifying comedy, for only in the tragedies of Webster do we find such an accumulation of evil, cynicism and vicious characters. Yet the play was a great success, as it deserved to be. Burbage, Heminge, Condell, Lowin, Sly and Cooke were the 'principal comedians' who first performed it, and took it to Oxford and Cambridge, to which universities Jonson dedicated the quarto in grateful acknowledgement for their 'love and acceptance shown to his poem'. In this dedication Jonson promised, 'if my muses be true to me, I shall raise the despised head of poetry again, and stripping her out of those rotten and base rags wherewith the times have adulterated her form, restore her to her primitive habit, feature and majesty, and render her worthy to be embraced and kissed of all the great and master-spirits of our world'. Strange words to use when Shakespeare was writing the noblest and most splendid of his plays.

Jonson was now much in demand, and he and Inigo Jones were commissioned to produce a masque to celebrate the marriage of the Earl of Essex, only son of Elizabeth's favourite, and the Lady Frances Howard, daughter of the Lord Chamberlain, the Earl of Suffolk. English-born Alphonso Ferrabosco wrote the music, and Thomas Giles, now musical tutor to the princes, arranged the dances, and the masque *Hymenaei* was produced in the Whitehall banqueting-house on January 5th, 1606. The scene was a great globe of gilded countries and silver seas, which, turning softly, revealed the eight men masquers sitting in a mine of precious metals. The upper part of the scene was 'all of clouds, made artificially to swell, and ride like the rack', whence the women masquers descended to the earth—'not', wrote a spectator, 'after the stale downright perpendicular fashion, like a bucket into a well, but came gently sloping down'. And he added sardonically: 'I think they hired and borrowed all the principal jewels and ropes of perle both in court and citty. The Spanish ambassador seemed but poore to the meanest of them.' It may be that memories of this masque partly inspired the writing of Prospero's speech about the dissolution of the cloud-capped towers and the great globe itself, leaving not a rack behind. The next night, Twelfth Night, was a foot-tourney or 'barriers', in which sixteen champions of Truth, led by the Duke of Lennox, tilted with headless lances across a waist-high barrier against the Earl of Sussex and the followers of Opinion, first in single combat, then three to three. Jonson supplied appropriate speeches for the contending parties.

The bridegroom and bride, in honour of whom such fabulous sums of public money were privately squandered, were aged fourteen and thirteen. Essex was to live to be a rebel as famous as, and more fortunate than, his father; the Lady Frances to become the most notorious woman of the corrupt Jacobean Court. Already the seeds of the great scandal were beginning to stir. A few weeks later there was an accident in the tilt-yard, and James's attention was drawn to the injured man, whom he recognised as Robert Carr, a former page of his in Scotland, now a charming youth of about twenty. The King was so infatuated by Carr's good looks, high spirits and accomplishments that he at once took him into favour, knighted him and gave him the Sherborne estate that Raleigh had tried to convey to his wife. It was not long before the precocious Countess of Essex was infatuated too, much to the consternation of Carr's inseparable friend at Court, Thomas Overbury, a young Warwickshire writer of Oxford and the Middle Temple, no doubt well known to Shakespeare.

Because of the unfortunate *Eastward Ho!* affair the Revels Children were not invited to Court in the winter of 1605, though they did not lose financially, for one of the syndicate somehow managed to masquerade as 'one of the Masters of the Children of Pawles', and brought them to Whitehall with two of the Blackfriars plays to entertain the Princes Henry and Charles. However, his triumph was short-lived. In March the Revels boys produced *The Isle of Gulls* by John Day, the man who had killed his fellow dramatist, Henry Porter, 'in self-defence'. They should have known better, for the rival Arcadians and Lacedæmonians of the play stood patently for the English and Scots, and Damœtas, the royal favourite 'made great with others ruines', might equally well be taken for young Sir Robert Carr. As a result many of those responsible were thrown into Bridewell, and the company had to be reorganised. A London goldsmith, Robert Keysar, bought Marston's share in the venture, and acted as manager for the Children, who now became their own masters, renting the theatre from the syndicate. At the same time James completely severed the relationship between the Chapel and the Blackfriars theatre, 'for that it is not fitt or decent that such as shoulde

singe the praises of God Allmightie shoulde be trayned vpp or im-
ployed in suche lascivious and prophane exercises'.

The uneasiness at the increasing licence of plays was reflected in
the Act passed by the puritanically minded Parliament shortly after
the *Isle of Gulls* episode. According to this *Act to Restrain Abuses of
Players*, any player jestingly or profanely speaking the name of God,
Jesus Christ, the Holy Ghost or the Trinity was liable to the ruinous
fine of £10. The offence, it should be noted, was to *speak* the oath,
not to write or print it, and the effect on the published text of plays
was curious. In the case of Shakespeare, reprints of quartos earlier
than the Act were unexpurgated, yet in the Folio many of the oaths,
and some mere imprecations and asseverations, were suppressed or
replaced by euphemisms; for example, Mistress Page's 'what the
devil' became 'what the dickens', the first-known employment of this
euphemism. The two parts of *Henry IV* were the most heavily censored, though even here the purge was far from systematic and complete. Yet it is only what we should expect. The oaths would have been
deleted or altered in the prompt copies from which the text of much
of the Folio was set up, and the printer would select the most legible
version.

In the summer of 1606 the Queen's brother, Christian IV of
Denmark, paid a state visit to England. The Court was already at
Greenwich because of the plague, and on July 18th James went down
to Tilbury to greet his brother-in-law. Christian was ten years
younger than James, a cheerful, vigorous man of thirty, as passionately devoted to the improvement of his country as to the pursuit of
his own pleasures. The visit was not an unqualified success; Christian
resented James's estrangement from his sister, and was infinitely
wearied by the perpetual pursuit of innocent animals, while James
was jealous of Christian's prowess at running at the ring, a sport on
which he particularly prided himself. Nor were relations between the
two Courts much happier. The Danes found the English reserved, as
some of them no doubt were, for the austerer Elizabethan element
among the English courtiers was shocked by the coarseness of Danish
manners and heavy-headed revelling. On the 24th James carried
Christian into Hertfordshire to stay—and hunt—for a few days with
Salisbury at Theobalds. As they entered the Fountain Court they were
greeted with speeches by the three Hours sitting upon clouds—in
English for James, in Latin for Christian. Jonson was the author, and

no doubt he had a hand in the extraordinary charade of *Solomon and the Queen of Sheba*, devised by Salisbury. That memorable scene was ironically described by Elizabeth's godson, Sir John Harington: 'The Lady who did play the Queens part did carry most precious gifts to both their Majesties, but, forgetting the steppes arising to the canopy, overset her caskets into his Danish Majesties lap, and fell at his feet, tho I rather think it was in his face. Much was the hurry and confusion: cloths and napkins were at hand to make all clean. His Majesty then got up and would dance with the Queen of Sheba; but he fell down and humbled himself before her, and was carried to an inner chamber, and laid on a bed of state, which was not a little defiled with the presents of the Queen which had been bestowed on his garments; such as wine, cream, jelly, beverage, cakes, spices, and other good matters. The entertainment and show went forward, and most of the presenters went backward, or fell down, wine did so occupy their upper chambers. Now did appear, in rich dress, Hope, Faith, and Charity: Hope did assay to speak, but wine rendered her endeavours so feeble that she withdrew, and hoped the King would excuse her brevity: Faith was then all alone, for I am certain she was not joyned with good works, and left the court in a staggering condition. Charity came to the Kings feet, and seemed to cover the multitude of sins her sisters had committed; in some sorte she made obeysance and brought giftes, but said she would return home again, as there was no gift which heaven had not already given his Majesty. She then returned to Hope and Faith, who were both sick and spewing in the lower hall.' 'I think the Dane', commented Harington, 'hath strangely wrought on our good English nobles, for those whom I could never get to taste good liquor now follow the fashion and wallow in beastly delights. The ladies abandon their sobriety, and are seen to roll about in intoxication.' Harington was no Puritan, but he was sufficiently an old-fashioned Elizabethan to be shocked by the laxity of the Jacobean Court. When the old Queen lay dying he had written to his wife, 'I find some less mindful of what they are now to lose, than of what they may perhaps hereafter get'. And this is what they had got. It is not so difficult, after all, to understand why dramatists turned to satire and to tragedy.

The King's players were called upon to give three performances before their Danish guests; the last, on August 7th at Hampton Court, almost certainly being *Macbeth*. If so, it would be a triumph for James, an important point in the silent but strenuous rivalry between the royal brothers. It may even have hastened the departure of Christian, for suddenly deciding to curtail his holiday, he was speeded from Gravesend on August 11th by a shower of fireworks. The Paul's boys had also given a play, 'at which the Kings seemed to take delight and be much pleased'. It was their last Court performance, and may indeed have been their swan-song, for soon afterwards their plays were sold to the publishers and their little theatre 'neere St. Paules Church' was closed.

James had fallen in love with Theobalds at first sight, when he stayed there on his progress from Scotland, and ever since, having given Greenwich to Anne and Richmond to the Prince of Wales, had coveted it for himself. The house had been begun by William Cecil in the year of Shakespeare's birth as an unpretentious residence for his younger son, Robert, but by the time of the Armada had been expanded into a virtual palace for the reception of the Queen. Built of red brick, with white-stone dressings, it enclosed two courts, one of which, Fountain Court, had a square tower at each corner, each tower having four turrets surmounted by a golden vane. Here were the state apartments, fancifully and extravagantly decorated. In the open gallery were scenes illustrating the history of England; the walls of the Green Gallery displayed its coloured counties, no doubt after the designs of John Speed; across the ceiling of the Presence Chamber a sun pursued its course among the painted constellations, on the walls were pilasters in the form of oak trees, from whose branches depended the shields-of-arms of the nobility, and its celebrated chimney-piece may have inspired Iachimo's description of Imogen's bedchamber. Then, and not least in James's eyes, there was a famous park of deer. It was in the Great Gallery, more international than the others in its mural embellishments, that, after dinner on May 22nd, 1607, Robert Cecil, Earl of Salisbury, delivered the keys of his father's house to his royal master, or rather, as Jonson courteously arranged it, to his royal mistress. For again Jonson was entrusted with the now essential pageantry. The Genius of the House, sadly attired and in pensive posture, lamented the fate of his lord, 'now in the twilight of sere age'—Salisbury was, in fact, just turned forty—who would have to seek a habitation new. When, however, he was assured by Mercury and the Fates that his present master was but a beam compared to the great sun that was to illuminate the house, he was so ravished that he flew

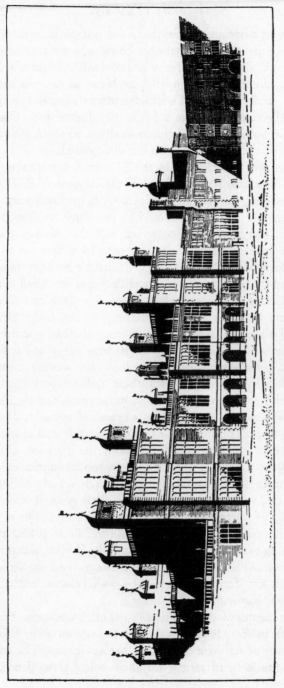

THEOBALDS FROM THE SOUTH WEST

Restoration by John Summerson, 1954

with fervour to surrender it. Salisbury did not go unrewarded, the price being the means to build another house, and the royal manor of Hatfield. There, although Mercury had admonished him that he had 'with mortar busied been too much', he began at once to build the present great Jacobean house. Theobalds was now another royal palace, and it was there, eighteen years later, that James died. Charles I delighted in it, but under the Commonwealth it was sold, split up and in the course of the next century all but disappeared.

The Queen was so enchanted by the Theobalds entertainment that she ordered Jonson to write a sequel to the *Masque of Blackness*, in which the twelve daughters of Niger, with five additional sisters (whereof their sire had store), should be recovered to their original fairness. This was ingeniously contrived, and the *Masque of Beauty* presented on January 10th, 1608. It was to have been on the 6th, but ambassadorial wranglings leading to a squabble between James and Anne, delayed the production and Twelfth Night was filled with two plays by the King's. A month later came *The Hue and Cry after Cupid*, written by Jonson for the marriage of the Lady Elizabeth Radcliffe and Viscount Haddington, the man who had rescued James from the clutches of Gowrie in the mysterious affray at Perth eight years before. Jonson strongly approved of 'the worthy custom of honouring worthy marriages with these noble solemnities', particularly when he was commissioned to write them, and in *The Hue and Cry after Cupid* he added a new element of comedy, a false- or anti-masque, to act as a foil to the serious spectacle and music. The conversation of the Graces was disturbed by the irruption of twelve boys, 'most anticly attired', who 'fell into a subtle, capricious dance, to as odd a music, each of them bearing two torches, and nodding with their antic faces, with other variety of ridiculous gesture, which gave much occasion of mirth and delight to the spectators'. The red cliff, symbolising Radcliffe, which parted in the middle to reveal a silver globe containing the masquers as the Signs of the Zodiac, was the work of Inigo Jones. The music was by Ferrabosco, and the dances by Thomas Giles and Jerome Heron, who, as Cyclopes, beat time to them with their hammers.

Both these masques were produced in the brick-and-stone banqueting house built in 1607 to replace the wooden one set up by Elizabeth for the reception of Alençon early in the heroic eighties. The cost was defrayed by the City in return for their being given Blackfriars,

Whitefriars and other liberties that had lain outside their control. James's new 'Great Hall' stood only for ten years before it was destroyed by fire, and Inigo Jones began the present splendid Banqueting-House in Whitehall.

Shakespeare had no need to augment his income by writing such ephemeral affairs as masques, but though his plays were the ones most frequently acted at Court where he would be a well-known figure, Jonson must by now have been even better known. And yet he was a recusant, charged at this time with the offence of not attending church regularly and even with being 'a seducer of youth to the popish religion', the penalty for which was death. It is an admirable illustration of the gap between Elizabethan-Jacobean theory and practice, for though the Exchequer might come down heavily on anybody who was financially worth pursuing, the law was but laxly enforced in the majority of cases. Another recusant who appeared on the same list was the former companion of Marlowe, Thomas Lodge, last of the University Wits, now an elderly physician with an Avignon degree and the author of a *Treatise on the Plague*. His prescription, the application to a plague carbuncle of a fowl from which the tail feathers had been plucked, was still the orthodox treatment at the time of the fearful epidemic in Charles II's reign. It was not very effective. Less fortunate than Jonson, he was persecuted for his recusancy and driven from the country for a time, but died in England in 1625.

In one way and another the elder generation of dramatists was going. Exquisite John Lyly and fat, chronically impecunious Henry Chettle died in 1606, and were shortly followed by the man who may perhaps be said to have begun the great dramatic revolution, Thomas Sackville, Earl of Dorset, Lord Treasurer, builder of Knole and part author of *Gorboduc*. In the same year Marston's dramatic career came to an abrupt and inglorious end. In March 1608 the touchy French ambassador complained to Salisbury about the treatment of contemporary French history in Chapman's *Tragedy of Byron*, the story of Charles, Duc de Biron, who had been executed for treason as recently as 1602. Moreover, he reported in his dispatches how, a day or two before, James and his Scottish favourites had been satirised on the stage by the same company. The distressing details were added in cipher: how James had been made to draw the coverts of heaven on bird-back, to beat one of his gentlemen for calling off the hounds and then been described as drunk at least once a day. Both of these were

Blackfriars plays, and the second one, unfortunately lost, was almost certainly the work of the reckless Marston. The King threatened to close all the theatres, but was bought off by the adult companies' offering to pay a heavy fine—the kind of proposal to which James was always amenable—and undertaking never again to represent contemporary history on the stage. Marston, however, was committed to Newgate, and is next heard of as a reputable clergyman in Hampshire. Perhaps his wife had at last converted him, for he had married the daughter of one of James's chaplains. Jonson adds a satirical footnote: 'Marston wrott his Father-in-lawes preachings, and his Father-in-law his Commedies.'

The old guard were going, but the new men were coming in. One was John Fletcher, son of a former Bishop of London, and cousin of the poets Giles and Phineas Fletcher. Now in his late twenties, he had already written the pastoral *Faithful Shepherdess* for the Queen's Revels, and theirs perhaps as well was his *Woman's Prize, or, The Tamer Tamed*, a sequel to *The Taming of the Shrew*, in which Petruchio is himself tamed by his second wife. Another of the new men was Francis Beaumont, at this time little more than twenty. He came of a good Leicestershire family, and after Oxford and the Inner Temple began to write for the stage, being helped at the outset of his career by Drayton, a friend of his father's. In 1607 his *Woman Hater* was published, one of the last plays written for the Paul's boys, and to the same year belongs the innocent burlesque of *The Knight of the Burning Pestle*, 'in eight days begot and born', for the Queen's Revels. Jonson took the two aspiring dramatists under his wing and they responded warmly by writing commendatory verses for *Volpone*, thus for the first time linking their names together. In the following year, 1608, the famous collaboration—and cohabitation—began, for, according to Aubrey, Beaumont and Fletcher 'lived together on the Bancke Side, not far from the Play-house, both batchelors; lay together; had one wench in the house between them, which they did so admire; the same cloathes and cloake &c betweene them'. The partnership lasted only till the marriage and retirement of Beaumont five years later, and was productive of only some half-dozen plays, yet so successful were they that their names became imperishably associated, and when fifty of the plays of which Fletcher was at least part author were published in folio, they were all ascribed to 'Francis Beaumont and John Fletcher, Gentlemen'.

The arrival of Beaumont and Fletcher marked the beginning of a new era in the drama, and their partnership set the Jacobean pattern. Signs of decadence had already begun to appear. Though there is nothing wrong with spectacle as such, the extravagant masques with which Jonson and Jones were delighting the Court were corrupting the taste for plays, and the time was coming when nothing would please that did not appeal as much to the eye as to the ear and mind. The mischief was that the demand for spectacle spread to the public theatres, and even in *Timon* Shakespeare had to pander to popular taste by introducing a masque of Amazons. Nor is satire necessarily a morbid symptom, but in excess it suggests that all is not sweet, all is not sound in the world it reflects in its distorting glass. Nor again is a preoccupation with tragedy an unhealthy sign, but many of the plays being written were no longer concerned with evil as a problem but only with evil as a stimulant, and were tragic only in the sense that the vicious characters with which they were crammed came to violent and gruesomely spectacular ends. The tragic emotion of terror was giving place to mere horror, and pity to a relish for the macabre.

The Puritans were once again, and with more justification than before, taking the offensive. In 1607 one of the Paul's plays, *The Puritan*, had been published—incidentally, as written 'by W. S.', an ascription that led to its being included in the Third Folio of Shakespeare's plays. It is a comedy based on apocryphal stories from the life of George Peele, and ridicules the Puritans in the persons of the hypocritical Nicholas Saint Tantlings and Simon Saint-Mary-Overies. William Crashaw, preacher at the Inner Temple and father of the poet Richard Crashaw, replied in a sermon preached at Paul's Cross. 'Thus', he thundered, 'Hypocrisy, a child of hell, must bear the names of two churches of God, and two wherein God's name is called on publicly every day in the year.' And he went on to attack ungodly plays and interludes in general, for 'what are they but a bastard of Babylon, a daughter of error and confusion, a hellish device (the devil's own recreation to mock at holy things) by him delivered to the heathen, from them to the Papists, and from them to us?'

Some of the playwrights were themselves perturbed, and in his Epistle to *Volpone* Jonson admitted that there was too much ribaldry, profanation and blasphemy in dramatic stage poetry, at the same time protesting that his own plays were free from 'such foule and unwashed Baudry, as is now made the food of the Scene'. Heywood, too, in his *Apology for Actors*, written apparently in 1608, had to protest against the licentiousness of some of the players, and the abuse 'lately crept into the quality' of liberal invectives against all the estates, though he submits that such violent railing is mainly put into the mouths of children, and that the adult companies, and his own company in particular, are comparatively free from such offences. No doubt Jonson and Heywood were anxious to safeguard themselves from prosecution under the Act to Restrain Abuses and to forestall criticism of their own productions, but that they were at such pains to do so is an indication of uneasiness.

Now Beaumont and Fletcher were not concerned with satire; they kept ever on the windy side of the law, and from the point of view of the government were irreproachable. Nor were they concerned with violence and the macabre; on the contrary, they were all sweetness and moderation, and their unwholesomeness was of a more refined and insinuating nature. Seeing that the Court and its fringes wished merely to be entertained and not made to think or be deeply moved, they revived the unfashionable romance, but with a general softening of its ingredients. They were both considerable poets, but their poetry is over-sweet; they were fertile in the invention of variations on a standard theme, but action and plot bear little relation to character; their puppets are so much rubber that can easily be squeezed into any of the surprising situations in which they find themselves, and made to utter appropriate sentiments according to a code of conduct agreeable to over-leisured courtiers. To Beaumont probably belongs the credit, if such it may be called, of inventing romantic tragi-comedy, a new kind of drama in which a young and very innocent heroine is exposed to various forms of humiliation, the more indecent the better, and a sigh rises from the breast and a delicious tear gathers to the eye of the spectator, without the inconvenience of any emotional disturbance. Even their so-called tragedies are no more disquieting, for all rough and awkwardly protruding tragic elements have been kneaded into a comfortable and feathery pathos. To Beaumont's prettiness Fletcher added his own sweetness and nastiness. The Elizabethan dramatists were far from squeamish, and their plays —Shakespeare's not least—abound in grossness and obscenity; but their ribaldry is generally frank and their bawdry genuinely funny, whereas with Fletcher and the later Jacobean and Restoration playwrights they become a hole-in-the-corner affair; grossness declines into prurience, obscenity into salacity and the manly Rabelaisian jest is emasculated into smutty innuendo and an adolescent snigger. We have only to compare *The Tamer Tamed* with *The Taming of the Shrew*, *The Faithful Shepherdess* with *As You Like It*, to appreciate the change that had come over the drama in the last ten years.

All this, of course, is the dark side of the picture, and does not mean that Beaumont and Fletcher—it must always be remembered that Beaumont worked with Fletcher only for a few years, though long enough to set the pattern—were incompetent dramatists and themselves degenerates. They could write exquisite lyrics and enchantingly pathetic blank verse, and as far as we know were admirable men and delightful companions (though Jonson thought Beaumont conceited, he loved him as he loved Fletcher and Chapman), and had they belonged to the generation of Shakespeare and Marlowe might have been formidable rivals. As it was, they were born too late, were too ready to exploit the laxity of the Jacobean Court, and by so doing set the seal of degeneracy on the great virile Elizabethan tradition that they had inherited. They created a demand and gave their audience what it wanted, so that in the years between Shakespeare's death and the closing of the theatres at the outbreak of the Civil War the performances of 'Beaumont and Fletcher' given by the King's Men outnumbered those of Shakespeare by three to one. And even after the Restoration Dryden could write solemn nonsense about Fletcher writing better than Shakespeare 'betwixt man and woman'.

The year 1608 is a turning-point in the history of the theatre. The Children of Blackfriars paid severely for their impudence in presenting two reigning monarchs on their stage, Henry IV and James I. Some of the boys were thrown into prison, arrangements were made for winding up the affairs of the company, and in August Henry Evans surrendered the lease of the Blackfriars theatre to its owner, Richard Burbage. Yet, after all, the company managed to keep going under Robert Keysar and his new partner, Philip Rosseter, who found new quarters for the boys only a few hundred yards from their original playhouse. These were in the buildings of another dissolved priory, at Whitefriars, a disreputable district west of the City walls, between Fleet Street and the river. Keysar must have acted on the assumption that the King's gusty fury would be as brief as it was violent, and that Rosseter, as one of the royal lutenists, was the man to restore the fortunes of the boys. Nor was he disappointed; during the Revels of 1608–9 he brought them to Court three times, their first appearances there for four years, and in the following season the Children of Whitefriars gave no fewer than five performances at Whitehall.

But the survival of the many-hued, chameleon-like Children was a matter of minor interest. The important thing was that the King's Men now had a private theatre which they could use as an alternative to the public Globe, presumably in the winter months, when performances in an open playhouse must frequently have been an ordeal for actors and spectators alike. They were the first company of adult players to perform regularly indoors, under conditions similar to those in the Great Chamber at Whitehall, and their more intimate surroundings and much smaller and more select audience involved considerable modifications both in their style of acting and in their plays.

A standing audience is far more volatile and unstable than a seated one, and it was one thing to declaim to an assembly of two thousand across an open yard crammed with gaping groundlings, and quite another to address an educated company of two hundred, all of whom were seated. If we are to assume, as I think we should, that Shakespeare himself was speaking when he made Hamlet coach the players in the art of acting, he had already taught his own company a more temperate manner than the traditional ranting style inherited from the miracle and morality plays. But it was still inevitably formalised, every emotion having a corresponding action or gesture to convey the general sense of the words to those who could not understand them, or were too far away to windward to hear distinctly. Such a convention would be as intolerable as it was unnecessary in a small theatre, and there can be little doubt that the King's Men adopted a quieter and more natural style of playing in the Blackfriars theatre, a style more in the manner of the boys who had preceded them. Indeed, 'to strengthen the King's service', as Burbage put it, they admitted two of the boys, now young men, as sharers in their company. It happened that Sly and Lawrence Fletcher died a few weeks after their acquisition of the theatre, and to bring up their number again to twelve they elected into their fellowship William Ostler and John Underwood, both of whom had been Children of the Chapel in the old days under Nathaniel Giles, when they had played in the first performance of Jonson's *Poetaster*. They seem to have stayed with the company until they joined the King's, for some of the 'children' were now so only in name—Nathan Field, for example, was still with them, and he was twenty-one. The King's Men, therefore, had two new players who could teach them a lot about acting on the Blackfriars stage.

Having found the players, the next thing was to find the playwrights and the plays. *Tamburlaine*, to take an extreme example, was no more suitable for a small stage than are the great stylised figures of medieval clerestory glass for the windows of an aisle. Shakespeare's recent plays, the great tragedies with their titanic figures, large as legend, were written for the open amphitheatre of the Globe, and would lose much of their majesty and grandeur if huddled into the compass of a room. How, even, could they persuade an audience to imagine a few square feet of stage to be the vasty fields of France? Shakespeare would have to return to romantic comedy, something after the pattern of *Much Ado, As You Like It* and *Twelfth Night*. Then there was Jonson, an old hand at writing for the Blackfriars stage, but he was busy with his masques; Marston, too, had written mainly for the Paul's or Revels boys, but he was in gaol. However, there were two new men who had already written, for the Children, a new type of play eminently suitable for the private stage, and the King's Men engaged Beaumont and Fletcher to write for the Blackfriars theatre, and the famous collaboration began.

Thus, in 1608, the leading company of actors had a new theatre, a new type of player and a new type of playwright. It was a second dramatic revolution, and a disastrous one, for though Shakespeare was yet to write the most perfect of his plays, the great Elizabethan drama that had been nurtured in the public theatres was finished. The private playhouse soon became financially more important than the public, the Blackfriars than the Globe, and in the year of Shakespeare's death the Cockpit in Drury Lane was roofed and converted into a private theatre for Queen Anne's Men. The stage was literally set for the rapid declension into Caroline drama and the cleavage of the old composite and stimulating audience into classes, the courtiers frequenting the exclusive private houses and the masses the decaying Globe, Fortune and Red Bull.

For Shakespeare himself the year 1608 was a turning-point. For one thing, he was one of the housekeepers in the Blackfriars theatre, entitled to a share of one-seventh of the profits, which, or at least the total takings, four years later were said to be a thousand pounds a season more than at the Globe. Then in 1607 his elder daughter

Susanna had married a highly esteemed Stratford physician, John Hall, and in the following February his first grandchild, Elizabeth, was born. Here was a theme to inspire the plays that he was to write for his new theatre, and having finished the crowning glory of *Antony and Cleopatra* for the Globe, he turned from tragedy to tragi-comedy, and applied the golden poetry of his prime to *Pericles* and the story of Marina, the fresh-new seafarer born in a storm.

In September his mother died. A few weeks later John Milton was born in Bread Street, Cheapside, next door perhaps to the Mermaid Tavern, and Ben Jonson celebrated his return to the Protestant fold by draining the chalice at his first communion.

XIII

1609–1611

TRAGI-COMEDY AND ROMANCE

SHAKESPEARE'S company was now producing more than half the total number of plays presented at Court, in the winter of 1608–9 giving twelve performances—altogether worth about £300 to each sharer—as against the Queen's five, Prince's three and Black-Whitefriars three. One of the last of these was Middleton's *A Trick to Catch the Old One*, originally written for the Paul's boys, a Jonsonian kind of comedy reduced to farce, a lively and amusing account of how a profligate and his mistress outwit a couple of elderly usurers. It was the best play that Middleton had yet written, but quite devoid of the poetry and passion that make *Volpone* a masterpiece, and we can understand why Jonson said that he 'was not of the number of the faithful, *i.e.* poets, and but a base fellow'. At this time Middleton was writing another comedy of London life, *The Roaring Girl*, with Dekker, whose *Gull's Hornbook* was on the point of publication. This is a satirical essay in which Dekker offers ironical advice to a gallant as to how he should behave himself in a playhouse and other public places if he wishes to attract attention to himself by his bad manners. The groundlings had been admitted to the yard in the late eighties or early nineties, and, yet further to swell the takings, round about the time of the building of the Swan in 1595, vainglorious gallants had been allowed to flaunt their feathers and tobacco-pipes on the stage itself, where they could hire a stool for sixpence or a shilling. It was a profitable, though distracting, arrangement for the players, but infuriating for the playwrights, as also for the groundlings, who sometimes drove them off by hooting, hissing, spitting and even throwing clods picked up in the yard. Dekker was a playwright, not a player and sharer in theatre profits, and his protest at the irresponsible wrecking of his work throws valuable light on the conduct of the Jacobean theatres:

Present not yourself on the stage (especially at a new play) until the quaking prologue hath (by rubbing) got colour into his cheeks, and is ready to give the trumpets their cue that he's upon point to enter: for then it is time to creep from behind the arras, with your *tripos* or three-footed stool in one hand, and a teston mounted between a forefinger and a thumb in the other.

Before the play begins, fall to cards, and throw the cards (having first torn four or five of them) round about the stage, just upon the third sound, as though you had lost.

It shall crown you with rich commendation to laugh aloud in the midst of the most serious and saddest scene of the terriblest tragedy. If the writer be a fellow that hath epigrammed you, you shall disgrace him if, in the middle of his play, you rise with a skreud and discontented face from your stool to be gone: no matter whether the scenes be good or no, the better they are the worse do you distaste them: and being on your feet, sneak not away like a coward, but salute all your gentle acquaintance that are spread either on the rushes or on stools about you, and draw what troop you can from the stage after you.

Marry, if either the company, or indisposition of the weather, bind you to sit it out, my counsel is then that you turn plain ape, take up a rush and tickle the earnest ears of your fellow gallants, to make other fools fall a laughing: mew at passionate speeches, blare at merry, find fault with the music, whew at the children's action, whistle at the songs: and, above all, curse the sharers.

It may be that Shakespeare refused to have spectators on the stage when his plays were performed—the mere thought of Dekker's gallant playing the fool in the last scene of *Lear* makes one indignant— but they were on the Blackfriars stage when the King's produced Jonson's *The Devil is an Ass* in 1616, and it was not until Caroline times that they were finally banished from all the theatres.

The year 1609 saw the publication of three of Shakespeare's works—the last to be published in his lifetime—each with its peculiar perplexities. The riddles of the *Sonnets* have never been, and probably never will be, solved. Who was the 'sweet boy' with a 'woman's face' to whom the majority of the poems were addressed? Was he the 'Mr. W. H.' of the publisher's enigmatic dedication? If so, was he William Herbert, Earl of Pembroke, or Henry Wriothesley, Earl of Southampton, or somebody of whom we have never heard, or merely a fiction? And who was the dark lady, Shakespeare's mistress, who left him for his friend? And who the rival poet? And then, when were they written? Some of them at least before 1598, when Francis Meres mentioned them as circulating among Shakespeare's private friends; and there are those who claim that the main sequence was finished soon after Armada year, twenty years before their publication. *Troilus and Cressida* may have been written some ten years before the appearance of the quarto, the first issue of which stated that it had been acted by the King's Servants at the Globe, and the second that it had never been 'staled with the stage'. Possibly the play had been given privately at the Middle Temple on one of their Grand Nights, under the direction of Richard Martin, 'Prince d'Amour', who may have contributed the facetious *Epistle* to the second issue. The first two acts of *Pericles* are so inferior to the last three that it is impossible to ascribe them to Shakespeare, and that they were not his is suggested by the fact that the play was not included in the Folio until the third edition in 1664, and then only as an afterthought. And yet *Pericles* contains some of the finest of Shakespeare's late poetry. Indeed, the three quartos of 1609 afford splendid examples of his three main styles. There is the early lyrical poetry of the *Sonnets*, a poetry of ceremonious line and phrase, within which the labials are triumphantly and perpetually varied:

> Yet nor the lays of birds, nor the sweet smell
> Of different flowers in odour and in hue,
> Could make me any summer's story tell,
> Or from their proud lap pluck them where they grew:
> Nor did I wonder at the lily's white,
> Nor praise the deep vermilion in the rose;
> They were but sweet, but figures of delight,
> Drawn after you, you pattern of all those.

Troilus and Cressida has the parallelisms, coupled words and peculiar form of imagery—a noun or, more characteristically, two, followed by a prepositional phrase—that link the poetry of *Henry V* to that of *Hamlet*:

> her wanton spirits look out
> At every joint and motive of her body.
> O, these encounterers, so glib of tongue,
> That give a coasting welcome ere it comes,
> And wide unclasp the tables of their thoughts
> To every ticklish reader, set them down
> For sluttish spoils of opportunity,
> And daughters of the game.

In *Pericles* verse has become a plastic medium, shaped almost with a potter's hand, line and metre being swept together, thrown and moulded into forms of infinite variety; and it is at the same time a counterpoint of interwoven assonance and rhythms, as in silver-voiced Marina's self-description:

> I am a maid,
> My lord, that ne'er before invited eyes,
> But have been gaz'd on like a comet: she speaks,
> My lord, that, may be, hath endur'd a grief
> Might equal yours, if both were justly weigh'd.

It was a bad year for the players. The theatres had been closed in the previous July, when plague deaths had risen to more than thirty a week, and they remained closed throughout 1609, the worst plague year since 1603. The King's Men went on tour, but were back again in London by the late autumn, when they put in six weeks of strenuous private practice (for which they were generously paid) in preparation for the Court season. They would need every minute of the time, for they were engaged to give thirteen performances—out of a total of twenty-five—at Whitehall that Christmas. Two of their new plays may well have been *Cymbeline* and *Philaster*. Shakespeare was now writing with the Blackfriars theatre in mind, and making his first essays in tragi-comedy, something in the manner of Beaumont and Fletcher; but in *Cymbeline* he almost came to grief in the last act, when the characters have to explain to one another a series of errors that are no mystery to the audience. Beaumont and Fletcher managed a similar theme much more tidily in *Philaster*, but the two plays admirably illustrate the difference between Shakespeare and the young collaborators. Shakespeare, passionately as ever, identifies himself with the leading characters, and out of his poetry creates Imogen and Iachimo, but Beaumont and Fletcher create nothing but a romantic day-dream, a superficial affair of misfortune, sweet pathos and indecency. The 'lascivious young lady' and 'wanton old lady' were to become almost stock characters in the plays in which Fletcher had a hand, to the great satisfaction of the Stuart courtiers.

Chapman had just finished *The Revenge of Bussy D'Ambois*, the tragedy of Bussy's stoical brother, forced into the role of revenger by all the stock Elizabethan apparatus of ghosts and visions, but it is unlikely that the Whitefriars Children brought the play to Court, for Chapman's *Byron* had been one cause of their temporary undoing. More probably they brought *Epicœne*, a delicious piece of foolery in prose, and the first play that Jonson had written since *Volpone*, three years before. Presumably his favourite, Nat Field, played Morose, 'the gentleman that loved no noise'. Now a man of twenty-three, Field was himself an aspiring dramatist, and his first play, *A Woman is a Weathercock*, was one of the five performances given by the Whitefriars company that Christmas. In his Epistle to the Reader, published in the quarto, he wrote, 'thou know'st where to hear of me for a year or two, and no more, I assure thee', as though he had no intention of remaining a player. Yet he was destined, like his former colleagues,

Ostler and Underwood, to finish his brief career as an actor with the King's Men.

Jonson had been too busy with *Epicœne* to produce a masque for the Revels at the beginning of 1610, but for the previous year he had written one at the request of the Queen. This was the famous *Masque of Queens*, in which Anne appeared as Bel-Anna, Queen of the Ocean, and eleven ladies of the Court as Queens of times long gone. Very wisely, Jonson made them draw lots for their parts. Among them were the Countess of Bedford, the vicious young Countess of Essex, and her beautiful sister, Lady Catherine Howard, who had recently married Salisbury's son, Viscount Cranborne. As a foil to the queens, Jonson devised an anti-masque of eleven witches, led by Ate carrying a torch made of a dead man's arm, a spectacular scene obviously inspired by *Macbeth*. Jonson himself had prescribed the scrupulously correct properties of vipers, bones, poisons and other ensigns of their magic, but 'the device of their attire was Master Jones's, with the invention and architecture of the whole scene, and machine'. This was an elaborate contraption, for the witches and their flaming hell suddenly vanished, to be replaced by a glorious and magnificent building figuring Chaucer's House of Fame, on the top of which were the twelve masquers sitting upon a pyramidal throne. Even this, being *machina versatilis*, as suddenly changed, and revealed Fame herself, who ordered the witches to be bound to her chariot wheels. The performance was to have been given on Twelfth Night, but the rivalry of the representatives of the Most Christian King of Spain and the Catholic King of France necessitated its postponement. Queen Anne was openly Spanish in her sympathies, and the French ambassador, La Boderie, had been slighted on the last two occasions. But now there were rumours of a *rapprochement* between France and Spain, and James was particularly anxious not to offend Henry IV. Unfortunately the Spanish position was strengthened by the presence of an Ambassador Extraordinary, who took precedence over an ordinary envoy like La Boderie, and the only thing was to wait for the Spaniard's departure. For a whole month the Court waited. Then on February 1st he went, and on the next night, Candlemas, Jonson and Jones presented *The Masque of Queens*.

Although Jonson wrote no masque in celebration of the year 1610, he and Jones devised the entertainment for Prince Henry's Barriers, held on Twelfth Night. Prince Henry was now nearly sixteen, a

clever, active and serious-minded boy, a great favourite at Court and
with the people, though not with his father, whose hunting he found
almost as detestable as his swearing and tippling. 'No sportsman',
James called him. He was, however, a good horseman, ambitious to
excel at all knightly exercises, like his pattern of chivalry, Henry IV,
and before the King and Queen and the whole Court he issued a
challenge to all the knights of Great Britain. For a week he kept open
table at St. James's, and then on Twelfth Night he and his six supporters, one of whom was the Earl of Southampton, met fifty-eight
opponents at the Barriers in the banqueting-hall. But first the Lady of
the Lake was 'discovered' beside an ample sheet of water, then King
Arthur as a star above, and after thunder and lightning (of which
Jonson so much disapproved in the public theatres), Merlin rose from
his tomb and called up Meliadus (Prince Henry) and his six assistants.
After a masterly two-hundred-line summary of English history, leading up to the sleeping Chivalry's reawakening at the mention of
Meliadus, the Barriers took place, and the ceremony concluded with
appropriate prophecies by Merlin about the royal children, Henry,
Charles and Elizabeth, all of which were to prove most dreadfully
and tragically false. This was Henry's first appearance in arms, and
must have been a severe ordeal for a boy of sixteen, for that night he
gave and received thirty-two pushes of pike and some three hundred
and sixty strokes of sword.

It was to be Prince Henry's year, for in the summer he was created
Prince of Wales. On May 31st he sailed down the river from his
palace of Richmond, to be met by the Lord Mayor and a worthy fleet
of London's citizens. Anthony Munday devised a pageant in which
John Rice, a boy actor with the King's Men, representing Cornwall
as Corinea on a whale, greeted him at Chelsea, and Richard Burbage,
symbolising Wales as Amphion on a dolphin's back, saluted him at
Whitehall. On June 4th the ceremony of creation took place in the
Parliament House, and on the following night Samuel Daniel,
assisted in 'the artificial part' by Inigo Jones, presented his *Masque of
Tethys*, in which the masquers were the Queen as the wife of Oceanus,
and thirteen nymphs of as many English rivers, clothed in sky-blue
and cloth of silver. There were no major ambassadorial complexities
this time, for news had just arrived of the assassination of Henry IV,
and there was no question of inviting the French ambassador.

Prince Henry had been so delighted with *The Masque of Queens* that he had asked Jonson to give him an autograph copy with explanatory annotations. This proved a labour of some difficulty, for Jonson had drawn on the store of his prodigious memory, but at last he tracked down all his recondite allusions and authorities and presented his manuscript—itself a work of art—to the Prince. At the same time he dedicated the quarto to him, with an Epistle in which he wrote: 'Amongst the rest, your favour to letters, and these gentler studies that go under the title of *Humanity*, is not the least honour of your wreath. . . . Poetry, my lord, is not born with every man, nor every day: and in her general right it is now my minute to thank your Highness, who not only do honour her with your care, but are curious to examine her with your eye, and enquire into her beauties and strengths.' Jonson's, then, was not the only poetry honoured by Prince Henry. Chapman, who had dedicated to Essex the first part of his translation of the *Iliad*, found a patron for the complete work in the young Prince, who promised him three hundred pounds and a good pension during his life. Even Raleigh wrote from the Tower to say that it was 'for the service of that inestimable Prince Henry, the successive hope, and one of the greatest of the Christian World' that he undertook his *History of the World*.

Nor was Henry's patronage confined to literature. At the beginning of 1611 he took Inigo Jones into employment as his Surveyor, and for him Jones is said to have built a cabinet room at Whitehall to house his collection of pictures. Some of these would be by Robert Peake, whom he had recently appointed as his Painter. Hilliard was now an old man, and English painting was mainly in the hands of four men, three of whom were foreigners and related to one another by marriage. The eldest of the group was John de Critz, son of an Antwerp goldsmith who had settled in London in Mary's reign. His sister married the younger Marcus Gheeraerts, whose father, also a painter, had fled from Bruges in the sixties, and his niece was the second wife of Isaac Oliver. All painted in a similar decorative and enamelled style, and probably from the same workshop, where they were joined by Peake, who in 1610 was associated with de Critz in the office of Serjeant Painter. The fine portrait of King James at Greenwich is attributed to de Critz, who painted numerous portraits of Salisbury, one of which was for Sir Henry Wotton, ambassador at Venice. Wotton, inspired by the Byzantine murals of St. Mark's and Torcello, had the picture copied in mosaic, a singular work that is now at Hatfield. Gheeraerts is the probable painter of the famous 'Somerset House Conference' of 1604, when Shakespeare as a Groom of the Chamber attended on the Constable of Castile. The English and Spanish commissioners face one another across a table, the inscrutable Cecil, as he then was, leading the English side, composed of the Earl of Northampton, as villainous as he looks, Charles Blount, Earl of Devon, perhaps less bibulous than he looks, the venerable Lord High Admiral Nottingham, hatched in silver, who had just relinquished the patronage of his company of players to Prince Henry, and, equal with him in honour as in age, the Earl of Dorset, author of *Gorboduc*.

Music, too, came within the ample scope of Prince Henry's patronage, and by 1611 John Bull, who had recently resigned his professorship at Gresham College, was in his service as his principal musician, with an annual salary of forty pounds. This was the year in which Bull collaborated with the oldest and youngest of the musicians of the Golden Age, William Byrd and Orlando Gibbons, in the publication of *Parthenia*, a collection of virginal music. Byrd was then seventy—still a stout Catholic—and it was almost the last publication with which he was concerned; Gibbons was seventeen, and had just published his first work, *Fantasies in Three Parts, Composed for Viols*. It was shortly after this that Campion followed up his *Book of Ayres* of 1601, 'framed for one voyce', with two more. This time, however, his friend Rosseter was not associated with him.

Rosseter was too busy helping Keysar to manage the Whitefriars Children, and carrying through a delicate operation in conjunction with the King's Men, to buy off the competition of the Paul's boys. Apparently their Master, Edward Pearce, was threatening to reopen their theatre, but he was sufficiently discouraged by the offer of a substantial bribe of £20 a year from the two companies financially interested in private theatres. Keysar had not been mistaken in his man when he took Rosseter into partnership to help restore the fortunes of the Children's company, for it was owing to his influence at Court that a new patent was obtained from James, whereby the boys were entitled once again to call themselves Children of the Queen's Revels. This was in January 1610. Still Keysar was not satisfied, Whitefriars had not the prestige of Blackfriars, and in February he brought a suit against the Burbages, and the other owners of the Blackfriars theatre, claiming a sixth of their profits since Evans's surrender of the lease. This, he maintained, had been a breach of

their agreement not to come to any arrangement with Evans preju-
dicial to the one-sixth share in the concern that he had bought from
Marston. This was not unreasonable, but when he claimed that the
Blackfriars' profits had come to £1,500 in the last twelve months or so,
he was on less certain ground. The King's Men merely denied the
profit, maintained that the theatre was in such a bad state of repair that
they had to take it over, and Keysar was driven to recover what he
could from Evans. What that amounted to we do not know.

It was in the following September that news arrived in London of
the wreck of the *Sea Venture* on the remote and uninhabited Bermudas.
In the summer of 1609 Sir Thomas Gates and Sir George Somers had
set out for Virginia with a small fleet, and supplies for the wretched
little colony of settlers at Jamestown. They were to assemble at the
Bermudas, but most of the ships went straight to Virginia, and only the
battered *Sea Venture* reached the islands. Some of the crew were
drunk and the ship was wrecked. The islands were popularly supposed
to be the abode of devils, but the strange noises came from nothing
more diabolic than the descendants of a cargo of Spanish hogs, wrecked
there nearly a hundred years before, when Juan Bermudez made his
involuntary discovery. There was no lack of meat and water, and,
though they were visited by storm and tempest, the castaways found
the air sweet, the climate temperate and the islands so eminently
habitable that they were occupied by the Virginia Company two years
later. Out of the wreck they built two pinnaces, and in May 1610
reached Virginia, where they found the settlement in such a deplorable plight that Gates sailed for England with a dispatch from the
Governor, and *A True Reportory of the Wrack* by William Strachey.
Shakespeare probably knew Strachey through his Stratford neighbour,
Thomas Russell. He listened to the strange story, read the romantic
Discovery of the Barmudas by Sylvester Jourdan, another of Gates's
companions, and the idea of *The Tempest* was conceived.

In April the Duke of Württemberg—the former Count Mömpel-
gart, and 'Garmombles' of *The Merry Wives*—had seen a performance of *Othello* at the Globe, but plague closed the theatres for the
second half of the year, and when, after their provincial tours, the
companies reassembled for the winter season, they found a new Master
at work in the Revels Office in the Whitefriars. Edmund Tilney had
died in August. He had been Master since the building of the first
theatres, served under six Lord Chamberlains, witnessed the great

dramatic revolution of the eighties, and seen the production of most of the great plays since then, possibly all Shakespeare's except *The Winter's Tale* and *The Tempest*. His career was an enviable one; no wonder John Lyly had coveted his office. But Lyly was dead, and the new Master was Tilney's nephew, Sir George Buck, who, as his uncle's deputy, had for the last few years exercised most of his functions, including the recent one of licensing plays for publication. *Lear*, *Pericles* and *Troilus* were all published by his allowance. Buck remained Master until he lost his wits in 1622, when he was succeeded by the persistent Sir Henry Herbert, who, at the Restoration, was still there to claim the office, though the theatres had been closed for eighteen years.

For the Revels of 1610–11, Buck called for three performances by the newly formed company under the patronage of Prince Charles, the Duke of York's, three by the Queen's, four by Prince Henry's, and fifteen by the King's. The Queen's had recently—perhaps that winter—produced Webster's first great play (if *The Revenger's Tragedy* really is not his), *The White Devil*. As melancholy and full of corruption as a graveyard, it is great by virtue of its poetry and the dazzlingly dramatic lines, grotesque or homely, of dying men:

> There's a plumber laying pipes in my guts; it scalds.

>   they'll re-marry
> Ere the worm pierce your winding-sheet, ere the spider
> Make a thin curtain for your epitaphs.

> I am i' the way to study a long silence.

>   I have caught
> An everlasting cold; I have lost my voice
> Most irrecoverably.

The play had taken long in the writing, yet it was not a success, 'since', wrote Webster in the quarto, 'it was acted in so dull a time of winter, presented in so open and black a theatre, that it wanted (that which is the only grace and setting-out of a tragedy) a full and understanding auditory'. Though the Queen's Men had done their best, as Webster gratefully acknowledged, the uncapable multitude at the Red Bull wanted their blood and thunder neat, and poisoned it, and Buck does not seem to have asked for a performance at Court. It would have found a sufficiently understanding auditory there if the Countess of Essex had been present.

In his Preface, Webster paid generous tribute to the work of his contemporaries to the 'full and heightened style of Master Chapman, the laboured and understanding works of Master Jonson, the no less worthy composures of the both worthily excellent Master Beaumont and Master Fletcher; and lastly (without wrong last to be named) the right happy and copious industry of Master Shakespeare, Master Dekker, and Master Heywood'. Plays by Shakespeare, Jonson and Beaumont and Fletcher would account for most of the fifteen performances given by the King's Men. *The Winter's Tale* was new and probably one of them. Another would almost certainly be Jonson's recently written masteriece, *The Alchemist*. The plot is as simple as and similar to *Volpone*. During a season of plague in London, three swindlers take possession of a house abandoned by its owner, and make quick returns by practising on the credulity, greed and lusts of a lawyer's clerk, a shop-keeper, an eminent voluptuary and a pair of Puritans. The satire is less ferocious than in *Volpone*, but it is sharpened and set off by the same splendid semi-Marlovian poetry, as when Sir Epicure Mammon anticipates the sybaritic delights he will share with Dol, a common prostitute:

> We'll therefore go withal, my girl, and live
> In a free state, where we will eat our mullets
> Soused in high-country wines, sup pheasants' eggs,
> And have our cockles boiled in silver shells;
> Our shrimps to swim again, as when they lived,
> In a rare butter made of dolphins' milk,
> Whose cream does look like opals; and with these
> Delicate meats set ourselves high for pleasure.

Lowin, who now played Falstaff, created the part of Sir Epicure, 'with mighty applause', and presumably Burbage played Face, the leader of the gang. The old hands, Heminge and Condell, were in the cast, and the new men, Ostler and Underwood; and Robert Armin made his last recorded appearance with the company. A romance was budding among the fellowship, for young Ostler had fallen in love with Heminge's daughter, Thomasine, whom he married in 1611, and how close was the friendship between players and playwrights within the company is witnessed by their calling their first-born son Beaumont.

Beaumont and Fletcher's *Maid's Tragedy* may have been another of the plays in which Ostler and his fellows appeared at the Revels of 1610–11. It is one of their best, and, once we have accepted the conventions of their fairyland in which there is no apparent relation between speech and action, moving in a sweet and pretty sort of way. The characters do not get themselves into their desperate situations, but simply find themselves there, and then, by the falling rhythms of their speech, wring all the pathos of their plight out of words saturated with romantic and melancholy associations. Thus Aspatia, abandoned by her lover:

> Let all about me
> Tell that I am forsaken. Do my face
> (If thou hadst ever feeling of a sorrow)
> Thus, thus, Antiphila. Strive to make me look
> Like Sorrow's monument, and the trees about me,
> Let them be dry and leafless; let the rocks
> Groan with continual surges, and behind me
> Make all a desolation. Look, look, wenches,
> A miserable life of this poor picture.

This device of a redundant syllable at the end of a line and before a mid-line pause they took from Shakespeare, but so abused it that the virile mounting rhythm of blank verse was subverted into an enervated and effeminate falling one. Shakespeare employed it for a very different purpose; to set up a counter-rhythm that emphasised the assonance running through his verse, as in Cleopatra's lament for Antony:

> For his bounty
> There was no winter in 't; an autumn 'twas
> That grew the more by reaping: his delights
> Were dolphin-like; they show'd his back above
> The element they liv'd in: in his livery
> Walk'd crowns and crownets; realms and islands were
> As plates dropp'd from his pocket.

A token of the ever-growing demand for spectacle at Court was the politic insertion of a masque into *The Maid's Tragedy*, and there can be little doubt that the most eagerly awaited event of the Revels was Jonson's *Masque of Oberon*, one of the most charming of his inventions. Prince Henry, for whom it was written, played the Fairy Prince, emerging from his palace in a chariot drawn by two white bears, cousins, perhaps, of the one that dined on the poor gentleman in *The*

Winter's Tale. The Exchequer had to find £250 for composers, musicians and players, and £40 each for Jonson and Inigo Jones. Another £16 for Jones came from the Prince's privy purse, and more than £1,000 for mercers and other tradesmen. As these figures must be multiplied by twenty or thirty to bring them up to present-day standards, the masque was, as the Venetian ambassador mildly remarked, 'excessively costly'. The Queen's masque, *Love Freed from Ignorance and Folly*, which followed a month later, must have been equally extravagant, although there had been admirable resolutions to economise. Jonson and Jones each received another £40, Ferrabosco £20 for his music, and James instituted the order of the baronetage, 'that', as John Chamberlain put it, 'the Kinges wants might be much relieved out of the vanities and ambition of the gentrie'.

From his employment at Court, Jonson was now earning an income comparable to that of Shakespeare, derived from his shares in the Globe and Blackfriars theatres. He could afford to relax and write, or try to write, what he had always wanted to do, a successful tragedy. Sometime in 1611 the King's Men produced *Catiline his Conspiracy*, 'a legitimate poem', complete with chorus, and obeying all the rules of ancient tragedy. Jonson made no concessions to his public, and it was not a success. No ordinary audience could be expected to sit patiently through Cicero's oration of three hundred lines, even if Burbage spoke 'the prodigious rhetoric'. In a Preface to the quarto, Jonson turned with arrogant irony on 'the reader in ordinary', who was too ignorant to appreciate his work; it was to 'the reader extraordinary', like the Earl of Pembroke to whom it was dedicated, that he submitted himself and his favourite play. But it was his last tragedy.

There were publications more interesting than *Catiline* in 1611. In this year John Speed brought out his *Theatre of the Empire of Great Britain*, a splendid series of maps of the English counties, incorporating some of the work of Saxton and Norden. This was soon followed by his *History of Great Britain . . . from Julius Cæsar . . . to King James*, in which, incidentally, the old Puritan tilted obliquely at Shakespeare, the feigning and falsifying poet who had transformed that virtuous Lollard, Sir John Oldcastle, into a ruffian and a robber. Speed was able to devote his time to cartography and antiquarianism owing to the generosity of Sir Fulke Greville, like his friend, Sir Philip Sidney, one of the most enlightened of patrons. 'One great argument for his worth', wrote David Lloyd half a century later, 'was his respect of the worth of others, desiring to be known to posterity under no other notions than of Shakespeare's and Ben Jonson's master . . . and Sir Philip Sidney's friend.' Greville was a Warwickshire grandee, and it is quite possible that he befriended Shakespeare when he was a struggling dramatist. He was now busy repairing and rebuilding Warwick Castle, which the King had recently granted him.

It is not easy to assess the influence on Jacobean England of Serlio's *Architettura*. Sebastiano Serlio was a north Italian who spent much of his life writing a treatise on architecture, the first six books of which were published before his death in 1554, a seventh being added posthumously in 1575. The work was fairly well known in England, and influenced the building of the great Elizabethan country-houses, though indirectly on the whole, through *The First and Chief Grounds of Architecture* (1563) of John Shute, whose chief authority was Serlio. It was not until 1611 that an English version of the *Architettura* appeared, 'Translated out of Italian into Dutch, and out of Dutch into English, at the charges of Robert Peake'. Peake, it will be remembered, was Serjeant Painter to the King, and with his colleague, John de Critz, responsible for the painting of scenery for plays and masques at Court. Serlio had helped in the production of entertainments at the ducal courts of Italy, had himself designed a theatre, based on his knowledge of Roman models, and the second book of his treatise gives an ecstatic account of these things:

> Oh good Lord, what magnificence was there to be seene, for the great number of Trees and Fruits, with sundry Herbes and Flowres, all made of fine Silke of divers collors. The water courses being adorned with Frogs, Snailes, Tortuses, Toads, Adders, Snakes, and other beasts: Rootes of Corrale, mother of Pearle, and other shels layd and thrust through betweene the stones.

It reads like Jonson's description of an Inigo Jones setting for one of his masques, though it is of a satyric scene devised for the Duke of Urbino. Serlio adds illustrations of the three main types of scene: the satyric, a country road bordered with trees; the comic, an open place flanked by irregular blocks of buildings half Gothic in design; the tragic, a broad street leading up to a triumphal arch between severely classical houses and palaces. All are basically the same, with an open stage in front, from which the road leads back, rapidly diminishing in perspective. Serlio explains that the background is a painted cloth, and that the houses are made of thin boards and linen stretched on laths. It is the medieval multiple setting, elaborated, ordered and formalised according to classical standards. Inigo Jones would have read the *Architettura* in Italian, and had advanced some way beyond Serlio in stage design, but the publication of the English version may have given fresh impetus to his settings for masques, as well as to the production of plays at Court and the private theatres. It is an interesting coincidence that Serlio's book on classical architecture appeared in the year that saw the completion of Hatfield House, in which the Elizabethan-Jacobean style reached its culmination.

One of the most amusing, as well as illuminating books of the period was Thomas Coryat's account of his travels in Europe. Coryat had been a pupil of Camden at Westminster, and perhaps it was his old schoolmaster who inspired him to set out on a tour through France and Italy to Venice, where Sir Henry Wotton was ambassador, returning by way of Switzerland and Germany. This was in 1608, and three years later he published a light-hearted narrative of his adventures, as *Coryats Crudities*, 'Hastily gobled up in five Moneths travells . . . newly digested in the hungry aire of Odcombe, in the County of Somerset, and now dispersed to the nourishment of the travelling Members of this Kingdome'. The elaborately engraved title-page, a recent development of English printing, depicts his various modes of travel, by ship, cart and gondola, and even in a chair in which porters carried him across the Alps; but most of his journey was done on foot, and on his return to his native village he hung up his shoes in the church. The eccentric 'leg-stretcher of Odcombe' was one of the company of wits who frequented the Mermaid Tavern, or as he himself put it, one of 'the worshipful fraternity of sirenaical gentlemen, that meet the first Friday of every month at the sign of the Mermaid in Bread Street in London'. Other members of the fraternity were Jonson, Inigo Jones, Donne, Drayton, Campion, Richard Martin, Shakespeare, Fletcher and Beaumont, who wrote nostalgically to Jonson from the country,

> What things have we seen
> Done at the Mermaid! heard words that have been
> So nimble, and so full of subtle flame,
> As if that every one from whence they came
> Had meant to put his whole wit in a jest,
> And had resolved to live a fool the rest
> Of his dull life.

To give the book a puff, for Coryat was not a wealthy man, the members of the club wrote a number of scurrilous and mock-commendatory verses as an introduction. Shakespeare was not one of the contributors, probably because he was then on his way to retirement in Stratford, but there can be no doubt that he was one of the Mermaid circle, for the landlord, William Johnson, was a valued friend of his.

Donne's ironical lines in *Coryat's Crudities* were his first verses to be published, although most of his greatest poetry had been written more than a decade before, and must have been read in manuscript by many of his contemporaries. Perhaps the revolutionary and casual idiom, the impudent and homely imagery of his *Songs and Sonnets*— 'Busie old foole, unruly Sunne', 'The worlds whole sap is sunk'— influenced Shakespeare, and were in part responsible for his abandoning the conventional and literary imagery of his lyrical plays for one more natural, colloquial and dramatic, as in *Henry IV*, where feudal toughs squabble in terms of bees, wasps and ants, nettles and knitting. In any event, Shakespeare and Donne made part of their journey together.

After a period of wretched poverty, as his family increased and his wife's health declined, Donne was at length reconciled with and relieved by his father-in-law, who towards the end of 1608 made him an allowance. He now became a member of the literary circle that surrounded Lucy, Countess of Bedford, at Twickenham, and, like Jonson, addressed a number of verse epistles to her. Then in 1610 he found another patron. That year died the fifteen-year-old daughter of Sir Robert Drury, a wealthy courtier and politician, and though Donne had never seen the girl he wrote a long and extravagant elegy, *An Anatomy of the World*, commemorating the first anniversary of her death. Sir Robert was so pleased that he offered Donne and his family free quarters in his house in Drury Lane, and in the following year, when Donne continued the poem in *The Progress of the Soul (The Second Anniversary)*, took him abroad. *An Anatomy of the World*, published in 1611, offended the Countess of Bedford and other older patrons, and even his great friend Jonson remarked that 'If it had been written of the Virgin Mary it had been something'. Donne defended himself by protesting 'that he described the Idea of a Woman', and not Elizabeth Drury herself. The poem is, in fact, a profound and impassioned meditation on death, and a landmark in the progress of poetry and philosophy, for it leads up to the passage in which he shows that the new learning has undermined the old order:

> The new Philosophy calls all in doubt,
> The Element of fire is quite put out;
> The Sun is lost, and th' earth, and no mans wit
> Can well direct him where to looke for it.
> And freely men confesse that this world's spent,
> When in the Planets, and the Firmament
> They seeke so many new; they see that this
> Is crumbled out againe to his Atomies.
> 'Tis all in peeces, all cohaerence gone;
> All just supply, and all Relation.

Although it was almost a hundred years since Copernicus had advanced his startling theory that not the earth but the sun is the centre of our heavenly system, his hypothesis had made little headway. But in 1610 Galileo saw the mountains of the moon and discovered the satellites of Jupiter with his newly invented telescope, and for Donne's far-reaching mind there could be no further shirking of the Copernican hypothesis and its consequences. The stable medieval cosmology was collapsing, the world had lost its beauty, its immemorial proportion, and everything now was clouded with a doubt:

> If under all, a Vault infernall bee,
> (Which sure is spacious, except that we
> Invent another torment, that there must
> Millions into a straight hot roome be thrust)
> Then solidnesse, and roundnesse have no place.
> Are these but warts, and pock-holes in the face
> Of th' earth? Thinke so: but yet confesse, in this
> The worlds proportion disfigured is;
> That those two legges whereon it doth rely,
> Reward and punishment are bent awry.

An Anatomy of the World is the first poem in which the new scientific discoveries were, in Coryatian phrase, digested and dispersed, and must have made disturbing reading for those who understood its implications.

A reply to Donne's obstinate questionings was not long in forthcoming:

O Lord my God, thou art very great; thou art clothed with honour and majesty. Who coverest thyself with light as with a garment: who stretchest out the heavens like a curtain: Who layeth the beams of his chambers in the waters: who maketh the clouds his chariot: who walketh upon the wings of the wind: who maketh his angels spirits; his ministers a flaming fire: Who laid the foundations of the earth, that it should not be removed for ever.

In 1611 the Authorised Version of the Bible was published, after some four years of labour by fifty of the greatest scholars of the time. Fortunately they based their version on the earlier translations, from that of Wyclif and his followers to the *Bishops' Bible*, and though the outcome is a language that was never spoken by men, it is a tongue that even angels might envy. Yet the process had involved sufficient transmutation and incorporation of current usage to make the book essentially Jacobean, and the greatest prose work of that age or of any other.

According to the translators, the King had shown a 'vehement and perpetuated desire of the accomplishing and publishing' of the new version, the only book, incidentally of which this might be said. The suggestion had been made by the Puritan leader, John Reynolds, at the stormy Hampton Court Conference, but James now found himself facing a more formidable body than the assembly of divines whom he had dismissed with a threat of harrying out of the land. Parliament had not forgotten the deprivation of three hundred conscientious clergy, and their resentment had been increased by the indolence of their successors, the growing insolence of the bishops, the practice of non-residence and other abuses. To these ecclesiastical differences were added equally serious political ones. The Commons had at last realised that if they allowed the King's claim to levy impositions as he liked they would be reduced to impotence, and a fierce struggle developed. The quarrel came to a head at the beginning of 1611, and in February James angrily dismissed his Parliament, determined thenceforth to rule without their interference. He was encouraged in his perilous course by young Sir Robert Carr, who rightly feared that Parliament was preparing an attack on himself and the other Scottish favourites. In the following month James created him Earl of Rochester, and soon afterwards a Privy Councillor. He was barely twenty. At the same time the Court became aware of his intrigue with Lady Essex, an amour bitterly opposed by Sir Thomas Overbury, who warned his friend against the girl, for she was no more already noted for her 'injury and immodesty'.

The year was blessedly free from plague—there were, indeed, no further outbreaks in Shakespeare's lifetime—and the theatres remained open throughout 1611. In the spring and early summer, a London physician and astrologer, Simon Forman, attended a number of performances at the Globe, and recorded his impressions in his

Booke of Plaies. On April 20th he saw *Macbeth*, on May 15th *The Winter's Tale*, and, though he mentions neither date nor theatre, it was presumably at about the same time that he saw *Cymbeline*, either at the Globe or Blackfriars. They are the only contemporary accounts of a Shakespearean performance that we possess, and all the more exasperating, therefore, in being little more than summaries of the action. He took a professional interest in 'Mackbetes quen' who 'did Rise in the night in her slepe, & walke and talked and confessed all, & the doctor noted her wordes'. And he drew a moral from Autolycus: 'Remember also the Rog that cam in all tottered like coll pixci and howe he feyned him sicke & to have bin Robbed of all that he had and howe he cosened the por man of all his money, and after cam to the shep sher with a pedlers packe & ther cosened them Again of all their money And howe he changed apparrell with the kinge of Bomia his sonn, and then howe he turned Courtier &c. Beware of trustinge feined beggars or fawninge fellous.' Like any other competent astrologer, Forman was well aware of the day on which he was destined to die, and his end came, as he had foretold, on September 12th, while crossing the Thames in a boat.

Shakespeare was by this time in semi-retirement in Stratford, and Forman's suicide took place the day after the name of 'Mr. William Shackspere' was submitted as one of those who contributed towards the charge of prosecuting the Bill in Parliament for the better repair of the highways. The King pocketed the money gratefully, and his servants began rehearsal of their latest play, *The Tempest*.

MAGNIFICENT MARRIAGES

'Hallomas nyght was presented at Whithall before ye Kings Majestie a play called the Tempest.' Fortunately the Revels Account for the winter of 1611–12 has been preserved, and thus casually do we hear of the performance of Shakespeare's last and most perfect comedy. Then, four nights later, on November 5th, 'the Kings players' presented 'A play called ye winters nightes Tayle'. We do not know the names of all the plays given at Court that protracted season—it did not finish till the end of April—and of the twenty-two by the King's Men these are the only two of Shakespeare's to be mentioned. Others were Beaumont's and Fletcher's *A King and No King*, a tragi-comedy, or farcical melodrama, of inconsequent passions and narrowly avoided incest, Tourneur's lost *Nobleman*, and when Prince Henry joined his mother at Greenwich in January, the King's combined with the Queen's Men to give Heywood's *Silver Age* and *Rape of Lucrece*, a revival of the tragedy in the Epistle to which Heywood complained of the publication of his plays 'so corrupt and mangled, copied only by the ear', that he was ashamed to acknowledge them. The Queen's gave four more performances, two of which were of *Greene's Tu Quoque*, a comedy by 'Jo.' Cooke, of whom virtually nothing is known except that he was a 'worthy friend' of Heywood's. It is a lively farce of Bartholomew Bubble, who inherits a fortune, and, to show his breeding, when greeted with 'God save you', replies 'Tu quoque'. The actor Thomas Greene played the part with such success that the piece was immediately christened 'Greene's Tu Quoque', and Cooke's original title, *The City Gallant*, was forgotten. The Prince's and the Duke of York's each gave three performances, and the Whitefriars company, once again the Queen's Revels, presented *Cupid's Revenge*, a singularly unsavoury tragedy for boy actors, by Beaumont and Fletcher.

Another company made its first appearance at Court this Christmas. The Lady Elizabeth, only daughter of James and Anne, was now fifteen, and the King authorised the formation of a fifth royal company, under her patronage. Unhappily for them the real controller of their fortunes was not Elizabeth but Henslowe, with whom they signed a contract whereby he agreed to finance them, and for the time being took over the Swan theatre for their use. It was at the Swan that they produced Middleton's *Chaste Maid in Cheapside*, a robust comedy after the Jonson pattern, but already half-way towards the elegant obscenities of the Restoration stage. Allwit's soliloquy on Sir Walter Whorehound explains the situation:

> The founder's come to town: I'm like a man
> Finding a table furnished to his hand,
> As mine is still to me, prays for the founder—
> Bless the right worshipful the good founder's life!
> I thank him has maintained my house this ten years;
> Not only keeps my wife, but 'a keeps me
> And all my family . . .

The Chaste Maid was probably one of the three Court plays presented by the Lady Elizabeth's, a strange one to find under a princess's patronage, and in the company of *The Tempest*.

It was a troublesome as well as a busy time for Henslowe. Apparently the Fortune was specialising in lewd and correspondingly profitable epilogues, and the crowds that flocked to see them were the cause of frequent disturbances. The Middlesex justices made the most of the opportunity, and issued an order that all theatres within the City and liberties should 'utterlye abolishe all Jigges Rymes and Daunces after their playes'. The prohibition did not apply to Southwark, and it may have been partly to escape the control of the zealous Middlesex magistrates, partly to find a permanent home for the Lady Elizabeth's, that Henslowe embarked on a new venture. He had recently acquired Alleyn's share in the Beargarden, and as the old wooden amphitheatre on the Bankside was in a derelict condition, he contracted with a carpenter to pull it down and build on or near its site a 'Plaiehouse fitt & convenient in all thinges, bothe for players to playe in, and for the game of Beares and Bulls to be bayted in the same'. It was an ingenious idea, for he would have the best of both the worlds of entertainment. Baiting was more profitable than the drama—in three days the Beargarden had taken £14 to the Fortune's £6—and the theatre need never be closed, with gratifying effect upon the overheads. The model for the new play-bear-house, to be called the Hope, was the Swan, though the compromise involved essential modifications. The stage had to be easily movable to make an arena for the animals, and was therefore built on trestles, while 'the Heavens all over the saide stage' were supported without pillars set upon it. For various reasons the building was delayed, and it was the autumn of 1614 before it was ready for the Lady Elizabeth's.

With the £580 that his father-in-law paid him for his share in the Beargarden, Alleyn was able to complete his purchase of the manor of Dulwich, whither he moved from his old house on the Bankside, and in 1613 began the building of the College of God's Gift, which was to develop, as was his intention, into a great public school comparable to Westminster. In the previous year Heywood had published his *Apology for Actors*, containing a celebration of dead players—Tarlton, Kempe, Phillips, Sly—and, among so many dead, one yet alive, 'the most worthy, famous Maister Edward Allen'.

To his *Apology* Heywood appended an Epistle protesting against William Jaggard's recent reissue of *The Passionate Pilgrim* in a form even more impudent than the original edition, for not only was Shakespeare again credited with all the poems in the miscellany, but two newly published poems of Heywood's had been included as well. This looked, Heywood wrote, as though he had stolen them from Shakespeare, who, 'to doe himselfe right', had published them in his own name. He added modestly that his work was quite unworthy of Shakespeare, whom he knew to be much offended with Jaggard for presuming to make so bold with his name. Yet it was a great temptation to an easy-going printer to exploit the name of Shakespeare. Eight printings of *Venus and Adonis* and four of *Lucrece* had been exhausted, thirty-seven quarto editions of separate plays had been published, and a fifth quarto of 1 *Henry IV* was in the press. Jaggard was to go in for piracy in an even bigger way when, in 1619, he began the surreptitious printing of a collected, one-volume edition, happily frustrated by the King's Men. He was not the only culprit, for by 1608 six spurious plays had been fathered on Shakespeare by other publishers.

Yet none of these Shakespeare quartos had found its way into the Bodleian Library at Oxford. In 1610 Sir Thomas Bodley had begun the building of the new quadrangle, and in the same year concluded an agreement with the Stationers' Company whereby they were to supply his library with a copy of every book entered in their register. It thus assumed the status of a national institution until the foundation of the British Museum a hundred and fifty years later. But Bodley had been brought up in Geneva, whither his parents had fled to escape the Marian persecution, and as a boy had sat at the feet of Calvin. His librarian was made of the same stern stuff, though he dutifully catalogued all the books that arrived from the Stationers' Company, much to the dissatisfaction of Bodley, who wrote to him in January 1612: 'I would yow had foreborne to catalogue our London bookes till I had bin priuie to your purpose. There are many idle bookes, & riffe raffes among them, which shall neuer com into the Librarie, & I feare me that litle, which yow haue done alreadie, will raise a scandal vpon it, when it shall be giuen out, by suche as would disgrace it, that I haue made vp a number, with Almanackes, plaies, & proclamacions: of which I will haue none, but such as are singular.' Bodley died a year later, but his librarian followed his instructions. The plays of Shakespeare were not reckoned among the 'singular', among the 'one in fortie' worthy the keeping, and though the Folio of 1623 was too large a volume to be ignored, the first Shakespeare quarto play to be acquired was in 1659—the fifth, 1637, edition of *Hamlet*.

Possibly Shakespeare was in Stratford when his brother Gilbert died there at the beginning of 1612, but he had not yet severed his connection with London, where he seems to have spent an appreciable part of the next eighteen months. He was certainly there in May, when he was called as a witness in the suit of Stephen Belott against Christopher Mountjoy, with whom he had lodged some ten years before. Evidently he did not wish to get involved in the quarrel between the old tire-maker and his son-in-law, for though he admitted helping to persuade Belott to marry Mary Mountjoy, he pleaded that he could not remember the amount of the dowry that had been offered with her. A fortnight later came the news that the Earl of Salisbury had died at Marlborough on his way back from Bath, where he had been taking the waters. It was a disaster, for though Salisbury was no great statesman he was a great administrator; though he did nothing to avert the struggle between King and Parliament he was at least a stabilising influence, and very few men could have remembered a time when neither he nor his father was in charge of England's fortunes. There simply was nobody to fill his place, though there were at least two men who had no doubts as to their ability to do so.

Francis Bacon had just published a second and enlarged edition of his *Essays*, including that on 'Deformity', in which, according to Chamberlain, 'he painted out his little cousin to the life'. Salisbury, Bacon admitted, was an adept at the 'artificial animating of the negative', a man 'fit to prevent things from growing worse', but what the country needed, he suggested to the King, was someone fit to make them better. James agreed, rewarded Bacon with the Attorney-Generalship, and himself assumed the vacant office. There was now nobody to check his disastrous course of government by favourites. He made Rochester his private secretary, and with him, in the intervals of hunting, discussed and outlined his policy, leaving it to be carried out by the Privy Council, now little more than a merely administrative body.

By 1612 Beaumont was wooing a wealthy heiress, and on the point of marriage and retirement from play-writing. Fletcher was reduced to working on his own, and to this period belong his two unaided tragedies, *Bonduca* and *Valentinian*, both produced by the King's Men, with Burbage, Condell, Lowin, Ostler and Underwood as their principal actors. The veteran Heminge had dropped out. His last appearance had been in *Catiline*, perhaps as the catastrophically boring Cicero, but he remained with the company as business-manager until his death in 1630, and was their regular payee for performances at Court. But Fletcher, accustomed to the stimulus of a partner, was an author in search of a collaborator. There were plenty of possibilities; there was, for example, Henslowe's latest hack, Philip Massinger, not long down from Oxford, and it may be that Fletcher worked with him on the comedy of *The Captain*. But a more experienced and infinitely more desirable partner than Massinger might be available. Although Shakespeare had retired to Stratford, he might be persuaded to help in drafting a play and writing a few scenes, preferably those introducing the main characters and themes, leaving the rest for Fletcher himself to develop. In this he would be supported by the full weight of the King's Men. The loss of Shakespeare and Beaumont was little short of a disaster, and Shakespeare, who was not the sort of man to desert his former colleagues in a crisis, readily agreed to take Beaumont's place as Fletcher's partner.

The first fruit of this collaboration was *Cardenio*, based on the story of Cardenio and Lucinda in *Don Quixote*, an English translation of which by Thomas Shelton had just been published. The play has been lost, but was registered in 1653 as 'The History of Cardennio, by Mr. Fletcher & Shakespeare', and it was presented at the Revels of 1612–13. Probably Shakespeare stayed in London to work with Fletcher and see it through rehearsals; it is even possible that his presence was required at Court as a Groom of the Chamber, for on October 16th Frederick V., Elector Palatine of the Rhine, landed at Gravesend.

Frederick, a grandson of William of Orange, was a moon-faced youth of sixteen who had been chosen by James as a suitable husband for his daughter, or rather as a suitable son-in-law who would strengthen his ties with the Protestant powers of Germany. The Lady Elizabeth was exactly the same age, lovely and adorable as Frederick was unattractive and uncouth, a girl whom Sir Henry Wotton called 'Th' eclipse and glory of her kind', a princess whose grace and beauty were to earn her the title of the Queen of Hearts. She probably disliked the match as much as did her mother, though for different reasons. The Queen favoured a Spanish alliance—Elizabeth might have married Philip III of Spain—and she taunted her daughter with the name of 'Goody Palsgrave'.

Now began six months of festivity and pageant. On October 20th the first dramatic performance was given, appropriately by the Lady Elizabeth's, and a week later, a windy autumn day, Frederick was taken to see the Lord Mayor's show and the 'somewhat extraordinary' City pageant, *London's Triumph*, devised by Dekker. It was Dekker's last triumph for some time. A few weeks later he was once again in a debtors' prison, where he remained for the next six years, for Henslowe no longer thought it worth his while to advance forty shillings 'to discharge Mr. Dicker owt of the cownter', as he had done in the old days. Prince Henry was not present at the pageant. An over-strenuous game of tennis had been followed by a fever, and he was confined to bed. On November 3rd the Queen's Revels gave a performance of *The Coxcomb*, an old play of the Beaumont and Fletcher partnership, and on the 6th, at eight o'clock in the evening, Prince Henry died. The Court was plunged into mourning, for he was a prince universally beloved, likely had he been put on, to have proved most royally. A young man of eighteen, sensible, clever, warm-hearted and courageous, he would soon have been in a position to frustrate the designs of favourites, and even to deflect the course of his foolish father. But it was not to be, and Raleigh wrote prophetically: 'Of the Art of Warre

by Sea, I had written a Treatise, for the Lord Henrie, Prince of
Wales: but God hath spared me the labour of finishing it, by his
losse; by the losse of that brave Prince; of which, like an Eclypse of
the Sunne, wee shall finde the effects hereafter.' Donne's inventive
brain spun a frigid and ingenious elegy, James himself is said to have
written a ballad called 'The good Shepherd's sorrow for the Death of
his beloved Son', and when Chapman's *Works of Homer* appeared, it
was dedicated to 'The Immortal Memory of the Incomparable Hero,
Henry, Prince of Wales'.

The theatres were closed until further order, for 'these tymes doe
not suite with such playes and idle shewes'. Yet the marriage festivities had to go on, and after a month of mourning Frederick was
invested with the Garter, and on December 27th betrothed to
Elizabeth. Three performances were given by the Queen's Revels
that Christmas: *Cupid's Revenge*, which was so popular that it had to
be repeated a week later, and a revival of Chapman's comedy, *The
Widow's Tears*. Another revival was Marston's *Dutch Courtesan*,
presented by the Lady Elizabeth's as *Cockle du Moye*, from the name
of one of the characters. Prince Henry's received a new patent as the
Elector Palatine's Men, but, as an act of homage to their late patron,
made no appearance. All the other performances, twenty of them,
were given by the King's Men. According to the Chamber Accounts,
Shakespeare was represented by *Much adoe about nothinge*, *The Tempest*, *The Winter's Tale*, *Sir John ffalstaffe*, *The Moore of Venice*, and
Cæsars Tragedy. 'Sir John ffalstaffe' was probably the Second Part of
Henry IV, for, in reply to a demand for more, 'The Hotspur' was
produced. *Much Ado* was also repeated as 'Benedicte and Betteris'.
It would have been more than human in Shakespeare, careless though
he was of Court preferment, not to have been present at such a concentration of his plays on such an occasion. *The Tempest*, as we have
it in the Folio, for it was never printed in quarto, is a marriage play,
and it is probable that he adapted his original version, as acted in the
previous year, for presentation before the royal couple on the eve of
their betrothal. Certainly none of the other plays performed that
season had any claim to be considered peculiarly appropriate for the
marriage of princes. Nor is it altogether fanciful to think that Shakespeare himself played Prospero that night. Although he had not, as
far as we know, acted with his company for the last ten years, what
could have been more fitting than the appearance of the author as the

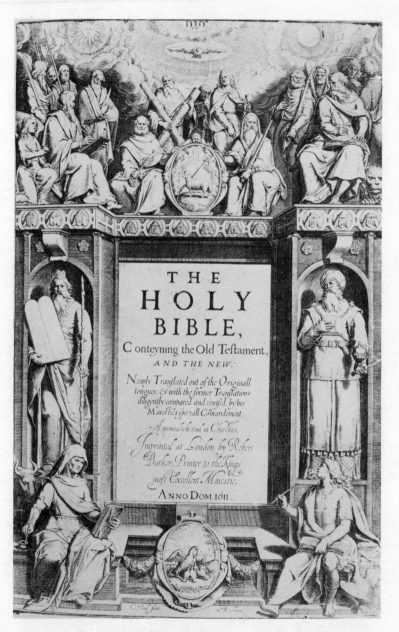

TITLE PAGE OF THE AUTHORISED VERSION OF
THE BIBLE, 1611

house
Temple stayres
Temple
Black freyars.
The Globe
Beere bayting h

THE SECOND GLOBE THEATRE AND THE HOPE (BEARGARDEN)
From the *Long View* of W. Hollar, c. 1640. (The names of the theatres are interchanged)

chief character in his last play, to bid farewell to the stage, and god-speed to the young princess setting out on the great adventure from which he was himself withdrawing?

Shakespeare, then, was probably present at the Revels, but Jonson certainly was not, though the King's Men gave a performance of his *Alchemist*. He was in Paris as tutor to Sir Walter Raleigh's seventeen-year-old son. The boy was more than a handful, 'knavishly inclined' Jonson called him, and with good reason. On one occasion he made Jonson dead drunk, put him in a cart, and had him dragged through the streets, at every corner exhibiting his stretched-out tutor and telling the spectators that there lay a more lively image of the crucifix than any they had. His mother was delighted when she heard the story; it was just like his father as a young man. But Sir Walter was of another mind. From Paris, Jonson took his pupil to Brussels, and by the time they returned to England the marriage festivities were over.

After Shakespeare, the plays of Beaumont and Fletcher were the most popular at Court, and the King's Men gave *The Maid's Tragedy*, *A King and No King*, *The Captain* and two performances of *Philaster*. Among their other plays were *Cardenio*, the anonymous *Merry Devil of Edmonton*, one of the numerous pieces later attributed to Shakespeare, and *A Bad Beginning Makes a Good Ending*, possibly by young John Ford. It was inevitable that somebody should combine the two degenerate and popular elements in drama, exploited by Webster and Fletcher, and it was to be under the hands of Ford that Elizabethan tragedy expired in a surfeit of horror, pathos and unnatural passions.

At the beginning of February 1613, when Shakespeare's last surviving brother, Richard, died at Stratford, the festivities reached their climax. On Thursday, the 11th, there were fireworks and 'fantastique or enchanted Castles, Rocks and other devises floting upon the water over against Whitehall'. The performance began with the discharge of balls of fire from the four castles floating on the river. Then from the ships were hoisted the figures of St. George, a dragon and a maiden. After a prolonged exchange of fire-balls the dragon exploded, leaving St. George and his damsel to play with fire until they, too, were consumed. The smoke cleared to reveal a mountain in eruption, and to the King's great satisfaction a fiery stag, pursued by hunters, plunged into the waters, where all exploded together. On Saturday afternoon a stately fleet of ships performed a river pageant representing the siege of Algiers and the battle of Lepanto. Then, on the 14th, Shrove Sunday, came the ceremony to which all else had been but prelude: 'The Prince Palatine and the lovely Princess, the Lady Elizabeth, were married on Bishop Valentine's Day, in all the Pomp and Glory that so much grandeur could express.' Her dress was white, her hair in tresses hanging down her back, and on her head a crown of gold set with precious stones, shining like a constellation. She was led to church by her brother, Prince Charles, her train supported by twelve young ladies in white, so adorned with jewels that her passage looked like a Milky Way.

> Up, up, fair Bride, and call
> Thy starres from out their severall boxes, take
> Thy Rubies, Pearles, and Diamonds forth, and make
> Thy selfe a constellation of them All,
> And by their blazing, signifie
> That a Great Princess falls, but does not die;
> Bee thou a new starre, that to us portends
> Ends of much wonder; And be thou those ends.
> Since thou dost this day in new glory shine,
> May all men date Records from this, thy Valentine.

Donne had returned from his foreign travels in time to write an *Epithalamion*.

After the marriage came the masques. Extra scaffolds were erected in the banqueting-house to seat the unprecedented throng, and ladies were warned that they would not be admitted in their farthingales. The wedding night was celebrated with Campion's *Masque of Lords*, in which Inigo Jones excelled himself by contriving a dance of stars among the clouds, though spectators found it tedious and more like a play than a masque. The next night the gentlemen of the Middle Temple and Lincoln's Inn presented a *Masque of Virginia* in the hall. The twelve masquers, with forty choice gentlemen, their torch-bearers and pages, rode on horse-back along Fleet Street and the Strand, accompanied by trumpeters, three carriages full of musicians, and a dozen little boys who served for an anti-masque. The entertainment was rapturously received, the dancing being beyond all that had yet been seen, and the King was so enchanted that he 'stroked the Master of the Rolls and Dick Martin, who were chief doers and undertakers'. It cost each Inn more than £1,000, of which Inigo Jones received £100, but poor Chapman, the author, was 'put with taylors and shoomakers, to be paid by a bill of particulars'. The other

Inns were not to be outdone. Each had a man fit to produce a masque. Beaumont was of the Inner Temple, Bacon a bencher of Gray's Inn, and the two combined, the one to write, the other to devise the setting of a *Masque of Knights*. They were less fortunate than their rivals of the night before. Their theme being the marriage of Thames and Rhine, they came by river from Bankside to Whitehall, making a gallant show with lights and lamps upon the water. But on reaching the Privy Stairs they found that the King was so wearied and sleepy with sitting up the better part of the two previous nights that he wanted above everything to go to bed. Bacon pleaded with him not, as it were, to bury them quick, but James replied that then they must bury him quick, for he could last no longer, and put them off until the following Saturday. They had their reward, for, whereas their rivals had played in the hall, they were allotted the more spacious banqueting-house, and after the 'ballet' helped to sweep the tables laden with comfits and thousands of mottoes. To make full amends for the postponement, James invited all the masquers to a solemn supper on the Sunday, though he did not pay for it. He and his company had won it upon a wager of running at the ring against the Prince and his nine followers. But the table was so crowded that some of those who paid for the feast could find no place and had not so much as a drink for their money. The ambassadors were particularly tiresome. The Frenchman claimed precedence of the Prince, his wife a place above the viscountesses, and the Venetian a chair above the carver, instead of a stool below. However, the masquers were well pleased with their entertainment, each being graced with kissing the Queen's hand and receiving an embrace from the King.

The young Elector was enjoying himself hugely and in no hurry to depart. The series of plays was resumed, and at the beginning of March Prince Charles took him to Cambridge to see a couple of Latin comedies. A visit to Oxford followed as a matter of course, but Frederick was back at Whitehall by the 10th to see a performance given by Prince Charles's players. This was the day on which Shakespeare bought a London house, the old gatehouse of the Blackfriars priory, close to the theatre. The next day he mortgaged the property to the vendor, apparently as security against payment of the balance of the purchase money. In this transaction he associated himself with three trustees: his colleague John Heminge, William Johnson, landlord of the Mermaid Tavern, and John Jackson, a wealthy merchant and one of the sireniacal gentlemen who contributed 'Panegyircke Verses' to *Coryat's Crudities*. Shakespeare may have lived in the house for a time, though presumably he bought it primarily as an investment, and sometime within the next three years let it to one John Robinson. On the 24th, the anniversary of the King's accession, there was the customary tilt, the occasion on which the Earl of Rutland appeared with a shield bearing an emblematic device designed and painted by Shakespeare and Burbage.

Still the Elector lingered and every day the expenses mounted. Already the Exchequer had had to find more than £50,000 in addition to Elizabeth's dowry of £40,000. James was on the verge of bankruptcy, and in a fit of economy dismissed the household appointed to attend his son-in-law. Frederick took the hint, and announced that it was time he returned to Germany with his bride. Their revels now were ended. Elizabeth left England to become for a few days Queen of Bohemia, and for the rest of her life an impoverished exile. Queen Anne, who could never have too many entertainments, set out on a protracted progress in the West Country. James went to Newmarket.

Among those who escorted the Prince and Princess Palatine to Heidelberg was the young Earl of Arundel, and with Arundel went 'our Kingdomes most artfull and Ingenious Architect, Innigo Iones'. He had just been granted the reversion of the highest of all architectural offices, the Surveyorship of the King's Works, though Chapman, when he thus described him, was thinking in terms of masques, for as yet Jones had built little more substantial than these pageants. Arundel was a man of cultured tastes, with a passionate desire to see Italy, to the monuments of which Jones would serve as guide, and once on the Rhine they turned south, and by August were in Venice. They wintered in Rome, where Jones spent his time annotating a copy of Palladio's *Quattro Libri dell' Architettura*, the drawings of Roman remains in which he compared with the originals, for his primary object was to make a first-hand study of classical architecture. He was the first Englishman to do so, for up till now Serlio's *Architettura*, Shute's version of it, or the strange variations on classical themes emanating from the Netherlands had served, and his research was soon to revolutionise the art in England. But he did not forget the medium that had brought him fame. Palladio had died in 1580 at his native Vicenza, where his last great work had been the building of the Teatro Olimpico, based on the rules of the Roman architect Vitruvius. Jones paid two visits to the town, where he saw the classical proscenium pierced by a large central arch flanked by smaller openings, beyond which perspective streets of buildings led away from the long and narrow courtyard of the stage. The Elizabethan theatre and its apron stage were doomed, for it was probably these momentous visits that inspired the idea of enlarging the central opening to form a permanent proscenium arch within which a greater scenical illusion might be framed. Jones was concerned mainly with the production of Court masques and plays, but his methods spread inevitably to the private theatres, where in Caroline times the picture-frame stage appears to have been evolved.

Shakespeare probably remained in London for some time after the conclusion of the royal wedding festivities. He had been working with Fletcher at a play of Henry VIII, and would naturally wish to see it on the stage. There is no external evidence to show that Fletcher had a hand in *Henry VIII*, but it is impossible to ignore the internal evidence of violently contrasted styles, the sinewy virility of Shakespeare's verse and the languishing sweetness of Fletcher's. On June 8th the King's Men presented their *Cardenio* at Greenwich as a special entertainment for the Savoyard ambassador, and a few days later produced *Henry VIII* at the Globe. It must have been at one of the first performances that, on June 29th, the theatre was 'casually burnt downe and consumed with fier'. The wadding from one of the guns, or chambers, discharged to announce the stage entry of King Henry, set fire to the thatch, and in little more than an hour nothing was left but smouldering timbers. The disaster inspired a rhymer with a doleful ballad, in which we get a vivid picture of some of the players:

> Out runne the knights, out runne the lordes,
>   And there was great adoe;
> Some lost their hattes, and some their swordes;
>   Then out runne Burbidge too;
> The reprobates, though druncke on Munday,
> Prayed for the Foole and Henry Condye.
>
> The perrywigges and drum-heades frye,
>   Like to a butter firkin;
> A wofull burneing did betide
>   To many a good buffe jerkin.
> Then with swolne eyes, like druncken Flemminges,
> Distressed stood old stuttering Heminges.

Jonson, just back from Brussels, was among the audience that so miraculously escaped by the two narrow doors:

> the Globe, the glory of the Bank:
> Which, though it were the fort of the whole parish,
> Flanked with a ditch, and forced out of a marish,
> I saw with two poor chambers taken in,
> And razed, ere thought could urge this might have been!

If we are to believe Sir Henry Wotton, fortunately—and how inadequate the word is!—'nothing did perish but wood and straw and a few forsaken cloaks'. Somehow the play-books escaped destruction. Half of Shakespeare's plays had never been published, and if the manuscript prompt-copies had been lost, *Twelfth Night, Macbeth, Antony and Cleopatra, The Tempest* and a dozen others might be no more than names to us to-day.

The rebuilding began at once, 'in far fairer manner than before', and by the end of the year the new Globe was almost ready to take the tiles with which it was roofed instead of the original fatal thatch. It cost the owners something like £1,700, and it may be that Shakespeare, rather than pay his part of the levy, now sold his interest in the playhouse, possibly in the Blackfriars, too, for there is no mention of theatre shares in his will. In any event, although he was working with Fletcher on another play, he must have left London soon after the fire to help defend his daughter Susanna against the calumny of the young Stratford scapegrace, John Lane, who accused her of having 'bin naught with Rafe Smith'. Susanna was cleared, and Shakespeare was free to get on with his part of *The Two Noble Kinsmen*, and to return to London if he wished.

It was fortunate for the King's Men that they had the Blackfriars theatre in which to perform while the Globe was being rebuilt, and it was there that they first produced Webster's *Duchess of Malfi*, apart from Shakespeare's, the greatest of all Jacobean tragedies. Webster has been called 'a Madame Tussaud laureate', and there is truth as well as wit in the gibe. His plays are chambers of horror indeed, though the figures are more than waxwork:

> This is flesh and blood, sir;
> 'Tis not the figure cut in alabaster
> Kneels at my husband's tomb.

And then, the man who created such a duchess and brought her to such an end could scarcely be graced with any title less than laureate:

> Pull, and pull strongly, for your able strength
> Must pull down Heaven upon me:—
> Yet stay; Heaven-gates are not so highly arched
> As princes' palaces; they that enter there
> Must go upon their knees.—Come, violent death,
> Serve for mandragora to make me sleep !—
> Go, tell my brothers, when I am laid out,
> They then may feed in quiet.

This production is of particular interest, for it is the only one in Shakespeare's lifetime from which we learn the parts taken by some of the actors. Burbage played Ferdinand, Condell the Cardinal, and Ostler, who died in the following year, Antonio. If the same plan was followed as in the revival after Burbage's death in 1619, some of the madmen were played by actors with comparatively major parts, and a boy trebled the parts of Cariola, the Doctor and an Officer. No doubt the tire-man and gatherers were conscripted to make a full complement of madmen.

While *The Duchess of Malfi* was being written and rehearsed, a tragedy of real life, in which the Countess of Essex played not the duchess, but the White Devil, was developing at Court. Sir Thomas Overbury, in his anxiety to put an end to the intrigue between her and Rochester, overstepped the bounds of caution. He told his friend frankly that the countess was no better than a whore, and wrote a poem, *The Wife*, describing the virtues that a woman should possess. But Rochester had now succumbed to the seductive advances of the countess; he repeated all that Overbury had said, and in revenge she contrived to get him thrown into the Tower on a charge of insulting the King. This was in April. The next step was to get a divorce from her husband, and, thanks to the interest shown by the King in the unsavoury details, this was obtained on September 13th. Two days later Overbury died in the Tower. After a decent interval, to allow the mud stirred up by the divorce to settle, Rochester, created Earl of Somerset for the occasion, married his mistress, and the year 1613 was brought to an end with the wedding festivities, which almost rivalled those of the previous February.

While Jonson was abroad, Campion had filled his place as writer of royal masques and entertainments. His was the *Lords' Masque* of the

Lady Elizabeth's wedding-day; his, too, the *Entertainment* with which Lord Knollys had diverted Queen Anne at Caversham during her progress in the spring, and it was from him that the King demanded a masque for Somerset's wedding. This was the *Masque of Squires*, presented on December 26th, for which Campion composed 'divers choyce Ayres that may be sung with a single voyce to the Lute or Bass-Viall'. But he sorely missed the genius of Inigo Jones. As a substitute he employed the Florentine architect Constantine de' Servi, a secretive and unco-operative man, whose 'main invention' turned out to be far less imposing than Campion had intended. Jonson, jealous perhaps of his rival's ascendancy, furnished a short farcical piece for the occasion, apparently without any elaborate scenical effects, and on the 29th presented this so-called *Irish Masque*. Many thought his ridiculing of the Irish in bad taste, but it was just the sort of thing to please James, who ordered it to be repeated a few days later.

Shakespeare may have been in London at the time for rehearsals of *The Two Noble Kinsmen*. More probably, however, having started the action of the play, introduced the main characters and written the last act, he sent off his manuscript to Fletcher, leaving it to him to elaborate the middle scenes as he thought fit; then in the tranquillity of his Stratford study began Michael Drayton's newly published *Poly-olbion*, a poetical gazeteer of the fortunate isle, which had already been fifteen years in the making:

> Upon the midlands now th' industrious Muse doth fall,
> That shire which we the heart of England well may call,
> As she herself extends (the midst which is decreed)
> Betwixt St. Michael's Mount and Berwick bordering Tweed;
> Brave Warwick, that abroad so long advanced her bear,
> By her illustrious earls renowned every where
> Above her neighbouring shires which always bore her head.
> My native country then, which so brave spirits hath bred,
> If there be virtue yet remaining in thy earth,
> Or any good of thine thou bred'st into my birth,
> Accept it as thine own, whilst now I sing of thee,
> Of all thy later brood th' unworthiest though I be.
> Muse, first of Arden tell, whose footsteps yet are found
> In her rough woodlands more than any other ground. . . .

Poor Drayton; it was a loving but so distressingly pedestrian a pilgrimage, and as yet he had got no further north than his native Warwickshire.

THIS INSUBSTANTIAL PAGEANT FADED

T H E Somerset wedding festivities covered the twelve days of Christmas, though not all was at the King's expense. James looked for an
appropriate demonstration from the City, and with some reluctance
the Livery Companies responded to his pressure. It so happened that
in the previous September there had been a ceremony commemorating
the opening of the conduit that brought fresh water from Hertfordshire to Islington, one of the most important and beneficial under-
takings of the age, and for this Middleton had written his *Running
Stream Entertainment*, which was so successful that he was asked to
devise the Lord Mayor's Show of a month later. It followed almost as a
matter of course, therefore, that he was commissioned to write the
City entertainment for the Somerset marriage, and after a solemn
banquet on January 4th, 1614, he presented his *Masque of Cupid* in
Merchant Taylors' hall. The Inns of Court should now have followed
suit, but they were still ruefully paying for the royal wedding, and
Bacon stepped into the breach by financing a *Masque of Flowers*, presented on Twelfth Night by the gentlemen of Gray's Inn. It cost him
more than £2,000, but as a means of gaining preferment by ingrati-
ating himself with Somerset and the Howard faction, it was to prove
so much money thrown away.

Then the Queen had found an additional occasion for celebration,
the marriage of one of the Scottish ladies of her household to a
Scottish peer, and at Candlemas gave a 'magnificent intertainment'
to the King and the bridal pair at Somerset House, her London
residence. She admitted, or boasted, that it cost above £3,000. Part of
the entertainment was a pastoral play by Daniel, *Hymen's Triumph*,
'solemn and dull', according to Chamberlain, though he added generously, 'perhaps better to be read than represented'.

In addition to the masques there was the customary series of plays,
two each by the Queen's and the Lady Elizabeth's, fifteen by the
King's, and when all was over James felt his pockets and found them

empty. In desperation he called a Parliament to help him out of his difficulties, but the Commons were unsympathetic and no more amenable than they had been in 1611; the talk was all of the King's illegal Impositions, and after two months of bitter wrangling they were dismissed, nothing accomplished. Perhaps the 'voluntary' contributions proposed by the bishops would see him through, and it was another seven years before he had to submit to a similar indignity.

It was some time during the unproductive sitting of the Addled Parliament, in April or May, that the King's Men hatched their valuable venture and opened the second Globe. We should expect Shakespeare to have come up for the ceremony, particularly if he was still a shareholder, and the play chosen for the occasion to have been one of his own. As there was no new one, it may have been the next best thing, one in which he had at least a hand, though *The Two Noble Kinsmen* had been written primarily for the Blackfriars stage. If Shakespeare had not seen what Fletcher had done to his script since he sent it to him, he must have been shocked by the sub-plot of the gaoler's distracted daughter, which he had perversely woven into Chaucer's story of Palamon and Arcite. Tolerant though Shakespeare was, he could scarcely be expected to go on putting his name to plays that contained such revolting rubbish, and it was the last play that he wrote with Fletcher, or with anyone else. He was not letting the King's Men down, for Massinger was now an accomplished dramatist whose verse might sometimes be mistaken for his own, and he could take his place as Fletcher's partner. Then there was Webster, Middleton too, and Jonson, back from his travels, was again available.

During the nine months or so that the Globe was in reconstruction there were no plays on the south bank. The King's were at Blackfriars, the Queen's at the Red Bull, the Elector's (the former Admiral's and Prince Henry's) at the Fortune, and at Whitefriars the Queen's Revels had been joined by the Lady Elizabeth's and Prince Charles's, a loose combination brought about by Rosseter and Henslowe. Apparently the combined companies had a summer season at the Swan, the only theatre available on Bankside, for the Rose was derelict and the Beargarden was being rebuilt at the same time as the Globe. The autumn of 1613 to the spring of 1614, therefore, was a lean time for the watermen, whose main traffic was in Bankside audiences, and John Taylor, an indefatigable versifier who called himself 'the King's water-poet and the Queen's water-man', addressed a petition to the

King on behalf of his colleagues and competitors, praying that no theatres should be allowed on the north bank within four miles of the City. This fantastic plea seems to have been taken so seriously that the King's Men appealed to the Earl of Somerset, who had just succeeded his father-in-law, the Earl of Suffolk, as Lord Chamberlain. However, the opening of the Globe, followed a few months later by the Hope, relieved the situation, and nothing more was heard of the affair, save that the other watermen accused Taylor of accepting bribes from the players to let the matter drop. It may have been so, for your waterman was notorious for his duplicity: 'He is ever more telling strange news, most commonly lies. His daily labour teaches him the art of dissembling, for like a fellow that rides to the pillory, he goes not that way he looks.' The unflattering portrait comes from the *Characters* of Sir Thomas Overbury, which had just been published with *The Wife*, the poem that had led indirectly, or directly, to his death.

On the day on which Somerset became Lord Chamberlain, July 10th, John Combe died at Stratford, and was buried in the chancel of Holy Trinity Church. He left £5 to 'Mr. William Shakspere', and his friend was probably at the funeral, for there was nothing now to keep him in London. Perhaps it was he who recommended Gerard Johnson as a likely man for making a worthy funeral monument. One of the four sons of Gheerart Janssen, a Flemish refugee, Johnson practised his craft of stonemason and tomb-maker on Bankside, so that Shakespeare would be well acquainted with the man and his work. It is tempting to think that when he went up to London a few months later it was to commission Johnson to carve Combe's effigy and make his tomb.

It was from John Combe that Shakespeare had bought his Old Stratford estate, and he was now to be involved by his nephew, William, in a scheme for the enclosure of the neighbouring fields in which he held tithes, negotiations for which began that autumn. On November 16th he paid a brief visit to London, for on the next day Thomas Greene, Town Clerk of Stratford and a distant relative of his, who was already there, made a note: 'At my Cosen Shakspeare commyng yesterday to towne I went to see him howe he did', and Shakespeare told him that though the enclosure scheme was going forward, he thought nothing would come of it. He was just too late for the opening of Henslowe's new theatre-cum-beargarden, the Hope, and the production there of Jonson's *Bartholomew Fair* on October 31st.

Tradition has it that the King made Jonson write against the Puritans, who were again beginning to be troublesome. For a taste: 'What voice is heard in our streetes? Nought but the squeaking out of obscaene and light Iigges, stuft with loathsome and vnheard-of Ribauldry, sucked from the poysonous dugs of Sinne-sweld Theatres.' The people were actually singing and whistling the popular songs picked up at the theatres! Jonson needed no prompting to gird at the Puritans; he did not lik kill-joys and humbugs, as he considered them, and Zeal-of-the-Land Busy is his reply to 'the Brethren' who had gloated over the burning of the Globe and 'nosed it for news' as a bawdy-house destroyed by the hand of God. But *Bartholomew Fair* is anti-Puritan satire only in part, and Busy but one of the scores of characters who throng the scene, making it the most uproarious, boisterous and kaleidoscopic of comedies. The huge cast was supplied by the Lady Elizabeth-Queen's Revels-Prince Charles combine, led by Nathan Field, 'your Burbage, your best actor', as Jonson affectionately made the incomparable simpleton, Bartholomew Cokes, call him. The Induction, as usual, is original and excellent comedy, in which the author mockingly takes the audience into his confidence, particularly the groundlings, 'the understanding gentlemen o' the ground here'. The bookholder, having shooed away the shameless stage-keeper, dictates articles of agreement 'between the spectators or hearers at the Hope on the Bankside, on the one party, and the author of *Bartholomew Fair* on the other party, the one and thirtieth day of October, 1614'. Every man was to promise to exercise his own judgment, and not to censure 'by contagion', Jonson adding with grave irony that 'he that will swear *Jeronimo* or *Andronicus* are the best plays yet, shall pass unexcepted at here as a man whose judgment shows it is constant, and hath stood still these five-and-twenty or thirty years'. In return the author promised not to look back to the sword-and-buckler age, nor to introduce a servant-monster, like those who write Tempests and such like drolleries. All was to be topical and realistic; even the bear-garden-theatre was as dirty as Smithfield, where Bartholomew Fair was held, 'and as stinking every whit'.

We do not know what Shakespeare thought of Jonson's ambiguous reference to *The Tempest*. Perhaps he never read or saw *Bartholomew Fair*, for there was no quarto, and the Court performance was on the night after the Hope production. He can have seen little or nothing of the Revels plays, of which the King's gave only eight, for he was back in Stratford by December 10th and spent Christmas at New Place. He did not miss much, for, according to Chamberlain, an experienced judge, the plays were 'for the most part such poor stuff, that instead of delight, they send the auditory away with discontent. Indeed, our poets' brains and inventions are grown very dry, insomuch that of five new plays there is not one that pleases, and therefore they are driven to furbish over their old'. Shakespeare was already being sadly missed at Whitehall.

Although Shakespeare did not see *Bartholomew Fair* during his short stay in London, he would see Jonson and learn of his latest project, the revision and preparation of his 'Works'—plays, masques and poems—for publication in one folio volume. It was an unprecedented proposal, for only a fraction of the plays written were ever printed, and even if they were it was as quartos, carelessly turned out along with almanacs, pamphlets and other 'idle books and riffraffs'; no other dramatist had had the temerity to call his plays 'Works'— Heywood was to chaff him about that—and enshrine them in a monumenal folio. The news must have set Shakespeare thinking along similar lines; half of his plays had never been published, and a few of them would have to be revised if ever they were to be a success on the stage. What pleasanter work could there be in his retirement than the revision of these for production and publication? Heminge, as manager of the King's Men, 'driven to furbish over' inferior old plays, would bring all the pressure of his friendship and fellowship to bear in persuading him to follow Jonson's course, and it is more than likely that Shakespeare collected three or four of his manuscript plays from the bookholder at the Globe, and carried them back to Stratford in his pocket. One of them was probably *All's Well that Ends Well*, an old play, perhaps the 'Love's Labour's Won' of Francis Mere's list of 1598, which he had tinkered with shortly after writing *Hamlet*, and he now began a further revision, adding speeches in his latest style, and elaborate stage-directions similar to those in his last plays, written, in part at least, at Stratford. Explanatory directions were essential when he was not himself to supervise the production.

While he was thus engaged in preparing his plays for the press, and William Combe was beginning the unauthorised enclosure of the open fields at Welcombe, Jonson was producing his latest masque at Whitehall. His *Irish Masque* of the previous Christmas had been in honour of Somerset and his bride, but since then the favourite had lost ground; fortune had turned his head, and his old charm had given way to arrogance, petulance and self-conceit. His enemies at Court, and they were many, were not slow to take advantage. They introduced to the King's attention a young man of twenty-two, George Villiers, tall, slim, pretty, somewhat vacuous in expression perhaps, but all smiles and affability. James was enchanted, and Jonson's masque of *Mercury Vindicated* was specially written for the gracing of Villiers, whose long legs made him the most delicate of dancers.

One minor source of irritation between Somerset and the King was Donne. He had attached himself to the favourite in the hope of preferment, but when he suggested taking holy orders Somerset was unhelpful. Donne was a Lincoln's Inn man, and a lawyer was more serviceable to a courtier than a priest. Not necessarily, however, to a king. James wanted him as a royal chaplain, and in January the Bishop of London 'proceeded with all convenient speed to ordain him, first deacon, then priest'. But a royal chaplain should be a Doctor of Divinity. In March, while James was staying at his favourite hunting-lodge at Royston, he paid a visit to Cambridge where he saw a number of plays in Trinity College hall, being vastly diverted by the satirical *Ignoramus*, so much so that he returned for a second performance, to the mortification of the lawyers against whose profession the satire was directed. But James was not the sort of man to neglect the pleasures of the chase for the rigours of academic drama—*Ignoramus* was merely light relief in a wilderness of Latin. His visit had an ulterior motive, and in April, reluctantly and with a bad grace, the university granted Donne the coveted degree. A few days later he preached his first sermon before the Queen at Greenwich.

A week before, on April 23rd, Shakespeare's fifty-first birthday, the King had made Villiers a Gentleman of the Bedchamber, and on the following day had knighted him. The sun of Somerset was setting. Foul whisperings were abroad; all that summer the clouds of suspicion gathered and darkened the Court, until in September the storm broke. It was discovered that Overbury had been murdered in the Tower. With the connivance of the Governor, a gaoler 'well acquainted with the power of drugs', a physician's widow and an apothecary had slowly poisoned him with doses of copper vitriol. The four accomplices were hanged, and then the Earl and Countess of Somerset were brought to trial. The Countess confessed her guilt; she had suborned the Governor appointed by her great-uncle, the Earl of Northampton, and the murder was her method of ensuring that her adversary should 'return no more to this stage'. Somerset pleaded his innocence, and was probably no worse than an accessory after the fact, but both were found guilty. Their lives were spared, and they were sent to the Tower, where they remained for the next six years. It was against this sordid and inglorious background that Shakespeare passed the last few months of his life.

The Earl of Pembroke succeeded Somerset as Lord Chamberlain, and was soon called upon to exercise his functions in theatrical affairs. The lease of the Whitefriars theatre having expired, Rosseter secured a licence to build another private playhouse on the site of a porter's lodge within the precinct of the Blackfriars priory, for the use of the Queen's Revels, Lady Elizabeth's and Prince Charles's. By the end of September he had pulled down Porter's Hall, as it was called, and almost completed his new theatre when the Privy Council ordered him to stop; the Lord Mayor and Corporation had complained that the noise would disturb divine service. However, Rosseter went ahead, and the Queen's Revels performed a number of plays there before the venture was stayed. What was Henslowe's relationship to the enterprise is not clear, but the Lady Elizabeth's left no doubt as to his relationship with them, for they drew up a long, formal indictment, with appended 'articles of oppression against Mr. Hinchlowe'. Among other things he had 'Cunninglie put privat debts into the generall accompt', sold the company's apparel and properties without accounting for them, 'promised in Concideracion of the Companies lying still one daie in forteene for his baytinge to give them 50*s*.', and then given them only 40*s*. Altogether they claimed that he had defrauded them of £267, so preventing their escaping his clutches by repaying what they owed, and had actually said 'in these wordes, "Should these fellowes Come out of my debt, I should have noe rule with them".' Finally, 'within 3 yeares hee hath broken and dissmembred five Companies'. Evidently Mr. Hinchlowe had much to answer for, and the day of reckoning was very much nearer than he thought.

Meanwhile in Stratford the enclosure controversy was still unsettled, and in September Thomas Greene made the note, 'W Shakspeares tellyng J Greene that I was not able to beare the encloseinge of Welcombe'. John Greene was the brother of Thomas, now on the point of being superseded as Town Clerk by Francis Collins, a

Warwick solicitor, and it was for Collins that Shakespeare sent in January to prepare his will. This was while Jonson was presenting his latest masque at Whitehall, ironically called *The Golden Age Restored*:

> You far-famed spirits of this happy isle,
> That, for your sacred songs have gained the style
> Of Phoebus' sons, whose notes the air aspire
> Of th' old Egyptian or the Thracian lyre,
> That Chaucer, Gower, Lydgate, Spenser, hight,
> Put on your better flames and larger light,
> To wait upon the Age that shall your names new nourish,
> Since Virtue pressed shall grow, and buried Arts shall flourish.

But the Golden Age was over. The masque was repeated on January 6th, the day on which Henslowe died. He, it is true, was dross; and yet, in spite of his chicanery, he had been in no small measure responsible for the Age of Gold; he had built theatres, employed playwrights and financed the players; the Rose, the Fortune and the Hope were his; his too, he liked to think, had been the Admiral's who had produced the plays of Marlowe in the eighties, and by the end all the London companies save Shakespeare's were virtually his; and we, posterity, are even more deeply in his debt than were the players whom he so shamelessly squeezed and defrauded.

It was twenty years since Henslowe had lent £4 to 'Bengemen Johnson player', many of them for Jonson years of disappointment and adversity, but genius allied to integrity and an inflexible resolution had at length brought him to success and security where all else was unstable and unsure, where courtiers stumbled and favourites fell at a prince's whim. He was Court poet, and in February his position was publicly acknowledged. The King granted him a pension of a hundred marks a year, and he thus became England's first Poet Laureate in all but name, for as yet there was no official title attached to the office. In the following month, on March 6th, Francis Beaumont died. He was only thirty-two, and had he lived might have returned to writing for the stage, to the great benefit of Fletcher, for he was the better dramatist and the better poet. A fortnight later Raleigh was released from the Tower to prepare for his last fatal expedition to Guiana, leaving the prison quarters that he had occupied for the last twelve years for the reception of the Countess of Somerset. On the 25th King James celebrated the anniversary of his accession with a tilt, and on the same day Shakespeare signed his will. Since Collins had prepared the first draft, his younger daughter, Judith, had married Thomas Quiney, son of his old friend Richard, and he made a number of alterations, including the addition of a marriage portion of £100. Among the minor legatees were his 'ffellowes John Hemynge Richard Burbage & Henry Cundell', to whom he left 26*s*. 8*d*. 'A peece to buy them Ringes'. On April 17th his sister Joan's husband, William Hart, was buried; on the 18th, in Madrid, Cervantes received the sacrament of extreme unction, and on the 21st Donne preached his first Court sermon at Whitehall:

How desperate a state art thou in, if nothing will convert thee but a speedie execution, after which, there is no possibility, no room left for a Conversion! God is *the Lord of Hosts,* and he can proceed by Martial Law: he can hang thee upon the next tree; he can choak thee with a crum, with a drop, at a voluptuous feast; he can sink down the Stage and the Player, the bed of wantonness, and the wanton actor, into the jaws of the earth, into the mouth of hell: he can surprise thee even in the act of sin; and dost thou long for such a speedy execution, for such an expedition?

It appears to have been no speedy execution for Shakespeare. He died on the 23rd, at the beginning of his fifty-third year, and was buried in Holy Trinity Church on the 25th. Gerard Johnson was commissioned to make his monument.

While Shakespeare lay dying, William Harvey was delivering his epoch-making lectures at the College of Physicians on the circulation of the blood. A few months later the new Surveyor of the King's Works, Inigo Jones, fresh from his Italian travels, began the construction of the first classical building in England—the Queen's House at Greenwich. In the same year three new painters from the Low Countries, Paul van Somer, Daniel Mytens and Cornelius Johnson, began work in England, and the overwhelming of the delicate national tradition by the coarser international style of the late Renaissance. It was in 1616, too, that the colony in Virginia was firmly established, and the first English settlement made in India, the factory at Surat. The Middle Ages died with Shakespeare, after that wonderful half century covered by his life, when, refertilised by the seeds of the Renaissance, they flourished for the last time in the Elizabethan and early Jacobean age, like the Mexican plant that accumulates the energy of decades to celebrate its fatal flowering. The change was inevitable, for civilizations are as roses,

> alas, that they are so,
> To die even when they to perfection grow.

There were gains to set beside the losses, but so much was irrecoverably gone; and we cannot but remember such things were, that were so precious.

EPILOGUE

1616–1623

JONSON'S *Works* duly appeared in the splendid Folio of 1616, but it was another seven years before the plays of Shakespeare were issued in a similar, though more modest, collected edition. His revision and recension had been sadly incomplete when death had taken him, and he had handed over the work to Burbage, Heminge and Condell, the only men who had seen the birth of all the plays and knew all their histories. It was a formidable task for the three men mainly responsible for the running of two theatres and the affairs of the King's Company, even though they 'scarce received from him a blot in his papers'. Half of the plays were still in manuscript, many of them old and annotated prompt-copies, and if each editor prepared for the press an average of two a year, it was as much as could be expected. Burbage died in 1619, but two years later Heminge and Condell were able to send their 'copy' to the printer, curiously enough William Jaggard, whom they had recently prevented from piratically issuing what would have been little more than a collected edition of 'bad' quartos.[1] The Folio was registered in November 1623, and on sale before Christmas. It was dedicated to the Earl of Pembroke and his brother, the Earl of Montgomery.

Heminge and Condell had done this office to the dead 'without ambition either of selfe-profit, or fame: onely to keepe the memory of so worthy a Friend, & Fellow aliue, as was our Shakespeare'. They were the last of the original fellowship that had been formed thirty years before under the patronage of the first Lord Hunsdon. Richard Cowley had been buried on March 12th, 1619, and on the following day Richard Burbage died:

> Hee's gone and with him what a world are dead,
> Which he revivd, to be revived soe
> No more; young Hamlett, ould Heironymoe,
> Kind Leer, the greeved Moore, and more beside,
> That lived in him, have now for ever dy'de.

[1] In his recently published *The Shakespeare First Folio*, Sir Walter Greg argues that Edward Knight, book-keeper of the King's Men, did most of the work of editing.

The Workes of William Shakeſpeare,

containing all his Comedies, Hiſtories, and
Tragedies: Truely ſet forth, according to their firſt
ORJGJNALL.

The Names of the Principall Actors
in all theſe Playes.

William Shakeſpeare.	Samuel Gilburne.
Richard Burbadge.	Robert Armin.
John Hemmings.	William Oſtler.
Auguſtine Phillips	Nathan Field.
William Kempt.	John Underwood.
Thomas Poope.	Nicholas Tooley.
George Bryan.	William Eccleſtone.
Henry Condell.	Joſeph Taylor.
William Slye.	Robert Benfield.
Richard Cowly.	Robert Goughe.
John Lowine.	Richard Robinſon.
Samuell Croſſe.	Iohn Shancke.
Alexander Cooke.	Iohn Rice.

ACTORS' LIST FROM THE FIRST FOLIO

Nathan Field who had probably replaced Shakespeare as a sharer, died in the following year, and in 1623 the twelve members of the company were, John Heminge, Henry Condell, John Lowin, John Underwood, Nicholas Tooley, Robert Gough, Robert Benfield, William Ecclestone, John Shank, Richard Robinson, Joseph Taylor and John Rice. But shortly before the publication of the Folio, Tooley, Richard Burbage's former apprentice, was buried from the house of his brother Cuthbert, leaving 'unto Mrs. Burbadge the wife of my good friend Mr. Cutbert Burbadge (in whose house I do now lodge) as a remembrance of my love in respect of her motherlie care over me the Some of tenn pounds'. The company still performed at the Globe, though every year the Blackfriars was becoming more important, because more profitable.

The Elector's, too, were still at the Fortune, though at a different Fortune. The original theatre had been destroyed by fire in 1621, and a new 'large round brick building' had just been completed on the site leased to a syndicate by Alleyn, who had inherited the theatrical interests of his father-in-law. Henslowe's death had thrown the other companies into confusion, but after varying fortunes the three adult companies found a precarious refuge under the new roof of the Cockpit in Drury Lane. Queen Anne's death in 1619 was a further blow to the Queen's and the Queen's Revels, and though the boys held together after a fashion as the Children of the Revels, the men's fellowship gradually broke up.

At the turn of the century Bankside had been the centre of the theatrical world, and the Curtain the only playhouse open on the north bank; but the current had set the other way, and now the Globe was the only permanent theatre on the south bank. The Rose and Swan had become something in the nature of circuses, where acrobats, fencers and prizefighters performed, and the Hope was reverting to its original function as a Beargarden. The venerable Curtain still stood in Shoreditch, symbol of the heroic age, but it was to the private theatres in the neighbourhood of the Inns of Court, occupied first by the boys' and then by the men's companies, that polite society now was profitably flocking, to Blackfriars and the Cockpit, perhaps also to the Red Bull, which may have been roofed by this time, and plans were already afoot for building the Salisbury Court Theatre close to the abandoned Whitefriars and Porter's Hall. It was only ten years since Jonson had written of the glory of the Bank; now the scene was set

on the other side of the river for the elegant declension into Caroline
and Restoration drama.

Anthony Munday was the last surviving dramatist of the generation of the University Wits, but he was now seventy and no longer
active, save perhaps as an occasional writer of City pageants. Of
Shakespeare's contemporaries, Daniel was dead, Drayton, bogged
down in *Polyolbion*, had written nothing for the stage for the last
fifteen years, and Chapman, after the death or defection of one patron
after another, was in some distress and no longer a practising playwright. Of the generation of the 1570's, Middleton had just finished
his tragic masterpiece, *The Changeling*, and was now writing his anti-
Catholic *Game of Chess*, a play that was to get him into serious trouble.
But his work was nearly finished. So, too, was Webster's. Dekker,
released at last from his debtor's prison, was collaborating merrily with
some of the new men, but Heywood was in the middle of a decade of
silence, though he was yet to complete the series of two hundred and
twenty plays in which he had 'either an active hand or a main finger'.
Jonson, too, was going through a similar period. Since the production
of *The Devil is an Ass* in the year of Shakespeare's death he had
written nothing for the theatre, though many masques for the Court.
There he had renewed his partnership with Inigo Jones, who had
built the classical Banqueting House in place of the old wooden hall
that had been destroyed by fire. He had also walked to Scotland,
where he had stayed at Hawthornden with William Drummond,
whom he had assured that 'Shakspeer wanted arte'. Jonson himself
did not, in more senses than one, for on his return he was
awarded an honorary degree of Master of Arts at Oxford. But his
best work was in his Folio, and when he began again to write for the
stage *The New Inn* was hissed at Blackfriars. 'Beaumont and Fletcher'
was the man; that is, Fletcher and his anonymous collaborators,
whose plays were being turned out almost with the speed and precision of Henslowe's old workshop and at Court were rapidly superseding those of Shakespeare. Fletcher himself had only a few more
months to live, and the future lay with the new men, Massinger,
Ford, Shirley and Davenant, who at the Restoration was to set the
fashion of 'improving' and polishing the plays of Shakespeare. By 1623
Henry Herbert was Master of the Revels.

That summer the King knighted Herbert, at the same time giving
his elder brother George, the poet, a sinecure worth £120 a year.

George Herbert's friend, Izaak Walton, was a London shopkeeper, Robert Herrick, Jonson's poetical 'son', writing his early lyrics, Robert Burton had just published his *Anatomy of Melancholy* and Milton was a schoolboy at St. Paul's. The new Dean of St. Paul's was John Donne. He was also Edward Alleyn's second father-in-law, for six months after the death of his first wife, Henslowe's stepdaughter, Alleyn had married his daughter Constance. Donne was then fifty-one, Alleyn fifty-seven.

The seven years had taken a heavy toll of the musicians. Campion died in 1620, and 1623 took his great friend Rosseter, Thomas Weelkes and 'our Phœnix', William Byrd, oldest and greatest of the galaxy. Orlando Gibbons and John Bull followed a few months later, and the golden age of English music was over. 'Never wise man (I thinke) questioned the lawfull use hereof', Henry Peacham had written of music in his *Compleat Gentleman* of 1622, yet thanks, in part at least, to the zeal of the metrical-psalm-singing Puritans— they deprived the aged Tomkins of his post of organist at Worcester Cathedral—England had to wait fifty years for another composer of genius, Henry Purcell. Nicholas Hilliard and Isaac Oliver died not long after Shakespeare. They were soon forgotten, and their room was filled by the young Flemish painter, Anthony Van Dyck, already in the service of the King, though playing truant in Italy, where he was studying the work of Titian.

There had been great changes at Court. The Queen was dead; Raleigh, last of the heroic age—all but one, the ninety-year-old Lord Admiral Howard—had been sacrificed to the Spaniards on the block; Bacon had fallen, like Lucifer, never to hope again, and the King himself was falling rapidly into a premature senility. George Villiers, Duke of Buckingham, had gained complete ascendancy over James and Prince Charles, and was now king in all but name. At the beginning of 1623 he took Charles to Spain to bring back a Catholic princess as his bride. But the visit was a failure; the young men returned alone, and Protestant England went wild with joy. Buckingham, basking in his unaccustomed and accidental popularity, flew to the other extreme, and by the end of the year England was on the verge of war with Spain. Superficially the situation was similar to that of exactly forty years before. In the early eighties the outbreak of the twenty years' war had been imminent—yet what worlds away it was! Then, Sidney had been alive, and in the year that Marlowe and

Shakespeare arrived in London Drake had sailed into Cadiz Bay and destroyed ten thousand tons of Spanish shipping. Now, the raid was to be repeated by a force of ignorant amateurs and pressed jailbirds in rotting hulks, and instead of the crowning victory over the Armada was to come the calamity at Rochelle, when the fleet mutinied and watched its allies surrender to the enemy. It was the nadir of England's honour.

The country was on the eve of these humiliations when Shakespeare's Folio was published. His widow did not live to see the book. She died in August, and was buried next to her husband.

INDEX

DATE DUE

OCT 29 '74			
NOV 12 '74			
SEP 20 '75			
OCT 7 '75			
NOV 17 '76			
NOV 8 '78			
NOV 22 '78			
NO 24 '82			
AP 25 '84			
12 '90			
FR 19 '96			
MR 24 '96			
MR 26 '96			
MY 14 '98			
AP 18 '01			
AP 17 '02			
APR 0 2 2012			
DEC 03 2012			
GAYLORD			PRINTED IN U.S.A.